C

D

THE
TWILIGHT
of SPLENDOR
Chronicles of the Age
of American Palaces

by

JAMES T. MAHER

LITTLE, BROWN AND COMPANY

BOSTON   TORONTO

FIRST EDITION

T 11/75

Title page calligraphy by Samuel H. Bryant.

The author is grateful to Doubleday & Company, Inc., for per-mission to quote excerpts from *The Circus Kings: Our Ringling Family Story* by Henry Ringling North and Alden Hatch. Copy-right © 1960 by Henry Ringling North and Alden Hatch.

LIBRARY OF CONGRESS CATALOGING IN PUBLICATION DATA

Maher, James T
  The twilight of splendor.

  Bibliography: p.
  Includes index.
  CONTENTS: Whitemarsh Hall. — Ca' d'Zan. — Vizcaya. — San Marino. — Shadow Lawn.
  1. United States — Social life and customs — 1865–1918. 2. United States — Social life and customs — 1918–1945. 3. Palaces — United States. 4. Upper classes — United States. I. Title.
E168.M24 973.91 75–22292
ISBN 0–316–54385–3

Design by Barbara Bell Pitnof

Published simultaneously in Canada
by Little, Brown & Company (Canada) Limited

PRINTED IN THE UNITED STATES OF AMERICA

To
Seymour A. Slater,
Will Lorin,
and
(*In Memoriam*)
Marshall W. Stearns

CONTENTS

ILLUSTRATIONS

A. Whitemarsh Hall: The Clodions from the Hôtel de Botterel-Quintin, Paris, 1785. Courtesy of the Philadelphia Museum of Art.

Endpapers

B. The Clodions in one of the rotundas at Whitemarsh Hall. Photograph by Mattie Edwards Hewitt. Courtesy of Pennwalt Corporation.

Endpapers

C. Whitemarsh Hall: Pajou's *The Four Seasons* in the garden arcade-loggia. Photograph by Mattie Edwards Hewitt. Courtesy of Pennwalt Corporation.   *Endpapers*

D. "Autumn" (or "Bacchus"), one of Pajou's group *The Four Seasons*. Courtesy of the Philadelphia Musuem of Art.   *Endpapers*

PREFACE

This is the first of two books with a common theme. It sets out the chronicles of five American palaces completed between World War I and the Great Depression. The second book, now in preparation, will tell the stories of five earlier palaces, all but one of them built during the Vanderbilt era, a season of splendor that began late in the depression of the 1870's and lasted into the new century. Each chronicle is self-contained, and each of the two books may be read independently of the other. (There is, however, a web of circumstance that the stories share.) The priority given to the present book grew out of the availability of people who were willing to provide first-hand recollections of the later palaces.

This is a writer's book — a search. I took as my guide an observation (which I read as a remonstrance) by Pierre Lavedan, a distinguished French scholar, in his fine small book *French Architecture:* "No judgement can be passed on a building without a knowledge of how it was built." There is a bias in my sense of the word *how.* To me it is weighted with human intention, and all the strange baggage that intention carries with it, openly or concealed.

My search, then, has been to try to find out how the American palaces were built by studying a selected group of them. In consequence, this is not a book about architecture, decorations, and landscape architecture as such, matters in which, at any rate, I have no formal training or special competence, but rather about the people who commissioned the palaces, the people who designed them and decorated them, and the people who designed their gardens and grounds. It is about great fantasies greatly realized, about rich dreamers and their artistic advocates — about the elusive, vague, and sometimes onerous process by which visions are reduced to reality, a process that flowers with misunderstanding, contention, and costly mischance, and that sometimes fails, but which often results in houses and gardens of rare and enduring beauty.

The image of the palace lies deep in man's racial unconscious, glowing dimly in the primitive need for shelter, seizing the imagination, goading men everywhere in all times. It is an archetypal image fixed in the collective memory, one that gives rise to regal ambitions for power and glory, sweeping men beyond avarice into the world of emperors, beyond the rational kingdom into the realm of the gods. The palace transcends utility, exacting of man war and treasure, viciousness and high art. In common with the ancient liturgies of religion and theater it celebrates peril and triumph, marking one after another the seasons of passion and the wind-drift silence of death.

Its beginnings were sacred and secular at once, a confusion (to us) born of the rule of god-kings in the dawn of time — a confusion that lingers on to betray the ritual declarations of democratic constitutions. The first palace may well have been the shaman's hut, and the first estate fence the magic circle that surrounded it. And the earliest cadences to resound in its dark sanctuary may have come from a bull-roarer which captured in its tethered flight both the voice and soul of the wind, an aeolian miracle.

Man's vision of Heaven is a palace and its gardens, the latter the tormented exaltation of the Bedouin. From ancient times man has filled the ambient pictorial space of his paintings and sculpture with the architecture of grandeur. Thus from infancy have the dreams of children been instructed with fantasies of palaces, commonplace as family laughter. And thus does the smallest cave kept secret from parents, or the poorest chair tipped forward onto the floor and covered with an old rug, yield from its lightless depths ranges of gleaming sconces, vast gilded halls, and great stairs that turn back upon themselves as they climb to even more opulent chambers beyond.

Lucian, a witty, elegant, and skeptical Greek writer — a Voltaire of the second century — asked for all of us: "Is it possible, on seeing a huge mansion, everywhere lit up, glistening with gold and flowering as it were with paintings, not to want to describe it?" Of course not. Lucian's question, put with the attractive flourish of a lively mind, answered itself, and it still does.

The American palace is the heir of the shaman's hut. However, it has a more immediate historical root, one that was nourished in Rome at the beginning of the empire in the first years of the Christian era. There Augustus taught the world that architecture is the rhetoric of power. "I built," he wrote in his *Res Gestae,* a routine summary of the things he had done, "the Curia, and the Chalcidium that adjoins it, the Temple of Apollo on the Palatine and its colonnades, the Temple of Divus Julius . . ." The list is long, and Augustus is careful to point out that in his great building program he served as the model civic benefactor — "The cost to myself was 100,000,000 sesterces."

His contemporaries were well aware of the magnitude of his public projects, and at least one of them, the architect-writer Marcus Vitruvius Pollio, was awake to their larger significance. Vitruvius published *The Ten Books of Architecture,* the oldest treatise on the building arts still in existence, during the reign of Augustus (29 B.C.–14 A.D.). In his preface he praises "Imperator Caesar" (Augustus) for "the distinguished authority" of the new buildings he has commissioned, noting that they reveal "the greatness of [the empire's] power."

In his biography of Augustus, written a century after the death of the emperor, Suetonius says that Rome had been "unworthy in her architecture of the position she held in the world." But then, "Augustus so embellished her that his boast was justified: 'I left Rome a city of marble, though I found her a city of bricks.' " Eighteen centuries later it would be said of the greatest of the American palace architects, Richard Morris Hunt, that he "found Newport a town of wooden villas and left it a place of marble palaces." The observation was made by Maud Howe Elliott, the daughter of poet Julia Ward Howe, both of whom probably read Suetonius in Latin, and both of whom preferred the old summers of wooden villas and archery on the lawn to the new era of marble and costly splendor.

There is a direct line from Augustus to the American palaces. The near end of the line is anchored in the work of a distinguished amateur of architecture, Thomas Jefferson, designer of, among other projects, Monticello, the University of Virginia, a new Governor's Palace at Williamsburg — a classicist who urged that the Capitol in Washington be based upon a model from antiquity which had "the approbation of thousands of years."

One of the most honored of the surviving buildings erected in the provinces during the reign of Augustus was the Maison Carrée (completed 16 B.C.) at Nîmes in southern France, a small temple in which Greek precedent is completely assimilated in Roman innovations — "a perfect masterpiece of Roman classicism," in the view of the archaeologist–art historian Gilbert Picard. Jefferson fell under its spell, and he adapted it in his design for the Capitol at Richmond. He had Charles-Louis Clérisseau, a French architect who was noted for the excellence of his draftsmanship, order a plaster model of the Nîmes masterpiece for him, requesting that Ionic capitals be used in place of the Corinthian originals because of the "difficulty" of the latter. (Clérisseau is now remembered principally for having instructed the Scottish neoclassical architect-decorator Robert Adam in Rome, and for accompanying him to Spalato, where they reconstructed Diocletian's palace in a memorable set of drawings.)

When he was finally able to visit Nîmes and indulge his Augustan fancy, Jefferson, as he later recalled, spent "whole hours" gazing at the Maison Carrée "like a lover at his mistress." Clérisseau subtly tempered Jefferson's ardor when he edited the great Virginian's designs for the Capitol at Richmond (lowering the pitch of the roof, for example, thus suggesting a pediment with a trifle less magnitude, a bit more *mesure*).

Augustus, almost as a corollary to his lesson that the countenance of public buildings should be eloquent of power, also left the world a word — *palace*. After living close to the Forum for a time, he occupied a house on the Palatine, one of the seven hills of Rome. He thus put the imperial imprimatur on a precinct that had become a rich man's enclave. "From about 150 B.C.," Donald R. Dudley has pointed out in *Urbs Roma,* "the Palatine developed as a fashionable residential district, until by the time of Augustus it was the most favored in Rome."

But there was a measure of irony in Augustus's lexical rôle, for "he could not bear gorgeous palaces," according to Suetonius, who adds that when Augustus moved to the Palatine he lived "in the modest house of Hortensius, which was neither particularly big nor strikingly decorated. It had only short colonnades of Albanian peperin — a volcanic rock — and its rooms contained neither marble nor mosaic floors. [There Augustus] slept in the same bedroom, summer and winter, for over forty years." And his furniture would never have suited his neighbors — it "hardly reached the standard of elegance to be expected from a private person."

However, his successors, beginning with Tiberius, extended the lesson of Augustus to include the palace of the emperor: they would let the world know where the most powerful man in the empire resided. One by one they covered almost the entire surface of the Palatine with magnificent imperial residences, some built upon the foundations of the others. Each great house was more opulent than its predecessor, and each was called a *palatium* — a *palace* — from the name of the hill.

Finally, Nero's House of Gold pushed magnitude and splendor to their limit. Suetonius tells us that Nero's entrance hall "was designed for a colossal statue one hundred and twenty feet high," his own image. The triple colonnades of the palace "ran for a mile. There was, too, an enormous lake, surrounded by buildings made to look like cities. . . . Some parts of the palace were overlaid with gold, and studded with jewels. . . . The dining rooms had ceilings of ivory, with sliding panels to allow flowers and perfumes to be showered down upon the guests. The main dining room was a rotunda, which revolved slowly day and night, like the vault of heaven itself.

"When the palace was completed on this sumptuous scale, Nero's approval as he dedicated it was confined to the remark, 'At last I can live like a human being.' "

America's emperors would begin living like human beings about a decade and a half after the end of the Civil War.

History is easily distracted by a distant footfall, or a cry in the street, so historians organize the human past into *ages* and *eras* in order to get it to stick to the point, as it were.

Acknowledging the limitations of such conceits, one may say that the age of the American palaces began at 10:51 on the morning of January 4, 1887, for at that moment Cornelius (Commodore) Vanderbilt, the richest man in America, died at 10 Washington Place in New York City, a substantial house, but not a lordly one, with fine stables and an exercise ring adjoining it. To his heirs he bequeathed $105,000,000, a sum said to have been equal to that in the Treasury of the United States the day he died. His will was a shrewdly drawn instrument, the charter of a dynasty. His estate funded the beginnings of the age of the palaces.

The heirs of the Commodore played a crucial rôle as patrons of palace architecture and decoration. They were preceptors to an age. A quarry in North Africa, closed since Roman times, was opened to provide them Numidian marble for their wall panels. A Vanderbilt yacht dropped anchor at Livorno so that one of the family could go ashore and select the Carrara marble for her Newport palace.

Jules Allard executed in Paris and installed on Fifth Avenue a Vanderbilt *Régence salon* that revolutionized American palace decoration. A Philadelphia newspaper sent a Paris art correspondent to Eugène Oudinot's studio in Montmartre to examine the stained glass windows he was preparing for a Vanderbilt banqueting hall.

And Paul Baudry, after he had completed his work in the grand foyer of the Paris Opera, painted two ceilings for Vanderbilt palaces, one for Allard's *Régence salon* and the other for a Louis XVI music room (which Allard was also installing). These canvasses were exhibited at the Orangerie in the Tuileries gardens and were analyzed in the *Gazette des Beaux-Arts* by Charles Ephrussi, the magazine's founder-editor and one of the models Proust drew upon for Charles Swann in *Remembrance of Things Past*.

The decorator William Baumgarten, who managed Herter Brothers before starting his own equally prominent firm, once provided an intimate sketch of the archetypal palace patron, William Henry Vanderbilt, one of the sons and the residuary legatee of the Commodore. William Henry Vanderbilt doubled the value of the Commodore's estate in eight years and commissioned the greatest residential project of the time, a massive triple palace on Fifth Avenue for himself and two of his daughters and their families. At the time of Vanderbilt's death in 1885, Baumgarten told a reporter:

> Mr. Vanderbilt was the most liberal customer [Herter Brothers] ever had. I had most of the dealings with him . . . and always found him a most agreeable man to do business with. In ordering his work he never made any contracts with us. The cost to him of the three houses was a little over $2,000,000 [more than $20,000,000 in equivalent modern value], of which probably two-thirds should be set down to his own residence. . . . We have rarely had a customer who took such personal interest in the work during its progress. All the designs were submitted to him from the first stone to the last piece of decoration or furniture. Mr. Vanderbilt was at our warerooms or at our shops almost every day for a year. He spent hours in the designing rooms,

and often looked on while the workmen were busy in the shops, and gave them money and encouragement in their work.

Mr. Vanderbilt always showed liberality, but he had a good idea of the value of things. He had a rare manner of inspiring one to do his best. Mrs. Vanderbilt's bedroom, you know, was furnished and decorated by Allard of Paris, and Mr. Vanderbilt saw M. Jules Lefebvre personally [in his Paris studio] about the ceiling the artist executed for it. We submitted to him the designs by MM. Galland and Luminais for the drawing room and dining room ceilings.

So it was in the beginning of the age of the American palaces.

The demise of the age was brought on by the stock market crash of 1929. It lingered only briefly in the tenebrous chill of the Depression. Then, its symbolic memorial service came on the morning of September 25, 1939, when Shadow Lawn, a palace on which Hubert Templeton Parson had spent $10,000,000, was knocked down at public auction to the Borough of West Long Branch, New Jersey, for $100. Its *Dies Irae* was a long roll call of tax claims.

Who, one might ask, was Hubert Templeton Parson?

He was the president of the Woolworth Company in the 1920's. True, but the answer is an evasion for it conceals Parson behind a conventional public mask of the sort worn in biographical dictionaries and newspaper obituaries. It provides only a single clue to Parson the palace builder: the source of his money. Actually, the man was a fool whose foolishness was of so great a magnitude that it becomes (as one examines it) almost mesmeric. And one must have a knowledge of this costly foolishness in order to know *how* Shadow Lawn was built, and thus to judge it.

Parson spent perhaps $22,000,000 on architecture, decoration, landscaping, and the maintenance of four palaces and their grounds simply to please Maysie Gasque, his wife, whom he adored without reservation. And who was Maysie? A Brooklyn shopgirl whose early life remains a mystery, but whose disagreeable manner and skill as a seamstress are remembered. She spent $4,000,000 on the interiors of Shadow Lawn and then, in season, passed the hours putting up jelly in a little kitchen upstairs above the palace garage which housed three Rolls-Royces.

Thus, the twilight of splendor.

Like Lucian I am moved to talk about palaces, their gilded *salons* glittering with light or moldering in ruin. But it was a more practical consideration — a magazine assignment from an old and gifted friend, Don Gold — that led in a roundabout way to these chronicles.

And it was the practical concern of Alec Wilder, another old friend, that opened the last door for me. I sometimes imagine Wilder, composer, author, and a fierce and gallant gentleman, listening to Villon in some ancient *cour-des-miracles*. He leans against a wall stained by an age of Paris winters detached and brooding, his mind at work on a woodwind setting of appropriate French sonorities for the poem Villon is reading.

For Wilder is the natural advocate of those who embrace the jeopardy of chance, deliberately and bravely, or timidly and by default of good sense. He was the ardent partisan of this book at a time when, far from bravely, I had drifted well beyond the limits of prudence. I hope he will find herein some recompense for his kind trouble.

I have had great help in this project — and I have needed every bit of it. Elsewhere I have acknowledged my large debt to others. I should like to say here that in undertaking so complex a book I needed someone of easy expertise in architecture and decoration who could interpret my distress signals and set me right again without alarm or impatience. Ethan Ayer has been that good companion through long hours of talk — and anxiety.

I have also thoroughly enjoyed the companionship of certain writers whom I have gone back to many times, not only for specific information but for the special refreshment that lively intelligence bestows on one. I would mention John Summerson, Francis J. B. Watson, Pierre Lavedan, Pierre Verlet, Michel Gallet, Mario Praz, Allan Temko, Esther McCoy, and Svend Eriksen among them. And all the while I have heard ringing in my mind that devastating requiem for an age, *La Valse*. How brilliant and how frightening of Ravel to have brought elegance to madness. (I am afraid that too often the palace builders brought madness to elegance.)

The reader should know that the architects, decorators, and patrons in these chronicles belong to a history that has generally been proscribed by the academic modernists. Pity — for here is a world rich with human foibles, and achievement of an engaging sort. I have, for example, found much to admire in the architecture of Horace Trumbauer, but it would seem to me witless to exalt him; to deck him out with the academic pieties that, say, have all but divorced a Louis Sullivan from reality. Lewis Galantière has provided a brief text which speaks for measure in such matters: "Tilly says of Restif [de la Bretonne], in his *Mémoires:* 'One would compromise oneself if one were to praise him highly; and yet it is easy to be unjust to him.'" The academic establishment has, I believe, been unjust to Trumbauer — and to history.

I should like here to invoke the memory of Jake Falstaff (Herman Fetzer). When he had completed *The Book of Rabelais,* Falstaff wrote:

"Now that the work is done, it behooves me to say, in the words of the scribe who wrote the Second Book of the Maccabees:

"'And if I have done well, and as is fitting the story, it is that which I desired; but if slenderly and meanly, it is that to which I could attain unto.'"

ONE

WHITEMARSH HALL

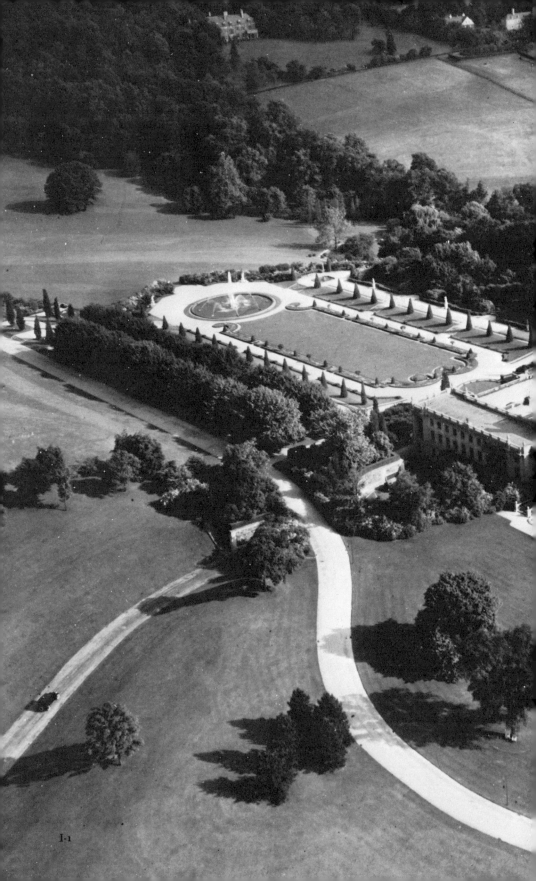

I-1

I-1   Whitemarsh Hall, an early aerial view. Photograph by Aero Service Division, Western Geophysical Company of America. Courtesy of Mrs. Helena S. Fennessy.

I-2   Artemis. Photograph by Mattie Edwards Hewitt. Courtesy of Pennwalt Corporation.

I-3   Lower fountain. Photograph by Mattie Edwards Hewitt. Courtesy of Pennwalt Corporation.

I-4   Front elevation.

I-5   Garden elevation.

I-6   Northeast elevation.

I-7   Southwest elevation. All elevations by Horace Trumbauer, architect; draftsman unknown. June, 1916. All elevations courtesy of Pennwalt Corporation.

I-8   Jacques Gréber's preliminary charcoal rendering of formal gardens. From *L'architecture aux Etats-Unis*, Paris, 1920. Courtesy of Editions Payot.

I-9   Formal gardens as actually completed. Photograph by Frances Benjamin Johnston. Courtesy of the Library of Congress (Frances Benjamin Johnston Collection) .

I-10   Plan of first floor with entourage.

I-11   Plan of second floor. Both floor plans redrawn for this book by John B. Bayley from Trumbauer's original floor plans (1916) now in possession of, and made available by, Pennwalt Corporation.

I-12   The foyer. Photograph by Mattie Edwards Hewitt. Courtesy of Pennwalt Corporation.

I-13   The reception room. Photograph by Mattie Edwards Hewitt. Courtesy of Pennwalt Corporation.

I-14   One of the rotundas. Photograph by Mattie Edwards Hewitt. Courtesy of Pennwalt Corporation.

I-15   The living room. Photograph by Mattie Edwards Hewitt. Courtesy of Pennwalt Corporation.

I-16   The ballroom: organ console and pipes beyond in the west gallery; the Boucher tapestry on the north wall. Photograph by Frances Benjamin Johnston. Courtesy of the Library of Congress (Frances Benjamin Johnston Collection) .

I-17   Stotesbury's bedroom. Photograph by Mattie Edwards Hewitt. Courtesy of Pennwalt Corporation.

I-18   Eva's bedroom. Photograph by Mattie Edwards Hewitt. Courtesy of Pennwalt Corporation.

I-19   Eva Cromwell in 1900, nine years before her first meeting with Stotesbury. Courtesy of James H. R. Cromwell.

I-20   Eva and Stotesbury at El Mirasol, Palm Beach, January 12, 1928. Underwood & Underwood News Photos, Inc.

I-21   The Stotesburys with Will Rogers and James H. R. Cromwell. Courtesy of Mr. Cromwell. Used with permission.

I-22   Eva. Pastel portrait by Douglas Chandor, 1926. Courtesy of James H. R. Cromwell.

I-23   Horace Trumbauer. Photograph from *Philadelphia and Notable Philadelphians*, New York, 1902. Courtesy of New York Public Library.

I-24   The Walnut Street mansion. Photograph from *Philadelphia and Notable Philadelphians*, New York, 1902. Courtesy of New York Public Library.

I-25   Jacques Gréber. Courtesy of Pierre Gréber.

I-26   Charles Carrick Allom. Photograph from *It Could Never Have Happened* by Alice M. Head, London, 1939. Courtesy of William Heinemann, Ltd.

I-27   Wingwood House. Photograph by Mattie Edwards Hewitt. Courtesy of Henry J. Magaziner.

I-28   El Mirasol. Photograph by Mattie Edwards Hewitt. Courtesy of the Pennsylvania Historical and Museum Commission.

I-29   The Tassaert group and the plaster nymphs (possibly by Pajou and Lecomte) from Whitemarsh Hall, in their present setting at the Philadelphia Museum of Art. Courtesy of the Philadelphia Museum of Art.

I-30   The ballroom, 1973. Photograph by Sam Nocella. Courtesy of the *Philadelphia Bulletin*.

Title page calligraphy by Samuel H. Bryant.

I-2

"Artemis, carved in limestone, at the head of the brushed gravel *allée*, framed by Norwegian maples."

I-3

". . . lead dolphins spouted thin silver arcs of water into the summer air . . ."

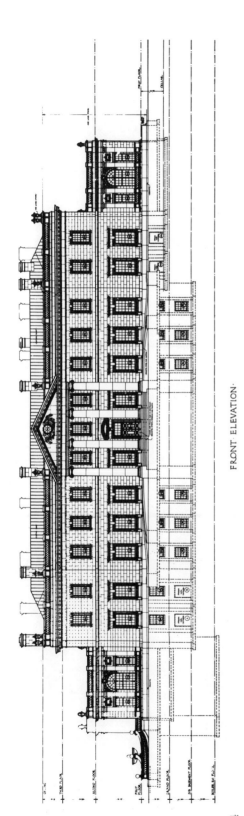

FRONT ELEVATION.

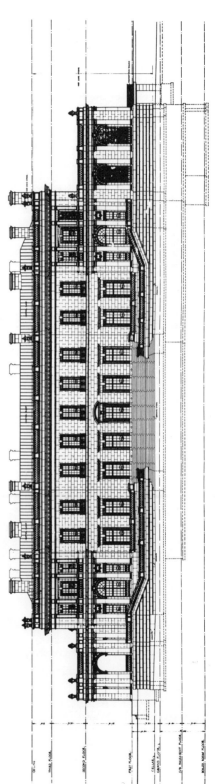

GARDEN · ELEVATION ·

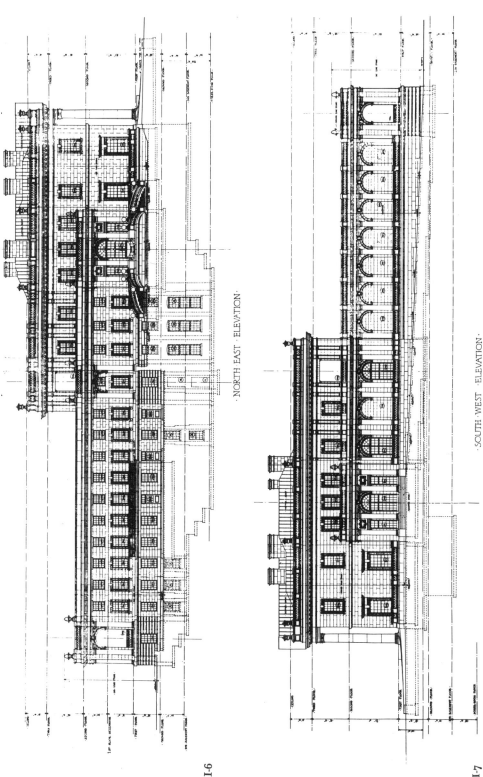

· NORTH EAST · ELEVATION ·

· SOUTH · WEST · ELEVATION ·

I-6

7

I-8

". . . lucid as geometry . . ."

I-9

"Clemenceau looked down the mile-long axial vista and was
reminded of Versailles . . ."

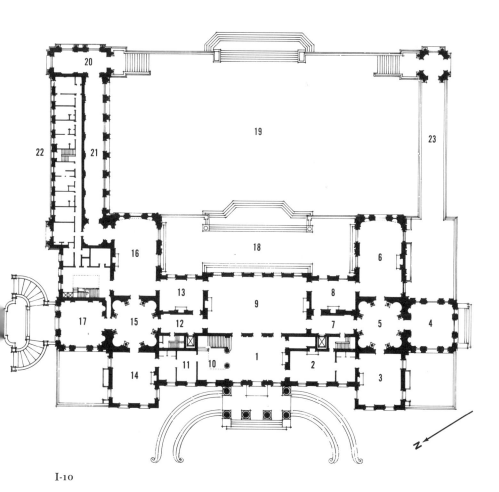

I-10

Whitemarsh Hall: First-Floor Plan

NOTE: Nomenclature from 1916 plans: Horace Trumbauer, architect. Material in brackets from James H. R. Cromwell and author.

1. Vestibule [Entrance Hall]. 2. Reception Room. 3. Library. 4. Loggia [West. Tea Room]. 5. West Palm Court [West Rotunda]. 6. Living Room [Principal Salon]. 7. Gallery Hall [West]. 8. Salon [West. Small Library]. 9. Great Hall [Ballroom]. 10. Stair Hall. 11. Men's Coatroom [Office]. 12. Gallery Hall [East]. 13. Salon [East. Breakfast Room]. 14. Billiard Room [Smoking Room]. 15. East Palm Court [East Rotunda]. 16. Dining Room. 17. Loggia [East. Summer Room]. 18. Terrace. 19. Upper Garden [Parterre Garden]. 20. Belvedere [East]. 21. Orangerie [Arcade-Loggia]. 22. [Service and Servants' Wing]. 23. Terrace [leading to West Belvedere]. 24. Belvedere [West].

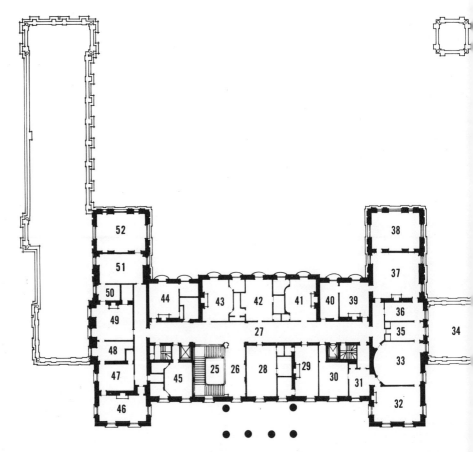

I-11

Whitemarsh Hall: Second-Floor Plan

25. Stairwell. 26. Stair Hall. 27. Gallery Hall. 28. Guest Room. 29. Guest Room. 30. Mr. S[totesbury]'s Dressing Room. 31. Mr. S's Bath. 32. Mr. S's Room. 33. Mrs. S[totesbury]'s Room. 34. [Mrs. S's Roof Garden-Terrace]. 35. Mrs. S's Bath. 36. [Mrs. S's] Dressing Room. 37. [Mrs. S's] Boudoir. 38. Loggia [West. Mrs. S's Empire Loggia]. 39. [Mrs. S's] Breakfast Room. 40. [Mrs. S's] Serving Room. 41. Guest Room. 42. Guest Room. 43. Guest Room. 44. Guest Room. 45. Guest Room. 46. Son's Sitting Room [James H. R. Cromwell's Sitting Room]. 47. Son's Room [Cromwell's Room]. 48. [Cromwell's] Dressing Room and Bath. 49. Guest Room [Converted to Mr. S's Cup Room]. 50. Bath [Daughter's. Mrs. Douglas MacArthur]. 51. Sitting Room [converted to Mrs. MacArthur's Room]. 52. Loggia [East. Mrs. MacArthur's Treillage Loggia].

I-12

". . . in the entrance hall the charming marble Tassaert once owned by Frederick the Great."

I-13

"The urbane eloquence of painted *boiserie,* adapted from Watteau and designed by Alavoine."

I-14

". . . the superb Clodions and the plaster figures that surrounded them . . ."

I-15

"Such were the legacies of great interior art that once made Eva Stotesbury's withdrawing room the most notable in Philadelphia."

I-16

". . . high chimneypieces with scrolled pediments that seemed to break above the cornice line . . ."

I-17

"... a bed whose plainness served as witness to
Stotesbury's Quaker upbringing ..."

I-18

"Her suite was designed for an *impératrice*."

I-19 "He was enchanted."

I-20 " 'Our pastime and our happiness will grow.' "

I-21 James H. R. Cromwell, Will Rogers, Eva, and Stotesbury under the portico at Whitemarsh Hall.

I-22

"She was a great lady."

I-23

Horace Trumbauer in 1902.

I-24

"Stotesbury's costly but staid mansion just off Rittenhouse Square on Walnut Street . . ."

I-25   Jacques Gréber.

I-26   Charles Carrick Allom.

I-27

Wingwood House at Bar Harbor.

I-28

El Mirasol at Palm Beach.

I-29

". . . Eva did not linger in the city. 'This will be my last visit to Philadelphia. I never want to see it again.' "

I-30

"It is the season of vandals . . ."

One may have been born in Philadelphia
. . . without ever presuming to call oneself
a "Philadelphian." . . .

Here will be an old abusing of God's patience and the King's English.

Aт Whitemarsh Hall, the stately Palladian palace that Edward
Townsend Stotesbury built in Chestnut Hill, one enters a semantic
wonderland in which the meaning of the great house shares with the
stone of which it was built the slow decay of ambiguity and the gray
ruin of time. There semblance and reality once merged in the nobil-
iary games of Old Philadelphia, and there splendor reigned — but
not in quite the way it appeared to. Only paradox remains: dust in
an empty reliquary. But one, listening attentively, may still hear in
stairwell and rotunda the soundless mirth of contempt.

The fine country house, a ducal Georgian presence, sober and
majestic, rises in stony silence above the Whitemarsh Valley. Once it
was common for two hundred, and sometimes as many as six hundred, guests to gather there for tea. Princes and statesmen visiting
the United States as guests of the nation slept in its gilded suites.
Cardinal Mercier, a leader of the revival of interest in the writings of
Thomas Aquinas and the prelate-hero of Belgium in World War I,
gave the palace his blessing during a visit there in 1919, an event
commemorated by a small engraved plaque attached to the top rail of
the back of a chair in the west loggia, the "tea room," which gave
onto the *boulingrin* (bowling green) garden.[1] In the autumn of
1921, Joffre, the hero of the Marne, came to Chestnut Hill to help
celebrate the formal opening of the house.[2] Then, one day late in
1922, Clemenceau, the premier who had rallied France against the
German invader, only to be ousted when the war was won, looked
down the mile-long axial vista that sloped gently away from the ter-
raced classical gardens of the palace and was reminded of Versailles,
perhaps with a certain rue.[3]

The chimneys are cold now, the fireplaces empty, and the lead dolphins that once spouted thin silver arcs of water into the summer air have been torn from their supports in the dried-up pool, almost ninety feet in diameter, at the lower end of the *tapis vert,* a four-hundred-foot carpet of turf now clotted with weeds. In the moonlight a statue draped in the baroque folds of a magisterial robe stands near the temple portico of the palace entrance, but it watches not. Its head has been severed from its shoulders. At the upper end of the garden *allée,* Artcmis, carved in limestone, lies face down in the frozen winter mud, toppled by the alien reflex of madness from her high stone base. It is the season of vandals: the past slips stealthily toward ruin, outwitting the eye of a lone watchman.[4]

A forgotten civilian gas mask lies three stories underground in a dank subbasement passageway. Its eyeless goggles and coiled breathing tube remind one that during World War II the vast structure — a hundred and fifty rooms measuring one million five hundred thousand cubic feet with one hundred thousand square feet of floor space — had served, first, as a fireproof stronghold for ninety vanloads of art, including French furniture, medieval ivories, renaissance bronzes, gothic tapestries, and five hundred paintings, that had been shipped down from the Metropolitan Museum of Art in New York City, and, second, as a temporary industrial research center.[5]

Today, no one pauses in the sunlit geometry of Gréber's boxwood *parterres* or looks down from a bedroom window on the cursive symmetry of his *broderies.* No one stands in the cool limestone refuge of the west belvedere looking with pleasure across the upper garden to Trumbauer's patrician loggia, the shadows of its arches ranged along an outdoor gallery of four life-size statues — *The Four Seasons* — carved in stone by Pajou. No one stops in the entrance hall to admire the charming marble Tassaert of *The Sacrifice of the Arrows of Love on the Altar of Friendship,* once owned by Frederick the Great. No eye examining the sculpture in the rotundas at either end of the long *enfilade* in the palace is now seized by the superb Clodions, which like the matching pair in the Musée des Arts Décoratifs (Palais du Louvre) had come from the Hôtel de Botterel-Quintin (1785) in Paris.[6] No one stops to praise the plaster figures holding gilded cornucopias that surrounded them, figures attributed to Pajou and Lecomte, one set of which Madame du Barry had displayed at her inaugural *fête* for Louis XV at her new *pavillon* at Louveciennes in 1771 only six years before Washington encamped at Whitemarsh on the eve of the Battle of Germantown.[7] No one now turns to the quicksilver music of a young woman humming "Blue

Room," then watches as her cloche disappears down the maple *allée* into the murmuring flow of guests.

The silent requiem of time fills the palace. One hurries through the dour twilight of abandoned rooms and voiceless corridors where the invading winter rain now turns to ice. Gone is the luminous elegance of the Georgian interiors — white and gold paneling, gilded capitals, stucco swags and festoons, and high chimneypieces with scrolled pediments that appeared to break above the cornice line — adapted by Allom from historic precedent and executed with a skill of like precedent in his London workrooms. Gone as well is the urbane eloquence of marbled Empire pilasters, cool treillage walls, and painted *boiserie* (adapted from the leaves of a Watteau screen) designed by Alavoine and executed in Paris with the nuance and measure, the cultivated certitude, of traditional French craftsman- ship. Such were the legacies of great interior art that had once made Eva Stotesbury's *grand salon* and boudoir, withdrawing room and guest chambers the most notable in Philadelphia.

It was said of her that Eva was "ambitious," as, indeed, she was. However, hers were gracious, if inconsequential, dreams, filled with a generous tumult of receptions. Measured against the long history of Philadelphia (whose merchants organized the first bank in America only several years after Jules Hardouin-Mansart had completed the Grand Trianon at Versailles for Louis XIV), Eva's season of tri- umph — 1921 to 1938 — was brief.[8] Its peculiar splendor is now faint as a rubbing from an ancient gravestone, and as easily misread.

Only the shadows at Whitemarsh Hall remain as they once were; shadows in which Old Philadelphia, coarsened by its long tenure of privilege, gathered beyond Eva's hearing and snickered. If one is to understand the queer chronicle of Whitemarsh Hall — its subtle and elusive failure in the midst of brilliance — one must watch the old families carefully as they manipulate ambiguity with the stubborn nonchalance of a saint rehearsing innocence. As with faith, so too with the secular divinity of Old Philadelphia: it imposes nullity on the witness of reason.

II

EDWARD T. STOTESBURY was the head — "the resident senior part- ner" — of Philadelphia's most famous, and prestigious, banking house, Drexel & Company. He was also a senior partner of J. P. Morgan & Company in New York. The two firms were actually two branches of a single organization, a historic copartnership that became the most powerful American financial institution of the age. John Pierpont Morgan, Sr., "The Great Pierpont Morgan," as one of his biographers, Frederick Lewis Allen, called him, or "Morgan the Magnificent," as John K. Winkler, another of his biographers, designated him in an obvious reference to Lorenzo de Medici, *il Magnifico,* was "the ranking partner" of both firms until his death in 1913, at which time he was succeeded in rank by his son and namesake, who was known with somewhat less awe simply as J. P. Morgan, Jr.

In the last dozen years of his life, Stotesbury got caught up in a web of society news, some of it amusing and all of it trivial, the cause and conditions of which will presently become clear. He was fed into journalism's great cliché machine and, to use a later image already nearing abuse, every printout was a caricature. The king became his own fool. In 1929, nine years before his death, the Associated Press distributed to its member newspapers a routine standby obituary on Stotesbury. Although it did take brief notice of his incidental rôle in the seasonal entertainments of society in Philadelphia and at Palm Beach and Bar Harbor, the lengthy obituary provided a balanced account of his singular career in banking and civic affairs. It pointed out, for example, that Stotesbury had been prominent in international finance at least since 1909, the year he went abroad to consult in the multinational funding of the historic loan the West made to China at that time. However, the obituary was folded away in clipping-file envelopes at the same time that Stotesbury had become that easiest of marks for whimsical reporting, the aging playboy. One news account did, in fact, quote him as saying at Palm Beach, "I want to learn how to play," a statement that has since been dismissed by a member of his family as "a ludicrous invention." The statement is authentic enough, but its authenticity is that of a 1926 musical comedy. (One can almost hear Stotesbury breaking into Sandy Wilson's hymn for aging playboys, "Sur la Plage," as he goes into a soft-shoe number with a dozen schoolgirl-chorines on the palm-fringed beach.)

During the years in which society-news headlines made it appear that Stotesbury was dreamwalking through a Broadway libretto, the public was led to forget that he had long been in the front rank of the financiers who created the corporate structures, small private governments, that provided the fiscal base for the swift growth of American industrial technology. Horace Mather Lippincott, a conservative historian of Philadelphia and its northerly environs, has observed that Stotesbury was "one of the small group of men from various countries which settled the financial policies of nations. Thus he wielded incalculable power and influence."[9]

Before he became a key figure in the network of Morgan firms — Drexel & Company (Philadelphia), J. P. Morgan & Company (New York), J. S. Morgan & Company (London), and Morgan Harjes & Company (Paris) — he had become known as the man who knew more about "commercial paper" than any other banker in Philadelphia.[10] It was this early reputation that served as the foundation of his career. However, it was an arcane distinction, one that might well have baffled anyone other than an expert in banking.

What did it mean? The *University Dictionary of Business and Finance,* compiled by Donald T. Clark and Bert A. Gottfried, defines commercial paper as "any of the various forms of short-term, negotiable, credit instruments which arise out of business transactions, including bills of exchange, drafts, acceptances, notes, etc. There are no exact limits to the application of the term, but in financial circles it is generally used to refer to credit which has a term of six months or less, and which is for an amount of $50,000 or less." Twenty-two types of commercial paper are then listed and defined. One turns to "bills of exchange" and finds thirty-four types defined. Six types of "drafts" and twelve types of "acceptances" are also defined.

A layman tracing these definitions of credit instrument forms is quickly bewildered. They are as confusing as definitions of money, or explanations of the international gold market. In the end, one gives up, settling for a homemade overview: whatever its purpose, whatever form it takes, whatever its time limit, a piece of commercial paper is based upon a promise to pay, and such a promise leaves the party who accepts it a hostage to dishonesty and misfortune — in sum, to chance.

One doesn't have to be an expert in commercial paper to perceive that its risks are great. Stotesbury's eminence as a banker without peer in issuing, buying, and selling commercial paper distinguished him as a superb technician, part financier and part mage, in an ancient art. According to Lippincott, Pierpont Morgan once observed that Stotesbury "knew more about the details of banking than any other man in the United States," which is to say, tritely to be sure, that in his prime Stotesbury was the banker's banker of American finance. What the elder Morgan, and his contemporaries, appear to have been telling the nonbanking world was simply that Stotesbury was recognized in the financial community as a man who came near to genius.

In October, 1907, when Pierpont Morgan was reaching his historic decision to compel his fellow bankers in New York to join him in a common effort to end the financial panic that had stricken Wall Street and was threatening the nation, he quietly sought Stotesbury's support for his bold scheme. He took a train down to Philadelphia, and the two senior financiers conferred in secret over dinner at Stotesbury's costly, but staid, mansion just off Rittenhouse Square on Walnut Street, the most fashionable neighborhood in the city.[11]

Stotesbury, a fifty-eight-year-old widower who entertained with somewhat grave elegance, had already had dinners there for Presidents William McKinley and Theodore Roosevelt. In several years, William Howard Taft would become the third president to dine with Stotesbury at his Walnut Street residence, a house laden with the swollen furniture and dark hangings of Victorian *décor*.[12] And there Stotesbury would soon preside at memorable midnight suppers for Mary Garden and Nellie Melba during his years as the leading supporter of opera in the city, an incidental career in which he personally loaned Oscar Hammerstein $400,000 against a mortgage on the impresario's new Philadelphia Opera House (later renamed the Metropolitan Opera House) and then became the owner of the theater after Hammerstein's financial collapse fifteen months later in April, 1910.

The dinner conference between Stotesbury and Morgan went well, and Morgan returned to New York ready to act with the support of Drexel & Company. Exercising power of a kind and degree not even the president could summon, Morgan, at a series of meetings climaxed by a gathering at the Morgan Library on the night of November 2, 1907, succeeded in persuading a group of leading bankers, brokers, and trust officers to bring Wall Street's hysteria, and their own communal avarice, under control.[13]

Stotesbury's crucial role in Morgan's strategy has never been recognized by Morgan's biographers, most of them New Yorkers. He has remained the invisible man of the crisis. In contrast, his position in eastern seaboard society was inherently a visible one. In 1890, he had been listed in the first Philadelphia edition of the *Social Register,* and in 1897 his name had been added to the New York edition. In June, 1894, the Philadelphia newspapers had mentioned him, along with John Cadwalader, George W. Biddle, and Richard Vaux, all members of Old Philadelphia families, as being of "the local four hundred," a reporter's catchphrase which, despite its indifferent arithmetic, had first gained currency in New York newspapers about a decade earlier. Thus, by the turn of the century, Stotesbury's high station in society had been publicly documented.

Stotesbury served as the treasurer of the Republican National Committee for the successful presidential campaigns of Roosevelt (1904) and Taft (1908). Twice he was offered presidential appointments, but turned them down: once to the cabinet post of secretary of the treasury, and once to the post of ambassador to the Court of St. James's in London. Supposedly, his shrewd caution as a banker — it was said of him that "he never made a bad loan" — led him to avoid the vulnerabilities of high public office. However, one of his few confidants has put the matter in a different perspective: "Mr. Stotesbury simply believed that it was more important to be a big man in Philadelphia than just another cabinet member."

Stotesbury was the civic man par excellence. He kept the opera going. He served on the arts council. He oversaw the finances of the Boy Scouts. He commissioned the outstanding pioneer French *urbaniste* Jacques Gréber to prepare the first designs for the Franklin Parkway, the axial focus of the city. He served as a trustee of the city's great center of learning, the University of Pennsylvania (from which he received an honorary doctor of laws degree of 1922). He provided the executive energy and direction that finally got the protracted construction of the Philadelphia Museum of Art on a fixed schedule with an opening date that was met. The list could be extended into a meaningless roll call of service with familiar organizations. But, the important point to be made is that Stotesbury, compelled by an inherited Quaker sense of duty, worked at his civic tasks.

His favorite rôle seems to have been his service as the head of the city's parks commission. He devoted himself to the creation, extension, and maintenance of Philadelphia's parks for many years. Whenever he passed the uniformed park police in his carriage, and later in his automobile, they saluted him. "He always drew himself up and proudly returned the salute," his confidant has recalled. "What you have to remember about Mr. Stotesbury is that he was a Philadelphia boy from the day he was born until the day he died. He loved this city."

The Associated Press wrote of him that "no Philadelphian was as widely known throughout the nation and abroad." An unwary outsider knowing Stotesbury's reputation in finance and civic affairs might have been led to assume that he was universally respected by his fellow citizens. However, Old Philadelphia would have disputed the assumption, for even though he was, undeniably, a Philadelphian, he was, just as undeniably, not a *Philadelphian*. Indeed, the honor of being a *Philadelphian* — a "birthright *Philadelphian*," to put a fine point on the matter — was not the city's to bestow: it was conferred by God, or sometimes, under the pressure of historical inevitability, by His surrogates, the managers of the exclusive Assembly balls, say, or by the admissions committee of the Philadelphia Club. And in the end, it was the bitter pleasure of the *Philadelphians*, practicing paradox among the teacups at Whitemarsh Hall, to seem to embrace Stotesbury while denying him the full favor of their rarefied company. Here, one needs a guide, and it is one's good fortune that E. Digby Baltzell, a Philadelphia-born sociologist, has taken a thorough, detached, and sometimes amused look at Old Philadelphia.

In his illuminating study, *Philadelphia Gentlemen: The Making of a National Upper Class* (republished as *An American Business Aristocracy*), Baltzell leads the outsider through the alician games, serious as liturgy, once played by Philadelphia's old families. "Within the fashionable and sometimes snobbish world of Proper Philadelphia . . ." he writes, "there are, of course, a few 'old families' who consider themselves, and are reverently so considered by others, to be 'first families.' In local upper-class vernacular, the 'first families' are simply known as *Philadelphians* [here italicized for ease in differentiation]. One may have been born in Philadelphia, and one's ancestors may have been there since colonial times, without ever presuming to call oneself a Philadelphian, at least within the city's loftiest circles. This rather esoteric use of the term *Philadelphian* is altogether confusing to the outsider."[14]

It is the language of aristocratic madness: one has encountered it before — beyond the looking glass. Shakespeare, addressing another matter, has both warned and armed the outsider in his blunt summary: "Here will be an old abusing of God's patience and the King's English."

III

M<small>Y</small> hatred of democracy is stronger than my love of country," Sidney Fisher, an archetypal *Philadelphian,* once observed in the diary he kept between 1834 and 1871. In *The Perennial Philadelphians,* a witty portrait of Old Philadelphia, Nathaniel Burt describes Sidney as "a gentleman of. . . the best family connections, and not enough money, who led a rather querulous and useless life." He "dabbled at law and poetry," and worried constantly about money, "but he could not lower himself to making any."[15] Fisher was, as he observed in his diary, deeply annoyed by "the vulgar, nouveau riche people who are now crowding into society," and he lamented the fact that "the good, respectable old-family society for which Philadelphia was once so celebrated is fast disappearing and persons of low origin and vulgar habits are introduced because they are rich."[16]

The new rich — the Tartars at the gate: it is a theme that absorbs him. Its variations spin on and on through generations of Old Philadelphians — music for a fantasy: a timeless leitmotiv for those whose Tory persuasions lead them to see no difference between the sacral and the familial, whose talisman is divine power held by the corporate few, and who celebrate the presence of God not so much in their temples as in their mirrors. The old families of Philadelphia, like their Tory models in England, abjured enthusiasm, suspected enterprise and intelligence (except when the latter addressed itself, say, to the comely periods of the *Georgics*), and, scorning success, made a virtue of mediocrity. Worn clothes and threadbare ideas: both were seemly, both were approved.

Stotesbury, the very model of success — his income for 1919 was $5,585,000, and he was known to be "the richest man at Morgan's" by 1927 when his wealth reached $100,000,000 — offended their articles of cloister on almost all counts.[17] He could not, for example, have been mediocre, even had he tried: his was not the impulse of the gentleman underachiever. One may question the quality of his intelligence — he never read a book, and he confused the New Deal with the Terror and Roosevelt with Robespierre — but, as has been noted, he had a remarkably keen mind for the complexities of finance, and his palaces in Chestnut Hill, Palm Beach, and Bar Harbor were monuments to the triumph of the Protestant work ethic.

Stotesbury addressed himself to profit, and its advantages, while Old Philadelphia sat spellbound in its moldering glory. It had had competent men among its numbers, and it could count great men on its family rolls. However, its celebration of them had become a form of incantation to ward off newcomers, and their claim to recognition. Lawrence Stone has observed in *The Crisis of the Aristocracy, 1558–1641*, a title appropriate to the heirs of Sidney Fisher, that "a class is not a finite group of families, but rather a bus . . . [that is] always full, but always filled with different people."[18] However, the *Philadelphians* didn't want any newcomers riding on their bus, even in the back. Unless, of course, it was to their advantage to invite the newcomer, and his new money, aboard.

The need for fresh money is the eternal condition of withering social stock, its vigor spent, its intelligence decayed by the exemptions of power. Old Philadelphia might look to England for its precedents and rituals, but its true model was to be found in the families of the *ancien régime* in Paris, a nobility without a court, inbred and insolvent. By the time Stotesbury arrived on Rittenhouse Square during the Victorian twilight, *le gratin*, the upper crust of the Faubourg Saint-Germain, had become obliged to contract rich marriages. Its luster was dimming, its noble patents had become tarnished by fiduciary matchmaking.

Tribal inbreeding, whether in Philadelphia or Paris, may lead to rather odd results. Philippe Jullian has observed that the men of *le gratin* "were more elegant than the women and the women . . . more cultured than the men,"[19] an amusing condition, but one that promised little for the longevity of the tribe. Jullian might, of course, have been describing the *Philadelphians,* for, like the *ancien régime,* Old Philadelphia remained an island within, proud, obtuse, and dangerous when provoked, touched as it was by the natural paranoia of privilege. It had long ago assumed the patent of aristocratic sanction — the power of exclusion — and it had no intention of giving it up, as the Knickerbockers, less clearly defined and much less strong-willed than Old Philadelphia, had been forced to do in New York. The Knickerbockers had yielded their power of exclusion (which, at best, they had exercised with little more than uninspired clumsiness) to the new rich of Fifth Avenue when the Vanderbilt palace era began at the end of the depression of the 1870's.

It was, of course, the prerogative of the old families to invite selected non-*Philadelphians* to join their games: in such invitations lay the roots of Old Philadelphia's ludic ambiguities. They did, for example, invite Stotesbury to the Assembly, a fact that duly impressed Lippincott, who wrote: "[Stotesbury] rose by sheer ability and industry from an office boy to be a partner in one of the world's greatest banking houses, and he went to the Assembly ball." No true *Philadelphian* would doubt which was the greater accomplishment.

The Assembly is a rigorously exclusive ball held each winter — twice each winter in an earlier era when the dances were known as the First Assembly and the Second Assembly. The earliest of the Philadelphia Dancing Assemblies was organized in 1784, preceding somewhat the similarly distinguished St. Cecilia's balls held each winter in Charleston. As early as the eighteenth century, the corporate phrase "The Assembly" had begun to evoke in Philadelphia a measure of awe which Struthers Burt has defined: "The Assembly exercises an altogether extraordinary power, both social and material, in the city, and to say you belong, which mustn't be said at all unless absolutely necessary, and then in the most casual manner, is exactly like announcing your rank in a country of hereditary titles."[20] One may hear in the quotation the distant voice of a catechist instructing an elite.

Stotesbury's daughters married into the Assembly, and he and his second wife, Eva, were invited to dance with the *Philadelphians* when he was sixty-six. Several legends surrounding Stotesbury's invitation have survived: their want of invention will be examined presently.

Beyond the Assembly, managed by men but dependent for its existence upon the presence of the women of Old Philadelphia, lay the world of the clubs, ruled by men and inhabited by them alone. There one encountered the *Philadelphian* at his most subtle, and ambiguous. There he welcomed and denied Stotesbury at once.

Stotesbury belonged to many clubs, among them the Philadelphia Art Club, the Radnor Hunt, the Philadelphia Cricket Club, the Merion Cricket Club, the Germantown Cricket Club, the Racquet Club, the Rose Tree Hunt, the Pennsylvania Club, the Rabbit Club, the Corinthian Yacht Club, the Philadelphia Country Club, the Huntingdon Valley Country Club, the Bachelor Barge Club, and the

Farmer's Club. The last named was the most exclusive dining club in Philadelphia, a distinction it had enjoyed since before the Civil War.[21]

Stotesbury devoted himself primarily to the Union League Club, where, Lippincott has noted, "he met most of his friends and where he was very popular." According to tradition, the members of the Union League Club run Philadelphia and have done so for generations, no matter which political party holds office. Historians of the city and most residents agree that it is the most important club in the city.[22] Stotesbury became a member in 1882 and served as president five times, declining further nomination after 1923.

But, there was a purer air to be breathed, a rarer company to be enjoyed in the exclusive club world of the *Philadelphians,* and both were to be found at the Rittenhouse Club and the Philadelphia Club. In the halls of these two clubs, Old Philadelphia decided who among the new men, with their new money, were worthy to be welcomed aboard the bus.[23]

Stotesbury was invited to join the Rittenhouse Club. He was thus elected to the elite, or so he appeared to have been, for custom dictated that he would then, in due course, be invited to membership in the Philadelphia Club, the ultimate measure of acceptance by the *Philadelphians.* He had made the Assembly, the Farmer's, the Rittenhouse, and he had been elected president of the Union League five times. Membership in the Philadelphia Club — "the hallmark of gentlemanly antecedents and business achievements,"[24] in Baltzell's phrase — would finally place Stotesbury among the elect few as a gentleman, and a millionaire. He had only to wait.

However, the years passed and the ultimate invitation from the Philadelphia Club did not come. Old Philadelphia, patient and cunning, let time run out. Stotesbury had been excluded.

One may presume that Sidney Fisher snickered. Certainly his heirs to privilege did, for it is their anxious rudeness one may still hear in the shadows of the ruined stone at Whitemarsh Hall.

Louis XIV once chided a courtier at Versailles for daring to arrive for a royal appointment, not late, but at the last possible moment. "I almost had to wait," the Sun King said, and turned away.[25] Looking at the king's back, the courtier did not have to be told that the royal audience had ended. Old Philadelphia turned its back on Stotesbury at the threshold of the Philadelphia Club.

Applying the alician logic of the *Philadelphians,* one might say that his failure was not that he had been born in the wrong bed but that he had not been born in the right one.

IV

BEFORE Wall Street there was Third Street, and the succession of outstanding moneymen from whom Stotesbury was ultimately to learn his trade. One should briefly recall them, and the tradition they created, in order to fit him into his own history, as it were.[26]

In 1838, eleven years before Stotesbury was born, Francis Martin Drexel, a successful painter of portraits and miniatures who had emigrated from the Austrian Tyrol, opened the small brokerage on Third Street in Philadelphia that was to become Drexel & Company. Philadelphia had been the American capital during the Revolution, the capital of the new republic from 1790 to 1800, and the capital of Pennsylvania until 1799.

Third Street, which lay only a step away from the waterfront countinghouses of the great importers, had been to the United States what Lombard Street was to London, the financial center of the country, a distinction it was to retain through the early decades of the nineteenth century. And, like Lombard Street, Third Street had become the symbol of a small but enormously important world — the vital, bustling, innovative, and aggressive world (completely non-*Philadelphian* in its vigor and conquests) of money changers, money-lenders, and merchant-bankers, the country's earliest brokers and financiers on a national scale.

There, against severe, almost insuperable, odds, Robert Morris and his associates had financed the American Revolution; Thomas Willing had served as president of the Bank of North America, "the first corporate banking structure in America," 1781–1791, and as president of the first Bank of the United States, 1791–1811; Alexander Hamilton as the first secretary of the treasury had developed the credit base of the new nation; Stephen Girard had founded the bank bearing his name and had financed the country's military operations in the War of 1812; Nicholas Biddle had served as president of the second Bank of the United States, 1822–1836, and had stood against President Andrew Jackson in a historic and extremely bitter struggle; and Jay Cooke had financed the Union Army in the

Civil War, and had enjoyed a monopoly as the broker for the sale of federal bonds until he was successfully challenged by Anthony Joseph Drexel, the son of Francis Martin Drexel.

Third Street has been called "the cradle of American finance." There, like Housman's mercenaries, the great Philadelphia bankers had "saved the sum of things for pay."

Such was the tradition, already fading, into which Stotesbury was born, and which would come to its inevitable end early in his career. Wall Street had begun to supersede Third Street by 1825, the year in which the Erie Canal was opened. The subsequent rapid growth of commerce in New York City, the great increase in international traffic in the Port of New York, and Wall Street's rôle as the broker for foreign investment, principally English, in the development of the country's railway systems foretold the end of Philadelphia's primacy as banker to the nation.

Because of the shrewd foresight of Anthony J. Drexel, his banking firm not only survived the historic shift, but prospered from it, ending up with one foot in Wall Street, where Stotesbury would be quite as at home as he was to be in Philadelphia's financial district.

T HE diligent hand makes rich."

Stotesbury learned William Penn's rule of work when he was a child. He was born in Philadelphia on February 26, 1849, to Thomas P. and Martha (Parker) Stotesbury; he was one of four children, three of them boys. His father was an Episcopalian, but it was his mother's church, the Society of Friends, that shaped his upbringing. He was named after Edward Young Townsend, a prominent member of his mother's Meeting. He attended Quaker schools until he was sixteen, and then studied for a year at a "business college" Thomas M. Pierce had recently opened in Philadelphia.

Stotesbury grew up in a neighborhood of Quakers who had gathered in "a large district about [their] Meeting House . . . in comfortable homes from which they went to Meeting on First Days in such great numbers that the pavements were crowded, morning, afternoon, and evening," Lippincott has recalled.[27] The material reward that Penn promised the diligent hand has moved Baltzell to the wry observation: "The ethic of the meeting house is congenial to success in the counting house."[28]

Stotesbury's father, a sugar refiner who had himself achieved a comfortable affluence, got Edward a job with Drexel & Company when he was seventeen. He started working for the bank in October, 1866, and advanced quickly from menial tasks — sweeping, cleaning inkwells, running errands — to his apprenticeship as a clerk. His starting salary was $16.60 a month. His second Christmas at Drexel's brought him a $200 bonus from the bank, and his salary was increased to $500 a year. "It was the beginning," he remarked long afterward with eloquent brevity.

Fiske Kimball, the first curator of the Philadelphia Museum of Art, wrote a brief memoir on the Stotesburys, published after his death, in which he told an anecdote that revealed Anthony Joseph Drexel's high opinion of his young clerk.[29] Drexel was the head of the bank. His daughter Emily had married Edward Biddle of the most prestigious family in the city. Drexel brought young Biddle into the bank, gave him a $150,000 interest, and made him a partner. "One day," Kimball wrote, ". . . Biddle came to Drexel saying, 'Your clerk has insulted me. Either he or I must go.' 'What clerk?' croaked Drexel. 'Stotesbury.' 'Then you'd better go.' And go Edward Biddle did." Some Biddles today treasure the belief that Edward, after the insult, but before his dismissal, felled Stotesbury with a single blow, a reflex known, ruefully, to his heirs as "the million-dollar punch."[30] Drexel bought back his son-in-law's interest, but the loss of his partnership cost Biddle many millions. Thus, in his first encounter with Old Philadelphia, Stotesbury was the innocent victor.

In May, 1871, Drexel invited J. Pierpont Morgan to come down to Philadelphia from New York for dinner. Morgan's father, Junius Spencer Morgan, the leading American financier in London, had only recently managed a spectacular $50,000,000 Franco-Prussian War loan to France, following the fall of Napoleon III at Sedan. The younger Morgan was thirty-four and Drexel forty-five (a bit young to have "croaked" at his son-in-law in the Biddle incident). After dinner, Drexel took Morgan into his library and there proposed that they become banking partners in New York City, while he continued to run his family's firm in Philadelphia. Morgan demurred. He was not in good health, he said, and he was thinking of retiring from business. Drexel urged him not to. Morgan said he would consider the matter, but that he would require a year off for travel and rest. Drexel agreed, and wrote down the major points of the partnership scheme on the back of an envelope. Drexel, Morgan & Company opened its doors in Wall Street on July 1 with the elder Morgan's blessing.[31]

Early in his dealings with his Philadelphia partners, Morgan observed that Stotesbury was "one of the brightest and most promising young men in the Philadelphia office."[32] In 1875, the partners gave Stotesbury an interest in Drexel & Company. The list of his promotions from that date is almost Handelian in its stately cadences:

On January 1, 1883, he was admitted to partnership in both Drexel & Company and Drexel, Morgan & Company. His initial share of the Philadelphia profits was two percent. In 1893, the year of Anthony J. Drexel's death, he became a senior partner in both firms. The Drexel era had ended; the Morgan era was about to begin. On December 31, 1894, Drexel, Morgan & Company was dissolved; the next morning, J. P. Morgan & Company, the new copartner firm, began business. Stotesbury was one of its original partners. In 1905, when he was forty-six, Stotesbury became the resident senior partner — the chief executive — of Drexel & Company, a position he held until his death.

Stotesbury's steady rise to success and wealth was tempered by early grief. On April 2, 1873, two years before the partners had voted to give him a participating interest in Drexel's, he had married Fanny Bergman Butcher, the daughter of Theodore and Ann (Powel) Butcher. When Stotesbury brought home the news that he was thereafter to share in the bank's profits he observed to his wife that he would probably, in time, become rich. Fanny Stotesbury, speaking to him in the Quaker manner, told him, "Edward, would that I could see more of thee than all thy money."[33] Eight years later, in November, 1881, shortly after the birth of her second child, she died. Lippincott remembers Fanny Stotesbury as "a beautiful and charming lady — gentle, gracious, and unworldly." At thirty-two, Stotesbury was a widower with two young daughters, one of them only a few weeks old.

VI

BALZAC has described the eternal banker: "lynx-natured, thinlipped, keen-eyed, hard-favored."[34] In his office, Stotesbury did his best not to impair the image. He was brisk in manner and speech, an unemotional little man, and vain; pardonably so, Lippincott thought. He was, the *Philadelphia Bulletin* once said, "somewhat distant and reserved to those who did not enjoy his confidence and friendship. To those who did, however, he was genial and sunny . . . a keen, well-versed conversationalist, and an appreciative listener."[35]

As a young man, he had collected watches, but his interest turned to gems and he acquired an expert's knowledge of their cutting and polishing. He became, Lippincott says, "so fine a judge of precious stones that Caldwell's [the jeweler to Old Philadelphia] would gladly have employed him as their buyer." His interest in gems lasted throughout his life, but his greatest enthusiasm outside banking was breeding, showing, and driving his outstanding stable of trotters. He "treated his horses like children as had his father before him at nearby Chelten Hills where they both learned to love horse-flesh as they drove about the beautiful countryside near their homes," Lippincott has written.

Every summer at the Philadelphia Horse Show (which drew ten thousand spectators to Wissahickon in 1892) he competed "against the best [drivers] in the United States [and] usually carried off the blue ribbons in the 'Gentleman's Roadster' Class. . . . It was a very satisfying sight to see Mr. Stotesbury showing his horses in the ring. Immaculately attired and seated in a Brewster runabout he drove with the skill of a master . . . and [spoke] fondly to his horses. It was a picture of complete refinement."

One evening in September, 1914, Stotesbury was amusing some dinner partners with stories of his experiences as an opera patron. "I paid Mary Garden $1,800 a night, and made an engagement to pay her $80,000 in the course of the winter," he said, adding wryly: "The newspapers accused me of spending too much time in her dressing room, while on the other hand she described me as 'such a timid little man.' "[36] Mary Garden made her Philadelphia debut in 1908.

By that time, Stotesbury was fifty-nine and rich. He had only recently begun to collect portraits by Gainsborough, Romney, Hoppner, Lawrence, Raeburn, and other English painters. He had fallen under the spell of the mesmeric Anglo-American art dealer Joseph Duveen, who had induced him to give up his taste for French nineteenth-century anecdotal painters, whose work had long been fashionable among rich Americans.[37] Troyan's *Retour de la Ferme,* a much admired painting of this genre ("two cows with one and a half sheep in the background"), which Stotesbury had bought shortly after it had been auctioned for $65,000 at the Henry sale in New York in 1907, would soon disappear from his walls.

Within three years of Miss Garden's first appearance in Philadelphia, Stotesbury's mansion would house one of the three finest collections of English portraits in the world, pictures which, Fiske Kimball later said, "Duveen . . . unloaded on [him] at enormous prices."[38] Only the Georgian portrait collection owned by Henry Edwards Huntington at San Marino, California, would come to take precedence over Stotesbury's in the United States. Both men were Duveen customers, a costly distinction.

Stotesbury's collection deserved a proper English setting: one can now see that Whitemarsh Hall was the inevitable consequence of his first Gainsborough. Stotesbury, of course, could not have known that a Georgian palace was implicit in the Georgian paintings Joe Duveen was sending down from New York. Duveen, on the other hand, could not have doubted it, for he had a rare gift: he could, when it was profitable to do so, both sense and assist the inevitable. But in his early sales to Stotesbury, even Duveen could not have foreseen that he was to have an accomplice in properly housing the mature collection . . . a terribly grateful accomplice.

Family life on Walnut Street was changing. Stotesbury's older daughter, Edith L., was married to Sydney Emlyn Hutchinson, a *Philadelphian* of impeccable antecedents. On January 25, 1909, his younger daughter, Frances Bergman Stotesbury, married John Kearsley Mitchell III, another *Philadelphian* and heir to a distinguished name in Old Philadelphia, one to which, disguised as "Mr. Marshall," he was to add a peccant stain. "Marshall," presently exposed as Mitchell, was the wealthy Philadelphia lover of Dot King (née Anna Marie Keenan), a New York "butterfly" who was found murdered in her bedroom on March 5, 1923. Miss King had, in her turn, been keeping Albert Guimares, a Puerto Rican of no known family distinction, who thus shared in the benefits of Stotesbury's generosity to his children and their husbands.[39] When Frances Stotesbury married Mitchell, the Philadelphia newspapers reported that her father had made her a gift of $1,000,000.

After the marriage of his second daughter, no one remained at Walnut Street to have a punctual breakfast with Stotesbury before he hurried off to the bank at seven-fifty. He was sixty years old and for the first time since his own marriage thirty-six years earlier he was alone. A year passed, and early in 1910 he was boarding a ship in New York for a business trip abroad when he noticed William T. Eldridge, an old friend and well-known broker, on deck. Eldridge was seeing Mrs. Oliver Cromwell, a widow of one month, and her daughter Louise, who was soon to make her debut, off to Paris. He introduced them to Stotesbury. Then, certain that Mrs. Cromwell would find Stotesbury a concerned and diverting companion during the long days at sea, he bade them bon voyage.

Eldridge was the godfather of Mrs. Cromwell's younger son, James H. R. Cromwell, who, by his own account, "was being very bad at the time and had been put in boarding school." Cromwell has re-called what turned out to be his avuncular godfather's error in intro-ducing Stotesbury to his mother, a notably beautiful woman. "Poor Uncle Bill. The truth of the matter is that he felt very dearly toward my mother. But, it was the old story: never introduce your girl to your best friend."[40] Stotesbury had ample time during the crossing to become acquainted with Eva Cromwell. He was enchanted.

VII

Eva — Lucretia Bishop (Roberts) Cromwell — had been born in Chicago in 1865, and had graduated from St. Mary's School, Notre Dame, Indiana. Her father, James Henry Roberts, was a corporation lawyer who liked to recall that at the beginning of his career he had ridden the judicial circuits of southern Illinois with an older lawyer, Abraham Lincoln. Roberts was a partner in Chicago of Melville Weston Fuller in a law firm that numbered the Illinois Central Rail-road among its clients. In 1888, after giving consideration to both men, President Grover Cleveland appointed Fuller chief justice of the United States Supreme Court. According to a Cromwell family tradition, "the two men had flipped a coin to see which of them would go to Washington."

Eva met Oliver Eaton Cromwell, a descendant of England's Lord Protector, in Albuquerque, New Mexico, and they were married there in 1889. Cromwell's father, Charles Thorn Cromwell, a success-ful lawyer whose clients included the Vanderbilt railroads, and Eva's father were opposing counsel in a protracted action in a court sitting in Albuquerque. James H. R. Cromwell, who was named for his mother's father, has recalled that his grandfathers stood opposed as representatives of "the eastern and western railroad interests. The conflict concerned which group would control new trackage into California from New Mexico. The two men were completely different. Cromwell was hard drinking, profane, tough. Roberts was an extremely religious type, a teetotaler and polished intellectual who never swore. But neither hesitated to buy legislators, when and if they thought it necessary."

They were opposed not only in the courtroom but also outside it. Neither wanted his child to marry the child of the other. Something of the depth of Roberts's concern was reflected in his warning to Eva when he finally consented to the marriage: "Daughter, you must faithfully attend church every Sabbath to arm yourself against the godless Cromwells." Eva was twenty-four and Cromwell forty-one at the time of their wedding. Their married life was begun in a hotel in Albuquerque called El Mirasol (The Sunflower), a name that Eva would long afterward appropriate to her mansion in Palm Beach.

Charles Thorn Cromwell had been a member of the Union Club in New York City and the New York Yacht Club. His racing yachts had won a number of trophies, and he had been socially active for many years. When Oliver Cromwell brought Eva to New York they immediately entered into the exclusive world of Mrs. William Astor and the four hundred deemed worthy of her invitations. Eva bore her first child in 1890, and she and Oliver were listed together in the *Social Register* for the first time in 1891. They lived in the handsome Cromwell country home on Manursing Island in Long Island Sound off Port Chester, New York, the house in which their three children — Henrietta Louise, Oliver Eaton, Jr., and James Henry Roberts — were born. During her childhood, Henrietta devised a succession of playful names for her mother: *Eva* was the last, and most intelligible, of them. Eva enjoyed the name and kept it. In time, Henrietta, who had been named for her grandmother Cromwell, dropped her own first name, preferring to be known as Louise Cromwell.

Because of Eva's youth, she and Oliver became part of New York's "younger dancing set . . . whose centers of activity [were] the Meadow Brook, the Country, and the Tuxedo Clubs."[41] The members of this fashionable and exclusive group all belonged to old families of long standing in the Four Hundred. They dutifully paid their *devoirs* to Mrs. William Astor and dutifully attended the tedious ceremonies of the Patriarchs. However, by the end of the

1880's they had begun to tire of the Patriarchs' balls and midnight cotillion suppers — three each winter season — managed with dreary pomposity for Mrs. Astor by her chamberlain–press agent, Ward McAllister. They — Eva and Oliver Cromwell among them — were guests at a memorable ball given by Center Hitchcock and Edward H. Bradley at the new Hotel Waldorf on February 16, 1895, "one of the handsomest and jolliest balls ever given in New York," in the opinion of one enthusiastic reporter.[42]

The Hitchcock-Bradley ball was only one of several significant social events that season that heralded the end of the dull and exhausted reign of the Patriarchs, originally twenty-five in number, whom Mrs. William Astor had marshaled to control post–Civil War society and fend off the emergent lords of finance, transportation, and commerce with their frightening social aspirations. The grand strategy of the Fifth Avenue elders had been to create and maintain those exclusive events at which the daughters of proper society could meet and form alliances with the sons of proper society.

McAllister, who had managed these events, had died in 1893. He had fallen out with Mrs. Astor in his later years, and the night before his burial, while his body lay in the parlor of his house only a few blocks from her mansion, she had given a small but costly dinner for her tactical inner circle, a vulgar demonstration of contempt. The last Patriarchs' ball, managed by a committee, was held on March 2, 1897, at the Waldorf, with supper in the Empire Room, the most opulent banqueting hall in New York, twenty-four seasons after Mrs. Astor had first raised the shield of the Knickerbockers, and quasi-Knickerbockers, against the new rich. She had failed in her effort to keep the new rich at bay: Cornelius Vanderbilt II had become a Patriarch by the end of the 1880's. (A decent man, Vanderbilt absented himself from her dinner the night before McAllister's funeral, even though he was on the invitation list. Further, he served as one of the deposed chamberlain's pallbearers the next morning. He greatly esteemed good manners.)

Eva and Oliver Cromwell began to give their own splendid entertainments, and Cromwell, who had graduated from Columbia College in 1868 as a mining engineer, began to play the stock market with a reckless hand. He lost heavily, and Eva urged him to move the family to Washington, "to remove him from further temptation to speculate." There the Cromwell dinners were warmly praised by the diplomatic corps, and by Washington, Baltimore, and Philadelphia society. Eva's natural gifts as a hostess began to flourish, and she became widely known, while she was still in her thirties, for her command of the protocol and logistics of courtly receptions, as well as her aristocratic composure and graciousness.

Late in 1909, Cromwell suffered three successive strokes, the last of which, on December 21, was fatal.[43] He was sixty-one; the New York newspapers remembered him only as a "clubman" and "yachtsman." Reports were published that he had left Eva three houses and "an ample fortune." Two of the houses were journalistic fictions. The "ample fortune" was, in its implications, an exaggeration; but, so too was the rumor, circulated in society, that Louise was "penniless" when she made her debut, postponed by her father's death, in the winter of 1910–1911. Eva would be able to live comfortably, but it appeared that her days of lavish entertaining had come to an end. She went into mourning, withdrew from society, and decided to go to Paris with Louise. In New York, an old and dear friend, William T. Eldridge, took them to the pier and accompanied them up the gangplank. . . .

VIII

A T the beginning of May, 1910, several months after he had returned from the business trip to Europe on which he had met Eva Cromwell, Stotesbury bought the town house on Walnut Street that adjoined his mansion.[44] He had purchased the mansion in 1899 from the estate of Thomas McKean, namesake and descendant of a signer of the Declaration of Independence and himself a prominent figure in Philadelphia.[45] The large somber house, its walls faced with dark stone, stood on an oversized plot of land at the northeast corner of Walnut and Twentieth streets. A large horseshoe stair, ceremonial and imposing, led up from the sidewalk to an arched entranceway on the first floor, which was raised on a half-story podium-basement.

The mansion — No. 1925 Walnut Street — had been designed by Frank Furness, a well-known architect and *Philadelphian*.[46] Its decorative detail revealed the picturesque flair, amusing and eccentric, that later became the hallmark of Furness's public buildings. The adjoining town house at No. 1923 had been built by McKean's son, Thomas McKean, Jr., who had only recently died when Stotesbury bought it in a move to protect his corner property. Having no need for the town house, Stotesbury leased it.

Early the following year, work was begun at the mansion on an elaborate interior remodeling and redecorating program. The Victorian interiors were to be torn out "from cellar to attic" and new interiors designed and installed, a project that was to take two years (1911–1912) to complete. Although contemporary accounts would not be entirely clear as to details, some minor structural changes would also be made: a basement level entrance would be pierced in the wall on the Twentieth Street side of the house, a mirror-lined formal entrance hall would be installed, and a handsome ceremonial staircase would be set into the old structure.[47] It was an unusual project to have been undertaken by a sixty-two-year-old widower, particularly one who had never before been known to have shown so great an interest in architecture and decoration.

The work, quietly organized, brought together, according to family recollections, an unusual group of four men. The presence of each of them on the project has yet to be documented. However, because all of them, or their associates, were to play important rôles in the design and decoration of Whitemarsh Hall, they are discussed together here with certain provisos which will presently be noted. They were Joseph Duveen, Charles Carrick Allom, Lucien Alavoine, and Horace Trumbauer: art dealer, decorator-architect, decorator, and architect.[48]

Duveen, whom James H. R. Cromwell has recalled as having had "more charm than anyone I ever met except FDR," had by then replaced most of the French nineteenth-century paintings in Stotesbury's gallery with English portraits. No one can now recall how Duveen met Stotesbury, but it was a meeting Duveen could easily have arranged, for his clients already included several of Stotesbury's friends and associates, notably Pierpont Morgan. Duveen undoubtedly introduced Allom into the Stotesbury project.

Stotesbury and Trumbauer had already known one another for at least five years. In 1905, during Stotesbury's third term as president of the club, Trumbauer had carried out some alterations for the Union League. And in 1910, at the time Stotesbury was buying the house next door to his Walnut Street mansion, Trumbauer was designing a structural extension to the club, a project with which Stotesbury was much concerned, as he had been with the earlier work. (When the extension was completed in 1911, Stotesbury and his fellow members showed their esteem for Trumbauer by electing him to life membership in the Union League.)

Duveen knew Trumbauer as the architect for several of his clients, P. A. B. Widener, the Philadelphia traction magnate and capitalist, among them. Further, he and Trumbauer had recently become collaborators on another project. Alavoine had succeeded Jules Allard, a fellow Parisian whose firm he had bought out only half a dozen years earlier, as Trumbauer's favored decorator. His presence at Walnut Street was probably a concomitant of Trumbauer's presence.

All of these men were skilled in giving substance to the gilded fantasies of ambition, vanity, and power. Two of them were to be knighted by King George V, and all were to become wealthy. The two foregoing sentences might be separated by an equal sign: they are the equivalent values of an equation each of the unusual group understood better than most men, and which Duveen understood better than any man of his era.

Although the business records that might document the assumption were almost entirely destroyed in the fire-bombing of London in World War II, it is safe to assume that Allom had already begun to work with Duveen in England and America on decorating projects for Duveen clients. Their memorable collaborations, with Duveen as the prime contractor for the decorations and Allom's firm, White Allom and Company (later White Allom Ltd.) as the subcontractor, would one day include the interiors and furnishings for the palaces built by Henry Clay Frick on Fifth Avenue in New York and Henry Edwards Huntington, in San Marino, California. (The story of the latter is told in Part Four.)

Duveen and Trumbauer were then collaborating on the construction of the Duveen Brothers gallery on Fifth Avenue, begun in 1911 and completed in 1912. Trumbauer was serving as the American correspondent of René Sergent, a Paris architect. Sergent had based his drawings for the Duveen building on the *pavillons* of the Ministry of the Marine on the Place de la Concorde in Paris. This superb *palais,* one of an identical pair, was designed by Jacques-Ange Gabriel, perhaps the most gifted French architect of the eighteenth century, who "brought to its ultimate perfection the French classical tradition of François Mansart" with such masterpieces as the Petit Trianon at Versailles and the Hermitage at Fontainebleau.[49] In the colonnades he designed for the twin palaces on the Place de la Concorde, Gabriel had paid tribute to François D'Orbay's famous colonnade on the Louvre (long mistakenly attributed to Claude Perrault), which Michel Gallet has called French architecture's declaration of independence from the Italian baroque. Duveen wanted Gabriel's sober elegance: he chose his collaborators, living or dead, with subtle care. He knew that by inflating the egos of his American clients as they passed through the Fifth Avenue entrance of his replica of Gabriel's imposing facade he would be able to inflate proportionately the prices they would pay within — "by thirty to forty per cent," he confided to the Paris dealer René Gimpel, his brother-in-law and competitor. Gimpel dryly confided the matter to his diary, a distinguished record of a remarkable era of art sales.[50]

Duveen was the son of a British knight, Sir Joseph Joel Duveen, who had decorated Westminster Abbey for the coronation of a client, Edward VII, in 1902. Duveen himself would be knighted in 1919 (as already noted), made a baronet in 1927, and raised to the peerage as the first Baron Duveen of Milbank in 1933. The elder Duveen, who, with his brother Henry Joseph Duveen, had established Duveen Brothers in London in 1897, dealt in English, French, and Italian furniture, gothic tapestries, Italian velvet, Spanish leather, porcelains — a wide range of objects, many of them costly rarities — but only slightly in paintings. As late as 1900, the younger Duveen was still known primarily as a decorator and dealer in fine furniture (the ambiguous term *decorator* implying, in his case, no architectural or design ability).[51] However, he had by then started to move toward an emphasis on paintings, and the enormous profits they implied. His instinct for money was as remarkable as his instinct for paintings, although the former often imposed certain vague distractions on the latter. For example, his instinct for money sometimes exacted of him a cavalier detachment, a benign duplicity, one might say, in matters of authentication. However, even though his inventory of masterpieces was to become unexcelled, Duveen paintings, as well as Duveen sculpture and tapestries, would, in the years to come, rarely want for the equable company of Duveen consoles, commodes, *bureaux, bergères, fauteuils,* tables, and *canapés.* As many of his anxious clients, Eva among them, later testified, Duveen never let them down — one by one the state chambers and *salons* of their palaces were filled by him, usually with distinction.

When the work on Walnut Street began, Charles Allom was at the threshold of his primacy in London. Edward VII — the inventor, burden, and solace of the *Edwardians* — died that year. When he had moved into Buckingham Palace, Edward had taken a last distressed look at his mother's furnishings, *echt* Victorian, of course, and ordered: "Get this tomb cleaned up."[52] Now, with Edward dead, it was once more time to exercise the royal prerogative and move the furniture. King George V was crowned the following year, 1911, and Queen Mary promptly summoned Allom to redecorate some of the principal rooms of state in Buckingham and Windsor palaces. These crown projects, closely supervised by the queen, brought Allom his knighthood in 1913, as well as a long succession of private commissions in Great Britain and the United States. He was well prepared to handle the latter: his firm had had an office in New York, with a small staff, from about 1905. (White's achievements, whatever they may have been, beyond forming the company with Allom in 1893, are, along with his first name, now forgotten in the offices of White Allom in London.)

Horace Trumbauer could not, of course, be knighted. However, he would be awarded an honorary master of arts degree by Harvard University in 1915, in that era a worthy distinction. He is a difficult man to rescue from the past. He feared publicity, and deliberately saw to his own obscurity. From time to time since his death in 1938 he has been dragged into the public eye to serve as a target for the Puritans of modernism, who cite his work only to demean it. He has been stabbed more times than Caesar, and with far more self-righteousness.

Canards have flourished around Trumbauer's name, some vicious and some little more than absurd. One of the most recent of them combines both qualities by stating that he "was frequently intoxicated, and so he left most of his work on these houses [The Elms, 1899, Clarendon Court, 1903, and Miramar, 1913, all in Newport] to be done by Julian Abele, his gifted black servant" (*Rhode Island Yearbook 74*). Julian Abele joined Trumbauer's firm in April, 1906, seven years after The Elms was completed and three years after Clarendon Court was ready for its owner. He graduated from the University of Pennsylvania in June, 1902, and was president of the Architectural Society there in his senior year. He studied at the Ecole des Beaux-Arts, and he was elected to membership in the American Institute of Architects. A sketch of his career, not as a "servant" but as an architect and designer of still unrecognized distinction, will be found in Part Five.

Both Abele and Trumbauer were Francophiles devoted to French architecture and its history, and both may well have been acquainted with the "Mansarade," a broadsheet diatribe circulated against François Mansart, and with the slurs the Duc de Saint-Simon perpetuated in his *Memoirs* against Jules Hardouin-Mansart. Theirs was an art with a long history of malicious gossip.

IX

IN February, 1904, the *Architectural Record* published a professional evaluation of Horace Trumbauer's work. It serves us today as a lens, polished with unconscious irony, through which one can examine Trumbauer in relation to the architectural attitudes of his times, and is worth reviewing at length.

Philadelphia architecture at the turn of the century was, one gathers, the focus of much professional debate because of its undisciplined mixture of the formal and the picturesque, the dull and the quixotic. After observing that "one is quite at a loss for prototypes" of the city's more extreme examples of architectural eccentricity, the *Architectural Record* sets out for its readers what might be called the Philadelphia enigma:

> Probably it must always remain a psychological problem how a city that possesses a building like Independence Hall could produce and tolerate a monstrosity like City Hall, or how the same community could have raised to eminence a designer like Furniss [*sic:* Frank Furness, the architect of Stotesbury's Walnut Street mansion], and trained artists of such high personal distinction as Cope & Stewardson, the Days and Eyre. . . . An acute architectural observer has endeavored to explain the anomaly. His statement is worth quoting:
> "In truth, it is evident from the look of Philadelphia that there is no constraint upon the architects, either from the professional opinion, which elsewhere keeps designers out the maddest of excesses, or from a lay opinion that betokens an interest in the subject and, though ignorant, is willing to be enlightened."
> If this explanation . . . be correct . . . Philadelphia's salvation is to be wrought most speedily by the addition to the professional ranks of a number of well schooled architects, trained in the accepted traditions of the art — men whose education, taste,

temperament, and energy can be bent to the work of annexing Philadelphia to the general practice of the country at large. . . .

In presenting to our readers . . . the designs of Mr. Horace Trumbauer, it is hardly necessary to point out that they furnish proof that the very conditions which we have set forth above as necessary for the production of a better state of things architecturally have, as a matter of fact, arrived. . . . Anyone glancing at our illustrations without knowing [their] origin would not be tempted for a moment by any mark or sign to differentiate the work from *the good metropolitan work* [italics added] proceeding from the office of any of the larger architectural firms located in New York, Boston, or Chicago. . . . It is all the more remarkable because the designs represent the work of a young practitioner. . . .

The article then notes that Trumbauer's firm has had commissions in cities other than Philadelphia:

To say that this success is based in some measure, or even in greater measure, upon business ability than on purely artistical merit is to state what is probably true of most architectural firms that are working in a large way, or if we must so put it, on a metropolitan basis. . . . In this environment the artist is probably limited. . . . Under these circumstances recourse is most likely to be to the formula, to tradition and the standard. Facility becomes the prime requisite. Common sense and its equivalent in art — good taste — are indispensable.

These qualifications with a positive capacity for management, produce the successful architect. Clearly Mr. Trumbauer possesses these qualifications. If his work lacks the decided individuality which has hitherto marked the better class of work in Philadelphia, it is at the same time free from all eccentricity. It is never crude. It conforms to the prevalent standards of educated architects. His work exhibits the eclectic facility which is one of the characteristics of the modern American architects.

Indeed, perhaps, it is this facile response to the current mode [which is] as much at home with the "classic" as with the Elizabethan or the Old Colonial that is responsible for the absence of any very strong personal qualities [in Mr. Trumbauer's work]. The note of any leaning or predilection is almost wholly absent from the mass of work we present. It is extremely difficult to catch the designer, so to speak, "at" any of his preferences. That this impersonality, accompanied by the good qualities of sobriety,

accuracy, and good taste, should have come out of Philadelphia,
is not only a matter for astonishment, but for congratulation.

The projects that were used to illustrate the article were mostly
early Trumbauer palaces — vast, sober, and designed with solid
authority. The article itself has an odd attractiveness. It could not
have been written in America today, for it speaks with that lost gift, a
sense of measure: it is too balanced for modern taste, too just in its
praise and blame. It says probably all that can be said in a general
summary about the strength and limitations of Trumbauer's work.

Reading the article today, one may be reminded of Berlioz's review of Rossini's *William Tell,* a masterful essay in critical analysis,
measured and thoughtful.[53] We perish of aesthetic sermons — Americans love to deliver and to be tormented by them. We need a Berlioz
to remind us to savor intention before we damn it. Trumbauer's intentions were clear: he loved the past, and he used it with intelligent
devotion, and sometimes, particularly after 1904, with panache.
Ahead of him lay the age of the engineer, the world of the megabox,
conditions that have inspired some, but which could only have chilled
a man of Trumbauer's temperament. He could not have imagined
defining a house as a machine.

There were two ironies concealed in the *Architectural Record*
article. The first lay in the magazine's choice of Trumbauer to serve
as the model of the "well educated" architect "trained in the accepted traditions of the art," the man "whose education, taste, temperament, and energy" would lead Philadelphia architecture out of
its parochial rut and away from its tolerance of eccentricity. Trumbauer, one of six children in the family of a man of "meagre means,"
left school at sixteen to go to work as a messenger and office boy for
the architectural firm of George W. and William D. Hewitt.[54]
There he learned drafting in practical circumstances. Only a family
recollection of Trumbauer constantly occupied by drawing as a boy
remains to suggest why he sought work in an architect's office.

He never had a day of formal architectural education, a condition
that made him an extraordinary choice to lead his Philadelphia colleagues into the mainstream of American architecture. The opinion
of the *Architectural Record* that he had, in fact, already done so is an
astonishing professional compliment, and one that must have gone
down hard in other Philadelphia drafting rooms. His intuition for
the classical, for orderliness, logic, and rectitude in design, had grown

out of a background completely innocent of theory and classrooms. However, he was never to forget his educational limitations — nor would his fellow architects in Philadelphia let him. He was elected to membership in the Architectural League of New York in 1899, but he was not elected to membership in the American Institute of Architects, the leading professional society in architecture, until 1931, a deliberate affront that long disturbed him.[55]

The second irony lay concealed in the article's flattering comments about the "metropolitan" quality of Trumbauer's work. When Charles Follen McKim, who like Trumbauer had grown up in Philadelphia, completed his training at the Ecole des Beaux-Arts in Paris in 1870, he wrote to his father, James Miller McKim, a prominent Presbyterian minister and abolitionist, to discuss a problem: should he come home to Philadelphia to practice architecture, or try New York? Without directly suggesting what his choice should be, Miller McKim pointed out to his son the difference between the two cities: "One is a provincial town; the other a metropolitan city."[56]

Charles McKim chose the metropolitan city. In New York he became a founding partner of McKim, Mead & White, one of the most distinguished architectural firms of the era. His own work included three New York landmarks, the University Club, the Low Memorial Library of Columbia University, and the Morgan Library (in which, as previously noted, Pierpont Morgan forced the collaboration of his financial competitors in his effort to contain the panic of 1907).

Unlike McKim, Trumbauer had no choice in the matter: he learned to be an architect in the provincial town. The favorable comparison by the *Architectural Record* of his work with the best to be found in New York, Chicago, and Boston was a high professional compliment. By 1904, scarcely more than a dozen years after he had opened his own office, he had moved well beyond the provincial limitations that economic necessity had imposed upon him.

In July, 1890, when he was only twenty-one years old, Trumbauer had taken the bold step of opening his own office, a single room in the same building at 310 Chestnut Street in which he had been working for the Hewitts. His earliest independent work had included a hosiery mill, stables and barns, a general store, an office building, a "Lock Up" for the Borough of Jenkintown (the town along the Old York Road north of Philadelphia to which his family had moved when he was nine), and a number of houses, some of them for real estate developers William Le Coney, with whom he had a partnership arrangement in 1890 and 1891, and Wendell and Smith. His father, Josiah Blyler Trumbauer, although not a successful man, was remembered as an able salesman, a trait Trumbauer inherited. He secured a number of "A. & A." jobs (additions and alterations), one of them a commission that fortuitously determined his career as the leading palace builder of his time.

William Welsh Harrison, a millionaire sugar refiner, contracted with Trumbauer for extensive A. & A. work at Rosedale Hall, the country house he had recently bought from J. T. Audenreid on the Lime Kiln Turnpike at Glenside, north of Philadelphia.[57] The work was begun and completed in 1891 at a cost of $30,000. Not long afterward the house burned down and Harrison commissioned Trumbauer to design and build a fireproof castle for him. Trumbauer based his design, somewhat freehandedly, on Alnwick Castle, a border fortress near Newcastle in Northumberland, England, which had been much altered in the nineteenth century. The massive three-story granite house, with towers and battlements at its corners, was built upon a ground plan that was roughly two hundred feet square. It was begun in 1892 and completed in 1893 when Trumbauer was twenty-four. According to a contemporary account, it cost "in the millions" (probably an exaggeration) and "ranked in magnificence with Georgian Court and Biltmore,"[58] the former designed by Bruce Price for George Gould — a house greatly admired by Trumbauer — and the latter designed by Richard Morris Hunt for George W. Vanderbilt. Harrison's castle was said to have been the third largest house in America when it was completed. He called it Grey Towers. It is now owned by Beaver College.

Trumbauer's career in palace architecture was then furthered by a succession of commissions from the Elkins and Widener families of Philadelphia. The first of these came from George W. Elkins, for whom Trumbauer designed and built Chelten House, a stone and half-timber "Elizabethan" mansion in the Chelten Hills at Ashbourne in a section presently renamed Elkins Park.[59] The $60,000 structure was begun and completed in 1896.

Two years later, Trumbauer designed neighboring palaces in the Ashbourne area for William Lukens Elkins and Peter Arrell Brown Widener, the traction partners and investors who had by then established their families in the hierarchy of American wealth. Both houses were planned and built in 1898.

Elstowe Park, William L. Elkins's house, was described shortly after it was completed as an "Italian renaissance" mansion, a description that was no more, and no less, precise than most efforts to worry a specific image out of the design vocabulary of eclectic architecture. It had columns, arches, parapet-balustrades, large paired cornice brackets, hemicycle colonnaded porticos, and a Mediterranean roof of half-barrel tiles on its projecting entrance bay, all handsomely composed. But, its general countenance was alien to both Italy and the renaissance. It was faced with Indiana limestone and cost $119,000, a figure that, like the others given here, refers only to the structural fabric.

For the garden facade at Lynnewood Hall, P. A. B. Widener's massive "Georgian" house, Trumbauer provided a great two-story portico, with a lunette in its pediment. It was based on the portico of Prior Park, an English landmark near Bath, which, in turn, was based on earlier Palladian models.[60] The garden facade at Lynnewood Hall (later slightly modified) was authentic Georgian: the one-story colonnaded hemicycle porticos at each end of the long axis of the house were authentic Trumbauer — he used them at Elstowe Park, Lynnewood Hall, and Balangary, the palace designed and built a year earlier (1897) for Martin Maloney, another millionaire client, at Spring Lake, New Jersey.

Other commissions, residential, commercial, and institutional, were to continue to come to Trumbauer from the Elkins and Widener families. The residential work would include Miramar in Newport (1913) and 901 Fifth Avenue (1922), both designed in the French classical tradition by Trumbauer and Julian Abele, who had become Trumbauer's chief designer in 1909, for the former Mrs. George E. Widener, née Eleanor Elkins, who had married A. Hamilton Rice by the time Trumbauer built her New York town house. (Under the terms of her will, authentic French *boiserie* from a room in her Fifth Avenue mansion was reinstalled in the Philadelphia Museum of Art.) [61]

Trumbauer's clients had in common, besides their wealth, a remarkable loyalty to him. Men who were fearsomely exacting in the use of their money came back to him again and again with commissions of all types: residences, stores, hotels, hospitals, churches. And he was able to persuade them to let him build for them a succession of costly mansions, a number of which rank with the most distinguished houses designed in this country at any time. Over a period of almost four decades they entrusted to him the expenditure of many millions of dollars, a reliable measure of his professional diligence.

His success brought him considerable wealth, and might also have brought him public prominence had he not deliberately avoided it; Trumbauer was afraid that his lack of formal education beyond the tenth grade might lead him into some embarrassing gaffe, and possible ridicule. However, one may wonder whether he really wanted to be almost entirely forgotten in Philadelphia only thirty years after his death, a condition that did, in fact, come to prevail. In the middle 1960's, Charles Martyn, the librarian of the *Philadelphia Bulletin,* was astonished to discover that his files didn't hold a single clipping on Trumbauer. "I can't believe it," he told a visitor he was helping. "You know, my father helped with the interior woodwork at Whitemarsh Hall." And on August 2, 1964, the *Philadelphia Inquirer* published a feature story on Whitemarsh Hall in which the reporter said that when Stotesbury decided to build the house he "hired an architect named Harold Trumbauer." One is embarrassed for Trumbauer's sake, but it is difficult to decide which unintended slight is the worse: the indefinite article or the definite Harold.

X

Two commissions at Newport — The Elms (1899) for Edward Julius Berwind and Chetwode (1900) for W. Storrs Wells — reveal that Trumbauer had already begun to collaborate in the design and execution of the interiors of his palaces with two outstanding Paris decorating firms: Jules Allard et Fils and Lucien Alavoine et Cie.[62] Jules Allard had collaborated between 1880 and 1895 with Richard Morris Hunt on the interiors of some of Hunt's most famous palaces. His name may be found on the bronze statues reclining on the mantel-pediment of the chimneypiece in the *grand salon* at Marble House and his firm's abbreviation "AF" (Allard Fils) may be discovered painted into the ceiling decoration in the great music room at The Breakers, both at Newport, and both among Hunt's most widely admired commissions. Allard's name is also to be found on the lion-and-crocodile bronze on the terrace at The Elms.

Before turning to Lucien Alavoine's work for Trumbauer, one should try to understand the ambiguities that have given to the word *decorator* both its luster and its tarnish. Michelangelo and Raphael were decorators, but, in modern usage, so is someone who selects and purchases the rugs, furniture, and curtains for a client's living room.

Jules Hardouin-Mansart and Richard Morris Hunt were decorators, but so too is someone who "does" a sun porch in wicker and raffia for a customer. Michelangelo, Raphael, Hardouin-Mansart, and Hunt had one thing in common: all were architects. This connection, as will presently be seen, is a crucial one to understanding the meaning of *decorator*.

How, one may ask, can work of these artists, the design and execution, say, of the Laurentian Library, the chambers of Pope Julius II in the Vatican, the Hall of Mirrors at Versailles, and the interiors of Marble House, be equated with the purchase of a wicker "suite" under the general aesthetic heading *decoration?* It cannot be, but it is, and one must blame the confusion in meaning on recent history.

What, then, *was* a decorator — in France, say, in order to reasonably limit the search for a definition? Once, one could have given a fairly simple answer to the question, but after 1800 the answer began to change radically. It was the lot of the nineteenth century to muddy up a good many things that were perfectly clear in the eighteenth. For example, during the eighteenth century the needs of the court at Versailles had established the primacy of the architect in the world of the arts, an ordering of responsibility that extended to private architectural work and decoration in Paris.

"It must always be borne in mind," Germain Seligman has written, "that in eighteenth century France, architecture was the dictator and that all artists, with the exception of easel painters . . . submitted to the instruction of the architect to whom, as to the conductor of a great orchestra, no detail was too small to be considered with careful measure."[63]

Michel Gallet has, more specifically, pointed out that "the architect [in eighteenth-century Paris] often assumed total responsibility for a building, from buying the site to the disposition of the furniture. He prepared a mass of drawings, especially for the decoration. Chevotet filled a portfolio with them for a house in the Rue Saint-Martin and Boullée made some 200 for rooms in the Elysée, when they were occupied by Beaujon. An expert's report speaks of the quantity of designs usually rejected by clients before their final choice."[64]

The nineteenth century brought the rise of the middle class and with it the swift increase in number of the new rich: financiers, merchants, industrialists, speculators. The private sector became the primary consumer of architecture and decoration, and, in conse-

quence, these enterprises were completely reorganized. The traditional responsibility of the architect for decoration was diffused
among those who had earlier served as his subordinate collaborators
and suppliers in the decorative arts. The long-established division of
labor was realigned. One reads, perhaps with astonishment, that
upholsterers — tapissiers, a word that also means *tapestry makers,*
tapestry merchants, wall-hangings merchants, wallpaper merchants,
and so on — became the new decorators. But then, one also learns
that François Barbedienne, a prominent bronze *fondeur,* and Jules
Allard, a highly successful furniture maker, were decorators, too.

One wonders, who under the new dispensation held the pencil?
Who was responsible for the actual design of an interior: the floors,
the walls, the ceilings, the door and window surrounds, the cornices,
the coves, the great staircases with their wrought-iron and bronze
railings, and the chimneypieces (with which the design of a room so
often began) ? Under the old system, decoration took its logic from
the architecture of a house. After the diffusion of responsibility, it
assumed a new logic, one that remains a mystery. Design coherence, a
legacy of the classical tradition, began to disappear. Variety, innovation, and idiosyncrasy came to the fore, declaring the presence of the
new rich and their new taste. Victoriana and *art nouveau* joined in a
conflict for control of decoration late in the century.

The destruction of large swaths of central Paris for the construction of the great boulevards created by Haussmann for Napoleon III
during the Second Empire hastened the rise of the *antiquaire,* the
merchant who bought and sold old furniture, old stonework, or old
boiserie detached from the wall of *hôtels* marked for destruction or
modern renovation. Like their fellows in the decorative arts trades,
the antique dealers also called themselves *decorators.* Paradoxically,
one does not often see the word *décorateur* in the nineteenth-century
Paris directories — those who had taken over the decoration of houses
retained their old business designations as, say, *fondeurs* (bronze
founders) , *tapissiers, ébénistes* (fine furniture and cabinet makers) ,
or *antiquaires.*

As it worked out in practice, the new decorators hired architects
and draftsmen to handle the design of the interiors. French architectural historians point out that Pierre Manguin (also spelled
Maugain or Mauguin) was the architect of the famous Hôtel de la
Païva on the Champs-Elysée (1856) , but they do not feel it necessary
to add that Manguin was, in fact, an employee of the *fondeur* Bar-

bedienne, who "erected, furnished, and decorated" the *hôtel*, on whose ornamentation "virtually every important decorative artist of the day, including the young Rodin, worked."[65]

Allard had an arrangement with the designer Eugène Prignot, who also prepared designs in the 1850's for the furniture makers Jackson and Graham in London.[66] Many of Prignot's designs for individual pieces of furniture as well as for elaborate compositions of curtains, valences, *portières,* and *boiserie* were published, and furniture he designed won awards in major expositions in Vienna and Paris.

When he was completing the interiors of his Fifth Avenue mansion at Fifty-seventh Street in New York City, Cornelius Vanderbilt II, the most diligent of palace builders, chided Jules Allard for not allowing enough time for him to approve the design for a Louis XVI music room before work on it had to proceed in Paris. Later, Allard executed the great chambers — the music room and dining hall — at The Breakers, Vanderbilt's summer palace at Newport, from designs drawn by Richard Hermann Bouwens van der Boijen. They are among the finest private Second Empire rooms in France or America. Years afterward, van der Boijen designed the main staircase of the S.S. *Ile de France.* The commission for The Breakers had probably been given to him by Richard Morris Hunt, the architect of the palace. Both architects had trained at the Ecole des Beaux-Arts.

Allard employed, retained, and collaborated with architects and designers. However, despite this fact, and even though he decorated Hunt's most famous palaces in America, Allard did not list himself in the Paris directories as a *décorateur* until after 1900, by which time the term, in its vague modern sense, had come into general use. Year after year he continued his listing as an *ébéniste* and *tapissier.*

The rise of the merchant-craftsman as a major figure in the decorative arts in Paris tended to dim the aura of preeminence that had for so long attached itself to the royal architect. However, the primacy of the latter in decoration as well as in architecture was revived during the Second Empire by Napoleon III in his program to link the Louvre and the Tuileries, and in subsequent projects devoted to the imperial image. Hunt carried the concept to the United States in the 1850's. He had been broadly schooled in the arts — in painting and sculpture, as well as in architecture — and was thus singularly qualified to assume the traditional responsibilities of the architect-decorator.

Hunt's practice of providing the designs for the interior decoration of his residential projects was revealed in a landmark trial, *Hunt v. Parmly,* 1858, in which the jury established the legal right of architects to charge a fixed-percentage fee based upon the total cost of a commission. Five years later, the lawyer-diarist George Templeton Strong praised Hunt's decorations for the inauguration of the Union League Club House (May 12, 1863). During the Civil War, a committee of New York women raised funds for the U.S. Sanitary Commission for the medical care of wounded soldiers by organizing a large fair — the Metropolitan Fair — in temporary buildings at several sites in the city. "The Union Square buildings are far more effective than those in Fourteenth Street," Strong noted in his diary (April 6, 1864). "Their architect, White, has done his hurried job wisely and well. Dick Hunt has put all his taste and his indomitable energy into their decoration, and has produced a series of most artistic and splendid interiors at little cost." When his great palace commissions came after the severe depression of the 1870's, Hunt, the architect-decorator, carried his dual art to a remarkable level of achievement.

He had been the pupil and protégé of Hector Martin Lefuel, the architect chosen by Napoleon III to complete the work on the Louvre begun by Ludovico Visconti. When he set out to create American palace interiors based upon an authentic interpretation of those created in France during the sovereignty of the architect in the eighteenth century, Hunt turned to Paris and chose Jules Allard as his collaborator. The tradition in which Hunt and Allard worked, with its exacting demands upon designer and craftsman alike, then passed to Lucien Alavoine (and, of course, to other Paris firms whose work was also based upon the same aesthetic past, but whose lack of a significant rôle in the decoration of American palaces places them outside the present discussion).

It must, of course, be recognized that this transition expressed only the surface of events, for a tide of change ran against the tradition that Hunt, along with a handful of other American architects, represented. The economics of residential architecture had begun to reflect new consumer requirements created by the emergence of a vast middle class in the second half of the nineteenth century in America. Two commentaries serve to define and illuminate that change.

In 1886, George William Sheldon wrote in a short preface to *Artistic Country Houses:* "In the Renaissance of American art [which began] with . . . the Centennial Exhibition in Philadelphia . . . the architect has been conspicuous. . . . He has created the American country seat, and he rests upon it his claim to distinction." Elsewhere in the book, Sheldon added: "The most interesting general characteristic of the new era in American architecture is undoubtedly the fact that the architect has come to assume the responsibility of the entire structure for which he has drawn the plans, so that he is both decorator, and, to a certain extent, upholsterer [furnisher] as well."

If this development manifests Hunt's influence, as it may in some measure, the second commentary reveals that Hunt's vision of architecture was dead by the turn of the century, the victim of history and architectural economics.

In 1902, only sixteen years after Sheldon wrote, Russell Sturgis observed in the *Dictionary of Architecture and Building* in an entry headed "Decorative Art":

> The position of the architect is very singular, for, while many architects think much of the decorative part of their business, they have but little inducement to devote much labor or care to it. The principal [of the firm] is much too occupied to design: the pay required by the specially skilled designer would be high, and the man might be found capable of little else; there is little demand from the client who, generally, takes the scrolls and friezes which the architect's draftsmen copy unchanged from old work as being entirely satisfactory. The architect, therefore, even of the best intentions and the most serious good will, finds the task of applying true decorative art to his work on the whole beyond his strength or outside his opportunities.

An era had ended. A few highly individualistic architects — Bernard Maybeck and Julia Morgan, both of whom had studied at the Ecole des Beaux-Arts, to cite only two among them — would continue the architect-decorator tradition that Hunt had brought home from Paris before the Civil War. However, only an architect whose practice included a large number of palace commissions could carry on Hunt's unique practice of collaborating with a Paris *tapissier-décorateur* — which is to say, only a Trumbauer could collaborate regularly with an Alavoine.

XI

Lucien alavoine had begun in the late 1890's to participate with Allard in his large American commissions for Hunt and Trumbauer. Their firms cooperated at Marble House (1892), The Breakers (1895), The Elms, and Chetwode, all in Newport, Allard as the decorator, first for Hunt and then for Trumbauer, and Alavoine as the well-organized subcontractor who shipped the finished Allard interiors from Paris and sent over teams of expert craftsmen from his own shops to install them here. Allard had opened his first shop and office in New York in 1885 in partnership with Eugène Prignot. The New York branch had been known originally as Allard & Sons and Prignot. Alavoine had opened a New York office eight years after Allard in 1893.

In 1905, Alavoine bought out Allard's business and inventory in both Paris and New York. The purchase of the firm came almost exactly a quarter of a century after Jules Allard had executed his first American commission, a boudoir for Mrs. William Henry Vanderbilt, installed in the landmark palace her husband built at 640 Fifth Avenue between 1879 and 1881. (The commission had come from Christian Herter, the leading American decorator of the period, who had studied painting in Paris in the *atelier* of Pierre-Victor Galland. The Allard boudoir had a ceiling painting, *Aurora,* commissioned by Vanderbilt from Jules Lefebvre, who painted it on canvas in Paris and shipped it to New York, where it was mounted backward, the sun traveling from west to east.)

Alavoine had begun his career as an employee of Eugène Roudillon, whose work and address, 9 Rue Caumartin, had long been familiar to a few New Yorkers who went to Paris to buy fine furniture. Roudillon had bought out Emmanuel Ringuet-Leprince of the same address in 1855. Earlier he had bought out Gustave Gilbert, who had been in business from the middle 1830's.

Edouard Mamelsdorf, a wealthy entrepreneur, came to Roudillon one day to contract for the decoration of his Paris residence. Mamelsdorf was a native of Mannheim who had come to France and, in partnership with his brother, had invested in a variety of businesses, including lace making. Mamelsdorf Frères had offices in Paris, Lyons, Luneville, Mirecourt, Le Puy, Planen, Nottingham, and London.

Alavoine was assigned to carry out the decoration of Mamelsdorf's *hôtel.* The two men got on well and Mamelsdorf was greatly impressed by Alavoine's execution of the commission. He proposed that Alavoine establish his own decorating firm, but Alavoine said that he did not have enough capital. Mamelsdorf offered to back him, and thus became the silent partner in L. Alavoine et Cie, established in 1890.

Almost immediately, Mamelsdorf and Alavoine bought out Roudillon. The combined firm was known formally as "L. Alavoine et Cie (Maison Roudillon)" until after 1910. Martin Becker, the retired head of Alavoine in New York and the *président honoraire* of Maison Alavoine in Paris, has recalled that when he was an architectural student at the Ecole des Beaux-Arts — before he turned to decoration — he learned that Alavoine had been a success as soon as the firm started in business:

"The carriages of everyone of importance came to the cobblestone courtyard on the Rue Caumartin. Alavoine seemed to do almost every important piece of work that was being done at the time — even the interiors of the palace of the Emperor of Japan. I was told that Alavoine had a beautiful delivery carriage that was well known in Paris. Four superb horses, and the men in livery. Older men told me how magnificent it looked going through the streets of Paris making deliveries. Then the Americans came: Astor, Oelrichs, Berwind, Duke — they all visited Alavoine when they came over to Paris."[67]

In 1890 Edouard Mamelsdorf came to the United States and opened a branch of Mamelsdorf Brothers in New York. Not long afterward he met and married Lucie Gutherz, whose sister Lina was married to Nathan Straus, of Macy's, one of the outstanding merchants of the era. Mamelsdorf is today remembered by his American relatives not for his earlier business ventures but for his enthusiastic devotion to Alavoine's classical French decoration — "to great rooms filled with fine *boiseries* and fine furniture."

Flora S. Straus has recalled his pride in the rooms the firm designed and installed in town houses, apartments, and country houses in America. "But I recall especially the pride and pleasure Uncle Edouard took in the beautiful French room at The Plaza — the corner room," Mrs. Straus has said. The latter was one of the few perfectly decorated hotel dining rooms in America, splendid but warm, august yet charming, with a view on one side of the Plaza fountain and on the other of Central Park yielding to the turn of the seasons. Its secret was its sense of measure, a peculiarly French secret that generations of New Yorkers treasured. It has lately been altered, and its treasure buried.

In 1893 Mamelsdorf opened the American branch of Alavoine in New York, following the successful pioneering of Jules Allard. The volume of business established in America by Allard before the close of the 1880's had been very impressive. His books had carried the names of more than three hundred customers (who may have purchased a chair or a mirror) and clients (whose entire mansions he decorated for Hunt). Alavoine continued Allard's great success by serving as Trumbauer's collaborator. The American partnership firm, Alavoine & Company, was run for many years by Edouard Hitau, a distinguished decorator who served as a consultant to the Metropolitan Museum of Art for the installation of two of the museum's eighteenth-century French rooms, a small oval room from a house in Bordeaux and the *grand salon* from the Hôtel de Tessé in Paris. (Both rooms were the gift of Mrs. Herbert N. Straus; both were to have been installed in a house that Trumbauer had designed for the Strauses just off Fifth Avenue on East Seventy-first street, an intention never realized, for Herbert Straus died unexpectedly as work on the fabric of the house was nearing completion and Mrs. Straus gave the superb structure, its interiors unfinished, to the Catholic Diocese of New York.)

Alavoine & Company was managed by Becker after Hitau's retirement. The firm continued to enjoy much of the prestige that Jules Allard and Lucien Alavoine had established as the leading palace decorators in America before the turn of the century. Becker closed down the firm about 1965, eighty-five years after Allard had executed his first American commission, for Herter Brothers.

XII

D<small>UVEEN</small>, Allom, Trumbauer, Alavoine — of such was the unusual group of men, some or all of whom began to work together early in 1911 to convert Stotesbury's house at No. 1925 Walnut Street from a Victorian mansion into a French *palais* with Georgian manners.

By the time work had begun, Stotesbury's intimates had learned the reason for his sudden interest in elegant *décor:* he was going to marry again. The palace was being prepared for Eva Cromwell.

Indeed, she oversaw the changes. She had a regal sense of architecture and decoration, and a restless urge toward perfection in both. James H. R. Cromwell, a witness to the event, albeit a young one, has said that his mother was not only responsible for the complete renovation and redecoration of the Walnut Street house, but also for bringing together the men who carried out the costly program.

"My mother had an inherent gift for decorating," Cromwell has observed. "She loved it, but she knew what she wanted and examined the plans and sketches with meticulous care. And she was forever changing and improving. It was expensive!"

However, in 1911, Eva was still a newcomer to the logistics of palace decoration and its disconcerting magnitudes. Her limited experience led her to throw herself on the expensive mercy of Duveen. "I can never be grateful enough to him," she later told Fiske Kimball. "He taught me how to live."[68]

Time was short, the wedding was nearing, the palace must be rushed to completion. But the deadline passed. Max Bruell, Duveen's comptroller at the time, later recalled that "Duveen suggested [Eva] go away and leave the matter entirely up to him. Whereupon, he hired trucks, and the whole Duveen establishment was practically dismantled — the stuff going to Philadelphia. There, under Duveen's supervision, the entire Stotesbury house was redone. . . . At the time, Joe said that nothing would be returned — and nothing was."[69] The cost to Stotesbury was between $1,500,000 and $2,000,000. Bruell remembered that Stotesbury drew a series of $25,000 checks until the full amount was paid.

It was expensive.

XIII

As the wedding neared, Philadelphia newspaper readers learned that Eva, who was nearing forty-seven, was "noted for her rare graciousness of manner," and that although she ranked high among "the most beautiful matrons in Washington," her true beauty lay in "her coloring, expression and figure, and, above all, in [her] pervading human sympathy."[70] She also had the gifted hostess's sense of personal theater. Her drawing room on New Hampshire Avenue in Washington, where her wedding to Stotesbury was solemnized on

January 18, 1912, was "done in old rose after a Parisian design," and the walls were hung with silk.[71] Its Louis XV chairs were covered with cream and old rose tapestry.

The wedding was "one of the most important in this country . . . in several years."[72] President William Howard Taft was the principal guest. J. Pierpont Morgan was absent in Europe, but his wife, his son, J. P. Morgan, Jr., and one of his daughters, Mrs. William Pierson Hamilton, were there to represent him. As further evidence of his good wishes, he gave Eva a necklace of diamonds, graduated in size and set in links of platinum, with a diamond pendant "the size of a robin's egg."[73] His gift was said to have cost $500,000. Stotesbury's gifts to his bride included, in addition to the refurbished palace (not yet ready for occupancy) , a $100,000 sapphire necklace, and a rope of pearls that, if worn in a single loop, would have fallen to the floor.

It was widely reported at the time that Stotesbury also gave Eva $4,000,000. "I don't know how the story ever got started, but it's absolutely not true," James H. R. Cromwell has said. "Mr. Stotesbury was very generous to Mrs. Stotesbury. He particularly enjoyed giving her expensive jewelry, but he never gave her any large gift of money or securities."

A private railway palace car hurried Eva and Stotesbury to the millionaires' siding at The Breakers hotel in Palm Beach. They lingered in Palm Beach a month, bought some property there, and witnessed the arrival of two new dances, the Bunny Hug and the Turkey Trot, which, the *New York Times* (February 11, 1912) reported, "took the fashionable colony by storm." Change was in the air, both for the country and for Stotesbury.

The sixty-three-year-old banker was about to betray Balzac.

XIV

M RS. STOTESBURY/IS SEEN AT OPERA.

Eva made her debut in Philadelphia on Monday evening, February 12, in Box 27 at the Metropolitan Opera House. Under the foregoing headline, the *Philadelphia Inquirer* (February 13, 1912) reported that "the horseshoe of boxes and chairs in the parquet were filled with society matrons and debutantes." Little attention was paid to the opera, Jean Noguès's *Quo Vadis,* which Henry H. Krehbiel of the *New York Times* had dismissed as second-rate Massenet, "inoffensive to good taste." When Eva arrived — "early," according to the *Inquirer;* "twenty minutes late," according to the *Bulletin* — "scores of opera glasses" were turned on her. (She was in her box on time.) Her appearance caused "audible" comments.

She wore a purple opera cloak with wide bands of rolled white fox at the collar and cuffs. Her gown was of white satin "with a net of silver and crystal spangles." The pearls Stotesbury had given her fell from her neck in four loops; over them lay the Morgan necklace. On her head she wore a diamond tiara, "the most beautiful ever seen at the Metropolitan Opera House, or at the Academy of Music, for that matter," the *Bulletin* noted. At the intermission, the regular promenade of the theater was deserted as the audience crowded into the smaller passage behind the boxes to see Eva. Bemused by her regal appearance, the *Inquirer* recklessly predicted that Eva would "doubtless . . . assume a commanding position in local society corresponding to that she occupied . . . in Washington."

Above the glow of the faery queen the fog of legend gathered, but Old Philadelphia, a wary eye at the battlement, let it be known that the Stotesburys would *not* be invited to the next Assembly ball. Then, from the fastness of his bank vaults, Stotesbury sent forth word to the managers of the ball that if he and Eva were not invited immediately, "he would move Drexel & Company, and all its business, to New York."

Good legends vary. Stotesbury really told the managers that if he and Eva were not admitted to the Assembly, "he would call in all the commercial paper in Philadelphia and ruin the old families." Now (turn the pages carefully), Stotesbury actually called in a young partner, a *Philadelphian* with intimate Assembly connections, and said: "Get us in and you'll be the next head of Drexel's."[74] Before you knew it, the invitation came. And Ned and Eva framed it and put it up under floodlights in the foyer of Whitemarsh Hall.[75]

Legends have at least two qualities in common: they travel, and they endure. To paraphrase Schiller, what never happened cannot age. Dixon Wecter has noted that tales almost as venerable as the event itself are still told in Charleston about Yankee business émigrés who tried to force their way into the St. Cecilia balls, "the most celebrated . . . in America," by "threatening to fire their aristocratic clerks." However, the Stotesbury legend had come from New York, and, in its modern guise, was at least half a century old. In the

1850's, August Belmont, the successful head of his own bank and the representative in the United States of the Rothschilds, and his wife, Caroline Slidell Perry, the daughter of one great naval figure, Commodore Matthew Calbraith Perry, and the niece of another, Commodore Oliver Hazard Perry, were consistently ignored by the managers of the Assembly, the most exclusive society ball in New York in the years leading up to the Civil War. Finally, Belmont went to the managers and demanded an invitation. They turned him down. "I have been investigating the accounts of you gentlemen in Wall Street," Belmont warned them. "Either I get an invitation this year, or the day after the Assembly each of you will be a ruined man." Presently, the invitation arrived.

(Belmont was a Jew and a Democrat: Horace Greeley disliked him on both counts. On March 22, 1853, Greeley's *New York Tribune* first published the anti-Semitic canard that Belmont had changed his name from Schoenberg when he arrived in the United States in 1837. The facts were simple enough, but they would not have served Greeley's purpose: Simon *Belmont,* August's father, owned a freehold estate in the village of Alzey in the Rhenish Palatinate. Simon's father's name was also *Belmont.*)

In Old Philadelphia, faith took the great risk of consorting with farce. The floodlighted invitation in the foyer at Whitemarsh Hall? "Preposterous," Martin Becker, the *président honoraire* of Alavoine, said several years ago when he heard, for the first time, that some *Philadelphians* still insist on the tale. Either Alavoine or White Allom would have had to install the big theater lights. Becker shook his head and added: "Why do people believe these things?" Old Philadelphia has believed them for fifty years because the fables of hagiography instruct the young and reinforce the faith of their elders. In the summer of 1967, a committee of Catholic hagiographers suggested certain deletions in the Universal Calendar of Saints. One of the scholars pointed out, however, that "many questionable saints will be retained if we find the legends a worthwhile reflection on life and morals."[76] The *Philadelphians* found in the Stotesbury legends a worthwhile lesson: the Tartars were still at the gates.

XV

Ned and Eva danced at the Assembly.

Lord Chesterfield once observed to a Knight of the Garter who had made an error in his ceremonial dress, "You foolish man, you don't understand your own foolish business." One may say of those surrogates of God who managed the Assembly that they understood their foolish business. Whether they did so out of fear or a desire not to appear malicious, either of which motives would have been self-absolving, they invited the Stotesburys to join them as peers at the Assembly held during the 1912–1913 season.

That same winter, Eva invited society to share the splendors that Duveen, Allom, Trumbauer, and Alavoine had devised for her. Immediately the palace on Walnut Street was talked about, and praised. Long afterward the *Bulletin* looked back and observed, "Many historic entertainments were given [there]."

During the summer of 1915, Stotesbury terminated the lease on No. 1923 Walnut Street, the town house he owned adjoining his mansion, and ordered some radical structural changes. The town house and the mansion were combined, and a two-story $40,000 ballroom that extended through the old party walls and occupied space in both houses was installed by Trumbauer. The structural work began in October.[77] On January 19, 1916, the *Philadelphia Public Ledger* reported that the ballroom would be inaugurated that evening. The great room, with a built-in organ, had no equal in the city and few in the country. Its decoration was memorable: eggshell and gold-painted *boiserie;* a Georgian chimneypiece, said (incorrectly) to have come from Siena; superb French chandeliers in crystal; ceiling panels painted in the style of Hubert Robert, the romantic classicist (a painter, architectural designer, and superb decorator) ; and a Beauvais tapestry representing abundance, an inadvertent choric comment. A fountain splashed softly near the entrance to the ballroom, and one could pause for a moment on small stone benches to enjoy the expensive effect. Madame de Pompadour had come to Walnut Street, bringing with her her good taste and passion for elegance.

Hower, Duveen had apparently already suggested to Eva that her *petit palais,* splendid as it was, no longer suited the grand dimensions of her new life. Eva, secure in the wisdom of her mentor, mentioned the suggestion to Stotesbury. Before the year was out, Stotesbury had purchased three hundred acres adjoining his well-known stables, the Winoga Stock Farm, in Chestnut Hill. He then commissioned Trumbauer to prepare the preliminary sketches for a Georgian country palace.

"Something along the lines of Lynnewood Hall," one can hear Duveen suggesting. Trumbauer had completed P. A. B. Widener's vast Georgian pile at Ashbourne seventeen years earlier, and Duveen had greatly altered the nature of the art collection it housed. (The collection had originally been tended to, in part, by Henry Joseph Duveen, known to collectors and his nephew Joseph Duveen alike as Uncle Henry.) Widener died in 1915, and his second son, Joseph Early Widener, inherited Lynnewood Hall, its art, and Joe Duveen, whom he looked upon not so much as his principal dealer as his collaborator in perfecting the excellent Widener collection.

In 1913, Joseph E. Widener had brought Jacques-Henri-Auguste Gréber from Paris to design a setting of French classical gardens to frame the austere splendor of the palace. Gréber had received his government *diplôme* in architecture from the Ecole des Beaux-Arts in 1908.[78] Then, in 1910, he had come to the United States to design the grounds and gardens for Harbor Hill, Clarence H. Mackay's vast north shore estate at Roslyn, Long Island. Gréber's work for Mackay revealed his singular command of the art of landscaping. At Lynnewood Hall, his next large American commission, his designs included a fountain with lead figures cast from models carved by his father, Henri Gréber, a well-respected French sculptor.

Eventually, Jacques Gréber was to become one of the leading *urbanistes* of the period, a pioneer in urban planning who carried out municipal commissions in Paris, Neuilly, Montrouge, Marseilles, Ottawa, and Philadelphia. His gardens at Lynnewood Hall had made it clear to Trumbauer that he would be the ideal collaborator on the Stotesbury palace. He was to bring to Whitemarsh Hall a memorable distinction: its unsurpassed French classical gardens. He and Trumbauer prepared their earliest sketches for the gardens and the palace in 1915.

Gradually, it became apparent that Walnut Street had merely been a costly rehearsal: Eva now included Gréber in her formidable company. On April 11, 1916, the *Bulletin* let Philadelphia know what was being planned for Chestnut Hill: "PALACE FOR THE STOTESBURYS," its headline read. The story that followed gave the "palatial" dimensions that had come from Trumbauer's drafting room: the "main block" of the house was to measure two hundred eighty-three feet by one hundred feet, and the "wing" eighty-eight feet by thirty-three feet. The cost was to be "several hundred thousand dollars" — the figure, the first ever published for Whitemarsh Hall, and by far the lowest, was meant to cover only the fabric of the house (the completed structure before doors and windows are in place, and before interior finishing is started).

Eva respected Trumbauer, but she was not a passive client. On the contrary, she was exacting, strong-willed, and she knew in detail what she wanted. She was not "easy" to work with, as Trumbauer privately complained. They were to have one abrasive difference at Whitemarsh Hall, which will be noted shortly. Even before work started there she had leased Friendship Hall, a large house on the property bordering on the Stotesbury estate for use as her command post during the great project.[79] (Subsequently, she would move her post into Dale House on the estate proper, renaming it Whitemarsh Lodge.)[80] Her constant presence at the site was reasonable cause for alarm, but Trumbauer, who was also strong-willed, had a remarkable gift for guiding the restive enthusiasms of his rich women clients, and, when necessary, he could curb their more inappropriate whims. In the end, Trumbauer's professional fastidiousness was never really threatened, for Eva had excellent taste.

Trumbauer and Eva had already collaborated as architect and client on two major projects. They had a third under way, and a fourth would presently enter the sketch stage. Walnut Street had yielded Eva a converted palace with a ballroom unexcelled in the United States, according to contemporary reports. Trumbauer, Allom, and Alavoine had there provided her a *mise-en-scène* in which she could act out her rôle as a hostess without peer: the regal aspirations of the client and the regal ambience of her palace were in perfect accord.

The year before work began at Whitemarsh Hall, Eva, as ardent a builder as Alva Erskine (Smith) Vanderbilt Belmont had been at Oakdale, Long Island (Idle Hour), on Fifth Avenue (No. 660), and at Newport (Marble House), oversaw the design and construction by Trumbauer of Brooklands, a large Georgian house at Eccleston, Maryland, in the Green Spring Valley. Stotesbury had built Brooklands for Louise Cromwell Brooks, Eva's daughter, who had married Walter B. Brooks, Jr., son of a Baltimore first family, in 1911. Brooklands, designed and completed in 1915, was said to have been based upon Powerscourt, one of the finest country houses in Ireland.[81] (The attribution is benignly confused.) Published cost estimates for Brooklands, later renamed Rainbow Hill by Louise when she mar-

ried General Douglas MacArthur, ranged from $150,000 to $1,000,-
000, a range that suggests the figures came not from Trumbauer's
office but from a roulette wheel.

There were to be Palladian echoes at Whitemarsh Hall beyond
those assimilated in its classical design. In the second book of his
great treatise, *The Four Books of Architecture* (Venice, 1570),
Andrea Palladio remarks that "an architect is often obliged to conform more to the will of those who are paying the expense than to
the principles that ought to be observed." He laments the fact that
"the building profession is one in which every person has persuaded
himself that he is the master." But, with engaging tact he salutes at
once Heaven, his noble patrons, and his own skill, thanking God for
having favored him with clients of "such excellent judgement" that
they approved his designs.

Palladio's classical vision has survived and flourished, and so too, as
Thomas Hastings has observed, have the problems he faced with
clients of less than excellent judgment who believed themselves
masters of architecture. Hastings, the distinguished architect of the
New York Public Library as well as Henry Clay Frick's handsome
New York palace, both on Fifth Avenue, once advised a class in
architecture at Columbia University that it is sometimes necessary to
"interest a client about a closet" in order to save "a tower or a
dome."[82]

No doubt Trumbauer had had to give Eva some "closets" in their
first two projects, but when Whitemarsh Hall was still in the design
stage they had a difference on which he decided to stand firm. Eva
had had an organ in her much publicized ballroom on Walnut Street
and she wanted one in her new palace in Chestnut Hill. The new
ballroom was, in fact, being designed as a scaled-up version of the old
one, but Trumbauer ruled out the organ. Eva, studying the drawings, persisted: couldn't the organ console go somewhere else? In the
stairwell, say? No. Trumbauer refused to force it into the area at the
foot of the great stair off the foyer, which had been designed as an
elegant, uncluttered Georgian entrance hall.

Finally, Eva *ordered* him to find a place for the console and he was
obliged to conform for she was "paying the expense." He nudged it
into a space along the French style *enfilade* that extended the length
of the house. The revised drawings reassured Eva: the console and
pipes would stand in the west gallery just beyond one of the arches
leading into the ballroom.

She had prevailed.

XVI

O_N Saturday, October 20, 1916, the George A. Fuller Company broke ground for the foundations of Whitemarsh Hall.[83] That evening the employees of Drexel & Company gave Stotesbury a dinner to celebrate his fiftieth anniversary at the bank — the partners presented him with a gold vase. He was, Horace M. Lippincott later observed, "at the zenith of his career." And, as Henry M. Flagler had been at Whitehall in 1901, Stotesbury was in a hurry to get the palace completed, and, like Flagler, he had the large means it would take to rush construction. Ten months later the fabric of the house was almost complete, and Eva wrote to Trumbauer from her command post:

> Whitemarsh Lodge
> *August 6, 1917*
>
> Dear Mr. Trumbauer:
> I have never been able to find an expression in words for the majestic simplicity and beauty of the new house which is so satisfying, so thrilling in its loveliness that it sometimes brings tears to my eyes when I see it at sunset or in the moonlight. Only yesterday I happened upon the following lines written by a young soldier who returned from the trenches to Paris, and thus describes his emotion in looking again at the Louvre:
>
> > "Heavens, there's no mistake about it being good to look at! What order, what concert, what rhythm! I am flooded in the harmony of it. I bathe myself, piously, in this silent music."
>
> I send you this because I know that, being your own creation, the house must mean even more to you than it does to me, and you will value this tribute accordingly.
> Sincerely yours,
> [Eva R. Stotesbury][84]

This gracious letter is unusual in its wholehearted praise. Too often the palaces of the American rich echoed with the disappoint-

ment of unrealized fantasies, the blame falling to the architect. However, Eva was happy with her new palace, and she had the
thoughtfulness to say so. The warmth, intelligence, and candor of her
praise touched Trumbauer deeply. The letter was one of the few
souvenirs of his career still in the possession of his stepdaughter
when she died in 1974.

The date on the letter is astonishing, for it reveals that in barely
thirty-nine weeks the Fuller Company had nearly completed the
fabric of the great structure. The pace of the finishing and decoration was, however, to be much slower. England had been at war for
three years, and Allom had converted his London shop facilities to
the manufacture of high explosive shells. By that time, the United
States had been at war for about three months.

On January 26, 1918, scandal fell on the palace: a *Philadelphia
Bulletin* headline read: "STOTESBURY COAL FOR THE POOR." A wartime rationing official had "seized" a carload of coal bound for
Whitemarsh Hall, which was being heated so that plastering, interior
finishing, the installation of gas, water, and electrical systems, and
other fitting-out work could proceed. The seizure was ambiguous.
The official said that the George A. Fuller Company had immediately released the coal upon request. Then he added: "Of course, I
could have taken the coal anyway."

An investigation was begun, and on February 1 another *Bulletin*
headline announced: "STOTESBURY HOME LOANED AS HOSPITAL." The
state fuel administrator had found nothing wrong in the shipment of
coal to the Whitemarsh Hall job site, and he confirmed the coopera-
tion of the Fuller Company in diverting a carload to meet a local
emergency among "needy families." Out of the administrator's investigation a rumor had arisen: the palace was actually being rushed
to completion as a U.S. naval hospital. The rumor was not true, but
another, apparently intended as a canard, was soon whispered about:
Eva was getting the palace ready to receive the Pope, in the event
that Germany overran Italy.

After the Armistice, the fine plastering, cabinetwork, painting,
and gilding proceeded, based on Allom's designs. Duveen prepared
to install the Stotesbury paintings, and an excellent inventory of
French furniture, some of the pieces signed by master *ébénistes* of
eighteenth-century Paris. Much of the furniture, English as well as
French pieces, was moved from Walnut Street, where Duveen had

previously deployed it in 1912. As 1919 drew to a close, Whitemarsh Hall was almost ready for occupancy.

How much did the palace cost? Several hundred thousand dollars: *Philadelphia Bulletin,* April 11, 1916. $1,000,000: *Bulletin,* February 8, 1918. $2,500,000: *Bulletin,* October 9, 1943. Original cost of house alone — more than $5,000,000; plus cost of furnishings — around $7,000,000; total — $12,000,000: *Bulletin,* September 19, 1944. $3,000,000: Lippincott. Most costly residence ever built in Philadelphia: *Philadelphia: A Story of Progress* (Collins and Jordan). Figure most cited in newspapers, magazines, and books: $3,000,000. Where did it come from? Other newspapers, magazines, and books. The only documented figure available is that in the business records of the construction contractor: the George A. Fuller Company built Whitemarsh Hall "under a maximum cost guarantee, with the total contract being $686,000, including profit."[85]

Horace M. Lippincott, by far the most knowledgeable, sober, and accurate of Stotesbury's biographers, probably got his overall cost figure — "upwards of $3,000,000" — from Stotesbury himself, whom he knew for many years. Lippincott also made an attempt to compute the overall cost to Stotesbury of his second marriage: the cost of the five palaces, the jewels, the wardrobe (Eva arrived back in the United States from their honeymoon trip to Europe with forty-seven trunks of clothes and hats), and sixteen years of regal entertainments. "All this," Lippincott has written, "cost him more than $50,000,000." It may be testy, and perhaps not very gallant, to wonder whether his years with Eva were worth so great a cost.

They were. A confidant who saw Stotesbury daily has recalled that he had a special telephone on a small table near his rolltop desk on the partners' platform at Drexel & Company which was connected directly to the phone in Eva's office at Whitemarsh Hall. "Whenever *that* phone rang, he would run to it, and his face would light up. It was like the coming of the Almighty. He absolutely adored her."

XVII

O N the afternoon of Saturday, October 8, 1921, Eva opened Whitemarsh Hall to society. More than eight hundred guests, including, the *Bulletin* reported, "Philadelphia's social register, almost en masse," and Cardinal Denis J. Dougherty, only recently appointed a cardinal-bishop, "passed through the great iron gates that led to the miniature kingdom of splendor." The limestone walls of the palace gleamed in the autumn sun a mile away at the head of a broad turf vista which sloped upward on an easy gradient. In an exercise of *urbaniste* magic, Gréber allowed the arriving guests to look up through the three-hundred-acre *parc anglais* — an incomparable Georgian setting — to the imposing Palladian house before discovering the French classical gardens immediately adjacent to it.

Gréber's formal gardens at Whitemarsh Hall, lucid as geometry and eloquent of the ancient theatrical visions of architectural fantasy, may have been the finest example of French classical landscape art in America. Raymond de Passillé, writing in *La gazette illustrée des amateurs de jardins,* has observed in his analysis of the vast landscaping scheme that Gréber subtly modified the French classical design concept, which depends for its logic upon the availability of large areas of level ground, and adapted it through the use of certain conventions of English formal garden design, to the undulating terrain of the three-hundred-acre estate.[86]

Gréber's formal gardens embraced the palace, and were, in turn, extensions of it, roofless rooms that reached out to the vast informal, naturalistic parks beyond. For convenience, the Stotesburys thought of the palace as facing north, even though it was sited NNW by SSE. To the west of the house, on its long axis, lay a *boulingrin* (a smooth turf bowling green) garden, two hundred feet long and ninety feet wide with a circular pool at its end. At the opposite, the east, end of the house, also along the long axis, Gréber placed a *jardinet d'attente,* a charming, partially enclosed open-air waiting room, which one approached from the house by descending an exterior *cour-de-cheval* stair adapted from that at Fontainebleau. This garden, illustrated in a book on American architecture Gréber published in 1920, was destroyed within several years, possibly to open up the view of the handsome broken-oval staircase from the approach road.[87]

The ground plan of the palace formed a "U," its open end facing south. Within the "U" — in an area measuring two hundred feet by one hundred and ten feet — Gréber placed a pair of identical *parterres*. Straight gravel paths led from their corners to circular *jet d'eau* fountains at their centers. The lead *putti* clustered about the pluming jets were the work of Lynn Jenkins, an English sculptor who had begun to work in America. The geometric designs of the *parterres* were formed of panels of grass and bedded flowers bordered by specimen dwarf box taken from the gardens planted by Jérôme Bonaparte at Woodbury, Maryland, during his American sojourn.

Below this *parterre* garden — directly to the south — Gréber planted a superb *tapis vert* (green carpet, of turf), a work of deceptive simplicity based upon a complex adjustment of the terrain. (A 1916 charcoal rendering by Gréber illustrated the *broderies*, never planted, that he had originally designed to cover this area.) The floor of the *tapis* lay at a level almost twenty feet below that of the *parterres*. The overall dimensions of this majestic garden were five hundred feet by two hundred and fifty feet. The latter dimension included the sloping grass shoulders that rose from the long paths that framed the *tapis* to the parallel walks that lay on either side at an intermediate level.

Two radial gravel paths led to the intermediate level from the upper garden. A curved baroque stairway with a Neptune grotto fountain set in its stone retaining wall led, in turn, down to the *tapis vert.* A shaded maple *allée,* four hundred feet long, lay to the east of the long *tapis* on a parallel axis, and on a common horizontal plane with the ground story of the house. A statue of Artemis stood at the head of the *allée,* which was bordered by Norway maples.

Gréber made excellent use of balustrades, subsidiary fountains, garden statues, topiary trees (*arbor vitae* ten feet high cut in an inverted cone silhouette, or shaped to domal forms), and regal stairs that rose, divided, and rose again in separate flights. However, he employed these architectural devices with a restraint that emphasized the classical spirit of the garden. Guests moved along radial and axial paths, descended from level to level, and returned to intermediate and upper levels by variant stairs. They were entranced by the visual theater of constantly changing sightlines, and the perspectives thus revealed.

One could indulge private ceremonies of contemplation in this Gallic echo of the sacred park that Xenophon had planted and dedicated to Artemis, the model, all but lost to cultural memory, for all future gardens in the West. Then the eye could sweep (as Clemenceau's had done) down Gréber's long parklike vista: past the lead dolphins cast in Paris by Visseaux that ringed the great circular pool at the foot of the *tapis vert;* past the dramatic sculpture by Henri-Léon Gréber (*père*) that rose in limestone grandeur above a tall baroque pedestal at the center of four radial paths that crossed on the main axis of the vista; finally scanning the gatehouse a mile away, its stone so ghostly at dawn and in the evening haze.

Long after Stotesbury, then Eva, had died, the ordered beauty of Gréber's gardens lingered warmly in the memories of those who had been familiar with Whitemarsh Hall. *Versailles* . . . it was the model that most often came to mind. However, Pierre Lavedan, an outstanding historian of architecture, remarked on the design origin of the formal gardens with more scholarly precision. In a short tribute he wrote for *La vie urbaine* shortly after Gréber's death in 1962, Lavedan referred to Whitemarsh Hall as *"une sorte de Marly americain."* Marly was Louis XIV's favorite château, the one to which he retreated with a few chosen courtiers when he wished to rest from the formal rigors of Versailles.

Fiske Kimball has recalled that Philadelphia dismissed Gréber as "Jack Grabber."[88] Lavedan, France's most respected scholar of *urbanisme* (city planning), has served our intelligence with rather more breadth of insight: "About the man: intelligent, shrewd, cultivated, brilliant in conversation, always witty, often caustic, but otherwise courteous, and a good friend. About the city planner: artist to his fingertips, an unflinching taste, and perhaps that which defines him best, a sense of humanity. Here is the appropriate place to recall his definition of city planning: 'the art of ensuring a physical setting that will provide happiness for the greatest number possible.' "[89]

XVIII

IN the forecourt of Whitemarsh Hall, guests found themselves in front of an Ionic temple portico whose columns — four across the front — rose fifty feet to an entablature that supported a gable pediment. Here one came upon a succession of historic refractions: Rome interpreting Greece; Andrea Palladio interpreting the Roman past in renaissance Italy; English architects interpreting Palladio in England during the reigns of the four Georges; and, finally, Trumbauer, and his chief designer, Julian Abele, reinterpreting the Georgian achievement in Chestnut Hill.

Trumbauer had been to England since Lynnewood Hall had been built, and Abele had become his right-hand man. In consequence,

the Georgian style at Whitemarsh Hall was less austere than that at
the Widener palace, but no less observant of classical restraint. Here
he broke up the wall of the front facade with projecting ells, deep
enough for a bay of windows. The Georgian root of the design may
be clearly seen in an elevation rendering (undated) of a facade for
Lowther Hall drawn by James Gibbs, one of the most esteemed
architects and writers on architecture during the eighteenth century
in England. The elevation, now owned by the Royal Institute of
British Architects, was never executed. There is no way now of deter-
mining whether Trumbauer, or Abele, ever saw it, but the elevation
is remarkably eloquent of the Georgian neoclassical vocabulary of
Whitemarsh Hall. Trumbauer placed a one-story cube at each end of
Whitemarsh Hall on the axial center line of the interior *enfilade*. On
the three walls of each projection he used a familiar Palladian motif:
a large three-section window with an arched head on the center section. Such projections were a Trumbauer mintmark, much as his
hemicycle porticos with columns had been earlier.

Whitemarsh Hall had six stories. The main block had a basement
and three stories, the top floor concealed by a balustrade. The service
wing, with quarters for thirty-five servants, extended eighty-eight feet
south from the east end of the palace. It had three basements. The
various underground stories housed recreation and service facilities — kitchens, bakeries, ice-making machines, automatic bellows
for the organ, a tailor shop, a motion picture theater, boilers, water
wells, and so on — which made the house, with its own commercial
telephone switchboard, an independent village in the tradition of the
great north Italian renaissance villas. There were one hundred and
forty-seven rooms, two passenger elevators (paneled with mahogany), one hundred thousand square feet of floor space, and one million five hundred thousand cubic feet of volume. Secretaries, and the
servants of houseguests, were housed in the attic story of the main
block. So too were the Stotesbury grandchildren. Potted trees turned
the tiled areaway behind the roof balustrade into a garden.

The entrance facade with its temple portico, plainly molded
rectangular window surrounds, unornamented frieze band, Ionic
cornice, and classical urns atop the roof balustrade was all Roman
probity. However, the architectural countenance that looked upon
the *parterre* garden on the other side of the palace was one of Roman
elegance. There, arches predominated: the severity of straight lines
gave way to the semicircles at the heads of twenty-one open arches

and arched windows. The arcade loggia on the east side of the garden gave this range of the palace its special distinction. The loggia was a classic arcade made up of eight repeated open arches separated by engaged columns. There, the *order, concert,* and *rhythm* that Eva so admired in Trumbauer's palace were strikingly apparent.

Gréber's mixture of French and English formal traditions in his landscaping was reflected in Trumbauer's adaptation of a French *enfilade* to a Georgian plan, a subtle innovation. The general disposition of the first floor rooms owes much to Coleshill (*c.* 1650 onward), a classic Georgian house in Berkshire, but Trumbauer chose to subsume its axial hallway in an *enfilade* like that found in the garden range of rooms at Vaux-le-Vicomte (1657–1661) near Paris. He tricked the eye with a line of archways that clearly defined the *passage,* and guests at Whitemarsh Hall thus tended to remember "the long hallway." But, in going from the tea room at the west end of the house to the latticed summer room at the east end they actually traversed a room-to-room *enfilade,* passing through the west rotunda (thirty feet in diameter), the west gallery (past the organ console), the ballroom (sixty feet long), the east gallery, and the east rotunda (also thirty feet across). About a year after the house was opened, the straight-line view through the *enfilade* was permanently interrupted: the famous pair of Clodions had arrived from Paris for placement in the rotundas (one of them replacing a *Diana* borrowed temporarily from Duveen).

René Gimpel, the Paris art dealer who was married to one of Duveen's sisters, wrote in his diary on September 25, 1922: "Four statues by Pajou. *The Four Seasons,* at least life-size, are marvelous. They are at Nathan Wildenstein's [with whom Gimpel had had a partnership], who bought them for 75,000 francs from Ancel, a dealer on the quai Voltaire, who in turn bought them from Leroy, the Versailles dealer. I went to see them with Stotesbury from Philadelphia; Wildenstein asked him for 1,250,000 francs for them. I myself want one million francs from him for the two plaster groups by Clodion from the Doucet sale: life-size female figures holding basins."[90] On June 15, 1923, Gimpel notes that he had by then helped Wildenstein sell both the Clodions and the Pajous to Stotesbury, who paid $70,000 for each group.

Another statuary group, Tassaert's *The Sacrifice of the Arrows of Love,* was displayed in the entrance foyer of the palace between two Ionic columns with gilded bronze capitals. Guests saw it to their left as they entered Whitemarsh Hall. The columns served as an open screen between the one-story foyer and the stairwell, which rose through two stories to an attic skylight. The exquisite Tassaert was bathed in natural light by day; its theatrical setting grew more dramatic at night when the chandelier and wall sconces in the foyer were lighted. The handsome stair with its marble balustrade rose through two landings to the second floor; it provided an effective ceremonial backdrop. Across the foyer, whose decoration reminded experts of the work of William Kent, one of the greatest of the Georgian architect-decorators, the visitor could see a portrait of Stotesbury painted by R. L. Partington hanging above a mantelpiece. Heavy stucco swags were draped around the portrait on the wall surface.

During the decorating of the Georgian palace, Eva decided that she wanted French as well as English interiors. André Carlhian, a well-known Paris *antiquaire* and decorator who sometimes collaborated with Trumbauer in the installation of French *boiseries* (as he had done at Miramar in Newport) , is remembered as having decorated a room at Whitemarsh Hall which for reasons now forgotten was shortly stripped down to its rough finish. Eva then turned to Edouard Hitau of Alavoine to carry out her French decoration, thus beginning a cordial decorator-patron relationship based upon common aesthetic sympathies that was to last throughout her life. Allom continued his work on the principal state chambers and most of the guest suites, while Hitau designed and installed the French rooms, which included the reception room and, on the second floor, a *treillage* loggia, an Empire loggia, and a breakfast room.[91]

The "great hall" (ballroom) , which served Eva most frequently as a large reception *salon,* and the white and gold George III "living" (drawing) room were outstanding examples of Allom's aristocratic style. A set of tapestries from the time of Louis XIV which had once belonged to the Duke of Sutherland, and two old Beauvais tapestries woven from cartoons by Boucher and known as "the Chinese set" hung in the ballroom.

Allom's monumental chimneypieces with their high mantel shelves of colored marble and huge overmantels with fluted Ionic columns supporting scrolled pediments that seemed to curve up almost to the ceiling; his Adamesque stuccoed ceilings; and his *enfilade* arches springing from freestanding columns with classical entablatures (and with coffering in the intrados of the arches) were skillfully derived from the decorative vocabulary of Georgian designers and craftsmen. At last, Duveen's Gainsboroughs and Hoppners, Raeburns and Reynoldses, Romneys and Lawrences had a proper setting, some of them looking down like hierarchs from Sir Charles's theatrical overmantels.

French and English — statues and paintings; gardens and architecture; chairs and *panneaux:* the mix was a model of coherence drawn from a common classical root. The furniture, chosen by Duveen, "made an impression of great magnificence," Fiske Kimball, a guide of unexcelled scholarship in such matters, later remembered. "One scarcely realized how few of [the pieces] were actually authentic." (The furniture, one might note, was "authentic" enough for Kimball to borrow it for an exhibition of "The Stotesbury Collection" at the Philadelphia Museum of Art in 1932.)

The family and guest suites on the second floor were, again, a mixture of historical styles, well designed and executed. An axial hall linked the second-floor suites; it ran above the *enfilade.* The west wing was occupied by contrasting master suites: Eva's looked south into the gardens, and she enjoyed a privileged view of Gréber's *broderies* and long axial vista; Stotesbury's bedroom looked north out over the Whitemarsh Valley. Eva had a sitting room, boudoir, bathroom, bedroom, roof garden, and breakfast room — the detailing and the materials used (marble, bronze, gold, parquetry) were stunning. Her suite was designed for an *impératrice.* Some of the rooms in her suite — her bedroom and boudoir — were installed by Allom; the others were designed by Alavoine. ("My mother came to depend more and more on M. Hitau," Cromwell has recalled. "She had complete trust in his taste.") In contrast with Eva's bedroom — a chamber of costly but restrained classical Georgian elegance with a parquetry floor *à la Versailles* — Stotesbury's room was almost austere in its simplicity. He may have had more than a hundred pairs of shoes in his closets, but he slept in a bed whose plainness served as witness to his Quaker upbringing.

Similar but less opulent suites filled the west wing; they were occupied at one period by Cromwell (the Whitemarsh Valley side) and his sister Louise, then Mrs. Douglas MacArthur (the formal garden side). Four guest suites were ranged along the terrace side of the house overlooking the *parterres,* and three others overlooked the valley. Each had its own stationery, call buttons for maid or valet service, and daily menu, and each guest was assigned a personal chauffeur. (Eva had a personal hairdresser on her staff as well as a resident *couturier* who preserved his designs in large folios.) After a stay at Whitemarsh Hall, Henry Ford is supposed to have said, "It's a great experience to see how the rich live." And when he was asked to define the style of the principal rooms of the palace, John Russell, an expert New York furniture restorer who had learned his exacting art in Vienna and Paris, innocently provided an echo of Ford's jape. Studying a set of photographs of the Whitemarsh Hall interiors, Russell broke into a smile. "I will tell you what it is, what style," he said. "It is pure twentieth-century American rich. And it is *per*fectly beautiful!"

Eva ruled her domain with rare executive skill. "She ran her household with more efficiency than any factory I was ever in," Cromwell, who sold Dodge Brothers for $160,000,000 in cash in the 1920's, has observed. House parties were frequent; sometimes guests were brought to receptions by private train from Philadelphia; teas for six hundred were not uncommon; Eva often seated forty for dinner (always at small tables) ; and the State Department came to depend upon her hospitality and knowledge of protocol in planning the itineraries of foreign guests. One can make a hasty projection: during the eighteen years between the opening of Whitemarsh Hall and Stotesbury's death, Eva probably entertained an average of two hundred people every two weeks at her seasonal palaces in Chestnut Hill, Palm Beach, and Bar Harbor. More than one hundred thousand guests availed themselves of her hospitality, some of them many times, of course. She was, by any measure, one of the greatest hostesses of American history.

Eva's composure was absolute: "A nervous hostess makes an unhappy guest," she once observed. An old friend remembered that "Eva never talked long to anybody, but she made each guest feel as if he or she were the only one asked."[92] And she always welcomed each guest by name. "Mrs. Stotesbury possesses great charm," Arrell Widener, the grandson of the original master of Lynnewood Hall, wrote in a memoir, "and she has an invaluable social asset in [her] remarkable memory. She apparently has never forgotten a name, and this endears her to everyone."[93]

On February 12, 1912, the Rev. Dr. George Dungan had addressed ninety ministers at the weekly meeting of the Methodist Preachers Association in Philadelphia. He "jarred" his colleagues, the *New*

York Times reported, by observing to them that "Philadelphia is the most inhospitable city in the country." That same evening, Eva had made her memorable debut in her box at the opera as "the new Mrs. Stotesbury." And, as though determined to prove the Rev. Dr. Dungan correct, Old Philadelphia had begun to loathe Eva from the instant she made her regal appearance. But, as Fiske Kimball dryly observed, "few wished to be omitted from her parties."

Such ambivalence was a commonplace among the *Philadelphians.* Nathaniel Burt addresses it bluntly in his pages on Sidney Fisher's complaints to his diary about the vulgarity of the new rich. "All this [vulgarity], of course, does not prevent Sidney, or any other *Philadelphian,* then or now, from going to the houses of the horrid nouveaux riches, admiring the decor, eating the sumptuous repasts, and coming away to disparage," Burt writes.[94] Old Philadelphia didn't bother to "come away" from Whitemarsh Hall before disparaging Eva, and snickering at her, when, according to their own legend, she went from one work of art to another in the presence of her guests with "a mimeographed list" in her hand until she had memorized titles, artists, provenances, and so on. The image is, of course, second hand: a pale echo of Charles Dana Gibson with neither his satiric precision nor elegance. (Why, one may wonder, was a single copy of a list *mimeographed?*)

"My God, I wish you could have heard them," one *Philadelphian* who went to Whitemarsh Hall has observed. "I got sick of it. The truth was, she had too much money and they had too little. They just kept gnawing the same old bone, for heaven's sake." *Too little money* . . . but they had the key to the Philadelphia Club, and not all of Stotesbury's money, not all of Eva's parties . . .

The tapestry dims; eyes stare into eternity; mouths remain forever open upon the warp of time and the pain of jealousy.

Did Eva know? "Oh, yes, she knew," Cromwell has recalled. "But she considered the Old Philadelphians a destructive anachronism in the path of the growth and progress of their own city. And she thought American 'society' was an absurdity. I can remember her saying: 'I love to entertain the aristocracy of achievement.' And she did."

An expert in Old Philadelphia's ritual exclusion has observed that Eva's two closest friends in Philadelphia were Mrs. Alexander Biddle and Mrs. Alexander Van Rensselaer. "Now, of course, this placed Mrs. Stotesbury in the very highest circles here, a position she had enjoyed in New York, where, as you know, the Cromwells were part of Mrs. Astor's circle. She was welcomed by people of the first consequence — into their small gatherings, *en petit comité*. It was mostly very pleasant for her, if you can sense what I am trying to tell you. But then, she did marry Ned Stotesbury, didn't she?"

XIX

E_{VA} was a patron with a generous spirit, as her letter to Trumbauer reveals. She also showed in her sometimes tense relations with him a subtler, and somewhat rarer, gift — magnanimity in victory. A year or so after their difference over the organ console at Whitemarsh Hall, she asked Trumbauer to begin work on the preliminary sketches for a winter palace at Palm Beach. Eva had entered that small company of palace builders for whom one great residence is not sufficient, and whose purses were equal to the splendor of their architectural visions. She had now arrived at the full and final flowering of her remarkable career in the palace arts.

Trumbauer had already designed villas at Palm Beach for Mrs. Frederick Guest (1916) and John A. Phipps (1917–1918). He designed another Palladian palace for Eva, one, it is said, that would have challenged Whitehall, the vast quasi-Roman palace that Thomas Hastings had designed for Henry Morrison Flagler, the creator of Palm Beach. However, the fourth collaboration between Trumbauer and Eva was not to be built. Eva changed her mind. She commissioned Addison Mizner to design her winter palace, El Mirasol, which she opened in the season of 1919–1920.

Eva was thus to establish Mizner's romantic adaptation of Spanish architecture — an adaptation that yielded a relaxed and slightly whimsical Mediterranean elegance — as the court style of Palm Beach. She underwrote trips to Spain for Mizner, permitting him to sharpen his eye, and his imagination, at her expense. He has never been taken seriously by architectural essayists, and, almost in answer to their need to dismiss him and his work, a body of lore, engaging and absurd in equal measure, has grown up about his name. If he is remembered now, it is primarily as the architect who forgot to put staircases in his houses.

However, the jest is a tired one, and very old. Casanova accused

Jacques-François Blondel, an outstanding architect-theoretician, of building a three-story house in Paris without a stair. But, as Gallet suggests, Casanova was a biased witness, for he was the rival of Blondel for the favors of "the alluring musician Marie-Anne Bellotti." Flaubert is a more objective witness to the stereotypal nature of the tradition. When he published his *Dictionary of Accepted Ideas,* a droll lexicon of the foolish notions we are heir to, Flaubert included the following entry: "ARCHITECTS. All are idiots: they always forget to put in stairs."

For whatever reason, Eva did not invite Trumbauer to design the last of her palaces, Wingwood House at Bar Harbor, Maine, either. In 1925, Stotesbury bought the property there of the late Alexander J. Cassatt, who had been well known as the president of the Pennsylvania Railroad.[95] (Cassatt is today remembered in art circles for a more enduring distinction — he was the brother of painter Mary Cassatt.)

Eva commissioned a New York and Palm Beach architect, Howard Major, to design a house in the Maine colonial tradition to be sited near the water on the Cassatt property. He had already designed an addition to El Mirasol for her and within a few months was to publish *The Domestic Architecture of the Early American Republic: The Greek Revival,* a handsome collection of photographs of American neoclassical wooden houses for which he had written an introductory essay. However, despite Major's authority in the style, Eva was not satisfied with his design for her Bar Harbor house.

One day during the summer of 1926, before construction had begun, she was talking to Gustav Ketterer in the offices of the Chapman Decorative Company in Philadelphia when Louis Magaziner, a partner in the architectural firm of Magaziner, Eberhard & Harris, walked in. Ketterer, who is remembered for having decorated many of the costliest homes in Philadelphia, introduced Magaziner to Eva and said to him: "We were just talking about you. Mrs. Stotesbury has a problem about a summer house she is building at Bar Harbor and I was saying that I thought you were the best man to solve it."

Magaziner solved Eva's problem by designing what evolved into the largest residence in the colonial or federal style ever built in Maine, significantly modifying Major's house — which survived as the central block — in the process. Magaziner's son, Henry Jonas Magaziner, like his father an architect, has recalled that Wingwood

House was first planned as a small summer place, a retreat from the ceremonial exactions of Whitemarsh Hall and El Mirasol:

"But then, Duveen came to Mrs. Stotesbury with some fine English furniture, the collection of a nobleman who had recently died. She wanted the furniture, but there was no place for it in her Philadelphia or Palm Beach houses. So she had my father enlarge the main room in the Bar Harbor plans to accommodate it. The room, as it was redrawn, was huge, and it threw the rest of the house out of scale. Then, everything else was scaled up accordingly."

The elder Magaziner added two projecting gabled wings, two L-shaped arcades with terminal gazebos (one of them serving as a *porte cochère*), and a large L-shaped servants' wing. He cut into the central block on the water side of the house, adding a two-story semicircular portico with columns, and upstairs porches, "to cast some shadows and relieve the bulk." On the land side of the original house he added a two-story portico with eight columns that spanned the full width of the block. "He followed southern precedent," Henry Magaziner has observed, "but the columns and entablature are detailed with the slender proportions characteristic of the colonial in Maine, and not those of a southern plantation house.

"Mrs. Stotesbury was very much involved in the design. She would drive around Maine taking and gathering pictures of colonial houses which she would send to my father with her comments. For instance, she sent him some pictures of the Sortwell house in Wiscasset, which she thought was 'the loveliest house in Maine.' On one of the pictures — a postcard — she indicated several details with X's and wrote on the back: 'Facade for us, especially arches over window.' Sometimes he would have to explain to her that even though a detail might be charming on a small house it could be all wrong for a house of the magnitude of Wingwood.

"It wasn't always easy for him."

However, Eva once more tempered her demands with graciousness. She sent Magaziner, her last architect, two enlarged prints of the Sortwell house. On the back of one she wrote: "For Mr. Magaziner. A souvenir of his Rescue Work at Bar Harbor. August, 1926." On the back of the other she added: "With kind regards and sincere thanks for infinite trouble taken to help. Eva Stotesbury."

Eva and her fine Duveen pieces were handsomely housed. Guests came to Wingwood House in their private railway palace cars — the Mellons from Pittsburgh, and, appropriately, the Pullmans from

Chicago among them. Two hundred guests at a time came to dance in the great main room on summer evenings. The waterside retreat had three kitchens: one for Eva's formal banquets, one for ordinary meals and midnight repasts, and one for the servants.

Cromwell has recalled that his mother turned to Alavoine for the decoration of the principal rooms at El Mirasol, and possibly for some of the work at Bar Harbor. However, Howard Magaziner has remembered that Ketterer, who often furnished the houses his father designed, was the decorator primarily responsible for the interiors of Wingwood House.

There was to be one more Trumbauer house in Eva's life, but she was not to be its builder. It will turn up in due course. Perhaps it would be well to observe here that in her costly career as a palace builder, Eva's most memorable collaboration was to remain that with Trumbauer at Whitemarsh Hall. And it might be well to observe further that, ironically, not only did Stotesbury's purse survive Eva's building program, it increased.

In his recollections of his stepfather's extraordinary succession of architectural commissions in the war years — Brooklands (1915), Whitemarsh Hall (begun 1916), and El Mirasol (begun 1918) — Cromwell has observed: "The reason for these vast expenditures by Mr. Stotesbury was that J. P. Morgan, thanks to Henry Davison [a partner of Morgan & Company], had been appointed purchasing agent for the Allies and the profits of the firm were colossal. Mr. Stotesbury told my mother that his share in 1915 and 1916 exceeded $7,000,000 each year!"

XX

O UR pastime and our happiness will grow."

This verse, part of a longer quotation from Wordsworth, was carved in a frieze band along the bottom of the sculptured plaster vaulting of the smaller library at Whitemarsh Hall. Although the poet was praising the rewards of reading, his words provide a text for the colorful second youth of Stotesbury's life after he married Eva. In World War I he turned his Winoga stock farm into an emergency potato farm, sold his famous stable of trotters, and never replaced them. Eva introduced him to a new pastime: entertaining on a princely scale.

"In the early twenties," Lippincott writes, "he began to relax his attention to business. He lost some of his initiative; and advancing years, together with an exacting social life in which he became involved lessened his flexibility and vigour. He showed a tendency more and more to exercise a veto power in business. The day of adventure was gone for him by the thirties . . ." Balzac would have been amused at the "hard-favored" banker, by then in his seventies, playing with the fervor of a well-favored youth, his picture often in the newspapers: going to a costume ball at Palm Beach, escorting Eva to the opera, dancing at Bar Harbor, returning from Europe on the maiden voyage of the *Rex*, being voted one of the ten best-dressed men in America.

But, under the sounds of dancing in the night there ran the dissonant countermelody of rage. Adventure was gone for him . . . and Franklin D. Roosevelt had come onto the American scene. Stotesbury had controlled the Philadelphia Republicans at Kansas City for Hoover. He hated Roosevelt; he hated the New Deal; he hated having to pay a fifty percent fine for not filing his income tax. A liberal news broadcaster, Boake Carter, had suggested one evening during a news broadcast in the spring of 1932 that someone ought to plant a bomb at Whitemarsh Hall. Stotesbury was sure a mob would march out from the city, as one had once marched from Paris to Versailles. However, both he and Carter underestimated the good sense of the average Philadelphian.

"He *was* afraid of mobs at the depths of the Depression," Cromwell has recalled, "and I equipped the house with four Thompson submachine guns. I tried to persuade him that FDR's reforms were actually preventing a revolution, but Roosevelt had attacked J. P. Morgan and Mr. Stotesbury couldn't see it."

A wit of the day said that if a bomb were to go off among the guests at one of the Stotesburys' costly receptions, $5,000,000,000 in assets would be destroyed.

"True," Cromwell has observed. "If the remark referred to Mr. Stotesbury's Farmer's Club dinner which Ford, Firestone, and many bank, railroad, and other industrialists attended, the combined assets they represented would have *exceeded* five billions."

In 1932, Stotesbury decided to close up Whitemarsh Hall and go abroad. The specter of the mob was becoming chillingly real.

Item: "on a single day in April, 1932, one-fourth of the entire area of the state of Mississippi went under the hammer of the auctioneers."[96] Item: in a letter he wrote on June 14, 1932, a financier remarked that "the mention of revolution is becoming quite common."[97] Item: five thousand banks had closed, wiping out the savings accounts of nine million Americans.[98] Item: theater director Harold Clurman has recalled in his memoirs that "we could smell the depression in the air that historically cruel winter of 1932–1933, which chilled so many of us like a world's end."[99]

Wall Street was becoming a ghost town. John Brooks, its most penetrating and urbane historian, has written that soon there was to be "talk of the end of finance capitalism."[100]

Eva and Stotesbury prepared to leave. In April, the *Ile de France* and other transatlantic liners carried four thousand workingmen back to Europe.[101] One day during the following month, Kimball has written, "Morris Bockius, Stotesbury's old and trusted legal counsel, called to ask me if I could go out to the house that afternoon with a view of taking care of the works of art at the Museum that summer. . . . The Stotesburys were to close the house, disband the servants, and go [to the Riviera].

"Both Mr. and Mrs. Stotesbury were there. She was all graciousness, saying, 'We consider ourselves only trustees of our collection for the public.' . . . Beyond the loggia the parterre danced purple in the sunlight. 'Well, Morris,' said Mrs. Stotesbury to Bockius with a spirit which one could not fail to admire, 'if we never come back, we've had ten wonderful years of it.' "

That autumn the Stotesburys returned, but they did not open the palace before going on to Florida. "On New Year's Eve . . . they gave their traditional party in the ballroom [of the Barclay Hotel in Philadelphia]. It was the last gasp of the old regime," Kimball adds. "The guests danced to the strains . . . of *Happy Days Are Here Again.* . . .

"By the fall of 1933, the Stotesburys were again at Whitemarsh Hall and its splendors revived, though [Gréber's] parterres were never replanted."

Eva returned to entertaining, and Stotesbury, small and neat, always carefully attended to by his valet, never failed to appear at Drexel & Company, where day after day he shook hands with each partner upon his arrival.

The diligent hand . . .

XXI

STOTESBURY died at eighty-nine on May 21, 1938, at Whitemarsh Hall. A fellow banker observed the next day that he had been "a grand old Roman." But, the image was wrong: the patrician overtones rang false. Stotesbury may, indeed, have been a Roman, but he had become Shakespeare's "antique Roman." Wall Street insiders as early as 1927 had known him to be worth $100,000,000 — "the richest man at Morgan's." Lippincott estimates, conservatively, that he spent $50,000,000 on palaces and royal pleasures. In 1932 he suffered severe financial reverses. At that time he told Kimball that he would not be leaving his collection to the Philadelphia Museum of Art: *it would have to go into his estate and be sold*. However, a year or so later, one finds him spending large sums for modifications at Whitemarsh Hall and Wingwood House at Bar Harbor. And he told a reporter that he was spending $1,000,000 a year to maintain Whitemarsh Hall. (In the opinion of Augusta Owen Patterson of *Town & Country*, who wrote with authority on such matters, Whitemarsh Hall may have been the best maintained estate in both America and Europe. At one time, Marcel Deschamps, Gréber's assistant, supervised the daily work of seventy gardeners there.)

The mosaic is confusing. Stotesbury withdrew $55,000,000 from his account at Morgan's between 1933 and his death — a rate of withdrawal of more than $10,000,000 a year! His stepson, James H. R. Cromwell, who was then married to Doris Duke, had become a devoted New Dealer. One day in 1936 Stotesbury told him, "It's a good thing you married the richest girl in the world because you will get mighty little from me. I made my fortune and *I* am going to squander it myself; not your friend Roosevelt."

But where did the money go? What did he squander it on at so incredible a rate? Two years after his death, a probate inventory revealed the estimated net value of his estate to have been $4,000,000. (Newspaper accounts had predicted that his estate would be worth $50,000,000.) Stotesbury, had he lived another two years, would have been broke with three unmarketable palaces on his hands. He had, in fact, been on a financial suicide course. The antique Roman; his blade drawn against *himself*.

Horace Walpole once observed in a letter: "The dead have exhausted their power of deceiving." But Stotesbury still deceives us. He left Eva the lifetime use of Whitemarsh Hall, but the total income he provided for her from an estate trust was only about one-quarter of what it would have cost to run the palace. She immediately moved out and sadly dismissed her staff of forty, most of whom had followed her through the seasons from palace to palace for almost two decades.

Fiske Kimball watched angrily as Eva, trying to sell the famous Stotesbury collection of English portraits and the fine furniture, realized little more than ten cents on the dollar. "A butchery," he called one New York auction that included some of the portraits. Duveen, Eva's old mentor, was dying of cancer in London and could not help.

From the complex unraveling of the estate and the sale of her jewelry, Eva received enough to live quite comfortably. She went back to Washington, where her old friend Mrs. Horace E. Dodge rented her, for a nominal sum, a superb *hôtel* that Trumbauer had designed. She named the house Marly, and, exhilarated by Alavoine's urbane Parisian interiors and Trumbauer's elegant adaptation of the Hôtel de Rothelin in Paris, she began to entertain again.

In the midst of her auction difficulties, Eva had called Kimball one day and told him: "I thought I must sell the sculpture, but, at the figure I am offered, I would much rather give it to the museum in honor of Ned." Thus, the rare Stotesbury group — the plaster Clodions, the stone Pajous of *The Four Seasons,* the plaster nymphs possibly by Pajou and Lecomte, and the marble by Tassaert which had belonged to Frederick the Great — had remained in Philadelphia, even though she had not.

Eva died in Palm Beach on May 31, 1946, eight years after Stotesbury. She was eighty-one.

Eva had an instinct for palaces. She brought to rooms eloquent of grace and measure a rare felicity that transmuted them from art to life. Martin Becker of Alavoine, who had helped her to create the ambience of her inner world, with its dreams of guests, once paused, distractedly, while telling a visitor about Alavoine's work at Whitemarsh Hall. He was trying to convey the nature of the subtle gift a creative patron brings to a fine room — a gift that Eva "certainly had." He started . . . then paused again: "Well, the point is . . . she was a great lady."

XXII

IN 1800 when Abigail Adams left Philadelphia with her husband, President John Adams, to journey to the muddy banks of the new national capital on the Potomac, Baltzell writes, "She wept at the thought of leaving her gay and charming Proper Philadelphia friends." She had danced at an Assembly ball. "The dancing was very good," she had observed, "[and] the company the best."

In May, 1939, Eva Roberts Stotesbury, a widow of one year, made a journey in the opposite direction. Old Philadelphia had once awaited her arrival in the city — widow and bride: the new wife of Edward T. Stotesbury, the richest man in town. She had come in a palace car; now she left Washington in a Pullman. Old Philadelphia was no longer interested; it had already had its say . . .

The train arrived in Philadelphia and Eva went to see how Kimball had displayed her lovely Clodions and Pajous. He had placed them in the west foyer of the museum as part of "the principal body of French sculpture in America." Kimball thought they were a noble addition. Stotesbury was well remembered.

Eva did not linger in the city.

"This will be my last visit to Philadelphia," she told Kimball. "I never want to see it again."[102]

Eva took the train back to Washington.

She did not weep.

TWO

CA' D'ZAN

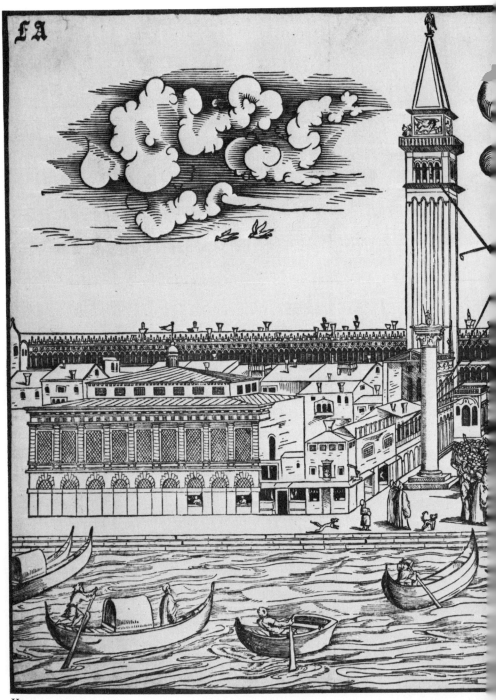

II-1

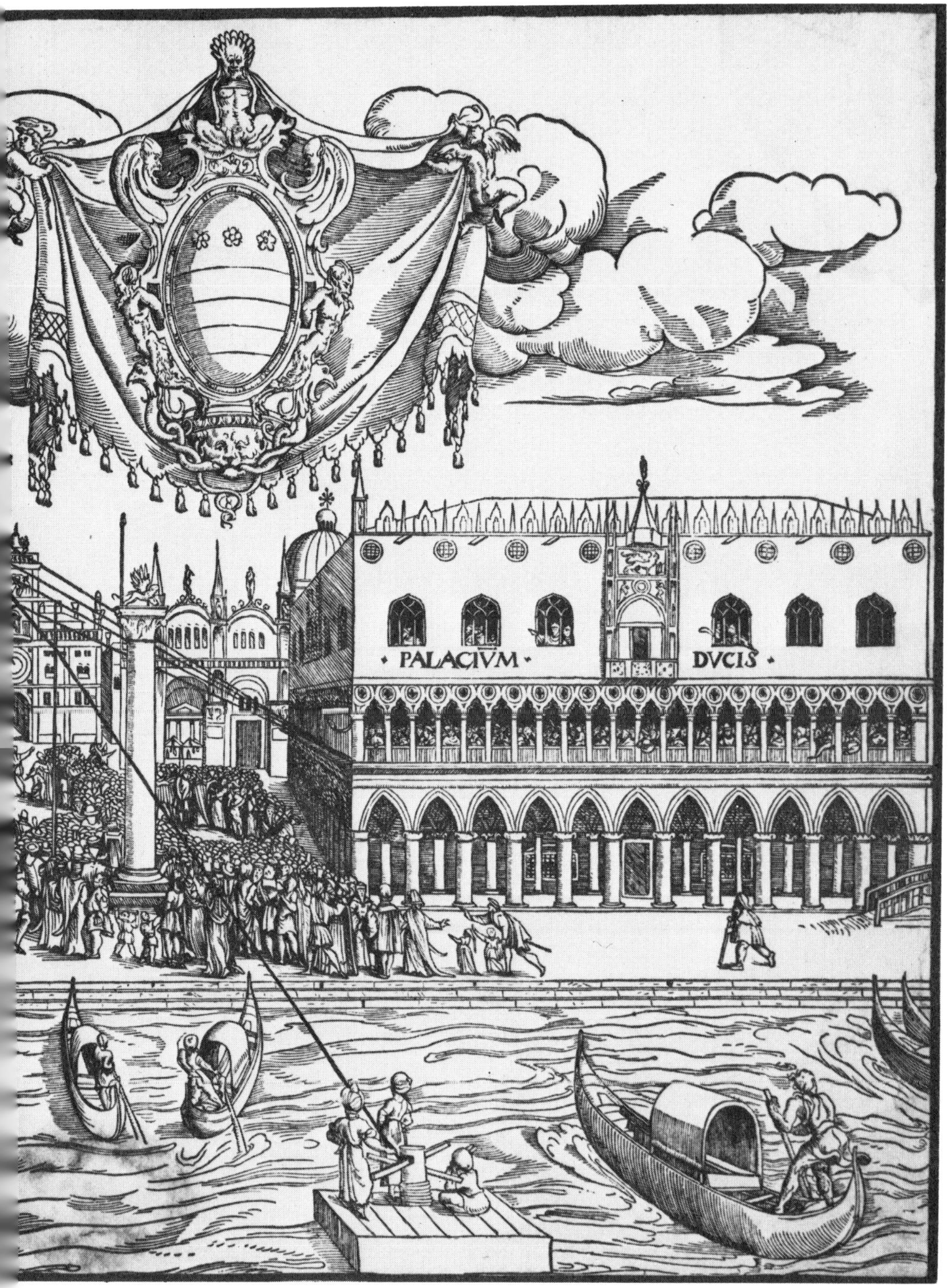
PALACIVM DVCIS

II-1 "View of the Piazetta with Rope Walker." Woodcut: 23″ x 14″. Artist unknown: Venetian, of the sixteenth century. Beyond the palace one sees St. Mark's (present building begun in 1063) , and in the left background the arcaded range of the Procuratie Vecchie along the north side of Piazza San Marco. The campanile soars in the center; its arcaded belfry is the goal of the rope walker. Courtesy of the John and Mable Ringling Museum of Art, Sarasota, Florida.

II-2 Ca' d'Zan from the bay. Courtesy of the John and Mable Ringling Museum of Art, Sarasota, Florida.

II-3 Intermediate watercolor rendering of Ca' d'Zan by Earl Purdy, on-site architect for Dwight James Baum. From *The American Architect.* August 20, 1926. Courtesy of *Architectural Record.*

II-4 The west end of the great hall, from the terrace. Photograph by Samuel H. Gottscho. (1931) . Courtesy of Gottscho-Schleisner, Inc.

II-5 The entrance facade as photographed in 1931. Mable was dead by then, but Ringling was still living at Ca' d'Zan. Dwight James Baum commissioned Samuel H. Gottscho, a leading architectural photographer from New York, to document the project. Courtesy of Gottscho-Schleisner, Inc.

II-6 Floor plan, first floor.

II-7 Floor plan, second floor. Both floor plans redrawn by John B. Bayley from Dwight James Baum's floor plans as published in *Country Life,* October, 1927.

II-8 Music room: detail of Byzantine columns. Photograph by Samuel H. Gottscho (1931) . Courtesy of Gottscho-Schleisner, Inc.

II-9 Dining room: ceiling detail. Photograph by Samuel H. Gottscho (1931) . Courtesy of Gottscho-Schleisner, Inc.

II-10 The Empire alcove adjoining John's bedroom. Photograph by Samuel Gottscho (1931) . Courtesy of Gottscho-Schleisner, Inc.

II-11 The cortile. Photograph by Samuel H. Gottscho (1931) . Courtesy of Gottscho-Schleisner, Inc.

II-12 John's bedroom. Photograph by Samuel H. Gottscho (1931) . Courtesy of Gottscho-Schleisner, Inc.

II-13 Mable's bedroom. Courtesy of the John and Mable Ringling Museum of Art, Sarasota, Florida.

II-14 Mable *c.* 1900; about three years before she married Ringling. Courtesy of Henry Ringling North.

II-15 The model (medium not known) for the so-called "Adam and Eve" terra-cotta panel on the entrance facade of the tower of Ca' d'Zan. (See II-5) . The panel was designed by Earl Purdy. Courtesy of Mrs. Earl Purdy.

II-16 Dwight James Baum. Pencil portrait by Joseph Cummings Chase. From *Country Life,* October, 1927.

II-17 The Ringlings' first house at Sarasota, on Shell Beach — purchased in January, 1912. Courtesy of Henry Ringling North.

II-18 John, mid-1920's. Courtesy of Henry Ringling North.

II-19 The Ringling summer house at Alpine, New Jersey. Courtesy of Henry Ringling North.

II-20 Mable Ringling, 1926. Two years later she was dead. Watercolor portrait by Savely Sorine. Courtesy of the John and Mable Ringling Museum of Art, Sarasota, Florida.

II-21 John Ringling, 1926. Watercolor portrait by Savely Sorine. Courtesy of the John and Mable Ringling Museum of Art, Sarasota, Florida.

II-2

"Ca' d'Zan stands above a tide-stained gondola landing ... a house of pied beauty and wayward design ..."

II-3

"A superb oval baroque stairway joining the terrace and the landing stage at the water's edge ..."

II-4

*"Then, out went the loggias . . . the shadows – deep, black, defining –
were gone."*

II-5

"The sunny charm of the palace is Mable's, the strutting bravura is
Ringling's."

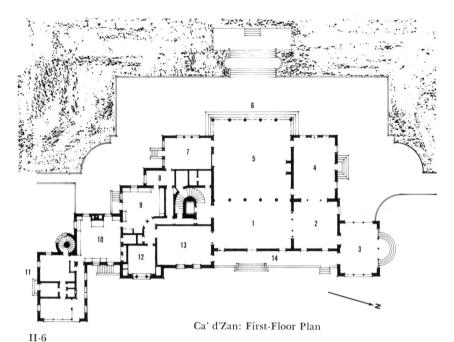

Ca' d'Zan: First-Floor Plan

II-6

NOTE: Nomenclature from undated plans (c. 1926): Dwight James Baum, architect. Material in brackets from guidebook and author. Darkened area represents Sarasota Bay.

1. Reception Room [Foyer]. 2. Lounging Room [Reception Room]. 3. Porch. [Solarium]. 4. Ballroom. 5. Great Hall [Cortile]. 6. [West (Bayside) Terrace]. 7. Breakfast Room. 8. Valet's Room [Pantry]. 9. Pantry. 10. Kitchen. 11. [Service Wing]. 12. Tap Room [Bar Lounge]. 13. Dining Room [State Dining Room]. 14. [Entrance] Terrace.

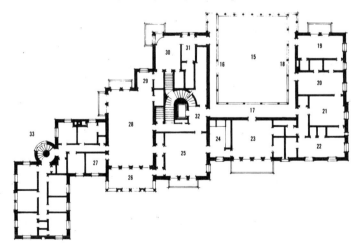

II-7   Ca' d'Zan: Second-Floor Plan

15. Upper Part of Great Hall. 16. [South Gallery]. 17. [East] Gallery. 18. [North Gallery]. 19. Guest Chamber. 20. Guest Chamber. 21. Guest Chamber. 22. Guest Chamber. 23. Guest Chamber. 24. Bath [Mrs. Mable Ringling]. 25. Owner's Chamber [Mrs. Ringling's Bedroom]. 26. Open Porch. 27. Owner's Bath [Mr. John Ringling]. 28. Owner's Chamber [Mr. Ringling's Bedroom]. 29. Alcove. 30. Private Office. 31. Guest Chamber. 32. Stair Hall. 33. [Servants' Chambers].

" 'It is a victory of fantasy
over logic, and the effect is
enchanting.' "

II-9

Dining room: ceiling detail.

II-10

The Empire alcove adjoin-
ing John's bedroom.

II-11

The cortile: " 'one of the most imposing rooms in the country . . .' "

II-12

John's bedroom.

II-13

Mable's bedroom:
"graceful, rococo, and
personal . . ."

II-14

" '. . . every other inch a gentleman.' "

II-15

"She was remarkably beautiful . . ."

II-16

"Buddy, get that god-damned architect."

II-17

"'. . . a comfortable, happy house to live in.'"

II-18

The Ringling summer house at Alpine, New Jersey.

II-19

". . . a master of patrician elegance . . ."

II-20

Mable.

II-21

" 'John, that's the first time I've
ever seen you with your hand in
your own pocket.' "

Sarasota likes you, John Ringling. You are a
good neighbor.

C A' D'ZAN, the winter palace of John and Mable Ringling, stands above a tide-stained marble gondola landing along the bay at Sarasota. It is a house of pied beauty and wayward design; a palace whose handsome intentions never got beyond the drafting room. Its architecture may remind one of a tale rich in circumstance and detail told by someone who has forgotten the point. In the long list of palaces, past and present, built in this country, Ca' d'Zan enjoys a droll distinction: it has been rescued from insignificance by its exuberant vulgarity. And vulgarity, it should be kept charitably in mind, has long served as an American equivalent of style.

The pale cream rose of Ca' d'Zan's stucco walls, and the warm earth browns and light buff tones of its simulated masonry — door and window surrounds, gothic tracery, and decorative panels, all cast in terra-cotta pretending to the vigor of carved stonework — glow in the Florida sun, a painter's light. Enameled buff and reddish-brown terra-cotta bricks, laid up in a diamond pattern on the palace tower, and *faïence* medallions and "targets" in soft red, yellow, green, blue, and ivory on dark grounds glisten in the clear air.

A deep terrace, almost two hundred feet in width, leads from the palace to the seawall, a thousand-foot-long revetment that keeps the shore front of the estate from sliding into Sarasota Bay. The terrace is paved with marble strips of varying textures and colors — Tennessee gray, rosso (red) Verona, sienna (deep yellow), Alaskan white with black veins, and Belgian black with white veins — laid in a chevron pattern. It is framed with a border of Italian serpentine, a marble of an aged bronze-green.

Part of the bay facade of the palace projects onto the terrace. A range of lacelike cresting — an echo of Byzantium: an alien place, an ancient time — runs along the parapet of the projecting *bloc*. Seen now in profile against the soft blue of the sky, the cresting is no more than a conceit, the decorative memory of battlements and siege.

Standing on the terrace, the visitor is at a disadvantage. He is confronted by a mélange of architectural forms that may appear strange — foreign, certainly — yet dimly familiar: images buried in a memory bank of movies and television commercials. What the visitor needs is distance. He might better recognize what he is looking at could he step from the marble landing stage into Mable Ringling's black and gold gondola (long ago destroyed in a storm) and draw off two hundred feet from shore. For, as one looks across the surface of the bay toward the palace, the exotic details of its architecture subtly reveal their origins. Mirrored upside down in the random run and fall of the water, flowing among the shifting blues and greens like the plural music of counterpoint, the ogival arches with their Saracenic double curves, the quatrefoils, the cresting, and the palace's bold sheath of color speak of one place only.

They are from Venice. But some damaging restraint was placed against them, and their ancient poetry — the sinuous lyricism of Venetian gothic architecture, shaped by a sculptor's eye and warmed by the polychrome vision of a race of painters — was not so much lost in translation as it was grounded before it had a chance to soar.

What happened? Part of the answer may be found in the miniature cast-concrete *putti* that line the driveway leading to the palace. Each nude *putti* stands on an individual pedestal; each is conventionally amorous, and ambiguous, knowing too much for innocence and too little for worldliness. Together they sound a festive warning to the visitor: *this is a palace dreamed by children*. It began with playful ambiguities. The rest of the answer will evolve in the pages that follow.

Ca' d'Zan is a fantasy that sought Heaven and got only as far as Limbo. It is delightful and amusing. It is also chastening, for it reminds one that a yearning for eloquence may lead to banality. It was dreamed in great magnitudes, then, its fantasy exhausted by financial reality, it was executed in a haphazard scale that left it ill-proportioned; somewhat "squashed" in the opinion of an architect who had been associated with its earliest design. John Ringling played the lordly role of the palace builder with a portfolio of securities that promised more than it could yield. In consequence, his architects beat a steady retreat from grandeur. Ca' d'Zan's stunted splendor reflects its owner rather than its designers.

John and Mable Ringling were fascinated by the Palazzo Ducale, the historic palace of the Doge, the ducal head of state of the ancient Venetian republic. The great palace was in part, but only in part, a dwelling. No one ever quite thought of it as a home until the Ringlings decided to re-create it in Florida. The Palazzo Ducale had been built by the Venetians to honor God and themselves, though not necessarily in that order. Their communal ego restrained the Venetians from becoming sentimental about God, whom they praised as a Fellow-townsman, first among them on sacred occasions. The monumental palace, one of the treasures of Western art, was a forthright compliment to a peer for His good sense in electing Venice to the salvation of earthly riches.

Ca' d'Zan quite as forthrightly praises John Ringling for running the best, and most successful, circus in America. The difference between Ringling and the Venetians — the Doges, churchmen, merchant-bankers, admirals, and the motley in the *piazetta* — was one of degree rather than of kind. For the *palatium Ducis,* as the palace is designated in the earliest known documents, looked out upon a plaza that groaned with a seemingly endless succession of carnivals, sacred and profane.

However, Ca' d'Zan, for all its exuberance, is a groundling: naïve, theatrical, and a bit of a shill. One blinks and sees grandeur. One blinks again and the rococo excesses of a gilded circus bandwagon dazzle the eye. Ca' d'Zan has an awkward vanity; not the sort one is moved seriously to blame. It is slightly comic in its pretensions — in its minaret-campanile, say, or in its maimed recollection of the monumental arcades of the Doge's Palace. Ringling ostensibly built it for his wife, a woman of uncommon beauty and even rarer graciousness. But John loved himself first. The sunny charm of the palace is Mable's, the strutting bravura is Ringling's. The palace — *Ca' d'Zan, the House of John* in Venetian patois — sings his name.

And yet, the music of Ringling's private *gloria* is not truly Venetian. It has nothing in it, say, of the undulant onrush of Vivaldi, a gifted son of the canals. The only music one discerns at Ca' d'Zan is the brassy wheeze of a calliope with its promise of cotton candy and transient wonders. *Step right up . . .*

II

Early in 1923, John and Mable Ringling returned from what had become for them an annual trip to Europe. For about thirty years, the war years excepted, Ringling had been going abroad in search of new circus acts. Mable had accompanied him on most of the trips he had made since he had first taken her to Europe on their honeymoon in 1904.

Their annual European tour had also become an art pilgrimage for the Ringlings. They visited galleries and museums, and looked at the important architecture, wherever Ringling's circus business took them — northern Germany, Berlin, Frankfurt, Naples, Venice, Paris, London.

His biographer, Richard Thomas, states that Ringling's earliest interest in art was "fostered" by Stanford White, who may have been the most admired architect-designer-decorator in the country at the turn of the century. Whatever White's rôle was in Ringling's education as an art collector — an inconclusive matter at best — it can only have been intermittent and of brief duration. White was a New Yorker, a lifelong resident of the city who was murdered there in the summer of 1906, while Ringling, who traveled with the circus much of the time, made his headquarters in Chicago from 1890 to 1907. (The Ringlings were, however, to call upon White to serve as a ghostly preceptor in the design of Ca' d'Zan, an exercise that will be examined in a later passage.)

When they toured Europe at the beginning of the 1920's, John and Mable Ringling were art *pilgrims* in the sense of commonplace piety the word traditionally evokes: that is, they went from museum to museum guided by faith rather than by the doctrines of art scholarship. For although he was to become a shrewd and knowledgeable collector, Ringling at that time was still a naïve amateur of art. It was, in fact, his lack of expertise that preserved him from the general prejudice against baroque painting that then prevailed in the world of art, a fidgety and often devious community that lives with its heart in Heaven and its hand in the till.

Ringling's limitations as a student of art were of the kind that the French poet-aesthetician Paul Valéry once indirectly praised. "In questions of art [Valéry wrote], learning is a sort of defeat: it illuminates what is by no means the most subtle, and penetrates to what is by no means the most significant. It substitutes theories for feelings and replaces a sense of marvel with a prodigious memory."[1]

Children of a world of marvels, the world of Clown and crouching beasts, of the high trapeze and death, of gilded bandwagons and rogue barkers, of the hunger of the vast throng for wonder and danger, John and Mable Ringling loved the marvelous. Learning had not wearied their eye. They had fallen under the spell of baroque painting and Venetian gothic architecture.

When she passed through customs in 1923, Mable carried, along with her other luggage, a large, specially made oilcloth artist's folio filled with prints, original sketches, photographs, brochures, and other visual memorabilia of Venetian palaces. In addition to reproductions of paintings by the greatest of the *vedusti* (view painters), Antonio Canaletto and Francesco Guardi, showing the Palazzo Ducale and the private *palazzi* ranging along the canals (which the Venetians called "houses," the Ca' d'Oro — House of Gold — first among them), the folio also held an array of drawings of architectural details:

Pierced quatrefoils, their pointed cusps framed in circles of stone; richly decorated window surrounds that rose in reversed-curve arches to spearlike points, their ogival profiles resembling a Saracenic onion dome; splendid loggias that stood one atop the other from gondola landing to cornice in the central bays of the palaces; slender balustrades that gave only the most poetic suggestion of security to balconies that hung high above the canals; and strange wall crestings in arabesque patterns that remind one still that Venetian gothic architecture, as Wordsworth wrote of the city itself, "once did . . . hold the gorgeous East in fee."

Mable had asked Venetian artists to sketch these details for her so that she could show them to an American architect, for Ringling had decided to build a palace at Sarasota. The drawings were dream fragments, insubstantial perhaps to the eye of a customs inspector, but vividly real to Mable and John. Once home in New York, the Ringlings stayed only briefly in their luxurious apartment at 636 Fifth Avenue near Fifty-first Street before hurrying south on their private railroad palace car, the Jomar (named for themselves: *John Mable Ringling*). The journey to Florida was one they had made each winter for a dozen years; seven of the trips had been made aboard the Jomar, which the Pullman Company shops had completed for Ringling in 1916.

The Ringlings had first visited Sarasota in the winter of 1910–1911 on the recommendation of two old circus men who thought it would be an ideal place for them to vacation while the Ringling Brothers

Circus, and the Barnum & Bailey Circus, not yet combined, were being refurbished at their respective winter quarters in Baraboo, Wisconsin, and Bridgeport, Connecticut.

The Ringlings had liked Sarasota immediately. During their first visit they went to see The Oaks, the large winter residence that Mrs. Berthe Honoré Palmer, the widow of the wealthy Chicago hotel man, Potter Palmer, was completing at Osprey, just south of Sarasota. It was the first costly seasonal dwelling to be built in the area. Some years later the *Sarasota Herald* observed that to Mrs. Palmer, one of the leading society women in America at the turn of the century, "belongs the honor of having first discovered the charm and beauty of Sarasota."[2] She had brought her own architect, Thomas Reed Martin of Holabird & Roche, down from Chicago. The house he designed for her is remembered by his son Frank C. Martin, also an architect, as having been "in the California bungalow style . . . spread all over everywhere." Achille Duchêne of Paris, one of the most respected landscape architects of the era, designed extensive gardens for The Oaks.

In January, 1912 — during their second visit — the Ringlings succumbed to "the charm and beauty" of Sarasota: John bought a house and thirty-seven acres of bayside property along Shell Beach, about three miles north of the cluster of stores and offices that formed the downtown section of Sarasota. Henry Ringling North, the urbane memoirist (with Alden Hatch) of the Ringling family, and the heir, with his brother John, to the woes and joys of running its circus, remembers Sarasota during his childhood as having been a quiet, somnolent place, "half fishing village, [and] half western cow town."[3] His uncle John's house, where he spent much of his time, was a frame house, "a spacious place . . . with gabled roofs and columned verandas . . . a comfortable, happy house to live in."

When they moved in, the Ringlings built a seawall and drained the swampy land, and Mable began at once to set out a rose garden. Ringling heard that Mrs. Palmer was buying up thousands of acres of scrub-pine land along the coast. She was a keen investor who had already doubled the value of her late husband's estate. Ringling sensed the first swell of the coming land boom: he bought one hundred and fifty-four acres on the nearby keys: St. Armand's, Otter, and Longboat. He could look across the water to them from his seawall and envision the low skyline of future Ringling suburban developments rising in the gentle winter air.

III

THOMAS MARTIN also sensed the coming period of Florida growth. After completing his work on The Oaks, he opened his own office in Sarasota. In the years following, he received commissions to design a number of winter residences, large and small, some of which were illustrated in *Modern Southern Homes,* an architectural survey published by the University of Illinois. He designed houses in and near Sarasota for Dr. Fred Houtlett Albee, a distinguished surgeon and author of medical books, who devoted his later years to Florida real estate development; John J. McGraw, the well-known manager of the New York Giants baseball team who, upon Ringling's insistence, brought the team to Sarasota for winter training, thus enhancing the real estate investments each of them had made; and Samuel W. Gumpertz, a successful showman who invested heavily in carnivals and commercial beach resorts (Coney Island among them), and who was later to play a leading role in Ringling's downfall and insolvency.

By 1923, Martin had become one of the leaders in the community, one of the "Builders of Sarasota," according to the *Sarasota Herald.*[4] His staff by that time included "a dozen skilled artists, designers, and draftsmen," and was still growing, the *Herald* reported. Martin was the logical choice to design John Ringling's new palace at Sarasota.

It was John's decision to build the palace; however, Mable's rôle as his artistic surrogate is tacitly confirmed on one of the few drawings that have survived from the project, an intermediate version of the first-floor plan. It bears the legend: "RESIDENCE FOR MRS. JOHN RINGLING." Earl Purdy, who was ultimately to serve as the on-site architect of the palace, has recalled that "Ringling kept pretty much out of it. It was really Mrs. Ringling's project. We saw very little of him, but she was always on tap."

Mable (Burton) Ringling is remembered with pleasure, admiration, and affection. She was remarkably beautiful: in her early photographs one sees the clear definition and symmetry of feature, the cameo perfection that distinguished the Charles Dana Gibson girl. It is believed that Mable grew up on a farm near Moon's Post

Office, Fayette County, Ohio. She had little formal schooling. However, she later learned a good deal about matters that interested her. Purdy, who worked with her almost daily for two years, has recalled that "you couldn't fool her on Venetian painters, not for one minute." And although Purdy is among the most enthusiastic witnesses to her graciousness, he has also observed that she would not put up with bad work: "She really told off the workmen when she found something that provoked her. She could be a Tartar."

The tradition that Mable and one of her sisters worked for the circus is false: her name never appeared on the Ringling payroll. Another tradition holds that she met Ringling while she was working as a cook in a small rural restaurant in southern Ohio. John, so the story goes, came in, thought his meal fine, sent for the cook, and ended up marrying her. There are several variants of the tale which, one may assume, it pleased Ringling to embellish. The search for Mable's genealogy taxes the ingenuity of the researcher, as does the search for the simple details of her past. Such facts about her as the date and place of her birth and the date and place of her marriage to Ringling have yet to be documented.

Richard Thomas, Ringling's biographer, states that Ringling met Mable in July, 1904, while she was working as a cashier "in one of Chicago's best-known restaurants," and that they were married in December of that year and left for Europe a "few days" after the wedding on the S.S. *Kaiser Wilhelm*.[5] In searching for supporting data, one might assume that they were married in Chicago, Ringling's nominal residence at that time, or New York. However, no official record of the wedding exists either in Cook County (Chicago) or the City of New York. Henry North writes that his uncle married "Mable Burton of Columbus, Ohio," in 1903.[6] "She and her sister were dancers" in the circus, he adds.

Mable was courteous and amiable, qualities she displayed when she first met Thomas Martin at a social gathering not long after she hurried down to Sarasota on the Jomar with her folio of Venetian palace sketches. She was, of course, bursting with plans for her own palace, but, as Martin later told his son, "she talked only about The Oaks, which was, indeed, very flattering."

Several days later, Mable went to Martin's office and asked him to design the palace she and John wanted to build. She explained that they were very fond of the Palazzo Ducale in Venice, and that they wanted a reproduction of that historic building. Further, they envi-

sioned soaring above their Venetian gothic palace, in uncertain magnitude, the tower that Stanford White had adapted from the minaret-
campanile of the Cathedral of Seville and placed atop Madison
Square Garden in New York. White's tower was three hundred feet
high; the most familiar facade of the Doge's Palace, that along the
piazetta, is about two hundred thirty feet long. If Martin thought the
Ringlings' palace scheme absurd, he did not say so. Architects have
always been expected to reduce fantasy to reality.

How much of the great palace of the Republic of Venice did John
and Mable actually want? How much of White's tower? In the very
beginning there was a problem of *scale,* a basic problem that was
never to be satisfactorily resolved. There were in Venice private palaces, built by merchant-bankers in the long past, that took their
spirit, their grammar of decoration, as it were, from the state palace.
The Ca' d'Oro, the finest of these, could provide Martin a handsome
precedent for reducing the Doge's Palace to livable dimensions for a
couple with no children.

But these were matters that could be discussed over preliminary
sketches while client and architect searched for some rational design
program. First, Martin knew he would have to find out precisely
what Ringling himself had in mind, and how much he wanted to
spend. Ringling's office was the next one down the hall from Martin's
on the second floor of a Sarasota bank building. It should be easy to
arrange an appointment.

Martin had good reason to assume that his prospective client was a
very rich man. *Fortune* magazine has noted that Ringling "was listed
as one of the ten richest men in the world [during] his golden era,"[7]
a period that extended from about 1910 to the collapse of the
Florida land boom in 1926–1927. The listing may have been based
on an offhand estimate similar to those that rose during the 1920's
like free balloons from the brochures of Florida real estate developments. It profited "The John Ringling Isles," say, and "The John
Ringling Estates," that their promoter should be known as a man of
great substance. But one of the ten richest men in the world? "A wild
exaggeration," corrects Henry Ringling North, who, in collaboration
with his older brother, John Ringling North, a man blessed with
stubborn cunning, struggled with loving desperation to keep their
Uncle John out of bankruptcy in his declining years. In 1925, Ringling was reported to have been worth $100,000,000. "On paper,"
North cautions.

Nevertheless, Ringling was, indeed, a rich man. He ran, and

owned one-third of, "The Greatest Show on Earth," the Ringling Brothers and Barnum & Bailey Circus, which was by then in its fourth year of combined operations, touring the country almost without competition. His oil wells in the Healdton Field in Oklahoma had been paying out handsomely for ten years; in time they would yield him more than $7,000,000 in net profits. The shortline railroads he had built (and named with a barker's flair; one of them, the St. Louis & Hannibal RR did not at any point come close to St. Louis) were bringing him steady earnings, as were his movie houses, cattle lands, locomotives and railroad cars he had out on lease, and other investments. He was a one-man conglomerate.

But like other men who lived in the tenuous world of paper wealth based upon speculative securities, Ringling had a problem that was once remarked by Ralph C. Caples, a winter resident of Sarasota from 1898. Caples had been the general agent of the New York Central, an automobile company executive, and an advertising man. He had sold the house and land at Shell Beach to Ringling, and they often crossed each other's neighboring lawns at night to play bridge or poker. "There are twenty millionaires in Sarasota," Caples observed dryly to his dinner guests one evening, "but not one of them has a thousand dollars."

Ringling was a rich man when he and Martin met in 1923. Henry North recalls that two years later, his uncle, without even discussing the matter, turned down a valid cash offer of $10,000,000 made by a New York group for his land holdings at Sarasota. He was more than rich enough to ask Martin to design his palace.

At their first meeting, held about midnight at the convenience of his client, Martin learned nothing. Ringling, blinking rapidly and spitting out tiny bits of the end of an unlighted cigar, told Martin that all he *really* wanted was "just a little bit of a place." This was, of course, a florid understatement, one not to be taken seriously. How much did Ringling wish to pay for his little place? He left the matter hanging in the air. Martin had been presented with a rare opportunity to design one of the great American palaces of the era, but the project was footed upon ambiguities. He decided to proceed. Watchfully.

IV

THE first thing Martin did when he began to sketch the earliest preliminary designs for Ca' d'Zan was to try to talk Mable out of her tower. He failed. Then, because he had other, less grandiose but more realistic, projects to guide through his drafting room, he turned the Ringling project over to his son, Frank, and an experienced draftsman, John MacKintosh, who was then in his sixties.

Ringling was a night man who was used to striking the great tents of his circus while the world slept, and who loved to savor the pleasures of the Great White Way in New York in the early morning hours with such confidants as the wealthy speculator John Warne (Bet-a-Million) Gates and George Lewis (Tex) Rickard, the best-known boxing promoter of the era. At Sarasota, Ringling ate breakfast at three o'clock in the afternoon, then spent three hours, with the help of his valet-barber, bathing, shaving, and dressing. He was ready to start the day about the time most Sarasota families, including the Martins, were getting up from supper.

"One day Father called me into his office and said, 'Son, you're a damn sight younger than I am; *you* keep the appointments with Mr. Ringling at one o'clock in the morning.' That's how I found out he wanted me to take over," Frank Martin has recalled.

The younger Martin had served his apprenticeship as an architect with the highly respected Chicago firm of Burnham & Root. He tried to talk Mable out of her tower, as his father had. He too failed. She appeared daily in the Martin drafting room with her oilcloth folio. She was always more than welcome there. Forty-three years later Frank Martin still spoke warmly of her: "She was a brilliant woman, and she had the most wonderful personality."

Mable stayed on when Ringling went north that year, but when summer came she halted her visits to the drafting room in order to join Ringling at their summer place at Alpine, New Jersey, almost directly across the Hudson River from Yonkers, New York, and close to Manhattan. There, on ninety-six acres, they had a twenty-room house, two guesthouses, a garage, a greenhouse, and stables. Ringling is said to have spent $250,000 on the house and estate.

As the preliminary drawings for Ca' d'Zan began to accumulate in his drafting room, the elder Martin expressed his deep concern to his son over the fact that Ringling was making no effort to pay for the work. "We can't afford this job," he said. "If we stay with it, we'll go broke." He decided to close out the design phase of the work and withdraw. Frank Martin called in Asa Cassidy to prepare an oil painting — a large perspective rendering — of the palace based upon the preliminary plans and elevations. Cassidy was a successful illustrator who had done several *Saturday Evening Post* covers, and who was then busy creating imaginary bird's-eye views of the fantasy communities Florida land promoters were building on paper.

When the elder Martin turned the floor plans, elevations, and other drawings over to Ringling, along with Cassidy's three-foot by four-foot oil painting, he told his difficult client that the dream palace would cost about $465,000 to build. Ringling thought the cost excessive. Thus, for the first time, Martin learned how much Ringling wanted to pay for his Venetian palazzo; which is to say, he found out how much Ringling didn't want to pay. Ringling was a man who behaved as though he wished to prove one-half of La Rochefoucauld's maxim that "Pride does not wish to owe and vanity does not wish to pay."

"Father spent a long time trying to collect for the work we did — about a year's work, all told," Frank Martin has recalled. "Ringling was famous for never paying his bills, you know. Finally, it got to the place where Father had to mention the matter to Mrs. Ringling. She paid the bill."

One day toward the end of 1923, her dream abeyed, Mable spent her final day at Frank Martin's drawing board. When she left, she carried away her folio of Venetian souvenirs for the last time.

V

THE Ringlings next turned to an architect who was a master of patrician elegance: Dwight James Baum.

In January, 1923, Baum had been awarded the Medal of Honor of the Architectural League of New York, "for his achievements in designing country houses."[8] In March of that year, the magazine *Architecture* observed that "Mr. Baum . . . has been for some time a recognized leader among the younger men in the designing of suburban and country houses, and his work has invariably shown refinement and good taste."[9] His emphasis, the magazine noted, was on colonial, which he "adapted . . . to his own ends with charming results. . . . He is still a young man, the youngest to receive such a distinction."

Baum, a graduate of Syracuse University, had opened his office at Riverdale-on-Hudson, an affluent community he helped to develop, about eight years before Ringling came to him. He had designed many fine residences in the "Colonial, Tudor, Formal Georgian, English, and Dutch Colonial" styles. In *The Work of Dwight James Baum,* a book of pictures devoted almost exclusively to the architect's residential projects, Harvey Willey Corbett, a Fellow of the American Institute of Architects, wrote: "The best of his achievements in any single style is equal to the best from the pencil of specialists. Architecturally Mr. Baum is no ordinary fiddler, but a virtuoso in his own right." Baum once told *Country Life* magazine that he objected to "slavish copies" of older styles.[10] However, he objected equally to "self-conscious originality."

His middle ground, which was well secured by the excellence of his chief designer, John H. Thiesen, was enthusiastically sought out by wealthy clients, among them Robert Law, Port Chester, New York; Arthur Hammerstein, Whitestone, Long Island; John F. Murray, Old Westbury, Long Island; Frank W. Sullivan, Westerly, Rhode Island; Senator Ernest E. Rodgers, New London, Connecticut; and, Charles Evans Hughes, Jr., Anthony Campagna, and George Matthews Adams, all of Riverdale-on-Hudson, Borough of Bronx, New York City.

Baum's work, as well as that of John Russell Pope, the designer of the classical National Gallery of Art with whom Baum collaborated on the Hendricks Memorial Chapel at Syracuse University, and Addison Mizner, the court architect of Palm Beach, has been characterized by James Marston Fitch in his scholarly study *American Building* as "skillful, precise, and sterile."[11] Fitch further observes: "These upper-class ideologues, with their explicit dependence upon a discredited tradition, were eclipsed in the convulsive realities of the Depression." However, in fairness to them it might be pointed out that each of the three ideologues *died* during the Depression, an event of rather greater significance in the falling off of their popularity than their being eclipsed by a convulsion. Each, of course, had given his rich clients what he thought they thought they wanted, a not inconsiderable achievement when, say, the client wanted to reconstitute the Doge's Palace on Sarasota Bay.

Baum would certainly have been at home in the London of the

four Georges, helping to create the historic country places of Roman provenance that fixed in stone the classic temper of the English aristocracy. One cannot, however, imagine him in Venice, interposing his well-remembered probity between the wild visions of Lombard sculptors and the stone they sought to work. It is said that Baum "paled" when the Ringlings first revealed their plans to him.

VI

CHANCE had taken the Ringlings to Venice; intuition had led them to the enchantment of Venetian gothic architecture, a style quite unlike that which had been given the name *gothic* elsewhere. The distinctive architectural rhetoric of the northern masons who built the great medieval cathedrals — soaring vaults, gossamer ribbing, thrusting buttresses, and vast curtain walls of pointed windows that rose to flamelike tracery — is not generally found in the gothic of Venice. When it is, as in the case of the familiar Venetian quatrefoils, it is perplexingly transformed. Thus, the quatrefoil, which got to France from Spain, is set handsomely between ogival arches in Venice, a profile alien to the north.

In Venice, the most characteristic monuments of the gothic era are secular — the *palazzi*. They are, of course, excepting that of the Doge, private; their sorcery lies in their elegant gaiety, with its sensual undertone, a style not altogether apt for a church (even though the pious facades of the churches of Venice often threaten to break into a declaration of eastern Mediterranean passion, theatrical, byzantine, and altogether secular). It is a style that possesses rather than absorbs those who enjoy it. And in order to understand what it was the Ringlings wanted to build along their seawall at Sarasota, one must remember something of the Venice of history, and the work of its sculptor-architects, a supple work marked by a freehanded genius.

The ancient Republic of Venice may have been European, but its sea captains and merchant princes (many of whom served as supercargo as young men) knew well the marketplaces of Byzantium and Asia Minor, the "Orient" of romantic tradition. "A list of goods in which the early Venetian merchants trafficked arouses a sense of pure wonder," Mary McCarthy has written: "wine and grain from Apulia, gems and drugs from Asia, metalwork, silk, and cloth-of-gold from Byzantium and Greece. These are the gifts of the Magi."[12]

For centuries there was piled upon the quays of Venice the stone of a distant architecture which was greatly admired by the shrewd Venetian trader who, never forgetting the deal in hand, joyfully explored the pied and bravura beauty of the byzantine world. Columns strangely wrought and ornamented, and sculpture vibrant with the bizarre music of the Eastern imagination were sent home in the hold with other merchandise. And slowly the stone of the Orient melded with the stones of Venice: a wild grace from beyond the sea entered into the native genius.

One by one the great cycles of architectural style — byzantine, gothic, and renaissance — turned toward Venice, and each in turn was there transmuted. Venice looked east and west at once from its watery fortress of small islands, and the Venetian architect-sculptor was true to each style as it came to him — true, in his fashion. (He remained faithful only to Venice.) He seized the spirit of the style and discarded its husk. His was a poet's translation; it has been preserved in a number of "apparently careless compositions which," Samuel G. Wiener has written, "seem to mock the scholarly monuments of Rome and Florence."[13] In Venice, Wiener has further noted, "the byzantine style was expressed with a freedom not to be found elsewhere in Europe." And gothic was treated with the same spirit of improvisation.

Venetian gothic has for more than five centuries exuberantly declared itself to travelers principally through the astonishing presence of two monuments of Western art: the Doge's Palace, built by the Republic of Venice, and Ca' d'Oro, built by Marino Contarini, a fifteenth-century banker and cloth merchant. The latter was based upon the former; in fact, as John Ruskin observed in *The Stones of Venice,* "every gothic building in Venice which resembles [the Doge's Palace] is a copy of it." Thus, in deciding to use the Doge's Palace as the model for their own American *palazzo,* the Ringlings had gone to the root of Venetian gothic and its disturbing beauty.

The Doge's Palace is a strange and marvelous buiding which in its long career as a ducal residence, tribunal, and house of parliament has been stained by fire, blood, holy water, and tears, the raw materials of Venetian history. When it was first built, about 810 A.D. according to scholar Terisio Pignatti, the Doge's private residence — the *palatium Ducis* — was no more than a simple wooden building.[14] It stood on the same ground the palace occupies today. As the Republic prospered and grew, the palace was extended, remodeled, razed, rebuilt. In 1340, a building designed to house the deliberations of the High Council was begun adjacent to the *palatium Ducis*. The new structure, known as The Palace of the Three Elders, faced St. Mark's Basin. When it was finished in 1419, at great cost, it completely outshone the Doge's residence. Five years later, the High Council, deliberating in its new splendor, decided to "rebuild the [Doge's] palace more nobly, and in a way more befitting the greatness to which, by God's grace, [our] dominions [have] reached."

The old residence was razed. The north facade of The Palace of the Three Elders was opened up and its structure was extended in a uniform style along the *piazetta,* the lesser plaza that runs from the basin to St. Mark's Plaza. (One can still see where the original building ended: in the thirteenth quatrefoil from the basin the sculptured figure of Justice on a tondo fills the piercing and marks the old corner.) The new section was completed in 1443 and, in time, the entire building became known as the Doge's Palace.

The Ringlings must have stared many times at its long street-level arcade of broad pointed arches; its second floor arcade of double-curved ogee arches, the framing circle of a quatrefoil set between each in such a way that a part of the circumference of the circle and the concave section on either side of each arch flow upward briefly as one line; the vast wall above, covered with small panels of white and rose marble set like brickwork in a repeated diamond pattern; the great windows in the wall framed with the same pointed-arch profile seen below in the street arcade; the elaborately sculptured porch bay that rises beyond the coping of the wall in a surge of gothic fancy to a gable surmounted by a statue; and the playful cresting along the top of the wall.

What one does not "see," without deliberate calculation, is the number of symmetrically repeated details along the *piazetta* and *canale* exterior facades of the building which together extend more than five hundred feet. There are thirty-five pointed arches along the lower arcades; seventy ogee arches along the upper arcades; seventy quatrefoils (some of them halved) ; and *four hundred and ninety* slender balusters (some engaged to columns) . The shadows of the street arcades are deep, cool, and sober; the tracery of the upper arcades breaks up the arabesque of shadows into a lyrical design which, from a distance, may be seen as a long band of *punto in aria,* the superb Venetian lace first created by the wives of fishermen along the nearby lagoons early in the sixteenth century.

It is unlikely that the Ringlings counted the arches or balusters of the Doge's Palace. However, it is the rhythm — the mensural repetition — of its arches and foliar piercings, and the sustained figuration of their shadows, that gives the magnificent building its mesmeric quality.

Not everyone, of course, has been enchanted by the palace. Herbert Spencer, the English philosopher, would have been appalled at the Ringlings' wish to build a replica of it. Spencer dismissed the palace not so much as poor architecture as not being architecture at all. "Dumpy arches in the lower tier," he wrote, "and . . . dumpy windows in the wall above."[15] He was annoyed by the "meaningless diaper [repeated] pattern covering this wall, which suggests something woven rather than built; and the long row of projections and spikes surmounting the coping, which reminds one of nothing so much as the vertebral spines of a fish." In short, simply not a proper building. Another Englishman, Edward Gibbon, the author of *The Decline and Fall of the Roman Empire,* itself a monument of Western art, was even more severe. "The worst architecture I ever saw," he wrote of the palace and its companion structures on the adjoining plazas.[16]

However, a third Englishman, John Ruskin, awakened the English-speaking world (as Hippolyte Taine did the French) to the glories of Venetian gothic. Writer, critic-apologist, antagonist, crotchety dogmatist, and for a brief period a dictator of English taste, Ruskin led the architects of England and the United States on a pious chase after the mystical gothic truths he revealed. "If Mr. Ruskin be right," a reviewer observed when *The Stones of Venice* was published in 1853, "all the architects, and all the architectural teaching of the last three hundred years, must have been wrong."

"That is, indeed, precisely the fact," Ruskin replied.

The late Edoardo Arslan, an Italian scholar whose superb study, *Gothic Architecture in Venice,* summed up years of perceptive research, has in a single phrase revealed the paradoxical secret of the Doge's Palace, a building, he wrote, "which a great unknown architect put together in a synthesis without equal, a miracle of illogical coherence [and] beauty wholly new and original."[17]

A miracle of illogical coherence — in five words, Arslan takes us to the heart of Venetian genius (and, incidentally, lifts the forbidding and doctrinaire Ruskin from our backs).

Of such was the miracle that had left John and Mable Ringling stricken. One can only guess at the angry stiffening of purpose — of faith — with which John Ringling reacted when Dwight James Baum, a man committed to the rectitude of *logical* coherence, first tried to persuade him to build a proper Georgian mansion house by the sea.

Baum had much to learn about his new client.

VII

A circus man who had known Ringling in 1889 later recalled that John had then worn "a yellowish Stetson hat and a fawn-colored frock coat." Riverboat sharp. Later he showed a band of silk braid around the lapels of his dark suits, and another band above the cuffs of his sleeves. Discreetly snappy. After he had begun to travel abroad, John gave up his Stetson hat and sleeve braid. He began to enjoy the elegant and muted pleasures of Rolls-Royces and Saville Row tailoring.

He also began, possibly with the help of Stanford White, to look at paintings more perceptively. Henry Ringling North has recalled discovering "a perfectly frightful . . . picture"[18] in the storage rooms of Ringling's museum at Sarasota. They used to walk over from the nearby palace, and North would find, and bring out, the pictures his uncle wanted to see. One day he found "a painting of a nude female statue in a garden setting. . . . She made me think of Venus rising from a bed of concrete," North recalls. "Uncle John sat looking at [the picture], not exactly proudly, but nostalgically. 'This is the first picture I ever bought,' he said."

North's recollection tends to substantiate a persistent belief, possibly encouraged by Ringling himself, that long before he became a serious collector he was an enthusiast of barroom art, a genre of fleshly, improbably animated, and often garish nudes that served as the closet baroque of the Victorian twilight. If Stanford White did, in fact, influence Ringling's taste in painting it would be amusing to assume that he sensed in Ringling's admiration for barroom art the soul of an intuitive baroque collector and simply pointed him in the right direction. Years later, when he started to assemble his collection, Ringling had the good sense to acquire the expert services of Julius W. Böhler, a dealer with small galleries, or business addresses, in Munich, Berlin, Lucerne, and New York.

In order to clarify the story of Ringling's art purchasing, a tale somewhat confused by chronologies that have him buying important paintings during his bachelor years, that is, before 1904, it is necessary at this point to anticipate a bit and examine a valuable document. Böhler has left an unpublished and undated memoir in which he recalls Ringling with warmth and admiration, and tells of their tours, purchases, and minor disagreements. Although his recollections of dates is not always accurate, Böhler's account is useful for what it reveals about Ringling's decision to become a serious collector, and how he went about collecting. He says that he and Ringling met about 1923. At that time, he carefully points out, Ringling was not "very much interested in art" — as a customer, that it.

Ringling and Böhler went to Italy in September, 1925, to buy "works of art" to be used to embellish Ringling's real estate developments at Sarasota: "copies . . . of old fountains and all kinds of decorative stone work [that] could be bought cheap." Then, a curious shift took place. In Naples they bought a reproduction, cast in bronze, of Michelangelo's *David,* a casting that stands roughly two feet taller than the marble original now in the Gallery of the Academy in Florence. Ringling's bronze reproduction can today be seen in the court of the John and Mable Ringling Museum of Art.

On his last day in Naples before sailing home, Ringling confided to Böhler that "he and Mrs. Ringling had been pondering over what they should do for Sarasota, of which they were very fond." They had decided to build the museum that now bears their names. "I was thunderstruck," Böhler writes. Suddenly, his responsibility to Ringling had changed: he was no longer advising a real estate developer with an eye for attractive landscaping *décor,* but a man bent upon filling up a public museum that had yet to be built.

Böhler came to have great respect for Ringling's judgment in buying paintings. "He had a wonderful eye," Böhler writes of his client. "One day [in New York] he came up to me quite excited about a picture he had seen in a small gallery . . . which he thought was a Tintoretto." Böhler looked at the painting, but refused to buy it. He thought Ringling's hunch might, indeed, be right, but the picture had been badly painted over (a common depredation) and he was afraid that underneath it might be "a complete wreck."

However, convinced that it was an authentic Tintoretto, Ringling bought the picture himself, paying only $100 for it. Böhler then cleaned it. "To my surprise, and his delight, underneath the modern painting," he writes, "came out that beautiful sketch which is now in the Ringling Museum, and which Baron von Hadeln considered one of the finest things Tintoretto ever did." (Freiherr Detlev von Hadeln, whom Böhler inadvertently promoted to the rank of baron, was a highly respected German art scholar of that era.)

Ringling made many daring forays into an art market that was skeptical of his intelligence and taste. He was impatient, intuitive, and willing to take great risks. Against Böhler's advice, he paid the Duke of Westminster $100,000 for four huge paintings by Rubens in 1926. "I protested," Böhler recalled, "but he insisted and said that these four pictures would make the museum look like the old museums of Europe. . . . He said they would be wonderful in a room built especially for them. . . . Mr. Ringling was perfectly right."

During a buying trip in Europe in 1929, Ringling and Böhler examined a disputed Rembrandt entitled *Descent from the Cross.* No one dared to buy it: curators and connoisseurs were put off by the obviously forged signature and date — 1650 — which had been added to the painting long after Rembrandt's death. However, Ringling was convinced the picture was authentic, and so was Böhler. They compared it carefully with two Rembrandts of the same date in the National Gallery of Art in Washington. They were certain that "there must have been an original date and signature [in Rembrandt's hand] on the picture." Ringling decided to buy it. The price was $40,000. When it was cleaned, Böhler added, "it was found that the old signature was hidden under the new one," which apparently had been added after some nineteenth-century overpainting.

At one time a rumor was set adrift in Europe that could have closed many doors to Ringling: he was not a true collector, the rumor said, but was merely putting together a kind of touring art sideshow to make money. Many older European curators, dealers, and collectors could still remember, with distaste, that James F. Sutton, a well-known New York art dealer, had bought Millet's *The Angelus* in Paris in 1889, and had then sent the painting across the United States on a commercial exhibition tour from which he had realized $200,000 in admissions and another $10,000 from the sale of prints before reselling the painting in Paris.[19]

Ringling took his problem to an old friend, Governor Alfred E. Smith of New York. Smith, acting in his official capacity as governor, wrote a statement that vouched for Ringling's honest intentions as a collector whose goal was to create a public museum, thus dispelling the canard. Ringling went on buying. He accumulated more than five hundred paintings before he was forced by insolvency to give up collecting baroque masterpieces.

VIII

THE baroque artist's instinct for escape drives him to prefer 'forms that take flight,' " Germain Bazin, the curator-in-chief of the Louvre, has observed.[20] Indeed, as the baroque gave way to the rococo, the earth itself seemed to have become a centrifuge, hurling thousands of figures, sacred and secular, up the walls and vaults of churches, and out into the heavenly reaches beyond. Ringling's instinct was one with that of the artists he so admired. The center from which he was hurled by the fugal energy of his own ambition was Baraboo, Wisconsin, the Ringling homeplace for many years (and also the homeplace of the *Baraboobarians,* as Ringling later labeled his old fellow townsmen) . By the time he was thirteen, he had run away from home four times.

"He kept on running all his life," Henry Ringling North has remarked, adding, "However, he was not running away from things, but toward them."[21] Toward, one might note, success, money, and fame, all of which he acquired. Toward a palace filled with feasting friends, and the loving presence of his sister's children (but empty of children of his own, for he and Mable remained childless) . And toward the museum he conceived to perpetuate his name and that of Mable Ringling, whom he loved devotedly, if at times errantly.

There had been seven Ringling boys, Albert, August, Otto, Alfred T., Charles, John, and Henry, born in that order. Ida, their sister, who became Mrs. Henry W. North, was the last-born of the Ringling children. Three others had died in infancy. Their father, August Rüngeling, was an immigrant German harness maker who came to the United States "to escape the alarms and confusions of the revolutionary years of 1848." For convenience he adopted an approximately phonetic spelling of his name: *Ringling.* An advertisement in the June 23, 1858, issue of the *Baraboo Republic* announced the opening of "The One Horse Harness Shop" owned by "A. Ringling."

August Ringling had difficulty getting well located in his trade.

The succession of towns and cities in which he tried to establish a business footing reads like the back-and-forth route book of an old regional tent show: Milwaukee; Chicago; Milwaukee; Baraboo; Mc-Gregor, Iowa (where John was born, May 31, 1866, and named *Johann*); Prairie du Chien, Wisconsin; Stillwater, Minnesota; Baraboo; Rice Lake, Wisconsin; and Baraboo. The last time he returned to Baraboo, his sons built him a fine, large house in which he could retire.

Five of the boys — Al, Otto, Alf T., Charlie, and John — formed the partnership that led, ultimately, to the Ringling Brothers and Barnum & Bailey Combined Shows, "The Greatest Show on Earth." John, the youngest, lived the longest and became the best known. He was the most ambitious, wide-ranging, daring, imaginative, and able of the brothers. His extraordinary presence of mind, the hallmark of his style in life, was first demonstrated when he was seventeen and serving as a "Dutch Comedian" with the Ringling Bros. Grand Carnival of Fun.

Late one evening the brothers had to recover a trunk that had by accident been locked in a hotel parlor which was occupied for the night by a widow with a decent fear of circus people. It was imperative that the trunk be carried to the railroad depot before the train arrived to carry the Ringlings to their next scheduled town. The older boys, one by one, knocked politely on the parlor door. There was no answer.

Finally, John stepped up to the door, banged on it with his cane, and called out, "Quick, madam! I can still save you." The door opened, John shoved his cane into the opening, and the trunk was recovered as the train whistled its approach.

Henry North, writing from his own personal experience in such matters, has observed that "the man who ran a circus train had to be harsh and utterly ruthless, wise and sympathetic . . . [a] psychiatrist . . . a howling optimist, and a compulsive gambler."[22] John Ringling was all of these things: he was also gentlemanly, vulgar, sentimental, impeccable in his dress and person, and unpredictably sensitive. It has been said that people talking to one another about him could never quite be sure that they were talking about the same man.

Ringling took naïve pleasure in bragging about his lusty humors. He once told North how, in the days before he became wealthy, he and his older brother Charles had "tished" the girls in the expensive

Chicago bordellos which were famous for their costly furnishings and fine wines.

> Now . . . it was the custom in the higher types of places [Ringling told North], that there would be no discussion about payment. Anything like that would spoil the temporary romance. You would probably order a bottle of wine and sit around talking about anything but money. The girls all wore high silk stockings with round garters, and after you had warmed up a bit the big spenders would bring out a fat roll of bills, and pulling back the garter a little, slip the roll down a girl's stocking. . . . [But] I'd take a twenty dollar bill and wrap it around a big wad of tissue, so it looked like a big splendid thing. When the time came I would shove it down the girl's stocking and she would never know until afterward the nature of the gift.[23]

He also told North how he had tricked the night detective at the Palmer House hotel in Chicago and was able to sneak girls into his room there and keep them with him overnight.

However, when he first saw the nude male and female figures cast in low relief on the entrance facade of the tower at Ca' d'Zan, he was outraged. "Buddy," he bellowed at young North, "get that goddamned architect." That god-damned architect was Earl Purdy, who had designed the offending panel and supervised the execution of its nude figures, festoons, and cartouche. Ringling gave orders for a trowel of wet cement to be placed over the terra-cotta genitals of each figure, thus rendering their private parts absurdly public, as the Florentines had done when they imposed a gold fig leaf on Michelangelo's *David,* and as Mazarin had done when he both castrated and plastered over the nude statues in his great collection.[24] (The rude globs of cement at Ca' d'Zan were later removed at the order of A. Everett Austin, Jr., the first director of the John and Mable Ringling Museum.)

Ringling mistakenly insisted that he and Mable were, recognizably, the subjects of the reliefs. The female figure, Purdy has recalled, was taken from a print, and the male figure had been posed for by an employee of O. W. Ketcham, Inc., at Crum Lynne, Pennsylvania, the terra-cotta firm that cast the panel. Mable very likely knew all about these matters from her regular visits to Crum Lynne, but in her absence, Ringling roared his way through the *opera buffa* scene, playing the unfamiliar role of the gentleman of offended probity.

"His very inconsistencies," North has written, "his splendor and meanness, his arrogance and kindness, his lashing temper and his bubbling humor, which he kept when all else was gone, made him one of the most fascinating men I have ever known."[25]

One cannot imagine a more unlikely client for Dwight James Baum, a man remembered by his associates not so much as a human presence as a pale embodiment of propriety.

One rainy April morning during a visit of the Ringling circus to New York in the middle 1960's, North received a caller backstage and talked at length about his uncle. "He always wanted to know about my love life when I first started to date. What a guy." North laughed softly in his corner of a noisy office he was sharing with others of the circus staff. "He'd always ask me the next day how I made out. 'Did you get anywhere?' That's the first thing he'd ask me. Oh God, he wanted to know all the details. *All* the details."

The visitor was reminded of an amusing observation that Rebecca West had once made of Michael Arlen: "He was every other inch a gentleman."

IX

Baum learned quickly about his new client.

He started working on the second set of preliminary drawings for the Ringling palace late in 1923, probably shortly before the end of the year. Client and architect were opposed in temperament and taste. Precisely how they got together remains a mystery. The same might well be said of why they got together.

A colleague of Baum's has remarked that he could not remember ever seeing him laugh. Another of Baum's associates, John H. Thiesen, the chief draftsman and principal designer of the firm, who in his retirement has been preparing a study of church architecture in the vicinity of Mexico City, has recalled Ringling's earliest visits to the drafting room in Riverdale vividly: "He was a 'tough guy.' He'd come into the office with a cigar in his mouth, and when he talked he'd take the cigar out and spit on the floor. Mrs. Ringling, on the other hand, was a much nicer person."

Once again, Mable smoothed the way, and once again her Venetian folio came out. However, it wasn't needed. Baum bought a shelf of architectural books on Venetian gothic, and he went to Venice with the Ringlings to look at the Doge's Palace. He also visited San Simeon to see how Julia Morgan had accommodated the Venetian gothic arches, quatrefoils, and balusters William Randolph Hearst had purchased for *his* palace.

Baum's first set of floor plans were ready by January 8, 1924. At the beginning of the project, architect and client got on well. Ringling had Baum design a two-story headquarters for him in Sarasota. That same year, Baum prepared the plans for the El Vernona hotel in Sarasota, which was built by Owen Burns, Ringling's real estate vice-president.

Early in 1925, while the foundation work at Ca' d'Zan proceeded, ground was broken for the hotel. According to the Sarasota historian Karl H. Grismer, the El Vernona was formally opened with "a grand ball" on New Year's Eve in 1926. Burns, with an indifferent ear for Spanish inflections, had named the hotel for his wife. The contradiction in gender between *El,* masculine, and *Vernona,* feminine, was resolved a short time later when Ringling bought the hotel from Burns and renamed it, without ambiguity, the John Ringling Hotel.

Baum's first Sarasota office had been next door to the hotel. However, as soon as the interior work on the El Vernona was far enough advanced to permit the move, Baum relocated the office on the second floor of the hotel.

Once Baum had begun the preliminary drawings for the El Vernona, a succession of Florida commissions followed. The land boom was cresting. So, Baum sent Earl Purdy, a young architect who had graduated from Cornell University, down to Sarasota to head a staff of six draftsmen there and to supervise the work at Ca' d'Zan. The foundations for the palace, which incorporated part of the original Ringling seawall, had already been poured by the time Purdy arrived. Baum's name was becoming known in local business circles, and, by the end of 1925, the *Sarasota Herald* was referring to him as "a Sarasota architect."

Baum's Florida office turned out drawings for churches, apartment buildings, yacht clubs, residences, municipal buildings, and hotels in Sarasota, St. Petersburg, Tampa, Melbourne, and Lake Wales. Baum's best known public building in Florida is the Sarasota County Building. Its tower remains an area landmark.

During the unlikely honeymoon phase of his work for Ringling,

Baum was able to get Mable to agree to a diminished sixty-one-foot belvedere-tower for Ca' d'Zan, but on that point all further agreement ended. Mable once told Purdy, "Now, Mr. Purdy, *I'm* paying for this house. Mr. Baum thinks *he's* building it, but it's my house. I know what I want and I'm the one who's paying for it." Every architectural historian should be made to memorize the last sentence in Mable's declaration.

"Mrs. Ringling was not an ordinary woman," Purdy recalls. "She was quick and intelligent. Vivacious and very energetic. And she learned to visualize well."

She and Baum, like Sarah, Duchess of Marlborough, and Sir John Vanbrugh, the architect of Blenheim Palace, were destined to differ. The duchess had so disliked Vanbrugh and "the maddnesse of [his] whole Design" for the historic Marlborough country palace that, in the end, she barred him from Blenheim.[26] Mable did not bar Baum from Ca' d'Zan, only from the third-floor L-shaped recreation area that she improvised out of a large storage space that had relatively little headroom. She commissioned a friend, Willy Pogany, whose illustrations and opera and theater sets were much in vogue, to paint some Venetian carnival scenes, showing her and John in festival costumes, surrounded by their beloved dogs and birds, for the ceilings.

Pogany, who was widely admired for his ardent colors and blithe spirit, had designed the sets for the Metropolitan Opera's first American performance of *Le Coq d'Or*. He executed his *scènes de Venice* for Mable in New York and sent the canvases to Sarasota, where they were glued in place. They are unpretentious, apt, and charming, and they are known to have pleased Mable enormously. However, because the ceiling on which they are mounted is so low, the paintings are best seen while kneeling or, preferably, lying on the floor, a condition Baum would not have failed to mention had he been allowed to inspect them.

Purdy, in the tradition of the medieval mason, designed a small bust of Baum to be used as a finial on one of the balustrade posts of the belvedere at the top of the tower. It was cast in terra-cotta and shipped to Sarasota. "It was in place only one day when Mrs. Ringling discovered it," Purdy has recalled. "She called out to the construction foreman, 'George, bring a crowbar!'" Baum disappeared with one blow.

X

THIRTEEN days after Baum delivered his first set of floor plans, he had a revised set ready incorporating changes the Ringlings wanted. This was an augury of hundreds of changes yet to come. One of the artists who worked on the house recalls that "there was *hell* to pay every time Baum came down here. He and the Ringlings fought like cats and dogs over every change."

The little architectural material that remains — a few intermediate floor plans and several renderings of the principal elevations — suggests the nature, but not the number, of the changes. An open porch with ogee arches is added; then it is closed in. A turret stairway is reversed. The pipe organ console is moved from an appropriate position designed for it in the room north of the great hall out into the hall itself. The paving of the central hall is changed from a pattern of small tiles to a pattern of large black and white marble blocks laid on the diagonal. A superb oval baroque stairway joining the terrace and the landing stage at the water's edge disappears. The cresting on the tower disappears, as do the tower windows with their ogival surrounds. The main stairway, rectangular on plan, is changed to circle around the elevator shaft, a change necessitating wedge-shaped treads. (Mable had Baum reduce the number of steps between the first and second floors, thus lowering the ceiling and "squashing" the scale of the first-floor rooms.)

Whimsical changes are common in palaces. However, they are premised in their great cost upon the ability of the client to pay for them, and pay well. Ringling, as Thomas Reed Martin had sadly learned, would not pay, well or otherwise, even if he could. Every change was made to save money. As it turned out, Baum did not live long enough to get paid for Sarasota. Ringling asked him to reduce his fee; then, when Baum refused, Ringling forgot all about the bill. Finally, more than a decade later, Ringling's estate settled the matter with Baum's estate.

XI

O NE more change remained — the last and most damaging one. "I can't remember now why it was ordered," Earl Purdy said while discussing Ca' d'Zan several years ago. "Probably money . . . as usual."

The final change was an extraordinary structural alteration, demanded by the Ringlings, that almost nullified the whole point of Ca' d'Zan as a partial replica of the Doge's Palace. The Ringlings betrayed the very acuteness of eye they had sought to learn in the galleries of Europe and along the canals of Venice. They discarded the beauty — the *necessity* — of shadow.

Shadow not only defines the presence of an object, but also its *sense*. It is the rich, cool depth of the shadows in the long galleries behind the repeated arches and tracery of the Doge's Palace that gives to the building its affecting and memorable beauty. The shadows change continuously, slowly and subtly modifying the presence of the arcades as the day lengthens and the season changes. Were the arches to be filled in, the striking facades would become less than ordinary.

The architects in Baum's drafting room had provided the Ringlings an authentic replica of a section of the arcades of the Doge's Palace. The section was made up of five pointed arches, ten ogee arches above them, and ten quatrefoils, all scaled down from their Venetian prototype. This picturesque replica projected slightly westward from the house. (There were additional arches and tracery on the sides of the projection.) No attempt was made to go above two stories in the composition. Thus, the parapet cresting was drawn immediately above the quatrefoils without the great intervening wall of the Doge's Palace.

Behind the arches in each story, Baum provided a porch, or loggia, with a depth of about eight feet. It was these loggias that required the projection of the "Doge's section" from the rest of the facade. Thus, the design was true to the essential character of the arcuation of the original: the shadows would be present when the palace was completed. They are, in fact, present in the several renderings of the terrace facade of Ca' d'Zan painted by Purdy at various stages in the planning. Other things might have been changed, but the shadows behind the arches remained . . . until the moment that Ringling insisted on further drastic savings.

Then, *out went the loggias*. The structural logic of the inner wall — the wall at the back of the porches — no longer remained, so the wall itself was removed from the plans. The outer wall — the pierced wall at the front of the porches — was filled in. The pointed arches on the first floor became frames for French doors that opened onto the vast marble terrace. The ogee arches of the second-floor loggia-porch became windows. Both the doors and windows were filled with leaded panes of tinted English lac glass. The tracery quatrefoils of the second-floor loggia were filled in with painted staff, a stuccolike material. A superficial stencil of the Doge's Palace remained, but the shadows — deep, black, defining — were gone. What remained was a high curtain wall, an architectural screen that closed the west end of the great hall; a screen with the outlines of Venetian gothic arches and tracery incised upon it. Charming, of course, but a promise unkept.

The architects who worked on Ca' d'Zan — who tried to impose their professional skill upon it — are quite matter-of-fact about its shortcomings. "The whole house is bad architecture," one of them has said. "In the first place, it is bad planning. It is something of a freak, because when it comes down to it, it wasn't architecture at all. It was just a problem in collecting details and adjusting them to scale — as much as was humanly possible."

Another has summed up: "We all thought it lacked what should have been done. It might not have been too bad if it had been done in marble. But, even so, the scale is wrong and there was nothing we could do about *that*."

Henry Ringling North, who "loved" Ca' d'Zan but who also was well aware of its "excesses," has offered an affectionate apologia for the house:

"Ca' d'Zan . . . was neither ugly nor vulgar. It was so riotously, exuberantly, gorgeously fantastic, so far out of the world of normality, that it surpassed the ordinary criteria for such things and emerged a thing of style and beauty by its magnificent indifference to all the so-called canons of good taste. It was in fact, the epitome of its owner."[27]

There is in North's engaging flourish an echo of Victor-Lucien Tapié's salute in *The Age of Grandeur* to Lukas von Hildebrandt's design for the historic Belvedere palace in Vienna: "It is a victory of fantasy over logic, and the effect is enchanting."[28]

Seeing Ca' d'Zan today, one yields to the giddy feeling that Hansel and Gretel had wandered through the Piazetta di San Marco on their way to the forest and had picked up some charming, but vague, notions for their architect.

XII

ERRA-COTTA, a material made of baked clay and used from the time of the Etruscans for art objects and architecture, saved the day financially for Ca' d'Zan. "It allowed us to cut the cost down to about one-tenth of what it would have been if the same work had been done in stone," John H. Thiesen has recalled.[29] The molds and kilns of Oram W. Ketchum at Crum Lynne, Pennsylvania, near Philadelphia, provided most of the surface of the Ringling palace and much of its interior. "Ketchum did marvelous work for us," Thiesen has said. "It was really outstanding."

Ca' d'Zan is a polychrome marvel of baked earth. The decorative surrounds of the doors and windows; the frames and cusps of the quatrefoils; the decorative medallions; the simulated ashlar masonry; the simulated quoins; the twisted corner arises; the balusters both inside and outside the palace (more than four hundred of them, each a miniature column, based upon seven basic Venetian gothic molds) ; the brackets and cornices in the main hall — all are made of terra-cotta. Excepting a small area of rose-tinted stucco, the belvedere-tower is covered with terra-cotta, some of it tinted and glazed (faïence). In order to make sure that the colors were precisely what she wanted, Mable went to Crum Lynne herself a number of times: she is remembered climbing around the kilns there. Terra-cotta, versatile and economic, preserved for her the playful fiction of a Venetian gothic world on Sarasota Bay.

The fiction began at the small terra-cotta gatehouses at the entrance to the grounds on Indian Beach Road. One approached the palace through pines and palms and flowering oleander, poinsettia, hibiscus, and azalea, passing a guesthouse and swimming pool on the way. Two weathered lions, looking rather more witless than fierce, greeted one at the marble steps of the palace. The lions fooled no one, for the purpose of Ca' d'Zan was pleasure, and its spirit was one of vigorous hospitality.

Heavy walnut doors, aged by banging them with cobblestones

wrapped in burlap, were protected by a screen made of wrought iron and *repousée* (designed in Baum's drafting room and long incorrectly credited to Stanford White). Guests entered a foyer measuring forty-two feet by twenty-four feet that gave directly onto the great hall measuring forty-two feet by thirty-three feet, a cortile that rose two and a half stories to an internal skylight with English lac glass panels in pale hues that softened the intense Florida light: rose, ivory, lavender, and straw. Tinted panes were also used in the doors and windows of the hall facing the water to mediate the strong reflections from the bay (which would have been absorbed in the deep loggias of the original plans).

Tradition holds that the glass in the doors and the pointed bronze arched frames around the doors were brought by Mable from Venice. "I'm afraid not," Earl Purdy has said in discussing the matter. "We had the frames made to fit the plans, and we chose the window-panes." (The rumor that there are some panes of Tiffany glass in the French doors is correct. However, they are not original.)

The foyer and cortile were continuous, with only a screen of five pointed arches separating them. The six columns supporting the arches were covered with a veneer of onyx. Ringling had the onyx shipped from Lower California by Railway Express at cost of $4,000 to make sure that the raw concrete columns would be properly sheathed for the housewarming of Ca' d'Zan at Christmas, 1926.[30]

The ceiling of the foyer bears further evidence of his efforts to hurry the house along.[31] The canvas-covered panels of the ceiling between the walnut beams were painted by Robert Webb, Jr. Webb still had several panels to complete in the foyer when Ringling asked him to speed up his work. "You can see where I thinned things out a bit," he said several winters ago, pointing to the panels nearest the doorway to the lounge. There the antique gray tendrils of the conventionalized floral design are more attenuated against their dramatic renaissance red background than in the other panels.

XIII

ROBERT WEBB, JR., who was twenty-eight years old when he was put in charge of the decorative painting at Ca' d'Zan, was something of a rarity. He was an American artist (born in 1898) whose training included landscape painting and portraiture, but who had grown up with a compelling intuitive addiction to the decorative wall and ceiling painting of the Italian renaissance. He would have preferred decorating the walls and ceilings of a Medici palace to owning one. And, in consequence, he has shared with many fine decorative artists, past and present, foreign and American, the predestined anonymity of their strange, almost arcane, calling. What recognition he has enjoyed has been concealed in the unpublicized fraternal esteem of fellow artists and the architects who commissioned his work.

"I started out with a muralist, F. M. Lamb, up in Stoughton, Massachusetts," Webb has recalled. "That was when I was about fourteen — an apprentice. Then, Lamb loaned me to [John Singer] Sargent in 1915. I worked as Sargent's color maker while he was installing his murals in the Boston Public Library. He had painted them in England, you see, but once they were mounted, and he could see them in place, he made some changes, of course. I ground his colors for him, and he was pleased with my color sense and asked me to go back to England with him. But the war was on in Europe, and my parents talked me out of going.

"Then I worked with Lamb on the drop curtains for the Boston Conservatory, and on some theater drops he was painting. During the war I went in the navy and served as chief camouflage artist for the Fifth Naval District. After the war I came down to Florida and worked for Addison Mizner. He used to come around to the job in his pajamas with a monkey on his shoulder. A character, Mizner — but a great architect. He hired me, he told me what he wanted, and let me alone.

"Baum came over and looked at my work and Mizner loaned me to him, and I came to Sarasota. I lived in a garage on the estate with my wife and children. While I was here I worked closely with Mrs. Ringling. She loved Italy and the Italian people. It was easy for me to work with her. She knew what she wanted, and that was that.

"When Willy Pogany was doing the ceilings in the recreation room and the music room for her he came down from New York a few times. A short man. Glass eye. I enjoyed working with him. He painted those dance scenes in the coffers of the music room ceiling and I did the decorative work. I used twenty-three-karat gold leaf on the *sgrafitto*. We even went into business together. We had a sign: 'Pogany and Webb, Interiors and Exteriors, Painting and Decorating.' You could see it outside the El Vernona Hotel.

"That was one of my jobs too — the El Vernona. I look at it now and I can't believe it. You see, I've never been afraid of color, and

I'm still not afraid of it. I've been a colorist all my life, but I'm not sure I could ever get those colors at the El Vernona again. That was one of my outstanding jobs.

"Then I was borrowed for the interior of an octagon-shaped Baptist church in South Jacksonville. And after that Baum had me go up to Montclair, New Jersey, where I did another Baptist church interior. Harry Emerson Fosdick was the minister. I worked there with Lamb, my old teacher, on a series of murals. We painted them on Irish linen in Lamb's barn up in Stoughton. I also did the first floor of that YMCA Baum designed in New York City. And the Campagna mansion in Riverdale up there. That was Baum's too.

"After all that work for Mizner and Baum, I worked for twenty-three years for the Rockefellers as superintendent of painting and decorating at the colonial restoration at Williamsburg. They were very nice people to work for."

(In the middle 1960's, Webb was busy at Ca' d'Zan again, repainting ceilings and walls as part of the costly ongoing maintenance of the palace. "It costs a fortune to keep up," a member of the museum staff observed, jealous of the funds spent on the house. "The residence is our bread and butter, but sometimes I wish it would cave in so the money could go to the museum.")

"I really don't know how I got interested in the Italian renaissance," Webb continued. "I just walked into it naturally. I've always loved color. Maybe that's it. Most of what I learned about the way Italian artists decorated the walls and ceilings of the great palaces — the way they painted the beams, say — I had to pick up for myself, although sometimes I would run into an older painter on a job who taught me some things. There were some older painters here that I learned a lot from."

(Earl Purdy has recalled the fine work done for Baum at Ca' d'Zan and elsewhere by Leon Buehler, who was in charge of the decorative painting at the Ringling palace until Webb arrived from Palm Beach. Buehler was then in his sixties. "You can see some of his fine *sgrafitto* work in the lunettes above some of the windows on the outside walls," Purdy has pointed out.)

"Mostly I learned from color plates," Webb went on. "I bought over two hundred color plates from a German bookseller in New York. I can still remember how excited I was when he got those beautiful plates of the walls and ceilings of the Davanzati Palace in Florence. They were a revelation, you see.

"I never made a design ahead of time, and neither did the Italians.

I went ahead, just like they did, full scale. By the way, those decorations in the ceiling panels of the dining room were Mrs. Ringling's idea. One day she gave me this huge tray of priceless cameos [from the Gavet collection] and left them with me. I simply took the designs incised in the pins and brooches and combs she gave me and copied them on the panels. I had that tray up there on the scaffolding for about three months. That was her idea — using the cameos — and it made it very interesting for me.

"It was all freehand, except, of course, for the designs I used on the beams in the great hall. I painted those from stencils, but I cut the stencils freehand."

XIV

THE great hall, a covered court or cortile, was the center of gravity of the palace. It rose through the two principal stories to an inner skylight. Its high ceiling, except for its skylight panels of tinted glass, was covered with pecky cypress brought from the east coast of Florida. Webb had painted not only the beams and coffered panels of the main ceiling, but also the coffered ceiling of the balcony that ran around three sides of the hall (north, east, south) and the frieze of the architrave above the balcony columns. The fourth side of the balcony had been eliminated when the inner west wall of the cortile had been removed from the plans. The balcony provided access to the guest rooms.

Ca' d'Zan's great hall was "one of the most imposing rooms in the country as regards not only size, but treatment," *Country Life* magazine said in an article published ten months after the palace was completed.[32] French tapestries were hung over the balustrades of the balconies, and several costly Flemish tapestries were hung across alcoves on the balcony, niches that concealed the pipes of a large organ. An English Mortlake tapestry was hung on the wall in front of the organ console on the ground floor.

The console of the custom-built three-manual organ, which was designed to play automatically or manually, stood on a low platform near the south wall of the cortile. Ringling and Mable were both very fond of organ music. Their collection of Duo-Art automatic player rolls included "Chant d'Amour" (Stojowski) ; "Morning," from the *Peer Gynt Suite* (Grieg) ; "Good Bye" (Tosti) ; "Le Cygne," from *The Carnival of the Animals* (Saint-Saëns) ; "Even-song" (Martin) ; "Romance" (Schelling) ; "Andantino in D-Flat," the melody used for the song "Moonlight and Roses" (Lemare) ; "Largo" (Handel) ; and "Pale Moon" (Logan) .

On the rare evening when Ca' d'Zan had no guests, Ringling might put a roll on the organ, start the electric playing mechanism, walk out of the great hall, cross the marble terrace, descend the marble steps of the landing, and join Mable. Together they would sit back in her gondola and listen. The music would shake the house and echo across the bayside terrace in the soft twilight air.

Purdy has recalled the curious shopping expedition in New York City during the summer of 1924 on which Ringling contracted for the organ to be built. He and Ringling went to three showrooms where organs were demonstrated for them. Ringling listened, and Purdy made notes on the dimensions of the consoles. At the first two showrooms they heard some music from the classical repertoire, but Ringling was not moved to buy. "I particularly remember hearing Brahms," Purdy has recalled. At the third showroom, the salesman talked to Ringling for a few minutes, then sat down and played a thundering version of "The Parade of the Wooden Soldiers," a German march (1911) that had been featured in the Broadway musical *La Chauve Souris* (1922) and had then become a nationwide hit in a dance arrangement still being played by hundreds of orchestras in the summer of 1924. Before the last *holzsoldaten* had marched by in a cheerful roar of open stops and pedal tones, Ringling was sold. This single performance of the hit tune was worth $50,000 to the Aeolian-Skinner Organ Company.

XV

Guests who considered themselves connoisseurs found in the great cortile a small array of art treasures that they would have considered far more spectacular, in their rarity, beauty, and value, than the organ. These objects — five late fifteenth-century carved poly-chrome heads of saints; two early sixteenth-century French walnut *dressoirs* with panels of carved low relief showing scenes from the crucifixion on one and mythological scenes on the other; a large

French gothic chest; and two South German baroque statuettes of "bishop saints" carved in gilded wood — were from the distinguished collection of late gothic and early renaissance art formed in Paris by Emile Gavet during the second half of the nineteenth century.

They were only a few of the items from the Gavet collection that Ringling owned. (Some of the other objects — jeweled watches, *coquemars* (kettles), monstrances, reliquaries, *chasses* (cases), chalices, clocks, miniature wax portraits from the sixteenth and seventeenth centuries, antique engraved stones, Hispano-Moresque *faïence,* glazed terra-cotta, and *verre eglomise* (glass decorated with metal foil) — were displayed elsewhere in the palace, and a selection of them may be seen today in one of the guest bedrooms, which has been converted into a small gallery. The Gavet objects had traveled to Sarasota from Paris by way of Newport, where they were once on display in the Gothic Room at Marble House.

Beyond the gothic arch doorways in the west wall of the cortile — the curtain wall that served only as a picturesque structural screen — lay the vast bayside marble terrace. Guests could sit there in the winter sun on travertine benches, or look through a large telescope mounted on a sturdy tripod. The telescope pointed out toward the bay, and guests could see the causeway Ringling had built, named for himself, and deeded to the city.[33] Ringling could point out to them the growing community on St. Armand's Key which he was developing, and which he had also named for himself. Straight across the bay on Longboat Key guests could also see rising day by day in 1927 the structural steelwork of Ringling's Ritz-Carlton Hotel. Soon the hotel would become a $900,000 ghost in the winter moonlight, and the distant sidewalks of "The John Ringling Estates" would be covered by ranks of weeds, the silent witnesses of insolvency.

But the broad terrace was really a stage on which Ringling could publicly display the two arts at which he excelled — hospitality and showmanship. The two inevitably merged, as on those fine winter evenings when he invited his fellow townsmen to an after-dark concert. One evening he had seventy-five of them in for a barbecue and music, and some good news: he had decided to move the winter quarters of his circus to Sarasota starting in 1927.

On other evenings a large crowd would fill the space between the palace and the seawall just to hear the "Czechoslovakian Band of Prague, Bohemia," which Ringling had discovered at Coney Island in the summer of 1924 and had brought to Sarasota the following

January for the first of a succession of winter visits. (Thereafter, its bass drum bore the legend "John Ringling, Real Estate, Sarasota, Florida," during the band's annual summer concerts at Coney Island.) Ringling became the winter proprietor of the "Czech Band," and he lent it out freely in Sarasota for street dances, county fairs, church bazaars, and Sunday concerts. The band became an enormously popular community morale booster — all in the cause of Ringling's, and Sarasota's, real estate. "Sarasota likes you, John Ringling. You are a good neighbor," a letter to the editor of the *Sarasota Herald* declared on January 9, 1926. (An editorial in the *Herald* several months earlier had pleaded with Ringling: "We want to know definitely and positively" that the band will be back next year.) [34]

During the evening concerts at Ca' d'Zan, Ringling would conceal the band on his yacht, the *Zalophus,* anchored a short distance offshore. While his hundred or more guests waited, Ringling would keep the band silent until complete darkness had fallen. And *then,* ladies and gentlemen, on the very first downbeat the yacht came alight like a starburst, and the night was filled with music.

Ca' d'Zan required eight refrigerators, for Ringling loved nothing so much as to be surrounded by celebrant friends. Among those who came to dinner, some of whom have already been mentioned, were: James J. Walker, the dapper and sportive mayor of New York; Alfred E. Smith, the governor of New York; Will Rogers, then at his peak as a Ziegfeld Follies star; Florenz Ziegfeld and his wife, Billie Burke; Irvin S. Cobb, the humorist; Albert Keller, head of the Ritz-Carlton Hotel in New York; Julius W. Böhler; Detlev Moritz Georg Heinrich Wilhelm von Hadeln; Dr. Fred H. Albee; John J. McGraw; Karl Bickel, a United Press Associations executive; Willy Pogany; Ottokar Bartik, a Metropolitan Opera choreographer who planned many of the circus's "extravaganzas" for Ringling; Frank Phillips, founder of the Phillips Petroleum Company; W. J. Burns, head of the private detective agency bearing his name; S. Davies Warfield, whose niece would one day marry the abdicant King of England; and Tex Rickard, who was associated with Ringling in building the "new" (1926) Madison Square Garden.

While the palace was nearing completion, Savely Sorine, a fashionable Russian-American society portraitist, used the solarium as a studio. There he painted the portraits of Mable and John still to be seen at Ca' d'Zan. "Very good likenesses," Robert Webb believes.

When Ringling, whom Sorine portrayed with his hand in his suit coat pocket, showed his picture to Will Rogers, the comedian said: "John, that's the first time I've ever seen you with your hand in your own pocket," a drollery that had no lack of precedent.

Ringling's bedroom was larger than the ballroom, which was rather small by palace standards. And his bathroom looked like a Sienna marble quarry: the tub had been hewn from a solid block of the deep yellow stone; the walls were paneled with it; the floor was paved with it; and, the bowl and seat of the commode were painted to simulate it. Ringling bought a large oval mythological ceiling painting in Paris. He had an artist "extend" it to the edges of the rectangular bedroom ceiling. (It has since been returned to its original state.) Ringling's large twin beds, derived from the Egyptian vagaries of French Empire design, looked like ceremonial barges, beached and forgotten, far from the Nile. They were embellished with gilded bronze sphinxes, and looked at too closely for too long a time, they remind one of an observation made by Ralph Dutton in his study *The Châteaux of France*. "There is unquestionably a certain vulgarity about the high Empire style," Dutton wrote. "It caters clearly [to] those who would not appreciate delicacy and subtlety."

Mable's room showed rather greater delicacy: it was graceful, rococo, and personal. Her furniture was made of inlaid sandalwood; her bedspread had been made from the lace of her bridal veil and wedding gown. The room overlooked the colorful flora of the broad approach oval and swimming pool in front of the house. The principal guest room, a French apartment of muted grays with an abundance of carved ribbons and cupids, also looked out on the landscaped drive. Will Rogers was an early, if somewhat unlikely, occupant of the room. Rogers later told his friends that after the butler had left him in his suite it took him two and a half days to find his way to the dining room, a wisecrack that was certain to please his host.

There were six guest rooms on the second floor at Ca' d'Zan, and eight servants' rooms. Although the palace looked westward upon one of the most beautiful seascapes in America, only two of the principal bedrooms provided a view of the water. Ringling had an office on the second floor in which he kept a number of mementos, including eighty railroad passes and a silver *repousée* telephone. As he hoped they would, his guests always asked Ringling about the phone. Well, you see, John would explain . . .

In brief, the story was that Ringling had had a private audience with the Pope during which the two men talked about their common love for Italian painting. Throughout the audience, Ringling looked admiringly at the gold *repousée* phone on the Pope's desk, which, of course, the Pope could not dispose of inasmuch as it had been a gift to the Holy See. However, the Pope told his visitor (according to Ringling) that one of the cardinals had a silver phone just like it, which he might possibly part with. . . . And, there it stood on John's desk! A miracle? Yes, if sleight of hand is a miracle. Long after Ringling died, a sales receipt was found that betrayed him. The phone had been sent down from Solomon's in New York along with a shipment of rugs. It had cost Ringling $75.

Ca' d'Zan, like the telephone, was part miracle, part . . . whatever the eye of the beholder chose to see. What Mable saw on Christmas Day, 1926, when John gathered the remaining members of his family for a German housewarming dinner, was a *palace* — a perfectly lovely palace in which she and John would entertain their many, many friends during the long, clement Florida winters that lay ahead.

XVI

UNHAPPILY, Mable's seasons at Ca' d'Zan were to be few: she died in New York on June 9, 1929, the victim of acute diabetes and Addison's disease. And when she died, a curious thing happened: John Ringling's luck ran out. First, he married Emily Haag Buck, a beautiful widow. Each thought the other was abundantly rich: both were deceived. "Why they ever married is beyond all understanding," Henry North has written.[35] They separated within two years and were finally divorced (the protracted litigation lasting until after Ringling's death).

Then, early in 1932, Ringling suffered a blood clot in his leg. A newspaper incorrectly reported that he had had both legs amputated. Before the year was out, he had been cast down as the king of the American circus. A coalition of his relatives and friends, in a complicated legal maneuver, facilitated by Ringling's arrogance, ousted him as head of "The Greatest Show on Earth."

He was dumbfounded. Within a few months he had a stroke that paralyzed his right side and left him unable to speak. However, he regained his speech in about a month and a half, and slowly recovered control of all but a part of his side. Two years later he had a near-fatal heart attack. Ill and demeaned, he withdrew to his seawall at Ca' d'Zan, a mortally wounded ruler, bereft of power, whose callers were more than likely to be process servers. But in the most trying times he showed bursts of his old sinewy humor. Once, when the doorbell rang, he called out to his nephew, "Tell them 'Annie Doesn't Live Here Anymore,'" the title of a popular song that enjoyed a brief vogue in 1933.

Mable had died before the museum they had planned together could be completed. Now Ringling thought only of preserving intact his first-rate collection of several hundred baroque paintings. The museum which was rising a short distance from the palace was to bear both their names. He had already announced his intention of giving both the palace and the museum to the people of Florida. He hoped that the house would become a museum of Venetian art.

Despite his severe financial problems — made worse by the Depression — he refused to sell a single painting. He became obsessed by his vision of himself as the sole trustee of this unusual baroque treasure. His stubborn courage held, even when his creditors forced him to the brink of bankruptcy. There, John Ringling North, with the help of his younger brother Henry, performed miracles of financial levitation trying to save "Uncle John" from the inevitable plunge to bankruptcy and the automatic liquidation of his collection.

One evening in May, 1936, Ringling invited his friend Karl Bickel of the United Press, and his friend and lawyer Henry Wiliford, and their wives, to dinner. It was a sad evening, as Bickel later recalled it. After dinner, John took his guests into the great hall, dragging his right leg as he walked. They helped him put one of his favorite rolls on the organ.

All knew that Ringling had only the most feeble hold on Ca' d'Zan. He was close to involuntary bankruptcy. Twice recently he had barely escaped a court order to sell the palace to satisfy a large judgment against him. But, as his friends knew, time was against him. They were the last guests Ringling ever had to dinner at Ca' d'Zan. Late in the year, the court set a firm date for the sale of the palace: December 9, 1936. Five days before the public sale, Ringling died in New York City. He had $311 in the bank. His death was his final bit of sleight of hand: he had once more saved the house — this time for the people of Florida.

XVII

ONE day during the painful and bitter years of his decline, Ringling asked Henry North to drive him to Pensacola to see a circus parade. Neither he nor North had seen one in fifteen years. When they arrived, North settled his uncle comfortably on a balcony overlooking the parade route. John was the last of the Ringling Brothers — "the last one on the lot," he had said the day his only remaining brother had died.

North became absorbed as the familiar sounds of the parade drew near. The escort wagons, the tableaux wagons, and the menagerie wagons passed. North turned to look at his uncle. "He was sitting absolutely motionless in his chair and tears were streaming . . . from his eyes," North later recalled.[36]

Finally, after the horses, after the elephants, after the steam calliope had passed, Ringling pushed himself up out of his chair and leaned on North.

"Time to go, Buddy," he said.

THREE

VIZCAYA

III-1

III-1   "The whole place was magic." The palace and the formal Italian gardens of Vizcaya. Courtesy of the Miami-Metro Department of Publicity and Tourism.

III-2   Villa Rezzonico at Bassano del Grappa, northwest of Venice. Courtesy of the Italian Cultural Institute.

III-3   Clay model of Vizcaya by Menconi Brothers, c. 1915. From drawings by F. Burrall Hoffman, Jr. Courtesy of the Dade County Art Museum (Vizcaya).

III-4   Vizcaya from Biscayne Bay. Courtesy of the Dade County Art Museum (Vizcaya).

III-5   The tea house and uniformed gondolier. Photograph by Mattie Edwards Hewitt (1917). Courtesy of the Florida Historical Society.

III-6   Plan of grounds, Vizcaya. The plan shows complete architectural entourage, which is missing from the architect's "Ground-Floor Plan." F. Burrall Hoffman, Jr., architect. Paul Chalfin and Diego Suarez, landscape architects. From *The Architectural Review*, July, 1917. Courtesy of Mr. Hoffman.

III-7   "Ground-Floor Plan." F. Burrall Hoffman, Jr., architect. From *The Architectural Review*, July, 1917. Courtesy of Mr. Hoffman.

III-8   "Second-Floor Plan." F. Burrall Hoffman, Jr., architect. From *The Architectural Review*, July, 1917. Courtesy of Mr. Hoffman.

III-9   The music room. Photograph by Mattie Edwards Hewitt (1917). Courtesy of the Florida Historical Society.

III-10 Enclosed loggia — or tea room. The wrought-iron gates are from the Palazzo Pisani (1615). Photograph by Mattie Edwards Hewitt (1917). Courtesy of the Florida Historical Society.

III-11 East (bayside) loggia set for heavy weather. Everything has been brought in from the terrace, except a small pair of sunset guns. Model of a caravel — the *Vizcaya* — hangs from ceiling. Photograph by Mattie Edwards Hewitt (1917). Courtesy of the Florida Historical Society.

III-12 Entrance hall, in the Directoire style. Photograph by Mattie Edwards Hewitt (1917). Courtesy of the Florida Historical Society.

III-13 Organ screen. Drawing from Chalfin's drafting room, May 2, 1916. Courtesy of the Dade County Art Museum (Vizcaya).

III-14 The south gallery. (In the last of this section of illustrations, Burrall Hoffman is shown standing in this gallery, in 1972.) Photograph by Mattie Edwards Hewitt (1917). Courtesy of the Florida Historical Society.

III-15 The "Espagnolette" guest room. (Among the other guest rooms at Vizcaya were "Galleon," "Pantaloon," and "Lady Hamilton.") Photograph by Mattie Edwards Hewitt (1917). Courtesy of the Florida Historical Society.

III-16 Deering's bedroom. Photograph by Mattie Edwards Hewitt (1917). Courtesy of the Florida Historical Society.

III-17 "Anacreonic-Decorative Panel." One of a set of four panels painted by Chalfin. Architectural League of New York: 25th Annual Exhibition (catalogue), 1910. Courtesy of the League.

III-18 James Deering at Vizcaya, 1917. Photograph by Mattie Edwards Hewitt. Courtesy of the Florida Historical Society.

III-19 Diego Suarez, c. 1933. Courtesy of Mrs. Diego Suarez.

III-20 Paul Chalfin in 1915. Pastel portrait by Albert Sterner. Courtesy of the Dade County Art Museum (Vizcaya).

III-21 Deering's house at Neuilly. Courtesy of the Dade County Art Museum (Vizcaya).

III-22 F. Burrall Hoffman, Jr., 1917. Courtesy of Mr. Hoffman.

III-23 F. Burrall Hoffman, Jr., Baden-Baden, c. 1939. Photograph by Kuhn & Hitz. Courtesy of Mr. Hoffman.

III-24 Paul Chalfin, c. 1956. Courtesy of the Dade County Art Museum (Vizcaya).

III-25 Hoffman, age eighty-nine, standing in the south gallery. (See Illustration III-14 for an earlier view of the south gallery.) Photograph by Jack Stark. Courtesy of the Dade County Art Museum (Vizcaya).

III-2

Villa Rezzonico, the basic prototype for Vizcaya.

III-3

" 'The models fired my imagination . . .' "

III-4

" '. . . old traditions debonairly worn . . .' "

III-5

" 'I remember how much I wanted to get into one of the gondolas . . .' "

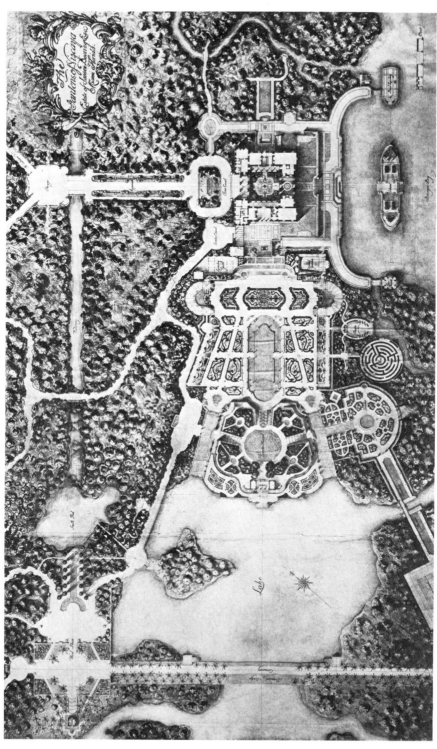

The gardens of Vizcaya.

III-6

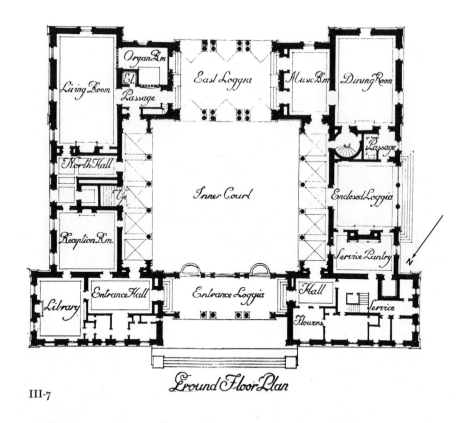

Ground Floor Plan

III-7

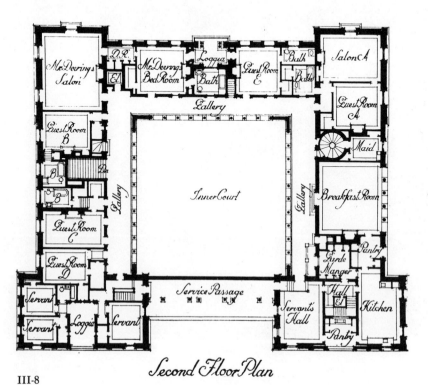

Second Floor Plan

III-8

III-9

The music room.

III-10   Enclosed loggia.

III-11   East loggia.

III-12

Entrance hall: view into entrance loggia.

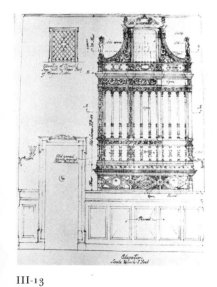

III-13

" 'Mr. Deering loved music . . .' "

III-14

The south gallery.

III-15

The "Espagnolette" guest room.

III-16

Deering's bedroom.

III-17   "He was a very private man."

III-18

"Anacreonic-Decorative Panel" by Paul Chalfin.

III-19

Diego Suarez.

III-20

"Few artists can have done as much for a patron."

III-21

Deering's house at Neuilly.

III-22

Hoffman with AEF in France.

III-23

Hoffman in Baden-Baden.

III-24

"Old and blind and burdened
with misfortunes . . ."

III-25

F. Burrall Hoffman, Jr., at Vizcaya, 1972.

> There is really no need for working, fixed
> as we are financially.

GEORGE W. PERKINS, who was to become known in Wall Street as
J. Pierpont Morgan's right-hand man, put together the International
Harvester Company in 1902, a virtuoso performance in capital organization whose peculiar distinction lay less in the field of finance
than in that of diplomacy. The principal parties, whose family-owned
companies and interests were combined by Perkins, were already
very rich. They feared one another, and they feared Morgan's reputation for watering the stock in his great trust ventures. However, they
wanted the additional millions that would come to them as the result
of the recapitalization of their combined companies. And, above all
other considerations, they wanted the princely convenience of world-
wide control of the enormous farm machinery market that the pool-
ing of their interests would insure.

They may jealously have advocated their separate interests, but
they were classical American capitalists: they wanted to free themselves of the rigors of competition. "The present fight [in the
marketplace]," one of them said, "is having a wearing and tearing
influence all around, making such people as ourselves work hard
when there is really no need for working, fixed as we are financially."[1]

Perkins, a man of tireless industry — "the only one in the [Mor-
gan] firm who really did any work," the eminent corporation counsel William Nelson Cromwell once observed of him — had made sure
in creating the harvester trust that none of the parties would ever
have to compete again. In so doing, he had merged the egos, the
power, and the ambition of two rich and formidable Chicago families, the McCormicks and the Deerings.

Four years later — by the summer of 1906 — he had reason to wish
that he hadn't. The giant trust, which had begun its corporate life

with almost eighty-five percent of the world's farm machinery business, was bogged down under an inefficient management made up of contending family officers, proud, unyielding, and unprofessional. *Primus inter pares:* each family, Deering and McCormick, saw itself as first among equals at the head of the corporation. The result, as Perkins candidly pointed out to them, was an organization that suffered from "too many 'millionaire officers' who were unwilling to work or take orders."

After having listened to their bickering for four years, Perkins, as his biographer, John A. Garraty, has observed, "was thoroughly fed up with the Deerings, whom he considered incompetent, and only somewhat less so with all the McCormicks," except the head of the family, Cyrus Hall McCormick. None of the family officers appears to have annoyed him more than James Deering, the third in command of the Deering interests.

William Deering, James's father, had founded the Deering Harvester Company, and by the 1880's he had come close to ending the long supremacy of the McCormicks in the farm machinery market. He was now in retirement in Coconut Grove, Florida, but, impatient with its poor dividend yield, he was threatening to dissolve the young trust.

Charles Deering, James's older half-brother, had graduated with distinction from the U.S. Naval Academy. After eight years of active service, he had, at his father's insistence, given up his naval career to help run the expanding family business. As early as the 1870's, during a visit to Paris, he had met the sculptor Augustus Saint-Gaudens and the painter John Singer Sargent, who was then studying with Emile-Auguste Carolus-Duran. He and Sargent became lifelong friends. Their warm relationship stimulated Deering's own latent interest in painting.

In 1893, he met Anders Zorn, a Swedish painter, and began another enduring friendship in the art world. Zorn was in Chicago for a year serving as the Swedish Commissioner of Fine Arts at the World's Columbian Exposition. Shortly after they met, he offered Deering the use of his studio in Paris. Encouraged by Sargent, Deering went to Paris to paint "for a season."[2] However, his father once more insisted he devote his life to business, and he returned to Chicago. When the International Harvester Company was formed in 1902, he was named chairman of the board of directors, an office he held until his retirement in 1910.

James E. Deering, named for his grandfather, was born in South Paris, Maine, November 12, 1859. His family moved to Evanston, Illinois, where he went to the Northwestern University preparatory school. He attended the university for one year (1877–1878), and the following year he went to the Massachusetts Institute of Technology, where he was enrolled as a "special student." He did not go on with college. By the time he was twenty-one he was working with his father and older brother.[3]

When the Deerings agreed to join the McCormicks in International Harvester, James was elected one of the three vice-presidents of the new company and was put in charge of its Chicago plants. He may have been an effective partner of the old family firm, but to George Perkins he was one of the "millionaire officers" who did not fit into the new corporate scheme. During the summer of 1906, "Perkins," Garraty writes, "[tried] to persuade Deering, whom he thought utterly useless, to drop his active contact with the corporation. 'Do you not consider that I am competent to run . . . the business?' Deering asked indignantly. Perkins could not answer this question, so he parried it."

After his meeting with Perkins, Deering may well have felt much as did the financier in a Wall Street anecdote related some years later to the financial writer and editor Clarence W. Barron, who wrote it down in his notebook:

"A gentleman of finance was descending the steps of the House of Morgan. A friend inquired: 'Why, what's the matter with you? You look so depressed.' "

The financier replied: " 'I have just been subjected to the unconscious arrogance of conscious power.' "[4]

The conscious power that Perkins held was singular: in the earliest stages of the negotiations that had led to the formation of the International Harvester Company, he had exacted from those involved an agreement that Morgan's would have "absolute control of the future organization of the Company."

Thus, whatever James Deering's feelings about his own competence, Perkins prevailed, and he "was able to force through the administrative reforms he considered essential." Within two years, the company was operating successfully, a condition reflected in the improved market value of International Harvester stock and the larger dividends it paid. Perkins had saved the trust, but James Deering was out of a job, as it were, for he was no longer responsible for plant operations. He was, however, to remain a vice-president for another ten years, a title he shared with two other founders of the trust, both of whom were also inactive.

Thus, by 1908, Deering was a rich man with a great deal of time on his hands. He was forty-nine years old and unmarried. He could move about as the whim seized him. He enjoyed travel and was as much at home in Paris or New York as he was in Chicago. He maintained residences, at various times, in New York at 10 West Forty-third Street and 22 East Forty-seventh Street; in Paris, at 9 Rue Saint-James, Neuilly; and in Chicago, at 1430 Lake Shore Drive, Evanston, his home and legal residence for many years. He was listed in both the Chicago and New York editions of the *Social Register*.

Deering was much attached to Paris, and his devotion to the French was earnest and greathearted. When Cyrus Hall McCormick had first wanted to sound out the Deerings on the formation of the harvester trust, he went to Washington to attend a reception for Jules-Martin Cambon, the French ambassador. McCormick knew that James Deering would be at the reception as a matter of course, and that he could there broach the delicate subject in a congenial ambience of Deering's choice.

In 1900, Deering had arranged for the exhibition at the Exposition Universale in Paris of a set of carefully executed scale models that traced the technical evolution of farm machinery in the United States. He then made a gift of the costly miniature machines to the Musée des Arts et Métiers in Paris. If the significance of Deering's tutorial gift now eludes us, it can be recovered from a paraphrase of an observation made at the time by President Emile-François Loubet that "France would starve to death except for the farming machines turned out in Chicago."[5] In 1901, France acknowledged Deering's practical affection by making him a chevalier in the Legion of Honor.

However, honors lists disappear quickly in the welter of history, a condition that must have pleased Deering, for he was a man who sedulously cultivated privacy. He became known to reporters as "the silent man of International Harvester," a phrase that was innocent of the irony that may now be read into it. Deering kept the American press at a polite remove, but he succumbed to Jules Huret, one of the most famous French journalists of the era and an early (1899) biographer of Sarah Bernhardt. For more than a decade, Huret's essays on politics, literature, theater, economics, and sociology had appeared in

Le Figaro, the Paris newspaper favored by the aristocracy, who could read in its columns extended accounts of their exclusive gatherings, some of them written by Marcel Proust, at that time a little-known writer on the arts.

Huret traveled widely in Europe, and in 1904 he came to the United States, sending back to *Le Figaro* a series of interpretive essays that were later collected in book form under the title *En Amerique de New York à la Nouvelle Orléans.* Huret's American pieces are remembered in France as having been *"très intéresants,"* but apparently they were not interesting enough to have been translated into English.[6]

In Chicago, Huret met Deering.

"In this city," he wrote, "which is generally supposed to be inhabited wholly by barbarians, I met more cultured men and more true courtesy and politeness than in New York. I have even discovered in one of the richest men in this fierce capital of business a mind as exquisitely cultured as one could imagine. I do not believe it is possible to find in all the aristocracies of Europe a nature more really distinguished than that of Mr. James Deering.

"I ask his pardon for speaking of him with such brutal publicity. But I am proud of my discovery of him, because it permits me to correct the too summary judgments that have been passed upon the American character. That a man as polished and cultured as he can exist in the terrible world of business makes up for the many things that are lacking [in that world]."

It may have amused Deering to know that any American who wished to penetrate his privacy and discover his rare distinction would have to read *Le Figaro* to do so.

On July 19, 1906, Deering was promoted by the French government to the rank of *officier* in the Legion of Honor, a tribute that may have redressed somewhat for him the low opinion of his management abilities expressed that same summer by Perkins. In commenting on the honor, *Le Figaro* republished the foregoing extract from Huret's 1904 essay, and then added the following new observations on Deering:

"There is no French visitor to the United States, whether on an official or a private mission, who does not return charmed with this cultured man. . . . [He] has been, since the project was first suggested, one of the warmest advocates of a treaty [of amity] between France and the United States. He has waged many campaigns, presided over many conventions, in support of this worthy cause, for which he has traveled hundreds of miles and spent a small fortune."

A New York newspaper translated Huret's flattering sketch of Deering and *Le Figaro*'s revelation of his role as an amateur diplomat. Thus, briefly, did Deering's mask of privacy slip, and thus could the quick eye of a few have learned that in the years leading up to the managerial reorganization of the International Harvester Company he was already deeply concerned with matters that lay well outside "the terrible world of business."

By the end of the decade, Deering was to add to them the most absorbing and memorable of his personal undertakings, the creation of Vizcaya, a one-hundred-thirty-acre Italian renaissance estate which he imposed on a vast hummock of tangled trees and vines and black marsh undergrowth along the edge of Biscayne Bay at Miami — an estate that once comprised the following:

A private harbor dredged to receive oceangoing schooners. A breakwater designed in the long tradition of decorative stone barges, but of a magnitude and artistry that excelled any previously known. A three-hundred-foot-long seawall. A gondola canal that wound through the estate. A lake, divided by a causeway. A boathouse to receive Deering's yacht, the *Nepenthe*. Two tea houses, one of French *treillage,* and the other of stucco and latticework. A large baroque casino. More than twenty-five miles of roadways and paths.

A forest of tropical trees, some native to the site, others imported. A large tract of farms with adjacent barns, pens, and service outbuildings. A partially hidden hamlet of north Italian baroque farmhouses for estate personnel. Ten acres of formal Italian renaissance gardens, with charming resonances of France in their *broderies* — humanist gardens unmatched in this hemisphere for their grandeur and carefully studied historical authenticity.

And the superb centerpiece of the estate, a four-tower, seventy-room baroque villa-palazzo of stucco and stone and red half-barrel tile roofs; a truly splendid house that evokes in plan and elevation many prototypes still to be found along the Brenta River, on Lake Como, and in the hills above Florence, but which, because of its fine command of scale and its assured avoidance of picturesque trifling, calmly reveals its own distinctive character.

If the villa ranks among the most successful adaptations of a traditional style to be found in this country, its interiors must be accounted unique in their brilliant blending of four centuries of Italian decoration, some of it of French provenance. They disclose a synthesis based upon uncommon decorative skill and subtle scholarship, a *mélange* serious in its intention but often playful, even when it assumes a curatorial precision.

This remarkable project, whose complex logistical problems — the construction of a railroad spur and the operation of a quarry among them — would appeal to Deering's arithmetical mode of thought, was to take him a dozen years to complete.[7] And, further, it was to cost him almost as much as Frank W. Woolworth paid, out of his own pocket, for his historic skyscraper during the same period.

M. Huret might have been surprised at the great enterprise of his "exquisitely cultured" friend.

II

STEP by step, vaguely at first, but with a kind of intuitive logic, Deering discovered and ordered his new role in life. He became a collector, but he was not content only with buying paintings, furniture, sculpture, and furnishings. He plunged into the world of architectonics, gathering together the fragments of a dream palace. He collected ceilings and cornices (plastered, beamed, carved, painted) ; mantels and chimneypieces (stone, wood, terra-cotta: molded, carved, gilded) ; towering door surrounds of carved stone; huge entry portals of weathered stone that once gave upon Italian garden and forest vistas; tall wrought-iron grilles and gates; doors large and small (molded, carved, painted, encrusted with bronze) ; *boiseries* (carved, painted, gilded) ; wall fountains; tile and marble floors; and entire roofs. No matter what their source or era, these decorative and structural components had one thing in common: romantic charm. They also shared an awkward lack: they had no common scale that would unify them architecturally. It would take a peculiar mixture of architectural skill and aesthetic sympathy to fit them coherently into a common matrix.

Deering's small circle of close friends knew him as a circumspect and judicious man, generous and thoughtful, but always deliberate. They might now have thought him benignly mad. He suffered from pernicious anemia and he rationed his energy carefully, but his friends could not have failed to notice how his health seemed to improve as he became progressively more involved in his imposing project. A new spirit marked his manner. "Those were really Deering's greatest years," one who observed him at the time has remarked. "He seemed so alive then. It was a time of great excitement for him . . . buying, and planning the house."[8]

He collected garden statuary, and he bought a huge public fountain, "which . . . reared its monumental sculpture and its *Baroque* basins above the *piazza* of [Bassano di Sutri] a town in the vicinity of Viterbo" near Rome.[9] The fountain became his as the result of adroit bargaining: he built a modern community water supply system in exchange for the masterpiece of sculpture, which was thought to have been designed by Vignola, "the leading architect in Rome after the death of Michelangelo."[10]

Deering made several long journeys in Italy to discover what it was he was after, and to buy it. He saw ancient castle-villas stained by the long seasons of history — structures whose dour towers linked by high curtains of stone had once defended enclosed courtyards. Vagrant boundaries in time, they marked the end of the feudal era and the dawn of a new age in which somber bastions slowly became gracious country residences. The long, abundant story of Italian *décor* absorbed him, revealing its calendar and aesthetic grammar: classical, renaissance, baroque, rococo, neoclassical, Directoire, and Empire.

A picture emerges from the little that is known of Deering's travels in search of Vizcaya: one sees a discreet but ardent figure hurrying across an ancient tapestry toward dim stone towers in the faded distance. But the image is only partly accurate, for his search took him not only into the Tuscan hills, the hamlets and towns above Rome, and the countryside beyond Venice — the vast plain and uplands (the *terraferma*) from which the original Venetians had been driven seaward to the watery safety of the lagoons by barbarian invaders — but also into the galleries and auction rooms of art dealers. And, he was not a lone figure on the landscape of his renaissance vision. Others were present in his long architectural planning sessions, on his trips abroad, and on his visits to the warerooms of *antiquaires* in New York, Paris, and Rome — experts who guided him, helped him refine the dangerous tumult implicit in the rapid growth of his plans, and who, in the end, boldly brought his great scheme down to earth. They will emerge in due course.

Vizcaya could have been an aesthetic disaster, a museum of incoherent, partially uttered thoughts. It became, on the contrary, an eloquent witness to the skill of the men Deering trusted with his costly reveries. It became, also, a tribute to his own cool resolution, his sense of measure. Unlike Hearst at San Simeon, a project of similar architectural and decorative complexity but of far greater magnitudes, Deering completed his palace. It grew well beyond his original intentions, and one is surprised that he was not completely overwhelmed (a vulnerability Hearst passionately indulged, and gave in to), for Italy is a tempting warehouse of marvels. But Deering, satisfied, called a halt: he was a reasonable man who knew his limitations.

The latter he had discovered early in his new career as a collector. Even before Vizcaya had assumed either name or form in his mind, he had made a commonplace, but humiliating, blunder. Acting entirely on his own, he had bought a painting, an "old master," that turned out to be "a fake."[11] It became embarrassingly clear to Deering that he lacked his brother Charles's knowledge in art. He made a decision, logical and precise: if he could not be an art expert, he would hire one.

Not long afterward he was in New York and he called on Elsie de Wolfe, "a great friend of his," who, in 1905, had given up a dubious career as the theater's leading "exponent of . . . the peculiar art of wearing good clothes well," and had since become the best-known interior decorator in America.[12] As early as August 28, 1887, the *New York Herald* had called attention to Elsie's diverting personal style in a report on a subscription ball at the Newport Casino under the headline "The Gayest Week of the Season." The *Herald* had noted that "the *chic* dancer of the evening was Miss de Wolfe." The *New York Times* of the same date had reported that she had just returned from France, where she had taken "a course of dramatic instruction." The *Times* had further noted that "her daily movements are duly chronicled in an evening contemporary."

Elsie had lived in the public eye from then on, a position she maintained by deliberate stratagems such as forcing her way into a Patriarchs' ball, one of the most exclusive of the winter rituals of the Four Hundred, and into the next day's headlines as well. Her loving companion of many years, Elisabeth Marbury, a highly successful playwrights' agent who had a remarkable gift for public relations, had guided her away from her girlish high jinks into news-making of a more sophisticated, if no less spirited, sort. Both were members, at least marginally, of the Four Hundred. However, they were also helping to create a new society in which wit, intelligence, style, creative achievement, and a lively interest in the arts took precedence over wealth and family status. They were, as Lloyd Morris has observed in *Incredible New York,* "creating a vogue for the most improbable of diversions — brilliant talk."

Frank Crowninshield, the urbane editor of *Vanity Fair* who neatly balanced detachment and involvement while serving at once as the *arbiter elegantiarum* and reporter-historian of the new society — the New York equivalent of *Tout-Paris* — late in his life told Geoffrey T. Hellman of *The New Yorker* that "in the old days society was so snobbish and narrow and limited that artists and writers and playwrights were not sought after. Finally it was discovered that they were more amusing, so the narrow society began breaking its neck to get into what was the forerunner of café society. It became *chic* to go to Alma Gluck's, Stanford White's, Bessie Marbury's, August Thomas's, Elsie de Wolfe's. That made a very charming society."[13]

The Sunday teas that Elsie and Elisabeth gave in what Elisabeth described as their "dear little house on the southwest corner of Seventeenth Street and Irving Place," just below Gramercy Park, brought together leading figures from the worlds of theater, painting, sculpture, the decorative arts, music, literature, journalism, and society. Because Elisabeth represented Oscar Wilde, Gabriele d'Annunzio, and Victorien Sardou — as well as all of Sardou's principal French colleagues — and maintained correspondent offices in London, Paris, and Munich, the teas usually included European guests prominent in the arts. "[Our house] was a glorified Ellis Island, and to many of our good friends it became the real port of New York," Elisabeth later wrote in her memoirs.

Comte Robert de Montesquiou, the "Prince of Aesthetes" (as his biographer Philippe Jullian has characterized him) , who was to serve Proust as one of the principal models of the Baron Palamède de Charlus in *Remembrance of Things Past,* came there during an American lecture tour Elisabeth had arranged for him, and observed Elsie's skill as an amateur decorator. She had completely redecorated the house, "bit by bit, need by need," as she recalled long afterward, unaware that she was laying the groundwork for a new career. Montesquiou's taste was rather more arcane, more *outré,* than Elsie's, serving as it did as one of the node points of the "aesthetic" and *art nouveau* movements. But, inasmuch as he was a friend and, in France, a neighbor (his house at Versailles was no more than a short walk from the Villa Trianon, the *pavillon* that Elisabeth, Elsie, and their good friend Anne Morgan owned there), and also a man of exquisite manners, he may well have joined other guests in their praise of Elsie's innate good taste and fine eye.

When Elsie retired from the theater in 1905 following the failure of Pinero's *A Wife Without a Smile* ("a play without an audience," Alice-Leone Moats later wrote[14]), friends encouraged her to become a professional decorator, and Elisabeth promoted her work with energy and shrewdness, an undertaking helped greatly by Elsie's own flair for publicity. (When Elisabeth later invented and coproduced a series of small-scale, intimate musicals at The Princess Theatre with librettos by Guy Bolton, lyrics by P. G. Wodehouse, and music by Jerome Kern — productions that revolutionized American musical comedy — she saw to it that Elsie designed either the costumes or sets for several of them.)

However, in the ordering of creative primacy, Elsie ranked well below the brilliant architect-designer-decorator Stanford White, the master of American palace architecture and decoration at the turn of the century. White himself had admired Elsie's work, and he had obtained for her her first major commission, the decorating of the Colony Club, which he had designed, and which had been completed on the eve of his murder in 1906. He had had to overcome the reservations of the women on the organizing committee of the club, and is said to have told them, "Give the order to Elsie, and let the girl alone. She knows more than any of us."[15]

The country had enthusiastically taken up her blithe, fresh, un-cluttered, and aery style of decoration, with its personal scale, inno-cent of grandeur, but always suggestive of sophistication in its vague echoes of historic precedent. Elsie had become the new woman, an American Sue Bridehead, the heroine of Thomas Hardy's *Jude the Obscure* (1895), whom Hardy, after being viciously attacked for daring to have dealt with her threatening presence in the world, later described as "the slight, pale 'bachelor' girl . . . who does not recognize the necessity for most of her sex to follow marriage as a profession."[16]

Elsie was independent, creative, glamorous. She had become a vital presence in American life. She generated a new spirit of personal freedom, bringing to her successful career an *élan* that verged on brashness, and a studied *panache* that tended to salute itself, qualities that endeared her to a nation that preferred a headline to a *mot*. She would not be suppressed, and men and women alike rallied to her, some of them to share the rigors and pleasures of a minor crusade, others simply to ride the bandwagon. She seemed to know everyone, and it was quite natural for James Deering, whose presence in her orbit remains unexplained, to turn to her for help. It is not known whether he told her about his embarrassing purchase of a fake masterpiece. However, he did ask her to recommend someone to serve as his art adviser, someone to monitor his collecting who would be free to travel abroad with him.

She recommended Paul Chalfin, a talented painter who had studied in Paris, Rome, Florence, and Venice, and who knew well the palaces and decorative treasures of those cities. Chalfin, who was then in his middle thirties, was unmarried and was, thus, free to travel at Deering's convenience. Elsie could not have made a better choice.[17] She knew, of course, that Chalfin's credentials were excellent, but she could not have anticipated how well he was to meet Deering's changing requirements.

She had, quite by accident, launched a remarkable career, brief but dazzling, that still perplexes those few who can remember it, however dimly.

III

PAUL CHALFIN (pronounced to rhyme with *dolphin*) was born November 2, 1874, in New York City, the last of the five children of Colonel Samuel Fletcher Chalfin, who had served as a military aide to President Lincoln during the Civil War, and Jane Voorhees (Connolly) Chalfin, an accomplished musician. His maternal grandfather, Charles Matthew Connolly, an old New York tobacco merchant and banker, had married Isabella S. Voorhees, who came of a family of "wealthy Dutch ship owners."[18] After the Civil War, Connolly had built a town house with an art gallery at 450 Fifth Avenue, diagonally across the street from the palatial residence that William Henry Vanderbilt had just completed at No. 459 on the southeast corner of Fifth Avenue and Fortieth Street.

Chalfin grew up in the affluent *milieu* of upper Fifth Avenue, a corridor of new brownstone mansions that extended north to Central Park. He was early exposed to good music well played amid the inherited paintings from his grandfather's collection that hung in his parents' house at 3 East Forty-seventh Street, an "elegant residence," according to a contemporary newspaper account.

Chalfin went to the Columbia Grammar School in New York City, then entered Harvard College in the fall of 1894. At the end of his sophomore year he left Harvard, and for the next two years he studied painting at the Art Students' League in New York City. Among his instructors there at that time, and later, were Charles C. Curran, Frank Vincent Du Mond, and possibly, although the records are not entirely clear in this point, the leading muralist Kenyon Cox, all of whom had studied in Paris. Chalfin, in his turn, then went to Paris and enrolled, probably in the fall of 1898, at the Ecole des Beaux-Arts. He studied in the *atelier* of Jean-Léon Gérôme, "the most sought-after and the most demanding of the instructors"[19] at the Ecole, as well as one of the most popular painters of the nineteenth century. Chalfin also studied with Henri Martin of the Beaux-Arts faculty, and with James Abbott McNeill Whistler, whose *académie* in Paris "caused a sensation in the studios" and drew a rush of young students to the Passage Stanislas, where it survived for only two years.[20]

By the time Chalfin returned home in 1901 he had experienced two quite different modes of instruction and the aesthetic philosophies they reflected: the disciplined French classical training of Gérôme and the vigorously individualistic teaching of Whistler. Lacking any examples of his student work, one cannot now assess either his skill or his intentions as an artist at that period of his life. He was twenty-six when he left Paris. His father had been dead for ten years, and his mother had moved to New Bedford, Massachusetts.

He returned to the Art Students' League in February, 1902, took classes for three months, then reenrolled in October, staying but one month. At some later date he advised the Harvard alumni office that he had become an instructor in "the architecture department" of Columbia University during the 1901–1902 academic year. However, the university has no surviving record of his having taught there at that time.

He may have cut short his painting classes in October in order to go to Boston to begin work at the Museum of Fine Arts there. Walter T. Cabot, who was then serving his fourth year as the curator of Asiatic arts, hired Chalfin sometime during 1902 as the acting curator of his department. Cabot was in ill health. He retired in 1903 and

Chalfin was named curator to succeed him. That year the museum published Chalfin's short descriptive catalogue of some of the Asiatic department's holdings: *Japanese Wood Carving: Architectural and Decorative Fragments from Temples and Palaces.*

However, Chalfin was not yet ready to give up painting and settle down in Boston as a curator. During 1904, he started work on a painting which, after many changes, he submitted to the judges of the biennial competition for the Jacob H. Lazarus Traveling Scholarship for painters, a prestigious award which was administered by the Metropolitan Museum of Art in New York, and which had been associated with the American Academy in Rome since 1897. The awards committee notified him in November, 1905, that he had been granted the current scholarship, and on February 12, 1906, he arrived at the Villa dell' Aurora in Rome, the home, at that time, of the American Academy. He was thirty-one years old.

During 1906, Chalfin spent eighteen weeks in Rome and thirty-two weeks in Florence and Venice studying and copying the work of Piranesi, Fra Angelico, and Tiepolo. In 1907, he studied in Rome for thirty-four weeks and in Paris and Florence for ten weeks. While in Florence that year he copied a lunette by Jacopo Pontormo at a nearby Medici villa — probably the lunette now entitled *Vertumnus and Pomona,* which, as Mary McCarthy notes in *The Stones of Florence,* was "painted for the big sunny upper room [the barrel-vaulted great *salone*] of Poggio a Cajano, Lorenzo's favorite villa." It is, she observes, "one of the most convincing and freshest bucolics ever projected by a painter . . . as strong in its design as a Michelangelo . . . and from it there transpires a breath of the natural farm life of the villa."

From Florence, Chalfin went on to Paris for a long stay — October, 1907, through November, 1908 — thus completing his Lazarus scholarship. No record exists of his principal interests in Paris. However, while there he completed a large (eight feet by thirteen feet) original painting, probably a decorative panel, entitled *The Poet.* In 1909, in recognition of his successful completion of his studies abroad under the terms of the Lazarus scholarship, Chalfin was namd a Fellow of the American Academy in Rome. He was thirty-five years old, and he may have been the most thoroughly trained painter in the history of American decoration. Studying had become his career.

One begins to suspect something of an aging *jeunesse dorée* about him. Indeed, Nathalie (Smith) Dana, who had delightedly explored the worlds of music and art at the turn of the century, provides in her memoirs, *Young in New York,* a swift glimpse of Chalfin that does reveal the affected wit of a golden youth who wants terribly to seem another Whistler or Wilde. On February 4, 1909, shortly after Chalfin had returned from Paris, an exhibition of paintings by the Spanish artist Joaquin Sorolla opened at the Hispanic Society of America under the sponsorship of Archer M. Huntington. It drew "the largest crowd that an art exhibit had ever attracted in New York" — just the sort of event that Nathalie Smith and her close friend Emily Spackman, who studied at the Art Students' League, would not have wanted to miss.[21] Emily, Mrs. Dana writes, was an enthusiastic student of Kenyon Cox, "a mural painter and a leading critic of art . . . [as well as] a favorite teacher" at the league. "Emily and I followed Cox in his enthusiasm for the Italian mural painters and for Rubens . . . [whom] we were proud to admire as his paintings shocked the Victorians." The Spackman family was in Europe when the Sorolla show opened, so Nathalie hurried uptown alone, looked at the pictures, returned home, and promptly wrote to Emily:

"New York is quite daffy over the Sorolla pictures. People flock up to 156th Street and make inane remarks about them. They are very brilliant out-of-door sketches, full of temperament, more stirring than monumental. Paul Chalfin says [that] when people ask him whether he has seen the Sorolla pictures he answers, 'No, but I find Mary Garden extremely unsatisfactory.' He is far too clever."[22]

One must try to *hear* Chalfin speaking, for his most remembered characteristics were his effeminate mode of speech and mannerisms. He is here, of course, being deliberately *chic,* a quality Elsie de Wolfe admired, and possessed in exhausting measure. In 1907, Mary Garden had brought home to America from Paris, where five years earlier she had sung the premiere of Debussy's *Pelléas et Mélisande,* the controversial new concept of the prima donna as a "singing actress." She cannot *sing,* her detractors said. She not only sings well, she can *act,* her advocates replied. Tempers quickened as she performed her famous dramatic rôles in New York: *Mélisande, Louise, Thaïs,* and, in the winter of 1908–1909, *Salomé.* Chalfin sided with the naysayers, if only for the sake of a witty turn.

He is far too clever — Nathalie Smith's youthful observation has, for us, a curious eloquence, but it is frustrating, for it implies much yet says too little. Fifty years later, while writing her memoirs, Mrs.

Dana felt constrained to add: "Paul Chalfin became an influence in the world of art." However, she throws no light on his "influence." Then, Chalfin disappears from her memoirs quite as suddenly as he had appeared.

About the time of the Sorolla exhibition, Chalfin became an art critic. He advised the Harvard alumni office that he had turned to criticism in 1909, but he failed to mention the name of the magazine, or newspaper, he was writing for. And he later told a reporter that during the 1909–1910 academic year he was again teaching at Columbia University, this time as an instructor in "design." And again, the university records in the matter are wanting.

During the winter of that school year, he accepted an invitation from Elsie de Wolfe to organize a lecture series on art, decoration, and architecture for the Colony Club, the women's residence she had decorated. The club had become a lively and important social and intellectual gathering place for business and professional women, as well as for those younger society women who had become concerned with matters of broader interest than the guest list of the recently deceased Mrs. William Astor.

Among the guest lecturers Chalfin selected was F. Burrall Hoffman, Jr., a twenty-eight-year-old architect who had been working in the drafting rooms of Carrère and Hastings on the designs for Mrs. E. H. Harriman's French renaissance *manoir* at Arden, New York (begun 1905, completed 1909). Hoffman came of a wealthy cosmopolitan New York family that had lived on a Louisiana sugar plantation as well as in New Orleans, Washington, and Paris. Wickham Hoffman, his grandfather, had been a general in the Union Army and had served as the secretary of the American legation in Paris during the Franco-Prussian War, the last days of the Second Empire, experiences he had written about in *Camp, Court and Siege* (1877). Murray Hoffman, his granduncle, had been a judge in New York's superior court and was long an active layman in the Episcopal Church.

Burrall Hoffman had gone to the preparatory school of Georgetown University, had graduated from Harvard College, and had been granted a *diplôme* by the Ecole des Beaux-Arts, where he had studied architecture in the *atelier* of Henri-Adolphe-Auguste Deglane, the codesigner of the Grand Palais des Beaux-Arts on the Champs Elysées. Deglane had also been consulted on the design of William A. Clark's house on Fifth Avenue, probably the costliest and most opulent Beaux-Arts palace ever built in America.

Hoffman's family had long enjoyed a position of quiet but substantial prestige in New York society. Carrère and Hastings had designed his father's house at 59 East Seventy-ninth Street, and when Alva Belmont reopened Marble House, her French classical summer palace in Newport, in the autumn of 1909 for two widely reported women's suffrage gatherings, she included Hoffman's mother among her dozen or so personal guests.

Hoffman was a substitute in Chalfin's lecture series. William Adams Delano, another Beaux-Arts architect, and a partner in the prominent firm of Delano and Aldrich, had originally been scheduled to give the talk on architecture. However, "one day, Paul Chalfin, whom I did not know, came to me," Hoffman has recalled, "and he told me Billy Delano was sick and asked me if I'd give the lecture at the Colony Club. I said I would, but when I got there — it was at the old building down on Madison, the one Stanford White did — I was scared to death. A couple old friends of mine took over and got me a drink. Two drinks, as a matter of fact. Then I gave the talk."

IV

O N the morning of February 2, 1910, readers of the *New York Daily Tribune* who were interested in such matters learned that an "interesting" new painter of promise had arrived in their midst. In the course of his long review of the twenty-fifth annual exhibition of the Architectural League of New York, Royal Cortissoz, the *Tribune*'s art critic and the most noted lecturer of the day on painting and sculpture, wrote:

"The painters . . . do not, on the whole, add appreciably to the solid value of the show. They make it gayer, it is true. . . . But conspicuously lacking is the decorative performance which instantly touches the imagination with a sense of fresh invention and technical authority. There is, in fact, but one arresting piece in this field, the large 'Anacreonic-Decorative Panel,' by Paul Chalfin, one of the more recent graduates of the American Academy at Rome. The touch of the true artist is visible in the copies from Fra Angelico and Pontormo which he shows and it comes out with exhilarating energy in this panel of his [which he had completed in Paris]. He has skill and taste, and though in draftsmanship and color he still wants distinction it is plain that he has the root of the matter in him. His talent is interesting, immediately detaching itself from the ruck."

Cortissoz's phrase "the touch of a true artist" may be read to imply that Chalfin might, in time, have ranked with the leading contemporary muralists, La Farge, Blashfield, Cox, Mowbray. However, something seems to have gone all wrong for him. Except for one remembered set of panels, which may already have been completed, one verified interior decorating commission (a *trompe-l'oeil* wall painting), and an undated, and unmounted, ceiling painting on canvas, Chalfin appears never again to have undertaken other large decorative paintings of the type for which he had trained from 1894 through 1908 — fourteen years.

Allyn Cox, the son of Kenyon Cox, and like his father a distinguished muralist, has thrown some light on what happened to Chalfin's career as a painter by recalling Chalfin's self-destructive behavior and the bitterness he felt over his failure to receive any commissions in the year following his return to America.[23]

Cox has enjoyed a long and productive career despite the successive waves of neophilia in American art that have sought to destroy the tradition upon which his work has grown. His commissions in the years following World War I included an overmantel panel for the New York apartment of Nathalie Dana and her husband, Richard B. Dana, Jr., the architect grandson of Henry Wadsworth Longfellow and Richard Henry Dana. In the early 1970's, Cox was still at work, painting the murals along the corridor leading to the House Dining Room in the Capitol, Washington.

"Chalfin was a very good painter," Cox has recalled. "He handled whatever he did with great skill. I remember that when I arrived at the American Academy in Rome to continue my studies, some of his things were still on exhibit. I was very impressed by them. My goal was to do as well as he had done, and I copied a lunette by Pontormo that he had copied when he was at the Academy. He was one of those people who have a great impact on others, and stimulate them. For instance, he had quite an effect on Nancy McClelland's work in the decorative arts.

"There were some Chalfin paintings around at one time. I remember once seeing a set of decorative panels he did in a show the Metropolitan Museum put on. They were good, but their subject matter was unattractive. Hospital scenes. Very morbid.[24]

"Chalfin came to my father's studio one day. I just sat to one side and listened. Chalfin told my father that people were not paying any attention to him. He could not sell his paintings, he said, and people were not giving him any commissions. He was bitter and angry. After a while he left, and when he had gone my father said to me, 'What he doesn't realize is that people don't like his work.'

"Furthermore, they didn't like *him*. That was the real trouble — besides his painting hospital scenes. He was a very talented but disagreeable man. I think that was the reason he so quickly lost the esteem of the people who might have helped him. He would say nasty things about other people, and their work. And that put people off."

At some point, Chalfin had to find some income. Kathryn Chapman Harwood, an authority on Vizcaya, has written that Chalfin became "associated with Elsie de Wolfe . . . in her New York Studio of Interior Decoration."[25] For whatever reason, Chalfin never mentioned this business association to his family, or to the Harvard alumni archivist. However, it was apparently not long after the Architectural League exhibit in January, 1910, that Elsie introduced Chalfin to James Deering, whose residence at 10 West Forty-third Street was listed that year for the first time in the New York edition of the *Social Register*.

A onetime student of Gérôme's and Whistler's, a former curator at the Boston Museum of Fine Arts, a Fellow of the American Academy in Rome, and a painter whose first work to be shown publicly had been saluted by the doyen of American art critics — such were Chalfin's credentials, and they could not have failed to impress Deering. For the next six years, Chalfin was to guide Deering's huge and complex project. By the end of that time, he would be launched with great fanfare upon a new career as an architect-decorator.

Thus, it would never be known whether Chalfin had the exceptional talent of a great muralist, for Vizcaya rescued him from his bitter frustrations as a painter, and from the ambiguities of an artist with no commissions. His career as a painter slipped quickly into the anonymous past of forgotten art reviews, and his work disappeared before it was known. Within a few seasons his paintings remained alive only as ghostly images in art gossip.

"Chalfin was a funny fellow," Burrall Hoffman has observed, "but he had great artistic perception. He knew good things. He had great imagination and wonderful taste."

A paradox had remained in Hoffman's memory:

"He was originally a painter, you know. But, there was something curious about that. I can remember everyone talking about his work at one time. That is, they talked about *hearing* about it. But no one saw it. Well, of course, some people must have. But I know that I never saw anything he painted. It was all rather strange as I think back on it."

V

THERE exists no orderly, unambiguous account of the events leading up to the design and construction of Vizcaya. However, it is possible to sort out a reasonable chronology — one, that is, that conforms to such verifiable data as deed records, and that also accommodates most of the contradictions that sincere but faulty memory, and the distracting inventions of vanity, impose on the matter. Presumption is, of course, a necessary constant of the process.

In the summer of 1910, Deering took his new art adviser abroad with him. The tradition that Deering spent twenty-five years collecting the materials, architectural and decorative, that would go into the making of Vizcaya is not true. "Everything that Mr. Deering bought for the place he got through Chalfin between 1910 and 1916," Hoffman recalls. And the distinguished photographer Nell Dorr, who observed the project at close hand almost from its beginnings, has recalled that "Mr. Deering would never buy anything until he had Paul's advice. He depended upon him entirely."

While they were en route to Europe on their first trip together, Deering revealed to Chalfin that he had decided to built a winter residence on Biscayne Bay at Miami. "At first," Chalfin later told a reporter, "[Mr. Deering] thought the architecture should be Spanish. We spent one entire winter [probably that of 1910–1911, upon their return from Europe] making plans for various types of Spanish houses, but one night, with his characteristic abruptness in making decisions [he] swept them all aside and we came to the determination that the building should be of the Italian villa type."[26] Deering and Chalfin then went to Italy "for a year to study and inspect the most characteristic types of villas to be found. Out of that trip eventually grew Vizcaya."

During their long journey in central and northern Italy in 1911, they discovered at Bassano del Grappa, northwest of Venice in the Alpine foothills, a seventeenth-century country residence — the Villa

Rezzonico — which they decided should serve as the basic prototype for Vizcaya. The Villa Rezzonico is one of the historic mansions of the Brenta River country — "the Brenta Riviera" — to which the Venetian aristocracy retreated each summer from the unbearable heat of their city palaces and the exhaustion of the long carnival season. This flight from Venice for an extended country holiday — *la villeggiatura* — became for the nobility an elaborate pilgrimage in luxurious *burchielli,* gilded barges many of which possessed a cabin "decorated with as much luxury as a drawing room."

Some of the earliest of the summer villas were no more than large farmhouses, but as time passed these gave way to "splendid palaces, set in beautiful parkland," in which the rich owners "pursued the crazy round of parties and pleasures" which, as Marcel Brion has remarked, they pretended in Venice to have wearied of.[27] Vizcaya was to be an echo of the most extravagant period of the *villeggiatura* of the Venetian nobility.

The Villa Rezzonico, an imposing and severe edifice, is said to have been designed in the 1670's by Baldasarre Longhena, "the only great Venetian architect of the baroque era."[28] Longhena had earlier designed the splendid building along the Grand Canal in Venice now known as the Palazzo Rezzonico (begun 1667) for the Priuli-Bon family. The Rezzonico family acquired the palace in 1750, and it was completed for them by the architect Giorgio Massari, who contributed his own designs for the unfinished sections. The traditional attribution of the design for the Villa Rezzonico at Bassano del Grappa to Longhena remains a matter of dispute among Italian scholars. Giuseppi Mazzotti in his *Palladian and Other Venetian Villas* cites the house as "a later work by Baldasarre Longhena." Contrarily, Renato Cevese says in *Ville della Provincia di Vicenza* that it "has been attributed to Longhena and Massari. The latter, on the basis of the formal values of the place, I consider more likely to be correct."

Whoever designed the villa followed the palace style of Venice in centering the plan upon a bisecting cortile. But, he departed from tradition by introducing into his design an "imperial staircase," a decorative and structural departure first employed in architecture only several decades earlier at the Escorial, the massive church structure near Madrid (an improvisation based, it seems, "on the sole precedent of unexecuted Italian drawings" patterned upon sketches by Leonardo da Vinci, according to Nikolaus Pevsner[29]) .

Probably because of the simple clarity of its symmetrical plan — a rectangle with a square tower at each corner; a tidy summing-up of the evolution of the ancient castle-villa — the Villa Rezzonico appealed to Deering and Chalfin, although Deering may have had some reservations about its severe countenance. Its worn stucco walls, two stories high in the central block and three in the towers, are broken only by rectangular windows, whose surrounds are barren of molding or ornament, and by the main door to the house, which is, Mazzotti notes, "powerfully framed by blocks of stone in strong relief on the bare facade."

As it turned out, Vizcaya was to escape the dour rigor of the Villa Rezzonico and achieve in its architecture a spirited yet serene baroque lyricism which it would owe entirely to the wit and resourcefulness of Burrall Hoffman, qualities encouraged by Deering's generous and intelligent patronage. Hoffman was to reveal at Vizcaya, his first palace project, a rather special gift for adapting and subtly recombining old forms in new ways — a case of "old traditions debonairly worn," to borrow a graceful phrase Robert Lowell has used to praise a fellow poet's work. In carefully examining Hoffman's work at Vizcaya, one is reminded of Monk Gibbon's observation about the work of Georg Dollman for Ludwig II at Linderhof: "His versatility was equal to the occasion."[30]

Hoffman's "occasion" began sometime in 1912 when Chalfin, whom, because they moved in different worlds, he had not seen since the Colony Club lecture, came to his office at 15 East Fortieth Street. "He asked me if I would be interested in doing a house for a client of his — an art collector. But he didn't tell me who the client was," Hoffman has recalled.

Hoffman had left Carrère and Hastings and in the fall of 1910 had opened his own office. He had then entered into association with Harry Creighton Ingalls, who was to become one of the best-known theater architects of the day. "Our first job," Hoffman has said, "was The Little Theatre [which opened in March, 1912]. Winthrop Ames asked Harry to design it — it was his project and I was the associate. That was the way we worked. We were not partners. We had the same arrangement on our next project, the Neighborhood Playhouse on Henry Street. When Chalfin later returned and offered me the commission to do Mr. Deering's house, that was my project and Harry was the associate."

Long afterward, in a memorandum on Vizcaya, Hoffman wrote: "Mr. Chalfin asked [me] if [I] would make plans for his client Mr.

Deering in such a way that use should be made of the many treasures of antiquity that had been acquired." Once the agreement was formalized, Chalfin took Hoffman to the warehouse of P. W. French & Company at Fourth Avenue near Thirtieth Street in Manhattan to see, in Hoffman's words, the "ceilings, mantels, grilles, statues, fountains, furniture, tapestries, carpets, and so on," that he would have to absorb into the fabric of Vizcaya, or effectively house in its rooms. Much of the costly, and still incomplete, inventory had been obtained from two art dealers, P. W. French & Company of New York, and Lavezzo and Brother, Inc., of New York and Chiavari, Italy.

Mitchell Samuels, one of the founder-partners of P. W. French & Company, had anticipated the unique problems that the complex project was going to face, and he had set aside several floors of his firm's midtown warehouse at 432 Fourth Avenue to receive and store Deering's purchases, domestic and foreign. There Hoffman discovered precisely what his problem was to be, for the dimensions of some of the objects he saw were to determine the magnitudes, and scale, of the house, while the configuration of others would dictate the architectonic detail of the rooms, and the floor plans, throughout.

The provenance of nearly every item in the collection of rare objects which had been gathered in the warehouse, or would soon be shipped there, was automatically entered in record books that Deering carefully kept. However, it should be noted, without bias, of course, that the attributions and authentications furnished to him by those from whom he bought have not yet been subjected to critical scholarly analysis.

VI

AMONG the principal objects Hoffman was going to have to accommodate in his designs were:

— A massive three-tiered French renaissance chimneypiece carved in white statuary limestone quarried at Caen. Enormous classic consoles of reversed volutes framed the fireplace section and supported the mantel shelf; four Atlantes, supporting a classical cornice, divided the chimney breast into three ornamented panels with strapwork motifs; and, above the cornice, two female figures, baroque in spirit and style, held a cartouche enframed in flowing scrollwork. (In

Deering's time an elk's head was mounted on the cartouche, suggesting the hunting châteaux of the French royal forests.)

This altarlike piece of architectural sculpture rose about twenty feet from the warehouse floor, a measurement Hoffman must instantly have noted. It was once said to have come from the Château de Régneville, and, according to Chalfin, it had originally been "made for the unfinished wing" of the historic Château de Chenonceaux, once the abode, successively, of Diane de Poitiers and Catherine de Medici, who had been, concurrently, the mistress and the queen of Henry II.[31]

Chalfin's claim that the chimneypiece had been carved in the seventeenth century needs further study. There was no "unfinished wing" at Chenonceaux. Mme. Margaret Pelouze, a Scotswoman who was married to Eugène-Philippe Pelouze, chairman of the Parisian Gas Company, bought the château in 1864 and commissioned the Dijon architect Félix Roguet to restore it to its original state before it was greatly altered by Catherine de Medici. Roguet removed a structural addition, of uncertain date, which may have housed the chimneypiece, which must also be considered as of uncertain date.[32]

— A set of wrought-iron gates from the Palazzo Pisani (begun 1614–1615) in Venice, a noble residence that now houses the Bendetto Marcello Music Conservatory. Again Hoffman was compelled to take particular notice of the height. The gates, the grille that surmounted them, and the arched stone surround that framed the entire portal also rose, *in toto,* about twenty feet from the floor — the height of the Chenonceaux chimneypiece. Thus was established the height of the principal chambers of the first story of Vizcaya — twenty-four feet, a measurement that conformed to the height of the *salones* in Italian palaces and villas of the sixteenth through the eighteenth centuries.

— A richly, but delicately, modeled plaster ceiling, dated 1750, which had been removed from the Palazzo Rossi in Venice. Its surface was divided into geometric fields by molded ribbing, each panel enclosing foliar and other traditional decorative details such as shells and arabesque scrolls. The central panel contained a circle of human figures — *putti* and gods. Chalfin (as he undoubtedly pointed out to Hoffman) hoped to freshen the colors of the ground and moldings — gray, gray-green, and golden yellow — and to extend the plasterwork from its outer edges. The added area would then permit the handsome ceiling to be used in a room larger than that from which it had been taken.

— A portion — about one-third — of a large beamed ceiling of traditional Venetian design with unpainted soffits and a frieze of carved and unpainted brackets. This partial ceiling also came "from a palace in Venice," but which one remains unknown. Chalfin planned to have expert craftsmen cut to size, carve, and stain the missing beams and frieze brackets for installation at Vizcaya. He was later to claim that the frieze section came "from a Venetian room by Sansovino," the leading architect of Venice before Palladio.

— "A table of Greek marble from the first century," which "might have been dug up at Pompeii or Herculaneum." The table was purchased from an antique dealer in Italy. It was said, perhaps imaginatively, that its heavy marble top and its two massive marble supports, carved in the shape of griffons, had been shipped separately to the United States from three different Italian ports. The table, it was further said, had for some unknown reason never been put together in Italy during the centuries since its discovery. Had it been, the Italian government would never have allowed so rare a treasure of classical antiquity to have left the country.[33]

— "The Empire bed from the Palace of Malmaison [which] formerly belonged to Maria Louisa," and which Chalfin would presently install in Deering's own bedroom at Vizcaya. The story of the disposition of the furnishings of the Château de Malmaison is a complex one that need not trouble us, except perhaps to note that some of the furniture, including an Empire bed, which was at Malmaison during the years Frederick William Vanderbilt owned the château may now be found in his mansion at Hyde Park, a national historic site. It may have amused Chalfin to have created, and left unsolved, a mystery: what was the bed of Napoleon's second wife, who would never have been admitted there, doing in the beloved private retreat of his deposed first wife?

— A handsome set of *boiseries* with "gold and painted decoration" which had been "taken from old Palermo rooms of the Louis XV period."

— A set of paintings Carl Vernet, who was known for his horse racing and battle scenes, had done for "the billiard room of Prince Ruspoli."

— "Four Venetian panel paintings on canvas of the Lady Hamilton period," Neapolitan in subject, but painted in Spain.

— A set of silk wall hangings woven at Lyons from a palm tree design, by Philippe de la Salle, one of the prominent decorative artists of eighteenth-century France. They had been sent directly to

Genoa upon completion. Long, long afterward . . . "a prominent family there had gone bankrupt and were obliged to dispose of most of their possessions. One of Mr. Deering's agents happened to be on the scene and bought the silk which had not been in use since the eighteenth century."[34]

— A rug "dating from the time of Ferdinand and Isabella [which] belonged to a series made for the Admiral [of Castile, Fadriquez Enriquez], another being now in the Metropolitan Museum, New York." The rug was "later given by [the Admiral] to a monastery at Burgos." The monastery, "falling upon evil days, finally sold it to a dealer, the same dealer from whom Mr. Deering's agents acquired it."[35]

— A rare *mille-fleurs* tapestry woven at Tournai about 1550, and another tapestry woven about 1460 at Ferrara by Flemish weavers. The latter is said to have hung in Robert Browning's house in Florence.

The tapestries may well have come from another floor of the P. W. French & Company warehouse, for Mitchell Samuels was already becoming one of the great tapestry dealers of the world. He had recently acquired the Charles M. Ffoulke collection and would shortly buy the J. Pierpont Morgan tapestries for his firm. Deering's large purchases of decorative materials played a significant role in the growth of Samuels's company, an old firm which had been operating as a new partnership for only four years as of 1912. Chalfin later told relatives that he had himself made so much money as Deering's artistic coordinator that he had been able to advance Samuels a large sum, which Samuels may have needed either to purchase the Morgan tapestries in 1916 or to buy out his partner, Percy W. French, in 1924.

VII

SAMUELS was born in 1880 and named for his birthplace, Mitchell, South Dakota.[36] As a young man in New York he had studied art at the Cooper Union and the Chase School of Art. He had met French while both were working for the W. & J. Sloane Company. French, who was nine years older than Samuels, had gone to the Harrow School and Oxford University before coming to the United States from England. He became an executive in Sloane's interior decorating department, and Samuels became the department's purchasing agent, a job that took him into collectors' homes, and the labyrinthine galleries, auction rooms, warerooms, workrooms, restorers' studios, and drafting rooms of the art market, and which determined his notable future.

Samuels was asked to settle a difficulty that had arisen between the store and Charles Mather Ffoulke, a rich tapestry collector and scholarly authority whose holdings included one hundred and thirty-five of the historic Barberini tapestries woven in Rome. Ffoulke lived in Washington and was confined to a wheelchair, but he managed to travel abroad in search of additions to his renowned collection. Samuels went to see him at his home, and Ffoulke shortly became the younger man's patron. With a $5,000 loan from Ffoulke, Samuels encouraged French to join him in a partnership.

In 1907 they bought out Sypher and Company, an art firm that in 1886 had succeeded Daniel Marley and Company. Thus, when P. W. French & Company began business, the partnership could trace its antecedents back to Marley's first art gallery on Ann Street, two blocks below City Hall, which had opened in 1840.

In time, Samuels was to become one of the most formidable, and knowledgeable, merchants in the international decorative arts world. He was to survive depressions and the severe competitive hazards native to his business. He even survived Joseph Duveen, the most powerful of the great merchants of art, who casually told several of his rich clients that he intended to "destroy" Samuels. (Once, not long after he had delivered some costly French period furniture to Arabella Duval [Yarrington] Worsham Huntington Huntington's palace at 2 East Fifty-seventh Street, Samuels got a call from her butler, who told him to come and remove his goods immediately. The butler, who was generously paid for such services, had alerted Duveen, who considered *his* clients to be *his* exclusively. Arabella had spent millions with Duveen, and although she dealt with Jacques Seligmann when in Paris, and with other art dealers, she still yearned to own more of the rare treasures she had seen in Duveen's princely gallery. He had only to chide her for trafficking with a lesser dealer, and Samuels lost his sale. Samuels, of course, could not object. When he arrived at Arabella's vast stone palace at Fifth Avenue and East Fifty-seventh Street, the present site of Tiffany's, he found his furniture sitting out in the open in the service court.)

In 1957, *Life* magazine observed that Samuels had by then sold $100,000,000 worth of art. That year his firm, which had been known as French & Company since 1924, had an inventory of 2,270 items worth $10,000,000. He could take clients through fifty separate showrooms in the building he had built on East Fifty-seventh Street. Twenty of them were complete period rooms, the most famous and valuable of which was the "Chopin room." This chamber, a remarkable museum piece, had been removed intact from the Place Vendôme in Paris. It had taken its name from the fact that Chopin had once occupied the *appartement* of which it was a part.

However, in 1912, both Samuels, then thirty-two years of age, and Chalfin, thirty-eight, were just beginning to learn about the peculiar problems of furnishing a rich man's palace entirely from the authentic past. Chalfin had not only to store the objects to be used at Vizcaya, but he had to have them constantly available for study. With Samuels's help, he arranged them into units, stage sets, as it were, that gradually assumed the aspect of rooms.

Objects great and small were grouped according to a scheme that Chalfin was slowly designing in his mind. An improvised architectural armature of temporary walls, partial or whole, even imaginary, had to be constructed against which doors could be stood and chimneypieces set, and from which *boiseries* could be hung, as fixed panels, and paintings and tapestries could be suspended by wires. Further, Samuels had to set up workrooms for the expert restoration that was required. And, space was going to be needed for the draftsmen who would reduce Chalfin's mental designs to working drawings.

The friendship Chalfin and Samuels developed during these years was to last throughout their lives. Samuels saw emerge in Chalfin the authority and flair of a man who was happily discovering that he was a very able decorator. Chalfin had the scholar-curator's grasp of the greater and lesser decorative styles of the past; a connoisseur's peculiar sensibility, which lies beyond taste (an intuitive felicity that led Chalfin, for example, to discern aesthetic perfection in a commonplace object; one, say, that had been ignored by collectors hunting only for treasure certified by great cost) ; and, an artist's eye which enabled him to compose from a wide range of historical elements a coherent *mélange* — a "new *milieu*," as one art critic was to put it.[37] He had an uncanny ability to find the hidden continuum of decorative aesthetics that links era to era.

VIII

WHEN Hoffman saw the skeletal "rooms" at the warehouse, his own eye began immediately that inenarrable process by which an architect creates the inner spaces of a house, and the great sheath in which he will enclose them. He did not go to the warehouse more than two or three times, preferring to work from measured photographs and drawings of the key architectural objects.

"I went down to Florida that winter [1912–1913]," he has recalled. "Mr. Deering had rented a house in Coconut Grove from Arthur Curtiss James, who also had homes in New York and in Newport. Paul Chalfin was also staying with Mr. Deering. I was surprised when I got there to discover that Mr. Deering's nearest neighbor was William Jennings Bryan."

Deering had just purchased — on December 31, 1912 — one hundred thirty acres of black marsh and hummock along Biscayne Bay below Brickell Point from Mrs. Mary Brickell, a pioneer resident. Miami was only sixteen years old. It had earlier been known as Fort Dallas, a settlement that had sprung to life (and changed its name) when Henry M. Flagler's Florida East Coast Railroad was extended there from Palm Beach in 1896. Mrs. Brickell did not think anyone needed as much land as Deering wanted, and she consented to sell the entire parcel only after Chalfin, as he later told a reporter, had convinced her that his patron intended to build a wide, paved public road through his proposed estate as a gift to the community. (The road is now part of South Bayshore Drive.)

"I spent several months down there that winter working on sketches and preliminary drawings," Hoffman has recalled. "I asked Mr. Deering why he had chosen that place to build and he said that he loved to travel and had been everywhere, even Honolulu, and that was the place he felt most comfortable. I remember he told me that he had paid Mrs. Brickell $1,000 an acre for the land, and I thought to myself at the time, 'He could get good land on Long Island for that kind of money.'

"I went up to St. Augustine to see some 'key' stone [a variety of Florida limestone found on the keys] which is full of coral. I liked it very much and we decided to open up our own quarry later on. It made a good stone for some uses — it aged well, for example, and hardened in the weather. But it was too soft to carve moldings properly. So we brought over stone from Cuba for the column facing and the molded window trim. The columns, of course, had cores of reinforced concrete.

"I went to Italy in the summer of 1913. I wanted to see for myself the villas along the Brenta — to look at them, and study them. What was really important was not a particular villa, it was discovering the baroque. It was a question of getting your eye in. I don't know why, but over here you don't get the same feeling of space and scale — the relative size of things. It's partly a matter of the north Italian light. I had made some preliminary sketches before I went over, and once I was there I discovered I had the scale wrong. For example, I had to redesign the loggias around the open court at the center of the house. I changed the number of arches along each loggia from seven to five. As a result, each arch was larger, and in better scale. That's what I mean by getting your eye in.

"I remember particularly finding a villa on Lake Como called the Villa Pliniana. It got its name from Pliny the Younger who, I was told, wrote about an intermittent spring on the grounds. I found a marvelous loggia there that opened on both sides — inward onto a court and outward, if I remember correctly, toward the spring and a steep hill beyond covered with trees. It was perfectly beautiful. At Vizcaya I adapted it to serve as the loggia between the inner court and the terrace along the bay."

While Hoffman was abroad, work at Vizcaya proceeded rapidly. The civil engineering survey of the land had been started by John J. Bennett shortly after the conveyance of the deed, and in 1913 Deering had personally turned the first spadeful of earth to begin the extensive site preparations, the draining and filling of the marshy ground. A great earth podium standing about twelve feet above the mean tide level of the bay was built up to carry the house, its foundations, and terraces. Also, a ten-acre platform of earth in the shape of an elongate trapezoid, with the short side next to the garden terrace of the house, had to be created to provide the base for the formal gardens with their various levels and grades. The "whole system of terraces and adjacent gardens" was to be "contained in an *enceinte* . . . nowhere less than four feet above the normal high tide."[38]

The magnitude of the project could be sensed by the residents of Miami in various ways. Hundreds of laborers had to be hired to work

on the site clearing . . . a railroad spur was built to the estate . . .
one day railroad flatcars arrived in the city carrying quarrying equip-
ment . . . suddenly, the "useless land" that Deering had been buying up at some distance from Vizcaya was opened up as a quarry to
supply some of the stone for the house.

In 1913, Miami had a population of 10,875. Close to ten percent of
that number were to find work at Vizcaya before the estate was completed. Some of Bennett's surveyors would continue to work there
until some time in 1923, when the landscaping of the gardens, interrupted by World War I, would finally be brought to completion, and
the great project ended.[39]

By the end of 1913, Hoffman had assigned Isador N. Court from
his office to serve as his representative at Vizcaya. (After a stay of
more than two years, Court was succeeded by G. A. Murtaugh.)
Harry Ingalls, Hoffman's associate on the project, went down to
Miami to supervise construction. Late in 1913, the *Florida Homeseeker,* a promotional publication distributed by Henry M. Flagler's
land company, principally to the guests, many of them affluent, of
Flagler's hotels, carried what may have been the first news story published on Vizcaya:

"One million dollars will be expended in the building of Mr.
James Deering's palatial winter home in Miami, according to estimates furnished. The mansion will probably take twelve or more
months to complete, as it will cover a ground space of 250 feet by 150
feet, and will be three stories high. It will be built of reinforced
concrete, it will be stuccoed white, and have a red tile roof."

The cost figure was the lowest ever cited for Vizcaya. It did not
include the cost of the gardens, for no one, including Deering himself, then knew what this latter cost would be. Nor could Deering
then have known that he was to be the patron of a masterpiece of
garden art.

IX

ONE day Mr. Acton called me to say that he had given one of his
villas for several weeks to a Mr. Deering of Chicago, and his art
adviser, Mr. Chalfin. He asked me if I would please show them
around some of the private villas and gardens that I had access to,

places that they would not have been able to see — Gamberaia, and Capponi, and places like that."

Diego Suarez, a retired architect and landscape architect, was speaking, in the spring of 1965, of his work as a young man at Vizcaya, and the odd sequence of events that had taken him there from Florence fifty-one years earlier.[40] He had been born in Bogotá, Colombia, in 1888, the grandson of the revolutionist-dictator General Francisco de Miranda. His mother was Italian, and after the death of his father she had returned to Italy with her children. Suarez had studied as "an architectural designer" at the Accademia di Belle Arti in Florence.

"I then practiced architecture in a small way, but I became very interested in garden design," he recalls. "During that time I became a good friend of Arthur Acton, an Englishman who owned the Villa la Pietra on the Montughi Hill in Florence. Mr. Acton was a disciple, you might say, of the great Henry Duchêne, and he had been engaged for several years in restoring the superb renaissance gardens on his estate, some parts of them going back to the seventeenth century. They had been destroyed during the stupid craze for naturalistic English gardens. Arthur Acton was my tutor. I went to his villa four or five times a week while he was at work carefully supervising the restoration. He gave me my teaching in classical Italian garden design, and he taught me Duchêne's ideals."

Acton was a prominent member of the old Anglo-Florentine community, which had once numbered the Brownings among its members. His wife was an American, the daughter of William Mitchell, the founder of the Illinois Trust and Savings Company of Chicago. Acton had been deeply impressed by the work and philosophy of Henry Duchêne, the French scholar-artist, who, during the closing decades of the nineteenth century, had led a spirited reaction against the *jardin anglais* vogue, which had caused the ruin of many superb renaissance gardens in Europe.

Duchêne, whose vision of a perfect garden rose from the historic designs of André Le Nôtre, Louis XIV's landscape architect, devoted himself principally to the restoration of the classical French gardens, some of them designed by Le Nôtre, of such châteaux as those at Champs, Langeais, Chaumont-sur-Loire, Sully, Villette, Breteuil, and Vouzeron.[41] Among his colleagues outside France with whom he corresponded was Frederick Law Olmsted, America's most distinguished landscape architect-planner.

His son and collaborator, Achille Duchêne, who was considered by one historian of the art to have been "the greatest landscape architect [*architecte paysagiste*] of our time," paved the forecourt and restored the water-and-*broderie parterres* on the terraces of Blenheim Palace, as well as restoring the historic gardens planted by Le Nôtre at the châteaux of Vaux-le-Vicomte, Maintenon, and Courances. The younger Duchêne also designed a number of magnificent gardens for American clients, among them Alva Belmont, her daughter Consuelo (Vanderbilt) Balsan (for whom he also designed residences in London and at Eze on the Riviera), Anna Gould, Mrs. James Speyer, Mrs. Potter Palmer, Harriet (Pullman) Carolan, Mrs. William K. Vanderbilt, Jr., Mrs. Cornelius Vanderbilt III, Mrs. Ogden Goelet, and Mrs. William B. Leeds.[42] (The classical French garden he designed for Hubert T. Parson's palace, Shadow Lawn, is discussed in Part Five of this book.)

Acton began his work at the Villa la Pietra two or three years after the death of the elder Duchêne in 1902. It was well advanced by the time Deering, who may have known Acton's father-in-law in Chicago, and Chalfin came to visit him late in May, 1914. Acton had several smaller villas on his extensive grounds and he turned one of them over to his American guests. Deering and Chalfin were by that time seriously studying the Italian renaissance garden. Construction of the house and seawall at Vizcaya had begun earlier in May before they came abroad. Chalfin's designs for the interiors were undoubtedly well advanced. The site for the gardens had been cleared and filled. The time had come for preliminary designs to be drawn for the vast formal gardens.

"I had designed about eight gardens by that time," Suarez recalls. "Two of them were important — to me, that is — and I took Mr. Deering and Mr. Chalfin to see them. One was at the Villa Schifanoia, which was then owned by Lewis Einstein and was later owned by Myron C. Taylor, and the other was a garden for Charles Loeser, the son of Frederick Loeser, the store owner. Charles Loeser, you will remember, was one of the first people to collect paintings by Gauguin, and Manet, and Cézanne. I remember seeing many Cézannes in his villa. He bought them around 1890 for about one hundred francs. Can you imagine?

"When we were visting the villas and gardens, Mr. Chalfin told me that Mr. Deering was building a great house in Florida, and he said that if I happened to come to the United States I should call on him and we would talk about the gardens. Shortly after that, Lady Sibyl Cutting, who owned the Villa Medici at Fiesole, said to me, 'We're going to the United States and you're not doing anything here, so why don't you join us.' Lady Sibyl was the widow of William Bayard Cutting, an American, and she was planning to take her daughter, Iris (you've read her I'm sure, Iris Origo) , to visit her grandmother at Bar Harbor — at Northeast Harbor, that is. It seemed sensible to me to join Lady Cutting's party; to go to New York, and then go on to Colombia, where I wanted to look into some family property. We were hardly on the ocean when we heard that the war had started.

"I was young and green when I arrived in New York, and I had very little money. I first stayed in a hotel on Broadway around Twentieth Street. Then I met a friendly Italian boy and we found a rooming house in Brooklyn where we could live for six or seven dollars a week. I addressed envelopes for the New York Telephone Company to earn my board.

"Then one day I was having lunch at the Ritz with Mrs. Albert Gallatin, whom I had known in Florence, and on the way out I ran into Mr. Deering and Chalfin in the lobby. Chalfin asked me to come to see him at his office. I remember there was a tremendous amount of furniture, and other things, a sort of warehouse. He first showed me the general layout of Mr. Deering's estate and then took me to the office of the architect, Mr. Burrall Hoffman. There I saw the architectural models of the splendid villa with its approaches, terraces, farm buildings, gate lodge, and boathouse. I could see at once that this was a project conceived in the great Italian classical tradition — the stately house and terraces, the loggias and lofty rooms.

"The models fired my imagination and when Chalfin asked me if I thought I was capable of designing Mr. Deering's gardens I knew it was a great opportunity to use all the knowledge and experience I had gained in Italy. Chalfin told me that my name would appear with his on the working drawings, but we had no formal agreement and, anyway, I was too young to think much about things like that. He paid me $25 a week and later I was getting $50.

"I had, of course, only a very limited knowledge of the site, but I went ahead and made a complete set of designs. Then a model of the scheme was made by a Mr. Marenzana of Menconi Brothers, a firm that made architectural and sculptural models. One day Mr. Deering came to inspect the model. It was only preliminary, of course, but he looked at it and said to both of us — to Chalfin and myself, that is — 'That's wonderful.' He seemed to appreciate the principal features.

"A few days later, Chalfin said to me, 'I want you to go to Florida to see the house under construction and study the site.' We went down together. It was early in 1915, and I remember that it was a complicated journey getting there. Mr. Hoffman met us at the site. The house was well along.

"Then came a terrible shock. I had made a great mistake, and I knew it as soon as I stepped from one of the main rooms out onto the south terrace overlooking the garden site. It was exactly noon and I looked straight ahead where the gardens would be, and *I couldn't see a thing*. I was blinded by light, for out there at the far end was a lake. It was like a mirror — a sheet of brilliant sunlight glaring in your eyes. And, following the Italian renaissance practice, I had designed a garden that dropped from terrace to terrace, from level to level straight down to that lake!

"While I was standing there the first thing that came into my mind was a curtain of green, a screen of trees, on a rise at the far end of the site, with a casino in the middle of them. You see, the casino would be raised on a little hill instead of sitting along the edge of the water. The eye would thus be led *up* instead of *down*. And at the same time the notion came for two long axial paths running, like the ribs of a fan, outward to the lake from the central point on the terrace where I was standing. The main axis of the garden would, of course, still run straight ahead as a continuation of the north-south axis of the house. Thus — I thought — Mr. Deering could stand on the terrace and look down the middle of the garden to a rising mound that would provide a plateau for the trees and the casino, or turn his head slightly and follow either of the level radial paths to the lake. Between the paths, and to either side of them, the individual gardens would be laid out, some of them hidden from the eye. I told Chalfin immediately that I had made a mistake and would have to start over."

Suarez had looked with an artist's eye past the noonday glare of Vizcaya down the long *allées* of history to the time of Xenophon and the beginnings of garden art in the West. Four hundred years before Christ, Xenophon had led an epic retreat of ten thousand Greek soldiers out of Persia and had then settled on an estate in Sparta on which he laid out a park to the goddess Artemis (Diana), making use of much that he had observed of Persian royal landscaping.

Thus, the Greeks appropriated the *pairidaeza,* the fabled gardens of the great kings of the "Orient," and the word *paradise* as well. The hellenistic garden then became a trophy of Rome and was spread to the far reaches of the empire. Later, the rebirth of the classical age in Florence rescued the muse-haunted Roman garden from the thickets of time, and it became part of the wave of humanism that swept north from Italy. Scholars consciously following the footsteps of Plato discovered that the most nourishing fruit of the quiet grove is human thought. And, just as it reinterpreted the architecture of the classical past, the renaissance found in what Georgina Masson has described as "the interpenetration of house and garden," a condition that had been implicit in landscape art since the earliest geometric water gardens of the *pairidaeza.*

Andrea Palladio, who has been called by one of his biographers, James S. Ackerman, "the most imitated architect in history," formulated a new garden logic out of the implications in the link between the ordered Roman house and its ordered paths, pergolas, terraces, and groves. He was, Adalbert Dal Lago has written in *Villas and Palaces of Europe,* "the first European architect to achieve an intimate relationship between a building and its landscape, conceived as integrated and reciprocally dependent elements. For the first time, the main axes of a building are extended without a break into the surrounding landscape."

Suarez at Vizcaya was the heir of the Palladian vision. Working closely with Chalfin he spent months drawing up his new plans for Deering's formal gardens, and once again Marenzana worked his sketches into plaster models. Suarez's designs included a "secret garden" (*giardino segretto,* a playful Italian landscaping conceit), a long turf island framed by water, a theater garden that differed from Acton's at the Villa la Pietra but evoked its spirit, a rose garden laid out to enclose the great "Vignola" fountain from Bassano di Sutri, a traditional maze, and the casino plateau with its water stair and framing arcs of trees. He prepared the detailed designs for all the *parterre* work — the exquisitely curved *broderie* patterns of clipped box and colored sand of both Italian and French precedent. He also made the preliminary sketches for the large sculptured breakwater barge. Hoffman then developed the barge sketches, and A. Stirling Calder, the father of sculptor-mobilist Alexander Calder, provided the decorative sculpture for the beguiling stone boat.

While he was redesigning the gardens, Suarez learned that his brother had been killed in action with the Italian army. "I told

Chalfin," he has recalled, "that I would have to go home and see my family. It was arranged that I would make further sketches while I was in Italy, so I made some drawings in the gardens of the Villa Corsini in Rome — mostly of the cascade. Then I brought my drawings back to the United States and incorporated them in the final designs."

During 1915, an oceangoing schooner arrived in the Vizcaya breakwater with the first shipment of furnishings and furniture from New York. Hoffman's work was almost completed. The house was roofed-in, the rough plastering was completed, and the rooms were far enough advanced for Chalfin to begin the final finishing (the hanging of the *boiseries,* ceilings, and so on) and the installation of the furnishings and decorative objects. The fabric of the house had cost $3,000,000. "The figure," Hoffman has cautioned, "did not include the garden, the grounds, or the art — none of the decorative treasures Mr. Deering had collected."

Slowly a transition was taking place. Even though the supervising architects from Hoffman's office would oversee the architectural work that remained to be done, the great palace was now becoming Chalfin's domain exclusively.

X

FROM 1914 onward, mesmeric rumors sped through New York's art galleries, interior decorating drafting rooms, decorative arts workrooms, and the editorial offices of magazines concerned with interior architecture and its restive child, interior decoration. Finally, all sense of editorial detachment was abandoned as Chalfin brought the great project to completion. For Deering's villa was much more than simply another huge American palace; more, even, than a costly evocation of the past. *It was the past:*

". . . hardly a modern door exists throughout it; not one new fireplace; hardly a piece of contemporaneous furniture has found a place in any of its rooms; nor a single commercial lighting fixture; not a material has been purchased from a dealer's stock, not a fringe, not a tassel!"[43]

Its earliest photographs, one magazine writer insisted, were "the outward and visible sign of the persistent and magnificent rumors which have been rippling through artistic circles for many months past."[44] "I want to say . . . that it's all true," a skeptical newspaper reporter wrote.[45] And the publisher of an architectural magazine assured his professional readers that "the interiors of this house should appeal to architect and decorator as containing more actual examples of old woodwork, furnishing, and detail than could be found in Italy in a six-months' study."[46]

Working directly from documents — authentic samples — provided by Chalfin, Cheney Brothers reproduced silk window curtains to serve as a "foil" to Philippe de la Salle's palm-tree wall hangings, and Edward Maag reproduced "fabrics for walls, curtains, and canopies . . . as well as tassels, fringes, and cords." John F. Patching and Company embroidered lace curtains from interpretive designs supplied by Chalfin. The Kent-Costikyan Trading Company provided sixteenth-, seventeenth-, and eighteenth-century "Persian, Caucasian, Asia Minor, and Chinese rugs." The G. E. Walter Galleries executed special lighting fixtures. The "marbles were given endless care" by John H. Shipway and Brother. "The upholstery was executed by P. W. French & Company." The "cabinet work, painting, and gilding were done in workshops created by Mr. Chalfin." And, "much of the iron work" was done by Samuel Yellin.[47]

Augusta Owen Patterson, the art editor of *Town & Country* magazine, summed up several years later the somewhat breathless reports inspired by this complex decorating project. She wrote in her book *American Homes of Today* that Vizcaya "was a sensation. Everywhere everyone seemed to know someone who was doing something for the Deering house. There were tales of weeks spent by expert fingers in constructing a grandly proportioned tassel to hang over a grandly proportioned bed: of ancient embroideries that were lifted from their tattered silken foundations to be applied with infinite patience and skill to modern fabrics. The rumors of . . . Venetian splendor . . . were endless."

Mrs. Patterson observed that "it is Mr. Chalfin who is most definitely associated with [Vizcaya's] exuberance." She was referring not only to the decoration of the palace, but also to its architecture and landscape architecture — to Hoffman's house and Suarez's gardens. All had somehow become Chalfin's: his was the magic name that glowed whenever people in "artistic circles" talked about Vizcaya, a subject that for several years seems to have absorbed them as much, say, as Mary Garden's performances had earlier.

Chalfin leads one into the mercurial world of the decorator, a world of desperate enthusiasms and irrevocable silences, a world in which the prevailing vogue founders under wildly giddy intensities it cannot survive, in which nuance is seduced by preciousness — a perfect ambience for folly, for pride and arrogance. Chalfin entered this world not as an apprentice, but as a prince of the realm — as Deering's artistic coordinator.

Deering appears to have kept a clear view of his role as patron: he did not forget why he had hired Chalfin. He did not pretend to abilities he did not have: he did not play the architect, the decorator, or the landscape architect, but he did become deeply, and happily, involved in his great project. He was an alert and critical patron. During one planning session, for example, he flatly rejected Chalfin's suggestion that Hoffman incorporate in the top story of the bay facade of Vizcaya the traditional range of small windows often seen in renaissance villas. Deering remarked that he didn't want his house "to look like a shoe factory from the sea."[48] Chalfin was trying to be archeologically correct, but Deering wanted no grimness, no matter what north Italian precedent might require.

It has been said of Deering's patronage that "of all the great houses in America probably none owes so much to its builder and owner as does Vizcaya."[49] The statement is a generalization of the sort we generously accept because it is so generously meant, but it would amuse, or possibly annoy, such career palace builders as George W. Vanderbilt, Cornelius Vanderbilt II, Alva Erskine (Smith) Vanderbilt Belmont, Arabella Duval (Yarrington) Worsham Huntington Huntington, William Randolph Hearst, and even Mable Ringling.

There is really no need to add so pious a blush to the portrait of James Deering as a princely builder. He was not a George Vanderbilt zealously studying and correcting the contract drawings for Biltmore House as they came from Richard Morris Hunt's drafting room, or working in the stone yard with the masons, or, finally, felling carefully selected trees to open mountain vistas with a rare skill taught him by Frederick Law Olmsted. Deering calls to mind someone else: Louis XIV at Versailles daily inspecting the progress on his historic château and gardens. The king observed in his *Mémoires* that, although he had no personal creative ambitions at Versailles, he wanted to "understand everything." As for reviewing the wearying details, "Mr. Deering left all that to Chalfin," Hoffman recalls.

Chalfin's responsibilities appear to have been without precedent.

He was Deering's collaborator in the original planning — a fellow dreamer. He was Deering's surrogate in the selection and hiring of an architect and a landscape architect. And he was Deering's decorator. He was not at all put off by the subtle complexities of his situation. On the contrary, his vaguely defined, but preeminent, rôle as Deering's aesthetic alter ego — as the artistic monitor of the project — led him, eventually, to exploit his relationship to his professional associates.

At Vizcaya, Chalfin discovered a career. The great chambers he there created are memorable, and they may well be unique. Each appears to the casual eye as a museum piece, a curatorial gem. But, Chalfin's artistic hand was quicker than the visitor's eye, for here theater prevails over scholarship, a deliberate choice on Chalfin's part.

Even though Vizcaya has become a public museum, Chalfin was designing the interiors of a private palace. He and Deering worked from a basic fantasy that might be stated thus: the Villa Vizcaya, built perhaps in the late fifteenth or early sixteenth century in an imaginary landscape where the Brenta River flows through the Tuscan hills into Lake Como, had been in the family for so many generations that it had undergone a long succession of both exterior and interior additions, restorations, and modifications, structural and decorative, all of them reflecting not only the changing times, but also the changing tastes of the family, whose members, one may assume, didn't always care to look back, but often wished (as Madame de Pompadour once had), to have only new furnishings around them — an Empire *guéridon,* say, or a completely *à la mode* chamber in "the Neapolitan classic of the late Directoire period."[50]

If one may paraphrase Willa Cather, the scholar classifies, but the artist arranges. Here Chalfin was living out the career as a painter he was never to enjoy, creating interior landscapes from a mythical past, synthesizing an eternal present. And here he revealed his unusual grasp of the Italian spirit in decoration. The incursions of northern Italy of Charles VIII and François I had carried the renaissance to France; in turn, the French had sent back to the peninsula some distinctively Gallic inventions which the Italians embraced, but with a difference. At Vizcaya, Chalfin, quite innocently, dramatized the difference. The eye grown used to the French interior architecture of the high Louis periods may well be astonished by, say, the *Italian* version of Louis XV decoration.

A verse from William Blake perfectly illuminates the difference: "The cistern contains: the fountain overflows."[51] Thus, the reception room that Chalfin assembled and installed at Vizcaya, its "woodwork and paneling from old Palermo rooms of the Louis XV period," *overflows* with an Italian exuberance that a French decorator — Nicholas Pineau at the moment he designed the *boiseries* for the *salon* of the Hôtel de Maisons in Paris, say — might have *contained,* a presumption encouraged by the consistent sense of measure of almost all French decoration.

Chalfin also revealed a somewhat different tradition in the entrance hall at Vizcaya — the tradition of the Greco-Roman decorative grammar that unified the varieties of neoclassicism which evolved in France and Italy (and England as well) following the archeological discoveries at Pompeii and Herculaneum during the eighteenth century. In France, a reaction against the rococo led to a revival of classical motifs in the Louis XV, Louis XVI, Directoire, and Empire styles. The last was a self-conscious attempt to codify decoration as a function of imperial ambition. It resulted in a didactic design program, and the creation of furniture that sometimes suggests the paradox of a studiously elegant Frenchman of Italian family connections murmuring *heil* with an Egyptian accent.

In England the Adam brothers instructed the return to classicism, creating a sober elegance that slowly became more and more attenuated with a consequent loss of Roman vigor. Italy heartily embraced, and immediately modified, the Directoire and Empire styles, turning them into familial elements of Italian decoration. (Chalfin particularly admired what he felt to be "the reticent coolness" of Empire. He designed Deering's bedroom at Vizcaya in "the Empire of Malmaison.")

A common restraint underlay the neoclassical movement, and it is this spirit of formal discipline refracted through the decorative arts of Italy and France that Chalfin skillfully revealed in the entrance hall at Vizcaya. There he combined an extremely rare set (possibly the only such in the United States) of panels of *papiers peints* — *La Gallerie Mythologique* — designed by Xavier Mader and blockprinted, with its *grisaille* relief realized upon an emerald green ground, by Joseph Dufour, a French master of wallpaper making; black and gold Directoire furniture made in Italy; marble paving laid in a diamond pattern; and a ceiling of decorated shallow coffers symmetrically disposed in geometric panels.[52]

Chalfin coursed delightedly over the centuries. As has already been observed, he had a remarkable ability to link the decorative distinctions of one era to those of another. Alva Vanderbilt Belmont had taught America the beauty of *témoignage,* the reconstitution of an actual period room or the creation of a room in a period style, an art, curatorial in the first instance and decorative in the second, that has been practiced for more than a century with varying degrees of scholarly and aesthetic purity. (*Témoin* means *witness,* and the aesthetic witness is as easily suborned as its human counterpart.) Chalfin provided at Vizcaya a superb text for a different way of looking at the decorative past, the art of *mélange:* the subtle, complex, and very risky practice of composing authentic objects from different eras into a coherent unity. An art critic remarked his "preciousness, flamboyance, and exquisiteness" at Vizcaya, but, in the end, praised his work there as "sensible and knowledgeable."[53]

One of his nieces, Mrs. Marianita C. Ranger, has recalled a curious contradiction in Chalfin's private decoration. The house at 349 Lexington Avenue in New York that he had bought and decorated in 1915 became quite well known in decorative arts circles, and in Chalfin's family. "I remember when my brother came home from his first visit to Uncle Paul's house," Mrs. Ranger has recalled, "he rushed in and exclaimed, 'It was like seeing heaven.' And it was. But, I noticed something fascinating during my own visits to the house: the rest of the place may have been dripping with tassels, but Uncle Paul's bedroom looked like a monk's room. Very simple and plain — even severe."[54]

If Chalfin wished to keep his inward asceticism a secret, Vizcaya was a perfect disguise.

XI

Not long before Deering formally opened Vizcaya, Gordon Mackay, a reporter for the *Philadelphia Public Ledger,* working from information quite obviously supplied to him by Chalfin, wrote that Hoffman had had to withdraw from the project "when the interior architecture was completed." The "press of business and other duties hampered Hoffman at this time, and he retired, *hurling the entire burden on the shoulders of his associate* [italics added], with Deering

as a coadjutor. . . . This . . . readjustment of authority with Hoffman's retirement, was a milestone in the career of Chalfin. He was
forced into the business of decorative designing to fill the necessities
of the Deering house. So rapid has become his vogue that he now
has the largest studio of this nature in New York City. Chalfin em-
ploys a force of fifty or sixty men." It was in this studio, the reporter
added, "that Chalfin also designed the gardens of Vizcaya."

The article suggested to the public what the decorating world had
already assumed: Chalfin was on the verge of becoming the heir to
Stanford White's unique prestige both as an architect and a decorator, arts that White, who had been murdered in 1906, had practiced with rare skill; with genius, in the opinion of many. In order to
understand the large implications of this suggestion, one might reread the comments that John Jay Chapman, essayist and poet, once
made on White and his work:

"He was a personality of enormous power, a man of phenomenal
force. He affected everyone he met. He, more than anyone else,
effected a revolution in American architecture which in a few years
reached and influenced millions of people. . . . His was the prevailing influence not only in architecture, but in everything connected
with the arts of design and decoration. He was the greatest designer
that this country has ever produced."[55]

Architecture, bookbinding, typography and layout, picture frames,
covers for *Scribner's* magazine, *The Cosmopolitan,* and *The Century
Illustrated* magazine, costumes for the wives of his clients, and
jewelry — White designed whatever caught his fancy, whatever engaged the enormous energy of his enthusiasms. He was an antiquarian who bought hundreds of objects — architectural and decorative —
in Europe and fitted them into the palaces he designed in New York
and Newport, at Southampton and Roslyn on Long Island, in Albany and Washington, and into their interiors, chambers that reso-
nated with his "rare skill in combining seemingly incongruous
objects" from Byzantium, renaissance Italy, rococo France, and classical Rome.[56]

If Chalfin were, in fact, the heir presumptive to White, such was
the astonishing complexity of the rôle he would have to fill, and such
was the intensity and scope, the creative rarity, he would have to
match.

Only four days before Deering opened his palace to his family and
a few friends, the *Miami Herald* (December 21, 1916) republished

Mackay's long feature story from the *Philadelphia Public Ledger*. Hundreds of thousands of words have been written in the years since about Vizcaya, but, strangely, Chalfin's architectural melodrama in which Hoffman had "hurled the entire burden" on him seems never again to have been mentioned in print. It is amusing to learn that Chalfin later allowed several episodes of *The Perils of Pauline*, the most famous serial melodrama of the silent film era, to be shot in a quarry on some property he owned in Connecticut. Had he not rescued Vizcaya at almost the last minute from unthinkable disaster?

It is less amusing to learn from Hoffman that until 1965 he had never seen, or heard of, the newspaper article published in Philadelphia and Miami during December, 1916. His sudden "retirement" from the multimillion-dollar project, and the lack of professional responsibility it implied, was a self-inflating fiction invented by Chalfin.

Hoffman had, in fact, completed his work on Vizcaya and had reported for military training with an army camouflage unit that was ordered to France shortly thereafter. The strange incident, with its troubling failure of ethics, marked the beginning of a protracted effort by Chalfin to expunge the names of Hoffman and Suarez from the history of Vizcaya. His own career as Stanford White's successor began and ended there, for he was never again to receive a commission of any real consequence.

One may trace in magazine and newspaper articles, in lectures and letters, and in a memorandum-deposition, Chalfin's obsessive need to claim Vizcaya all to himself. Finally, old and blind and burdened with grave misfortunes, he slandered Hoffman. The *New York Times* (March 15, 1953) quoted him as saying of Vizcaya, "Hoffman did the plumbing, I did the house." A court action for libel was averted when the *Times* (May 17, 1953) published an account of Vizcaya in which Hoffman and Suarez, as well as Harry Creighton Ingalls, were given full and accurate credit for their work there. It was the first time in thirty-seven years that Hoffman had been correctly identified in print as the "architect" of the project. The last previous correct professional credit had appeared in a series of advertisements by the original contractor of Vizcaya, the George Sykes Co., in *Town & Country, Country Life,* and *House & Garden* in June, 1916.

Immediately after the slander had been published, Chalfin protested in a letter to Chauncey McCormick, the husband of Marion

Deering McCormick, one of Deering's nieces and an heir of Vizcaya, that the quotation "could not be more inaccurate." He did not, however, protest to the *Times* nor, apparently, make any effort publicly to deny the statement. Twelve years after the event, Aline Saarinen, who had written the report for the *Times* in which the quotation had appeared (under her then married name, Aline Louchheim), recalled "the threat of a lawsuit" and the subsequent "retraction to avoid a lawsuit," adding: "The information I got was from interviewing people available at the time I did the piece." Mrs. Saarinen, who was much admired for the precision of her witty and urbane observations as a writer (*The Proud Possessors*) and television personality (the "Today" show), has since died. Of the principals involved in the incident only Hoffman is still living. Does he think Chalfin really made the remark? "Of course he did."

Hoffman had been the victim of an error in judgment he himself had made. When he reported for military service, he had turned over to Chalfin all responsibility for newspaper and magazine inquiries on the project. Chalfin began his egocentric campaign almost immediately in the July, 1917, issue of the *Architectural Review,* which devoted forty-eight pages of photographs and text to Vizcaya. The professional credits for the architecture, landscape architecture, and decoration which appeared at the heads of the three unsigned essays accompanying the illustrations failed to mention Suarez and Ingalls. However, Chalfin's name appeared three times: as associate architect, as the landscape architect, and as the decorator. Hoffman was listed, not as the architect, as he should have been, but as the associate architect along with Chalfin, that is, as Chalfin's coequal.

The anonymous analytical essays were presented to the professional reader as objective appraisals of the project, but they were, in fact, written by Chalfin. (His authorship was indirectly revealed by Augusta Owen Patterson in *American Homes of Today.*) Chalfin's rococo prose, elegant and arch at once, was equal to his goal of unrestrained praise for his own work. Without quite mentioning his own name, he saluted himself for having brought to Vizcaya "the energy and firsthand enterprise that a Vignola would have contributed to a Cardinal Gambara." Vignola was Michelangelo's successor in Roman architecture: a painter who became an architect, a landscape architect, a writer on architecture, and one of the most honored figures of the Italian renaissance. Only a man as expert as Chalfin was in these matters could have gratified himself with such precision. Later, in a series of ten signed articles in the *Miami Herald* — "By Paul Chalfin, Architect of Vizcaya" — he wrote thousands of words on the villa and its gardens without once mentioning Hoffman, Suarez, or Ingalls.

There is no need to trace further the details of Chalfin's efforts to publicize himself in *Vogue, Vanity Fair, Town & Country, Harper's Bazaar,* and elsewhere at the expense of his colleagues. One may well be tempted to find his brio amusing, but there is a peculiar sadness to it, and a disturbing irony. One must keep in mind that in order to further his already flourishing career, Chalfin would have to establish himself as an architect, as White had done. However, not only was he not an architect, he had never studied at any professionally accredited school of architecture.

Under New York state law he would have to meet certain educational requirements in architecture to get a license, unless he could demonstrate the equivalent professional experience. He turned to Deering, Deering turned to Hoffman, and Hoffman solved his dilemma. He allowed Chalfin's name to be linked to Vizcaya as an associate architect. The State of New York then waived its educational requirements for Chalfin and granted him a license to practice architecture. Thanks to Hoffman's *beau geste,* Chalfin was able to open an office as an architect in New York City, combining it with the drafting room he had established for the decoration of Vizcaya (which had required several thousand drawings). It was a large office with more than sixty employees, including Thaddeus Joy, an outstanding architect-designer on leave from architect Julia Morgan's office in San Francisco, and Ralph Calder, a brother of the distinguished sculptor A. Stirling Calder, who provided the figures and decorative carving for the breakwater-barge at Vizcaya. But Chalfin's brief season of radiance had ended: the firm was a failure. It closed down within three years.[57]

Hoffman, looking back, has recalled that when he saw the *Architectural Review* for July, 1917 (which caught up with him overseas months later), he wrote to Chalfin: "I told him what I thought of what he had done. I never spoke to him again." However, he has further observed that he had no reservations, no misgivings certainly, about his decision to support Chalfin's ambitions in architecture. He greatly admired Chalfin's work on the interiors of Vizcaya. But that was in a happier time — the war in Europe still seemed far away: Deering was still alive: the fabric of the great villa rising from swamp and hummock was daily nearing completion.

On Christmas Day, 1916 — with Chalfin launched upon his private fantasy — Deering's dream palace became a monumental reality. He drew together a select few friends and members of his family for a private Medicean housewarming. Only the gardens had yet to be completed.

XII

THE greater American palaces overwhelm the visitor first coming upon their opulence. The modern eye can barely function under the stress of such a visual overload of rich detail. At Vizcaya the problem is compounded. Not only does each room of the palace nearly exhaust the eye, but the gardens beyond present so various an ensemble of memorable detail that one succumbs to bemusement. Later, one begins to sort out what one has seen. However, something is bound to suffer on balance.

Oddly, what seems to get lost in the process, if one examines the testimony of visitors who have written about Vizcaya, is the house. It has never been adequately analyzed and interpreted. All generally agree that it is handsome and that it evokes the northern Italian villa of the baroque era. But, beyond that limited appraisal few writers have ventured.

Hoffman did his work almost too well. He started with the general concept presented to him by Deering and Chalfin, and he was even provided with a specific Italian prototype. However, the concept was only a rough hand map of a vision. The Villa Rezzonico provided the basic scheme for one of the house's four facades, and a traditional four-tower rectangular ground plan. But Hoffman then had to go on from there, which is to say, he had to design a house — a structure and its rooms, halls, stairs, service areas, and court — that would accommodate both Deering's vision and his warehouse inventory. In consequence, he radically changed the Villa Rezzonico ground plan.

One should note, for example, that at the Villa Rezzonico the central feature is not the open court Hoffman designed for Vizcaya, but a closed cortile that rises through two stories to the roof of the villa and is elaborately decorated with ceiling paintings and baroque sculptural detail executed in stucco.[58] The cortile bisects the long axis of the villa. It is not appropriate here to further extend this comparison of the two structures. However, it should be observed that they are different in almost every design particular.

Hoffman adapted the nearly identical entrance and garden facades of the Villa Rezzonico to the bay facade of the Deering villa. The changes he made in proportion, decoration, structure — in overall design — reveal a young architect with taste, imagination, and a newly found certitude in handling the early eighteenth-century *villeggiatura* style. One is reminded of the subtle, but authoritative, modifications that Horace Trumbauer made in appropriating the entrance facade of the Château d'Asnières to the garden facade of The Elms, the Edward Julius Berwind residence at Newport. Both adaptations reveal the subtle grace that can come only from a profound understanding of, and control of, scale and style.

Hoffman's changes at Vizcaya were bolder than Trumbauer's at The Elms, but they had to be in order to serve what one feels was Deering's wish to avoid the fortress severity of much north Italian traditional design. The modified triple-arch loggia from the Villa Pliniana on the ground floor of the bay facade at Vizcaya, and the Palladian loggia immediately above it on the second floor, tell one a great deal about Hoffman's inventive flair in adaptation. His skill in improvising on renaissance themes is further revealed in the broken segmental-arch pediment and pseudo-buttressing — large volutes and finiallike statues bearing down on high plinths — that rise above the parapet line to form a handsome baroque addition to the wall, one that conveys the Italian sense of bravura without succumbing to it.

Most country houses of whatever grandeur have two principal facades — those on the entrance and garden sides — and two subordinate ones. Because of the nature of ground scheme for Vizcaya, Hoffman had to design four entrance facades, and each has its carefully studied distinctions. As he circles the house, the visitor is charmingly misled by Hoffman: he sees four towers, but he does not at first notice the interesting adjustments the architect has made in them. The towers to the west — those first seen by Deering's guests — are shorter than those that rise above the bay. They are also of a different plan, and are subordinate in other details, for it was the view of the villa from the water (from his yacht, that is) that Deering wanted to be the most dramatic.

The colonnade on three sides of the inner court and the galleries above them, with their sloping lean-to roofs, are out of traditional whole cloth. They were studied against a number of prototypes. The main staircase leading from the north colonnade of the court to a midpoint landing, thence dividing and returning in parallel flights to the second floor, is based on the pair of *scalone d'onore* at the Villa Rezzonico, and its effect is no less imperial than theirs.

Throughout, the eye is beguiled by the adjustments in scale, the variety of accommodations, that Hoffman made in solving a long schedule of design problems. Deering's collection of architectonic components is there, neatly in place, its ghostly warehouse armature replaced by the substantial fabric of the villa. There is an air of effortlessness about the place, a rustic elegance in which Hoffman preserved the spirit of the postcarnival voyages of the Venetian nobility to "the Brenta Riviera."

XIII

IF William Randolph Hearst at San Simeon, issuing daily commands to his editors here and abroad, and accepting the *devoirs* of anxious film stars, saw himself as an emperor, James Deering in his palace at Vizcaya deliberately sought a less exposed, less public place among the *noblesse* of the world. *An attendant lord . . .* the phrase T. S. Eliot used to describe J. Alfred Prufrock suggests itself. Deering was not, of course, "deferential," but like Eliot's enervated hero he was certainly "cautious and meticulous." One seeks his measure and nature in literature, for his is a refracted presence. When Aline B. Saarinen visited Vizcaya as an art critic of the *New York Times* in 1953, she wrote: "Judging from his portrait by Zorn, James Deering was a small, immaculate, extremely elegant man, looking as an acquaintance said 'like a minor Henry James character, with white piping on his waistcoats.' "

Nell Dorr, the widely admired photographer-author of several memorable books of photographic essays, saw Deering frequently during the years he was building Vizcaya. Mrs. Dorr and her first husband, Thomas Koons, who worked for the general contractor of the project, lived with her husband's brother, Louis Koons, and Paul Chalfin on a houseboat Chalfin had designed and decorated. Louis Koons was Chalfin's secretary-assistant, and the companion of many years with whom Chalfin shared his New York house. The houseboat, the *Blue Dog,* was moored first in the lake at Vizcaya, then later in

Biscayne Bay at the foot of Flagler Street nearby. It served Chalfin as his headquarters in Miami.

Sitting in her garden in Connecticut on a September afternoon several years ago, Mrs. Dorr reflected on Deering with a mixture of amused detachment and sympathy, and exchanged recollections with actress Lillian Gish, an old friend, about an evening they once shared as dinner guests at Vizcaya:

"Mr. Deering was a dyspeptic man," Mrs. Dorr recalled. "People would be there for dinner, a dinner beautifully served on gold plate, and he would be eating a coddled egg. He was an odd mixture. The house was *not* for show, you know. No, no. Mr. Deering had no exhibitionism in him at all. And it really wasn't for entertaining, although he did entertain some. I think he built it solely for the joy of creating Vizcaya.

"He didn't seem to enjoy life the way ordinary people do. Actually, it was the collecting he seemed to enjoy most. Then, when the house was finished, he enjoyed it in his own way. But, he was a very private man and it would be hard to say what his pleasure truly was. Vizcaya was overpowering to him and his guests. It wasn't so much that the house overpowered his guests as the fact that he could never relax."

Miss Gish, who went to dinner at Vizcaya at a time when her performances in *The Birth of a Nation, Intolerance,* and other historic silent films directed by D. W. Griffith had established her as one of the most distinguished young actresses of the day, confirmed Mrs. Dorr's reflections on Deering:

"He was an astringent little man, and I don't think he was really comfortable with guests — perhaps he was with friends, but that is another matter. I can remember clearly the night we were there. I was visiting Nell and we went over for dinner. It was a lovely April evening and after dinner the gardens were full of fireflies. I was probably very romantic, and I remember how much I wanted to get into one of the gondolas and ride along the canal through the grounds. It was such a lovely night. But Mr. Deering took us right inside again to see a movie. It was a movie about microbes and germs. Can you imagine that? I suppose he thought it was entertaining. I had the impression that he was a man who wanted to have beauty around him in his house and gardens, but that he didn't know what to do with it. He wasn't able to *live* with it. It was simply there."

"He was such a properly dressed man," Mrs. Dorr then added.

"Fastidious. Always completely dressed: waistcoat, jacket, high collar, and tie. We used to tease about it. We wondered if he *ever* took off all his clothes at once, even to bathe. Then we'd all laugh and imagine that he didn't — that he took a bath partly dressed. And you know about that secret passage from Mr. Deering's bedroom to an adjoining guest bedroom? I guess we hoped, really hoped, that someday he would make good use of it. But we were romantic and Mr. Deering wasn't.

"There was no singing, no laughter there. There was nothing in the palace: it was an empty place. But he did like our children, and he did not seem to mind at all when they ran through the house. And I remember the gardens in the moonlight, too. And the fireflies. It was sheer magic. The whole place was magic. Everything except poor Mr. Deering. And there was not a magic thing about him."

Deering never married. "Many lovely ladies wanted to marry him, but he sidestepped them," a man who knew Deering and his social circle has confided. "One whom *he* wanted to marry later told me she always wished she had said 'Yes.' " However, a man who would entertain a young woman of uncommon beauty by showing her a film on microbes is unlikely to stir the mermaids to song. "I had the impression," Miss Gish recalled dryly, "that Mr. Deering certainly wasn't interested in women. But then, he certainly wasn't interested in men either. He was tied up in things that interested just him — whatever they may have been."[59]

After his responsibilities as the architect of Vizcaya had long been discharged, Burrall Hoffman returned to the palace several times as Deering's guest. "He was a marvelous host," Hoffman recalls. "He was a naturally hospitable man. An extremely kindly man. The last time I ever saw him was in Spain — in Seville in 1922. He was very cordial, and he made it a point to tell me how much he enjoyed the house. He said it had given him a great deal of satisfaction. Then he said, 'We're having a little dancing party this evening. Won't you come along?' And it was very pleasant." (Deering also went out of his way to thank Harry Creighton Ingalls for his work as the associate architect of Vizcaya.)

"Mr. Deering loved music," Hoffman has recalled. "He wanted an organ in the house, and he told me he wanted it installed in such a way that he could hear it during meals. He wanted the music to come through the court into the dining room upstairs. I also put a player piano in a little room off the circular stair, a small *entresol*. Music was piped in from the piano into the breakfast room through special ductwork. When we were planning the house, Mr. Deering was very concerned how the organ would sound, so I asked Mrs. Harriman if I could bring him to Arden to hear the organ installed in her house. We drove up and listened, then went somewhere nearby for lunch. Mr. Deering was very much offended that Mrs. Harriman hadn't asked us to stay for lunch. He couldn't understand such a lack of hospitality."

Life at Vizcaya followed a fixed routine. "It was a very formal house," Eustace Edgecomb, who had spent eight years working for Deering, recalled not long before his death several years ago.[60] "Mr. Deering was a very formal sort of man. We never saw him in shirt sleeves. Usually we were all out of the front of the house — all the cleaning done — about eleven o'clock in the morning. Only a maid stayed up front. But the butler, valet, and the two footmen would be in the servants' quarters on call, ready to answer the annunciator. Mistress [Ethel C.] Syer was the housekeeper, but she passed on and Mrs. [C. J.] Adair became the housekeeper. There were twenty-five [later increased to thirty-two] of us on the staff then under Mrs. Adair, with two chauffeurs to drive the Packards.

"Now, let us say that it was a cool day and Mr. Deering was giving one of his big luncheons. That was his favorite time to entertain. He would have twelve to twenty people in for luncheon, two or three times a week, and they would sit all afternoon and visit. The butler, an Englishman named Fred Leach, and Mr. Deering's valet, Arthur Hoad, would be in tailcoats, and the footmen, Henry Ratcliff, another Englishman, and Russell Young — he was from Kentucky — would be in blue with those striped vests: horizontal yellow stripes. These were the men who served the luncheons.

"It was pleasant. The servants could have fun in back — in their own quarters. There was a framed notice in the servants' dining room that read: 'Singing and Whistling Will Not Be Indulged in While Mr. Deering or Guests Are in the House.' I remember one day Mr. Deering was in the servants' dining room and he saw the sign. After he read it, he took it down. He didn't want to impose on the staff in their own part of the house.

"Mr. Deering usually arrived here in the middle of December and left about the middle of April. Sometimes he got here earlier, and sometimes he left later. Then he would go to Europe. I think, it's just my feeling, of course, but I think Mr. Deering enjoyed his boat more than he enjoyed the house. He had a yacht, the *Nepenthe,* and he would take two or three people on cruises through the keys, sometimes for two or three weeks. And he also had a cabin cruiser, the *Psyche,* that he used for fishing. He really enjoyed fishing.

"And there was always music, but I can't remember that anyone ever came to play the organ. Mr. Deering always used those automatic player rolls. And there wasn't ever any dancing — any music for dancing — as far as I can recall. I remember seeing Mr. Deering sitting with his friends and other people who came to visit. He would smoke a cigarette and sit there and watch the others with his feet crossed."

XIV

I remember one day," Mrs. Dorr has recalled, "when I was in the woods with the children — they were still quite little — and they found a wonderful tramp. He had old clothes and a beard. The children played with him and climbed in his lap and had such a wonderful time. When we went back to the house I got hold of Paul [Chalfin], whom we called 'Brother,' and I said, 'Brother, don't you tell Mr. Deering, but there is a wonderful tramp in the woods and the children adore him.' Then I described the man and told Brother what happened. He started to laugh and he told me, 'That tramp is John Singer Sargent.' "

Sargent had gone to Ormond, Florida, to paint a portrait of John D. Rockefeller, and had then continued on down to Cutler, to visit his old friend Charles Deering. The visit ended, he went on to Vizcaya, where he was fascinated by the renaissance evocations of the place, the semitropical light, and the brilliant colors of the flowers there. He painted a series of watercolors, including a portrait of Deering, during his stay. Not long afterward, he returned to England for the remainder of the war.

When the United States entered the war, Deering halted all work on the incomplete grounds and gardens. In 1919, work was resumed, and by 1923 the superb baroque gardens were finally completed. Two years later, Deering was dead.

Shortly after the war, he had completely redecorated his house in Neuilly on the outskirts of Paris. The enthusiasm which had sustained him through the creation of Vizcaya and the work on his Paris house seems to have held in check the fatal effects of the pernicious anemia he had contended with for so long. Then, the disease moved quickly toward terminal symptoms. A sentence from a letter he wrote in March, 1922, provides eloquent witness to the low key of life at Vizcaya: "I go to bed every night at six o'clock and try to rest as much as I can." By 1924 he had begun to use a wheelchair to get out into the gardens, and early photographs of the interiors of the house show the small pillows he used to shield himself against the least draft while sitting in the wicker furniture of the bay loggia. In the final summing up, one must recognize that only someone very close to him, someone who knew intimately the progress of his anemia and the effect it had on his life, both physically and emotionally, could truly reveal Deering. However, it may be safe to assume that his vision of splendor had helped him to survive until he could complete the great undertaking of his life.

In 1925, Deering became quite ill at Vizcaya and required several blood transfusions. The blood was supplied by his valet, Arthur Hoad. Deering recovered enough to make his annual trip to Paris. His secretary, Roger Comat, and Hoad accompanied him. However, in August, Deering became critically ill at Neuilly. After some weeks the crisis seemed to lessen enough to permit him to be taken home, a journey he profoundly wished to make. He was taken to Le Havre on the boat train, but when he was carried aboard the S.S. *Paris* he was in a coma from which he never recovered.

France paid a final courtesy to the dying man. When he was carried aboard the *Paris* he was put in "the deluxe suite" that had been reserved for Joseph Caillaux, the head of "the Caillaux Mission" which was then on its way to Washington. Shortly after daybreak on September 21 while the *Paris* bore through a great storm off Newfoundland, Deering died "from a complication of diseases."[61]

He alone knew how much he had spent on Vizcaya. The only verifiable cost figure now available is that for the fabric of the house: $3,000,000. As noted earlier, the first published cost figure for the house was a projected estimate of $1,000,000 (*Florida Homeseeker,* 1913). The cost of the incomplete estate was placed at $10,000,000 ($3,000,000 for the house, apparently; $7,000,000 for the grounds) at the time Deering opened the house (*Philadelphia Public Ledger,* December 11, 1916). A comprehensive figure of $15,000,000 was published in the mid-1930's, an estimate for the completed estate which appears to have been computed by Deering's heirs (*The Magazine of Sigma Chi*, February, 1936). By the 1950's "experts" were estimating the "total bill" at $15,000,000 to $20,000,00 (*Tropical Homes and Gardening*, August, 1953). More recently, the *New York Times* has estimated the "present value" of Vizcaya to be $50,000,000, apparently a replacement cost projection.

In the early 1930's, several years after the stock market crash, R. Milton Mitchill, Jr., the head of the combined American Art Association–Anderson Art Galleries, a leading New York art auction firm, undertook to sell the interiors of Vizcaya — the art, furnishings, and furniture. Wesley Towner in *The Elegant Auctioneers* has stated that Mitchill "called the contents of Vizcaya 'the finest collection in America today,' and predicted that it would bring between one and half and two million dollars." The collection was catalogued, but the auction was called off as the Depression grew more severe by the day.

Deering had willed Vizcaya to his nieces and nephews. Two of his nieces, Charles Deering's daughters, the late Marion Deering McCormick (Mrs. Chauncey McCormick) and Barbara Deering Danielson (Mrs. Richard Ely Danielson) bought out the interests of the other heirs in Vizcaya.[62] In 1952, preparatory to conveying the palace, gardens, and remaining grounds of the estate to Dade County, they had certain appraisals made. The value of the art and furnishings was appraised at $1,367,053 by Mitchell Samuels of French & Company. The twenty-seven acres forming the core of the estate was appraised at $1,400,000, and the contiguous land at $413,000.

The appraisals completed, Mrs. McCormick and Mrs. Danielson donated the art and furnishings of Vizcaya to Dade County — an outright gift of almost $1,400,000 — the entire inventory to become the property of the county on a deferred schedule based upon annual tax allowances. They also sold the house and approximately thirty acres of land to the county for $1,000,000. The sale was made "on a revenue bond basis to be paid through income derived from admissions and sales." In order to further the conversion of Vizcaya to a public museum — the Dade County Art Museum — Deering's nieces also advanced $50,000 to the county as "a starting fund." Their goal in the gift and conveyance was to establish Vizcaya as a permanent memorial to their uncle.

The museum was opened to the public on Sunday, March 8, 1952, with Robert Tyler Davis as its first curator. There is no precise way of stating the dollar value of the gift: how, for example, can one estimate the enormous revenues Mrs. McCormick and Mrs. Danielson might have realized had they subdivided, improved, and sold, parcel by parcel, the valuable bayfront property? If one were to take as a base the "present value" estimate made by the *New York Times* — $50,000,000 — and subtract from it the $1,000,000 Dade County agreed to pay for the museum land, then it was worth $49,000,000.

Whatever the precise value, the gift was a generous one. It was estimated at the end of the first quarter of 1971 that Dade County will discharge its entire revenue bond debt on the museum land by 1977, almost a quarter of a century after the conveyance of the gift.[63]

Deering might well be pleased that his palace and its interiors, his formal gardens and tropical forest, and his renaissance farm hamlet beyond — collectively forming a unique cultural and botanical treasure — have been preserved.

XV

CHALFIN might be said to have signed his name to Vizcaya in many ways, some of them subtle and allusive. One day while the estate wall was being finished, he found the plasterers running a continuous undulating line along its outer surface, the only decoration on the otherwise bare stucco. The line rose and fell only slightly on each excursion over its long course. Chalfin was annoyed to find the workmen using tools that would ensure a geometrically perfect result. He immediately banned the tools from the work site and encouraged the men doing the work to run the rise and fall of the line with only their eye to guide them. He thus preserved at Vizcaya the ancient freehanded mark of the artisan. And in so doing, he subtly preserved the presence of the painter: himself.

Hoffman has recalled the invigorating creative spirit that Chalfin brought to the project, a spirit, Hoffman felt, that arose from "his genius and vision." And he has expressed the belief that Chalfin "sustained" James Deering against his chronic illness during the dozen years it took to create Vizcaya.

Few artists can have done as much for a patron.

FOUR

SAN MARINO

IV-1

IV-1   ". . . a vision of Eden." The Shorb house in San Gabriel Valley. From Thompson and West's *History of Los Angeles County*, 1880. Courtesy of the Henry E. Huntington Library and Art Gallery.

IV-2   A wash rendering signed "A.T.L." (dated 1905 or 1906) suggests what Huntington originally had in mind for the palace at San Marino. (The actual rendering has been lost. This rough sketch of it was made by the author at the Huntington Library in 1965.)

IV-3   San Marino: south facade. Pen and ink rendering by Elmer Grey, c. 1910. Courtesy of Harold C. Chambers.

IV-4   North facade. Huntington is here seen standing outside the great stairwell bay, 1920. Courtesy of the Henry E. Huntington Library and Art Museum.

IV-5   Terrace. Courtesy of the Henry E. Huntington Library and Art Gallery.

IV-6   South facade: distant view. Courtesy of the Henry E. Huntington Library and Art Gallery.

IV-7   First-floor plan. Redrawn by John B. Bayley with entourage added, from original floor plan by Myron Hunt, architect. Original plan courtesy of Harold C. Chambers.

IV-8   The main hallway, Georgian with a French accent in its capitals — the pendant festoons. Courtesy of the Henry E. Huntington Library and Art Gallery.

IV-9   Dining room. The table is set for a luncheon given by Huntington for the Crown Prince and Princess of Sweden, July 23, 1926. (This is the only known interior photograph made at San Marino in Huntington's lifetime.) Photograph by Boyé. Courtesy of the Henry E. Huntington Library and Art Gallery.

IV-10   The library. Courtesy of the Henry E. Huntington Library and Art Gallery.

IV-11   4 West Fifty-fourth Street, original state. Taken by an unknown photographer from a window of St. Luke's Hospital, c. 1865. Courtesy of the Rockefeller Family Archives.

IV-12   4 West Fifty-fourth Street; new staircase, c. 1881. Photograph by Samuel H. Gottscho (1937). Courtesy of the Rockefeller Family Archives.

IV-13   Arabella's new bedroom. Photograph by Samuel H. Gottscho, taken in 1937, immediately before the demolition of 4 West Fifty-fourth Street. Courtesy of the Rockefeller Family Archives.

IV-14   5 West Fifty-first Street: the Mosle house designed by Detlef Lienau, architect, 1878. Elevation by Lienau. Courtesy of the Avery Architectural Library, Columbia University (Lienau Collection).

IV-15   The Colton mansion, San Francisco. From a contemporary woodcut. Courtesy of the Mariners Museum, Newport News, Virginia.

IV-16   Hôtel de Hirsch, No. 2 Rue de l'Elysée. Photograph by Henry Sorensen, Paris. Author's collection.

IV-17   Château de Beauregard, St. Cloud. Photograph taken c. 1873. Photograph from *Miss Howard and the Emperor* by Simone André Maurois, New York, 1958. Courtesy of Alfred A. Knopf, Inc.

IV-18   Ceiling panel commissioned from Elihu Vedder by Arabella for 2 East Fifty-seventh Street. Painted by Vedder in Rome in 1893. Courtesy of the Mariners Museum, Newport News, Virginia.

IV-19   2 East Fifty-seventh Street. George B. Post, architect. Courtesy of the Mariners Museum, Newport News, Virginia.

IV-20   The library staircase, original state. Courtesy of the Mariners Museum, Newport News, Virginia.

IV-21   The library staircase during demolition, 1927. Courtesy of the Mariners Museum, Newport News, Virginia.

IV-22   Elizabeth (Stoddard) Huntington. Courtesy of the Mariners Museum, Newport News, Virginia.

IV-23   Collis Potter Huntington: "the great persuader." Courtesy of the Mariners Museum, Newport News, Virginia.

IV-24 Arabella Duval (Yarrington) Worsham Huntington Huntington. Oil portrait by Oswald Birley, 1924. Courtesy of the Henry E. Huntington Library and Art Gallery.

IV-25 Belle. Artist unknown, *c.* 1868. Courtesy of Collis H. Holladay, Jr. Photograph by the Henry E. Huntington Library and Art Gallery.

IV-26 Henry Edwards Huntington as a young man. Courtesy of the Henry E. Huntington Library and Art Gallery.

IV-27 Huntington at Lake Vineyard. Left to right: Susan Patton Wills, George S. Patton, Jr., Ruth Wilson Patton, Henry E. Huntington, George S. Patton, Sr., and Hancock Banning. Photograph thought to have been taken by Anne Patton, *c.* 1903. Courtesy of the Henry E. Huntington Library and Art Gallery.

IV-28 Huntington at Redondo Beach baseball game, September 14, 1912. Courtesy of the Henry E. Huntington Library and Art Gallery.

IV-29 Myron Hunt. Courtesy of Mrs. M. K. Johnson.

IV-30 William Hertrich, *c.* 1929. Courtesy of the Henry E. Huntington Library and Art Gallery.

IV-31 Huntington in 1927, the year of his death, sitting on the veranda at San Marino. Photograph by George A. Watson. Courtesy of the Henry E. Huntington Library and Art Gallery.

IV-2

Original design for San Marino.

IV-3

" '. . . the most truly magnificent residence in the whole of California . . .' "   [219

IV-4   North facade.

IV-5   Terrace.

IV-6

“ ‘Standing long and white and low against its background
of soaring mountains . . .’ ”

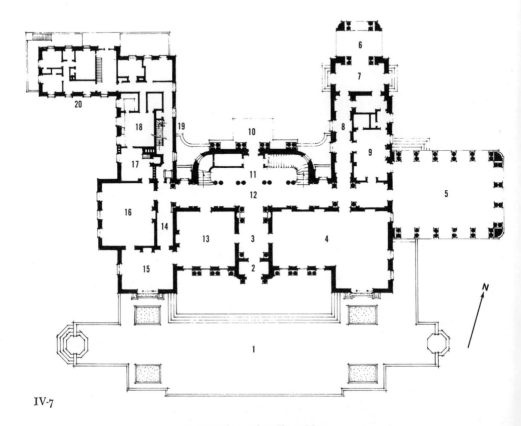

IV-7

San Marino: First-Floor Plan

NOTE: Nomenclature from undated plan (C. 1908): Myron Hunt, architect. No copy of the architect's second-floor plan is known to exist.

1. [Terrace]. 2. South Vestibule. 3. South Hall. 4. Library. 5. East Porch [Loggia]. 6. Porte Cochère. 7. North Porch. 8. North Corridor. 9. East Library [Office]. 10. Patio. 11. [Stairwell]. 12. Main Hall. 13. Large Drawing Room. 14. West Corridor. 15. Small Drawing Room. 16. Dining Room. 17. Butler's Pantry. 18. Kitchen. 19. Rear Stair Hall. 20. [Servants' Rooms and House-keeper's Office].

The main hallway.

IV-9

Dining room.

IV-10

". . . he had yielded most of the
library's shelf space to the Boucher tapestries."

IV-11

"Belle Worsham was about to enter the world of palaces."

IV-12

". . . a broad ceremonial staircase."

IV-13

Arabella's new bedroom.

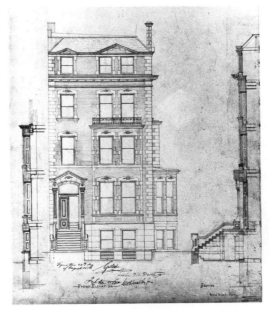

IV-14   5 West Fifty-first Street.

IV-15   The Colton mansion.

IV-16

"Then Arabella bought a palace in Paris . . ."

IV-17

Château de Beauregard.

IV-18

2 East Fifty-seventh Street: ceiling panel by Elihu Vedder.

IV-19

"... a wayward railroad station ..."

IV-20

The library staircase,
original state.

IV-21

The library staircase during
demolition, 1927.

IV-22

Elizabeth (Stoddard) Huntington.

IV-23

"The great persuader."

IV-24

"... haughty, severe, humorless, truculent, old."

IV-25

"... a young woman of uncommon beauty ..."

26

Henry Edwards Huntington as a young man in West Virginia.

IV-27

Huntington visiting the Pattons at Lake Vineyard.

IV-28

Huntington (center, white Panama hat)
at an employees' baseball game and picnic.

IV-29

Myron Hunt.

IV-30

William Hertrich.

IV-31

At home in Eden.

ONE

For fifty-four of her seventy-four, or so, years — the imprecision is one of many she still imposes on those who would inquire into her life — Arabella Duval (Yarrington) Worsham Huntington Huntington lived with the burden of a lie that made each of her days a hostage to strategy. And because even the most ordinary lie has in it the root of melodrama — providing, as it does, the strange nourishments of self-imposed jeopardy — one might think of her undiscovered fiction as a time bomb set, not to a given instant, but to the whim of fate; a weapon that could at any moment have exploded into ruin the world of costly elegance that she had created out of cheerless circumstance but uncommon native means: cunning, beauty, intelligence, courage, arrogance, and an impulse toward the high taste of the connoisseur. What she had originally lacked — money, social standing, and the imperative legitimacies of proper society — she achieved in abundance, and manipulated with the desperate skill of an impostor.

Shades of scandal and disaster rose before her at every turn. Her strategy must have presumed that they might materialize at any moment, arriving in the room with an unexpected caller, or with a letter addressed in a strange hand — appearing in the full view of all, or coming by stealth. They lay concealed in the sudden hesitations of conversation, silences eloquent of danger. Once, they brushed close to her with a subpoena, from which, forewarned, she fled in the night. They waited at her bedside while she slept.

The measured ticking of her deception, which she alone could hear, first came to her from beyond the front door of a rented three-story brick house in a "fashionable" residential neighborhood only six blocks north of Gramercy Park in New York in the first decade after the Civil War.[1] She had (at that fateful instant) just closed the door behind a man who was gathering information in the annual canvass of the city's residents. Innocent of his rôle, the anonymous canvasser was carrying away in his tabulation sheets a lie that would presently circulate in thousands of copies of the *New York City Directory*, each sturdily bound and bearing the formidable appearance of truth.

Later, the spectral presence came through the high, sunlit windows of her sumptuous *hôtel particulier* in Paris across the way from the gardens of the Palais de l'Elysée, windows through which the Comtesse de Montijo, whose daughter Eugénie had become the Empress of France, had once looked.

It ticked in the evening haze below her splendid belvedere-veranda overlooking Long Island Sound. It possessed the silence of her drawing room at San Marino in southern California, in which she had placed a superb Louis XVI *secrétaire* signed by one of the most honored of the eighteenth-century *ébénistes*, Martin Carlin. And she could hear it still as she lay slowly dying in her vast limestone palace on Fifth Avenue, in which she had hung Rembrandt's *Aristotle Contemplating the Bust of Homer*.

II

IN years past, visitors going through the exhibition hall of the Huntington Library at San Marino, California — a long reliquary-gallery whose treasures, secular and sacred, tend to revive even the most importuned sense of awe — were sometimes bemused into committing a small gaffe.

After pausing to examine such wonders as a French fifteenth-century Book of Hours ("profuse," the guidebook tells one, "in gold ivy-leaf pattern and brilliant colors"), a Latin manuscript Bible that belonged to Gundolph, Bishop of Rochester, England ("probably [copied] by a monk about A.D. 1077"), and a first edition of *Paradise Lost*, visitors came eventually to the east wall and were there confronted with a pair of portraits hung against the oak paneling on either side of a doorway across which a rope was hung during public hours.

One of the pictures was large and imposing: a portrait of Henry

Edwards Huntington, 1850–1927, the founder of the library and the owner of the palace-museum only a few steps away, both of which he had left to the public. The other portrait was somewhat more modest, both in size and treatment.

Visitors usually turned first to the Huntington portrait. It had been painted by Oswald Birley, a British artist who had been knighted for his portraits of the Royal Family. Birley knew what he was about. Huntington looks like a rich man who was at ease with his great wealth — a man who wishes the visitor, plain man or scholar, to enjoy the rarities he had brought together in his house and library. He appears to have been fastidious, sober, courteous. Despite the presence of old age and illness in the portrait, one could — and still may, of course — discern in it the discreet amiability that Huntington's closest associates have often remarked in their recollections of him.

Most visitors glanced only hurriedly at the smaller portrait on the other side of the doorway before leaving the gallery and its treasures. If they noticed anything at all about the other picture, it was the long hair that fell to the subject's shoulders. As they left the hall, murmuring "Thank you" to the guard at the exit, many of them would nod toward the smaller portrait and ask, "*Mrs.* Huntington?"

"No," the guard would answer, "but don't be embarrassed. Everyone asks the same question. Actually, it's John Milton. Mrs. Huntington's portrait is back there [pointing] where you came in. Same artist who painted Mr. Huntington. Done at the same time, in fact."

Absurdity nullifies awe, so the library decided to rehang the portraits. Arabella Huntington replaced Milton, and the poet was dispatched to the west wall. The tale, of which there are, of course, several versions, provides a double metaphor for Arabella's life. In the exchange of portraits she finally assumed what she undoubtedly considered her rightful place in the gallery, just as she had done in real life. Milton himself appropriately provided the second part of the metaphor in his title *Paradise Lost.* The desolate image precisely summed up a crucial moment in Arabella's early years, when, at nineteen, she became pregnant and was "abandoned." In time, however, her life became a *Paradise Regained,* thanks to the miraculous, if ambiguous, appearance of Collis Potter Huntington, Henry Huntington's uncle, in her disordered life.

Ultimately, as Collis Huntington's second wife, she came to live in splendor. She was the mistress of a Fifth Avenue palace, a San Francisco palace, a country house at Throg's Neck on Long Island Sound, and a handsome mountain lodge in the Adirondacks at Racquette Lake in northern New York. When Collis Huntington died in 1900, "controlling more miles of railroad than any man before him in history," he left her one-third of his estate, which, although never precisely evaluated, may have been worth a minimum of $150,000,-000, much of it in high-yield securities.[2]

Thus, at fifty years of age, Arabella became one of the richest women in the world. She also became, almost immediately, a familiar figure in the elegant, carefully guarded galleries of the leading art dealers in New York and Paris. Two brilliant and ambitious young "merchants of art," Joseph Duveen and Jacques Seligmann, began to attend Arabella and guide her growing sophistication in painting, sculpture, and *décor* in the early years of the new century. Duveen was soon to emerge as the dominant figure in Duveen Brothers. Seligmann had only recently (1900) moved from his first shop in Paris, in the Rue de Mathurins, to a *galerie* in the Place Vendôme. The move had been encouraged by the fortuitous patronage of Baron Edmond de Rothschild. The Duveens would also establish themselves on the Place Vendôme.

Duveen encouraged Arabella to spend several million dollars on art in a single luminously spendthrift year in Paris. Shortly thereafter, she bought two adjoining, and combined, *hôtels particuliers* on the Rue de l'Elysée, with an entry garden on the Avenue Gabriel. The huge duplex structure was known as the Hôtel de Hirsch. Arabella was well prepared for such developments, which were, of course, not altogether the product of chance. She had schooled herself, with the aid of tutors, in French history and literature, and, we are told, she came to speak French "like a native."[3] She had also diligently supervised the education of her son, Archer Milton Worsham, whom Collis Huntington, the boy's stepfather, had welcomed into his house. Although he did not adopt Archer, Huntington treated him unreservedly as a son. Archer, with his stepfather's approval, changed his name to Huntington.

So well did Arabella mold Archer's taste that when he was twelve and they were visiting the National Gallery in London he told her that he wished he could live in a museum. (William Randolph Hearst at the age of ten asked his mother to buy the Louvre for him.) Eventually, Archer was to spend almost his entire large fortune for the support of art and literature, principally that of Spain. In an almost literal sense his childhood dream came true: he seems rarely ever to have been outside museums, some of them monuments to his openhanded generosity. "Wherever I put my foot down, a museum springs up," he once remarked.[4]

Another one-third of Collis Huntington's fortune was left to his nephew and right-hand man, Henry Edwards Huntington who, in consequence of his development there of a transit network, public utilities, and vast real estate tracts, became known as "the man who built Los Angeles." Arabella ultimately married Henry Huntington, and thus became the mistress of two more palaces: a fine house in the French classic tradition, adapted from both urban and rural precedent, which Huntington had built for her at San Marino, California, during his protracted courtship, and a native example of the same style, the Château de Beauregard, at La Celle-Saint-Cloud near Paris, which he leased for her.

The latter was the Second Empire palace, now destroyed, that the mysterious "Miss Howard," the mistress of Napoleon III during his rise to power, had constructed upon the ruins of a seventeenth-century château. She had begun the project in 1852, the year she was deposed by Eugénie de Montijo. Miss Howard had loaned Louis-Napoleon Bonaparte five million gold francs, which, after he had established himself as the "Emperor of the French people," he repaid from the national treasury. A substantial part of the repayment went into Beauregard: a new château, new gardens, an aviary with five hundred birds, and a high crenelated wall entirely surrounding the estate's five hundred acres of park and forest. The emperor himself prepared the letters patent making his discarded English benefactress the Comtesse de Beauregard, a patent he then deliberately failed to execute.

Like Miss Howard, née Elizabeth Ann Haryett, Arabella Huntington knew the uses, and dangers, of mystery: she had effaced her past with the same zealous care exercised by the mistress of the emperor. So well had Elizabeth Ann guarded the secret of her modest beginnings, her unfortunate early pregnancy, and the birth of a son, whom she contrived to have the world accept as her younger brother, that it was not until 1955 that her astonishing story became known in its entirety. That year, Simone André Maurois, the wife of the biographer and novelist André Maurois, published a masterful exercise in research and biography, *Miss Howard and the Emperor,* telling the remarkable story in full. Miss Howard had originally gone to great trouble to make sure that the world would forget Elizabeth

Ann Haryett, but later, as Mme. Maurois makes poignantly clear, the world went to almost no trouble at all in forgetting "Miss Howard."

Arabella Huntington is not so much forgotten as misremembered, when she is remembered at all. She protected herself from the press so adroitly that, despite the fact that she had been married to two of the best-known men of the era, and had herself been one of the richest Americans of history, no accurate obituary of her could be written when she died.

No one who has written about her to the present time seems to have known the first name of the man believed to have been her first husband and the father of her son, her only child. Even the author of an admiring biographical sketch of her, prepared "from statements by her relatives and associates," was forced to refer to him vaguely as "a Mr. Worsham of New York."[5] He thus appears to have been partially expunged from the collective memory of Arabella's family and friends, retaining only his last name, a faceless, but convenient, legal identity. He fared no better on the document certifying his son's change of name to Huntington, an instrument which does not contain Worsham's first name "nor anything about him."[6]

No birth certificate has yet been found for Arabella; no entry in a family Bible. Nor has a baptismal record been located. Was she born in Alabama or Virginia? She gave relatives cause to propose both states to genealogists and researchers. She was born as early as 1847 or as late as 1852, depending upon the source that one uses. The inscription on her mausoleum reads, in part: "Born June 1, 1850, Union Springs, Alabama . . .* However, no municipal, country, or church document has yet been found in Union Springs, the seat of Bullock County, Alabama, which would confirm either her birth or residence there. Further, the U.S. Census for 1860 states, on the authority of her mother as the then head of the family, that every member of the household in Richmond, Virginia, of which Arabella was a part, was born in Virginia.

One could extend for several pages the contradictions, ambiguities, and doubtful facts that surrounded Arabella's life up to 1884, the year she married Collis P. Huntington (a marriage, incidentally, for which no license was issued by the County of New York even though the wedding was solemnized in Manhattan) .

* Hereafter, unless otherwise noted, when Arabella's age is given for a specific year, it will be computed from June 1, 1850. But, the reader should keep in mind that such age citations may well be inaccurate within a range of six years. The reader may add one, two, or three years to the cited age, accept it as is, or subtract one or two years.

However, David Lavender, the author of the most recent biography of Collis P. Huntington, *The Great Persuader,* published in 1970, has summed up the problem briefly, and well. His own dilemma can be deduced from the fact that when members of the Huntington family invited him to write Collis Huntington's biography, he was given unconditional access to the Huntington letters and papers, as well as to family recollections of personal matters, a generosity upon which no censorship was imposed. Thus armed, Lavender confronted Arabella only to back away warily. "Efforts to discover information about her background," he writes, "lead to such blank walls as to leave one wondering whether she may systematically have eliminated traces of her youth."

Who, then, was Arabella? The question leads to a labyrinth guarded, as it were, by the Birley portrait of her in the Huntington Library.

There one must start.

III

WHISTLER liked to say that "it takes a man a long time to look like his portrait." Arabella, to the contrary, looked exactly like her portrait the instant Birley had completed it: haughty, severe, humorless, truculent, old. She saw to it that the picture came out that way. Birley painted her during the year she died, 1924, and he sought, as Anders Zorn might have, and Giovanni Boldini would have, to turn her into a fashionable society woman — an aging but attractive *grande dame.* When Arabella, in spite of her increasing blindness, discovered what he was up to, she made him start over. The painting has its own eloquence.

Robert R. Wark, the curator of art at the Huntington Art Gallery, has observed that "it is certainly one of the most powerful portraits of the 1920's, but there are comparatively few women who would have the courage to present themselves to posterity that way." Unless, of course, as Arabella did, they too had wished to manipulate the response of the viewer — of posterity, that is. The dour portrait serves Arabella's purpose well. It is bleak and forbidding: funereal in its blackness — black satin coat, black velvet dress, black beads, black hat swathed with black satin that falls veillike on either side of her face then drops forward across her shoulders, black-rimmed pince-nez glasses. Her dark eyes shine with glacial asperity. They question the viewer: *what are you doing here?* Having intruded, one turns away in embarrassment. The picture has worked its magic.

There is another "portrait" of Arabella, richer, more complex, warmer, more alive, and, oddly, more bristling. But in order to see it one must read, ask, listen, weigh, and not be put off . . .

"Mrs. Huntington allows herself manners which even the Empress of Germany cannot afford," a disenchanted art dealer wrote of her. Another art dealer, the author of a memoir that charms one by its sensitivity and intelligence, contradicts him. He remembers Arabella as an old woman whom he knew well — she was, he tells us, self-effacing, and she had a ready sense of humor about her extremely limited vision. She carried herself with dignity, he recalls, noting that her great height added to her impressive bearing. Still a third dealer offers us a crude anecdote about her poor eyesight. One day a large rat approached her in a gallery where she was examining some Oriental carpets. She leaned forward in her chair and said, "Here pussycat."[7] (Are we meant to laugh?)

A doctor calling at San Marino never forgot her rudeness. When he introduced the nurse whom he had brought with him, Arabella turned away. Only when the doctor took her by the arm, turned her around, and again introduced the nurse did Arabella acknowledge the presence of the other woman. She loathed unexpected visitors she did not know. When Henry Huntington, the last of her husbands, wished to have the public, in small, selected groups, see his splendid collection of Georgian portraits, the finest in America, she said, "No." She didn't want strangers trooping through her house.

She disliked California, preferring New York and Paris. In consequence, Henry Huntington spent at least nine months a year away from his estate, and he felt deeply being deprived of its beauties. Not until after Arabella died was he free to spend Christmas there, with the children of his first marriage, and his grandchildren, around him. But Arabella's wishes had always come first. Los Angeles presumed that when she arrived at San Marino in 1914, a sixty-three-year-old bride, she would assume the leading rôle in society that her husband's commanding eminence in southern California assured her. She twice accepted invitations to lunch with the socially prominent ladies of Los Angeles, but that was all. She never invited them out to the palace. The legend that she aspired to high rank in Fifth Avenue society is absurd. She had good reason not to.

She was an exacting and difficult employer, "and to feel the full force of her displeasure must have been a terrifying experience," a staff member of the Huntington gallery has been led by his researches to observe.[8] She had a quick temper, and her first reactions could be devastating. A carpenter at San Marino once made a cage for one of the many birds in her aviary. She didn't like the cage, and in an outburst of petulance she had the man fired. Instantly. The next day, feeling contrite, she had him rehired. Another time she showed her genuine concern for the servants. When she learned that, because of poor ventilation, they would have sweltered in the quarters designed for them on the third floor at San Marino, she had a comfortable cottage built close by to house them.

On balance, the personal memories of her one gathers tend to be disagreeable. She saved a man's job after she had had him fired out of pique. She was nice to children — to her nieces and nephews. But these were hardly substantial blessings in a world that daily suffered her arrogance. No published memories, and none one hears, confidential or otherwise, give the slightest clue as to why the Huntingtons, uncle and nephew, adored her. But then, no man can answer for another's affections, and certainly not for his passion.

One must reflect upon, one must privately sense and test, the anecdotes, the memories, the opinions. First, one must keep in mind the fact that almost all of them are the product of the last few years of Arabella's life, her years with Henry Huntington. During all that time she was coming closer and closer to total blindness. The burden of her secret aside, she would certainly have begun to withdraw, to spare herself the problem of coping with the unfamiliar person, the stranger who must forever remain a dismaying blur. Thus, age and blindness added their demands to the habitual guardedness that a daring lie had years earlier imposed on her. A moat lay between her and the world. Few were welcome to cross it.

One comes at last to the heart of the paradox in the Birley portrait. Pretending to truth, the picture deceives. It interposes itself between present and past, deliberately obscuring a simple truth the artist might compassionately have suggested had he been let alone to do so: Arabella had been young once. This is no more than a truism, trite, to be sure, and so obvious that we are easily encouraged by Arabella to dismiss it as being of no significance to us. But it could lead to an engaging speculation, a charming possibility: Arabella may once have been beautiful. The portrait, stamped with her invisible imprimatur, conveys no such resonances of youth. For if it did, might not one wish to learn a great deal more about Arabella — about, that is, a beautiful, possibly sensuous and delightful young woman who had profoundly captivated, and influenced, two men of great wealth; both already married, and both willing to wait patiently to marry her?

A beautiful girl . . . "In 1869, at the age of eighteen, Arabella married a Mr. Worsham of New York. He lived only a short time after the wedding, leaving the widow with a son born on March 10, 1870."[9] Thus does the mythic Mr. Worsham, the man who first won Arabella, conveniently emerge from the mists, and thus does he conveniently return to them in the only serious biographical sketch yet published about Arabella.

One enters the labyrinth to begin a search that leads into old, and often remote, tax rolls, wills, tombstone inscriptions, cemetery registrations, family Bibles, deeds of trust, deeds of release, deeds of sale and bargaining, municipal hustings, police department personnel rolls, birth and death certificates, marriage bonds, change of name documents, New York fire insurance maps, specialized Civil War studies, gambling histories, the U.S. Census for 1850, 1860, and 1870, nineteenth-century newspapers, and the endless attenuations of genealogy.

One is fortunate to discover an experienced and well-informed guide, John G. Worsham of Richmond, Virginia, whose genealogical studies of his own family have necessarily led him into considerable research into Arabella's lineage. And yet, despite his scrupulous searches, he too remains thwarted by the deceptions, the contradictions, the family lore, and the Richmond gossip (a century old) — as well as the lack of certain crucial documents which may have been burned during the Civil War — that make progress through the labyrinth slow and discouraging.

At every turn one meets the Arabella of the Birley portrait — at every turn she asks, *what are you doing here?*

In the library of the New-York Historical Society (an organization that once numbered Collis P. Huntington among its patrons), one finds one's first solid footing. There, in the *New York City Directory* for 1873, one discovers this entry: "Worsham Bell D. wid. John, h 109 Lex av."

The widow Worsham: the entry is the earliest published document yet discovered that linked Arabella to a man named John Worsham. The entry now appears to have been a deliberate fraud, which was to serve as the base for a complex set of conditions, each of them, in turn, fraudulent in the degree that it was based upon the original deceit.

The next issue of the directory, dated 1874, carried the same entry, with the addition of Worsham's middle initial: John *A.* Worsham. The middle initial narrows the search for Arabella's first "husband." However, the more one learns about the shadowy "Mr. Worsham of New York," the more one becomes aware that his life was the stuff of myth, of legends and country ballads.

IV

JOHN ARCHER WORSHAM, the most conspicuous and picaresque descendant of "a family that settled in Henrico County, Virginia, by 1640," was the firstborn (1822) of the children of Archer and Margaret (Wingo) Worsham, who had signed a marriage bond in Amelia County, Virginia, in 1821.[10] By 1850, Archer Worsham, a "mail contractor," had established his family in nearby Dinwiddie County. However, Johnny, by then twenty-eight, had long been gone; but he had not yet settled down. When he was twenty-two he had already shown the weather eye of a young man on the move. Various county personal tax records show that he was circling around Richmond, and was slowly being drawn to the capital city on the James River.

In 1854 he bought some business property in downtown Richmond. The record of that conveyance reveals that he was at that time a resident of Petersburg, about twenty miles to the south. Two years later, in 1856, he and his younger brother, Washington J. Worsham, had become residents of Richmond, living together at the same address. Johnny had found a place in life for both of them; unwittingly, he was leading his brother to an early death.

The 1860 *Richmond City Directory* lists Johnny's place of business — 149 Main Street, upstairs — but not his occupation. The U.S. Census for the same year reveals that he was then a man of at least marginal substance: he owned real estate with a declared value of $4,000. He was thirty-eight years old, and still a bachelor.

Things were going well for him. In September, 1862, he bought "Mount Erin," a thirteen-acre parcel of land "with large Brick Dwelling House and other improvements thereon."[11] The small estate lay back from the east bank of the James just below the city boundary. Johnny, an emergent gentleman, paid $15,000 for it, a sum equivalent to approximately $150,000 today.

A great change had come to Richmond, and Worsham had profited well from it. The city was now the capital of the Confederate States of America. A war boom was on, bringing with it a variety of consequences. "When Richmond was the headquarters of the Confederacy," a historian of gambling in the United States has written, "some Southern wits rechristened it Farobankopolis. Food was scarce, flour sold for $125 a barrel, but parties and balls and the wildly popular faro games went on. . . . Prostitutes sauntered the shady streets and the gambler plied his trade 'glistening in fine clothes.' . . . An especially thick cluster of [gambling establishments] centered around Richmond's Exchange Hotel. . . . Johnny Worsham's place, where the wine was excellent and the play high, was the favorite resort of the Confederate dignitaries."[12]

Another historian records the frequent presence there of Judah P. Benjamin, Secretary of War for the Confederate States of America. Some of the Richmond gambling houses "spent ten thousand dollars a day for food, superbly cooked" (dollars, one should observe, that were severely inflated) , a third historian relates. "In the top places like Johnny Worsham's the decorations were engaging and the furniture 'luxurious.' "[13]

Johnny was the king of the faro bankers of the Confederacy, and, quite incidentally, a taste maker whose décor was remarked, and remembered. He was well liked, and his good reputation among government and military dignitaries rested on his honesty.

But there was a vicious underside to Richmond's wartime high life. "Holdups and murders took place openly in broad daylight," many of them the result of gambling debts and the high-tempered disagreements common among "the sporting fraternity."[14] One such disagreement had led to the death of Johnny's brother, Washington, in a "duel with pistols" fought in December, 1861.

On April 3, 1865, Johnny's little kingdom came down in flames. The Confederate Army abandoned Richmond, and the advancing U.S. Army occupied the city, setting fire to a part of it. Six days later, Lee surrendered to Grant at Appomattox Court House. The time of Farobankopolis had ended, and "most of Richmond's gamblers fled, some going to New York."[15]

One hundred days after Appomattox, Worsham, and a partner, bought a house just off Fifth Avenue on West Twenty-fourth Street in New York City. It lay precisely at the center of gravity of Manhattan's elegant new high life.

V

ABOUT six blocks east of Worsham's luxurious faro parlors in Richmond, Richard Milton Yarrington had been supporting a family of seven on a machinist's wages at the time of his death in 1859, two years before Fort Sumter. According to a burial document, Yarrington may also have worked as a carpenter.[16] His house at the corner of Nineteenth and Main streets was undoubtedly an inexpensive dwelling — possibly a humble one.

In 1839, Yarrington had married a childless sixteen-year-old widow, Catherine J. Maddox (Mrs. Edward M. Maddox). Catherine bore him five children. Four years after the birth of the last of their chidren, Yarrington died. He was buried in Shockoe Cemetery, Richmond, May 12, 1859. The U.S. Census taken the following year lists the surviving members of his family as follows: C. J. Yarrington, female, age thirty-seven; Eliza Page, seventeen; Emma J., fifteen; Carolina B., nine; Richard M., seven; and John D., five. The census indicates that Catherine was supporting her children by running a boardinghouse.

This is the family of which Arabella, by all accounts, was a member. However, she is not listed in the 1860 census as a member of the household. Depending upon the date of canvassing, she would have been either nine or ten years old the month the census was taken, too young certainly to have left home. A puzzling matter.

One turns for guidance to the biographical sketch of Arabella written by Cerinda W. Evans, a biographer of Collis P. Huntington and Librarian Emeritus of the Mariner's Museum, Newport News, Virginia. As already noted, this brief but useful work depended for its information upon Arabella's "relatives and associates." Miss Evans writes: "Arabella Duval Yarrington was the daughter of Richard Milton and Catherine J. Yarrington. . . . The Yarringtons were native of Alabama and Texas, but members of the family had resided in Virginia since 1850. There was an R. M. Yarrington — presumably her father — listed in the *Richmond Directory* from 1850 to 1856."

The rather odd reverse migration of the Yarringtons reported to

Miss Evans may have been the product of faulty memory. Richard
was a Virginian at least by 1839, for on April 1 of that year he and
Catherine Maddox had signed their marriage bond at Richmond.
And Catherine, as the then head of the family, told the census taker
in 1860 that every member of the household had been born in Virginia. It seems more likely that Richard actually descended from
some branch of the Yarrington family that first appeared in Virginia
in Middlesex County in 1709.

Miss Evans learned that Elizabeth Page Yarrington, apparently the
"Eliza" of the 1860 census, had married Mansfield Hillhouse, a member of the faculty at Rutgers College, and that "Arabella [had]
nursed her . . . during her last illness" in 1899. Of the other children, Miss Evans discovered that Emma had married a resident of
San Marcos, Texas; that Richard, his father's namesake, had become
"a prominent citizen" in the same city; and that John had become a
railroad executive and had bred and trained trotting horses on his
farm in Kentucky. John had first gone to work as a conductor on the
Chesapeake & Ohio Railroad in 1872, about two years after Collis P.
Huntington gained control of the road. Yarrington was then seventeen. Nine years later he had become the superintendent of the Lexington & Ashland division of the C & O, and he had continued to
prosper under Huntington until he had finally become a vice-president of the company Collis formed to administer all his railroad
interests east of the Mississippi.

Miss Evans seems not to have come upon any family memories of
"Carolina B. Yarrington," who was Arabella's age in 1860. Was Carolina B. actually Arabella D.? An error by the census taker? This
seems the likeliest possibility that can presently be put forward to
explain the curious discrepancy: unless, of course, Carolina disliked
her first name and simply changed it, along with her second name,
when she became old enough to exercise her wishes in the matter.
Arabella, undowered but spirited, possessed both the fire and the
willfulness of the southern belle of romantic tradition, and it is not
surprising to learn that she preferred to be known as Belle as a young
woman, even in formal listings.

Two years after the war ended, Catherine Yarrington took her
family to New York to live. Her reasons are not known. She may
simply have followed Arabella, who, according to a tradition in his
family, had followed Johnny Worsham there after the fall of Richmond. Arabella was seventeen. She was about to marry Worsham and
bear his child — according to her version of the events.

VI

Johnny worsham's handsomely furbished gambling rooms had been only a short walk from the lobby of the Richmond Exchange Hotel. The proximity of the two well-liked gathering places had demonstrated a simple truth that was well known to professional gamblers: the best faro parlors in any city were likely to be within walking distance of its finest and liveliest hotels. It was a truth that Worsham probably had much in mind as his train headed north to New York after he had taken prudent leave of the fallen Confederate capital. . . .

In 1851, the Metropolitan Hotel, a New York brownstone palace for one thousand guests at Broadway and Prince Street, had opened its door. Barely eight years later, in 1859, the Fifth Avenue Hotel, occupying the entire blockfront between West Twenty-third and West Twenty-fourth streets on Fifth Avenue opposite Madison Square, had been completed. At the moment each of these famous hotels registered its first guest it was rightly believed to be the finest lodging place in the United States. American civilization, restive and improvident, had merely hurried uptown, distributing astonishments of comfort and charm with a free hand.

Each of these hotels was the vibrant, dazzling center of its neighborhood: each gave to its milieu a distinctive aura of splendor and excitement. In order to follow Worsham after his flight from Richmond, one must know something about each of them, for both were bench marks in the peculiar topography of Johnny's New York, peculiar in that the slope of his private terrain was all downhill.

During the fifties, the Metropolitan Hotel attracted many affluent families to its handsome residential suites. Its structure almost completely surrounded that of Niblo's Garden Theatre, already a community landmark, and in 1853 the party wall separating the hotel and the theater was pierced to create a great dining hall, the scene of many famous banquets.[17] During the war a number of U.S. Government officials and army officers lived and worked there. And even though it came to be somewhat overshadowed by the Fifth Avenue Hotel during the sixties, it retained its substantial prestige for several decades.

The proprietor of the Fifth Avenue Hotel, Paran Stevens, who also ran the Revere House in Boston and the Battle House in Mobile, had a memorable flair for opulence, gaiety, and innovation. At the Fifth Avenue Hotel he introduced the first elevator to be installed in a lodging place, a matter of considerable public wonderment. His guests there, many of them men of international prominence, were no less awed by the costly decoration of the rooms, public and private, in his newest hotel. Further, his kitchen was famous and his menu envied.

The Fifth Avenue Hotel had that rarest of distinctions in an already crowded city: a view. It looked out upon the green oasis of Madison Square, a park around which lay a neighborhood of palatial residences. Across the square one could see the mansions of S. L. M. Barlow, a leading corporation lawyer and book collector; Leonard Jerome, Winston Churchill's American grandfather; and Mary Jane Morgan, a "genial, unpretentious lady" who would shortly begin to accumulate one of the outstanding art collections of the era.

Here Broadway slanted at a shallow angle across Fifth Avenue; here the exuberance of the former merged with the exclusiveness of the latter, a condition that gave rise to a new spirit of lively elegance. And nowhere was the liveliness more elegant than in the faro and roulette parlors of John Morrissey, the richest gambler in America, at No. 5 West Twenty-fourth Street, just opposite the uptown side of the Fifth Avenue Hotel. Morrissey's chambers were famous for their deep pile carpeting, brocaded wall hangings, and rosewood furniture upholstered with cut velvet. Fernando Wood, New York's millionaire proslavery mayor, August Belmont, and Cornelius (Commodore) Vanderbilt were said to have been regular guests at his late-evening suppers.

A few years earlier, Morrissey had been well known as a brawler who had hired out a vicious gang of Irish thugs to Tammany Hall on election days to terrorize opposition voters. One night he survived a famous, and particularly bloody, fight in a Broadway saloon, just a few steps away from a recently opened faro parlor on Leonard Street. Christian W. Schaffer, the keeper of another Broadway saloon and a partner in the new faro bank, was among the awed witnesses of the brawl. Schaffer got his gambling partners to hire Morrissey to keep order in their Leonard Street parlor.

Morrissey soon became a partner in the game himself, and there began his remarkable ascent in New York gambling, politics, and wealth. Within a decade he ran what was frequently accounted to be the most sumptuous gambling house in America, at 818 Broadway, adjacent to Grace Episcopal Church, then the most fashionable place of worship in New York. He had "washed his face," as a contemporary observed. Then, responding to the uptown trend, Morrissey settled across the street from the glamorous new Fifth Avenue Hotel. Within three years — he was a man who moved swiftly — he was serving in Congress.

Morrissey bought 5 West Twenty-fourth Street on December 23, 1863. On February 15, 1865, with the war drawing to a close, Morrissey's old partner, Christian Schaffer, bought a brownstone house down the block from him at 27 West Twenty-fourth Street. Schaffer purchased the house in his wife's name.

Then, Johnny Worsham came on the scene. On July 19, 1865, he and Schaffer together signed a purchase indenture for 17 West Twenty-fourth Street, only six doors west of Morrissey. There is no evidence that their partnership was based on anything more than a chance encounter and a common business background. They may have had their eye on Morrissey's carriage trade, a foolish ambition.

Their house was listed in the *City Directory* as Worsham's residence.[18] Schaffer and Worsham paid Joseph Seligman $27,000 for the house. Seligman, one of the great bankers of the day, had founded J. & W. Seligman, a leading commercial bank with branches in Paris, London, and Frankfurt. He had bought the house in 1855, and, being a man of probity, he probably disliked the recent changes in the neighborhood. He was "sojourning in Frankfurt" at the time he and his wife, Babette, signed the deed conveyance in front of the American consul. He may have been pleased to learn that Worsham was a "banker," as the gambler, by trade a faro banker, had himself listed in the *City Directory*.

Ten months after they bought the house, Schaffer and Worsham sold it for $54,000. They appear to have made a one hundred percent profit on the sale. Why they decided to sell the house remains unknown. Perhaps Morrissey did not welcome them in the block.

Despite the large profit on the sale of the house, Worsham was chronically short of capital throughout the time he stayed in New York. As early as 1866 he borrowed $13,000, securing the negotiable note drawn to the lender with a deed of trust on Mount Erin, his place just outside Richmond, and a piece of developed property in the heart of the city. The day the note was paid six months later he immediately borrowed $14,500, and again put up Mount Erin and the Richmond property as security.

After he broke up with Schaffer, Worsham moved to a small brick house on Prince Street near the Metropolitan Hotel, and by 1867 he had entered into another partnership, this one with James A. Bailey, who lived in the same house. Worsham & Bailey — "bankers" — operated at 138 Fulton Street. At a time when the movement uptown was taking on added momentum every day, Worsham was headed the wrong way: downtown, and downhill.

At the end of the war, gambling parlors of a new type had sprung up in great numbers in New York. They were called "Day Gambling Houses," and they were "conveniently located to business," most of them to be found in the blocks running "from Fulton Street to Wall . . . at a convenient distance from Broadway."[19] They opened at nine in the morning and closed at four in the afternoon, when the financial district went home for the day. The "bank" run by Worsham & Bailey was one of these daytime faro parlors.

Worsham, once the king of the Confederate faro bankers, was slipping badly, for these houses were considered far beneath the gambling mansions run by Morrissey and his peers.

The truth was, Johnny's luck lay buried in the ashes of Richmond.

VII

ABOUT the time Worsham was busy with his brief venture on Fulton Street, which lasted only a year, Catherine J. Yarrington moved her children from Richmond to 35 Bleecker Street in New York, possibly following Arabella and Worsham north. The two-story brick dwelling she rented lay half a block east of Broadway and two blocks uptown from the Metropolitan Hotel.

Mrs. Yarrington arrived on Bleecker Street sometime during 1867. She had operated a boardinghouse in Richmond, but an examination of the *New York City Business Directory* for the period 1866–1869 reveals no entry under "Boarding Houses" for her. She may, however, have rented out rooms in the house, a common custom at the time.

The neighborhood, until the war a fine residential area, was deteriorating rapidly. Business had taken over most of Broadway and had spilled into the side streets. Bleecker Street was becoming "Parisian," a bohemian quarter occupied by the demimondain. One spoke of its new residents — dancers, actresses, artists — with cautious daring.

Worsham could walk east from his house on Prince Street about fifty yards to the Metropolitan Hotel, proceed up Broadway two blocks, then walk half a block east to visit the Yarringtons. They were virtual neighbors.

By the end of 1869, Mrs. Yarrington had moved to 5 Bond Street. The move was a short one — through the block as it were — for Bond Street bounded on the north the same block that Bleecker Street bounded on the south. Mrs. Yarrington and her children were now located three houses from Broadway at the entrance to a dogleg passageway known variously as Shinbone Alley or Jones Alley. Only a few years earlier, New Yorkers had taken walks on Sundays up Broadway to Bond Street, then near the edge of the city, to see "the marble houses," twin dwellings faced with marble, the first such erected in New York City. And just a block uptown from Bond Street lay Great Jones Street, which let traffic into Lafayette Place, then still a cul-de-sac. There, John Jacob Astor had earlier established a family enclave. But Catherine had arrived on Bond Street after its golden days as part of "the most fashionable neighborhood" in the city had ended.

Sometime in July or early August of the year the Yarrington family moved to Bond Street — 1869 — Arabella became pregnant. She gave birth to a son on March 10, 1870. She named the boy Archer (Worsham's middle name) Milton (her father's middle name) Worsham.

At this point one is well into the labyrinth with only Arabella's published claim to have been the "widow" of John Worsham to guide one. Other records that might lead one out of the maze do not exist: there is no marriage license for Worsham and Arabella in New York County and no birth certificate for their son.

The U.S. Census for 1870 appears to establish that Worsham was living with the Yarringtons on Bond Street as of June 12 that year. But the pertinent entry is a marvel of confusion. For example, Worsham is listed as "John De Worsion," Arabella as "Bell De Wersion," and their three-month-old child as "John De Wersion" also. (All his life, Archer Huntington was quite certain his name was Archer, not John, and that he had been born in New York City, not in Virginia as the census entry states.)

Mrs. Yarrington is listed first as the head of the household, and, inexplicably, a Miss E. P. Ashburn, "Authoress," twenty-three, born in Richmond, comes second, ahead of the rest of the family. Emma Yarrington, twenty-one, is shown third. Her brothers, Richard, seventeen, and John, fifteen, are listed respectively as "At College and "At School." Four other males, apparently boarders or roomers, are also listed. Mrs. Yarrington, whose occupation was "Keeping House," is shown to have been the owner of $15,000 worth of property. (Other records suggest that the property was not in New York.)

The census entry creates the impression that Worsham and Arabella were married and living together on Bond Street with their infant child. However, it is clear that Worsham — his name completely garbled, his age incorrectly given, his middle initial missing, and his realty undeclared — did not himself give the information to the canvasser.

Presently, Johnny was dead, according to Arabella. But Worsham was, in fact, that greatest of embarrassments, a living ghost. On July 14 — only thirty-two days after the faulty data on him was posted on the canvasser's sheet in New York — Worsham was interviewed by a census taker at his house at Franklin and Fourteenth streets in Richmond. He was, according to the July 14 entry, back home and the head of a household that included his wife, Annette Worsham. And his name was "John A. Worsham."

The authenticity of the second census entry is supported positively by the *Richmond City Directory,* and negatively by the *New York City Directory.* The former shows him resident in Richmond in 1870, and the latter has no listing for him after 1868 (effective date) .

The strange array of errors in the New York census data suggests — perhaps *discloses* would not be too strong a word — that someone in the Yarrington household was trying to create a statistical, quasi-legal presence for "De Wersion," a presence that would in some measure legitimatize, in the absence of a marriage license, the apparent relationship of "Bell" and John as husband and wife.

Men's lives are filled with documents, a fact Arabella, as most of us might have done, had overlooked. When Schaffer and Worsham had sold their house on West Twenty-fourth Street in 1866, the deed of sale, conforming to state law, bore not only their signatures but also those of their wives, who thus signed away their dower rights in the property, a necessary condition of the sale. The conveyance registration reads in part: "John A. Worsham and Annette Worsham his wife."

Thus, Annette was Worsham's wife in 1866, and she was his wife in 1870, according to two valid documents, a deed conveyance and an uncontestable census entry. A third document, her death certificate, states that she died in Richmond on January 3, 1874, at thirty-four years of age, and that she was married at the time of her death. And a fourth document, the record of her interment at Hollywood Cemetery, Richmond, reveals that she was buried in a plot owned by Worsham and his nephew.[20]

And so, Arabella could not legally have been married to Worsham at any time between May 16, 1866, and January 3, 1874. Or, to narrow the matter, between 1866 and 1870, the year he "died." Arabella had invented his death. She appears also to have invented their marriage.

Let us complete Johnny Worsham's story before proceeding with Arabella's (which will include one more dramatic invention). On September 27, 1871, Worsham sold his remaining interest in Mount Erin for only $6,500. He was by then back at his old trade, and one can find him in the Richmond directories regularly between 1871 and 1877. Then, on May 28, 1878, the *Richmond Daily Dispatch* reported his death:

"J. A. Worsham, a leading member of the sporting fraternity of Richmond . . . died Sunday afternoon [May 26] at the residence of his nephew. . . . Mr. Worsham prided himself upon the reputation for fair dealing he had acquired in the long years of varying fortune during which he had been 'in the business.' . . . Many members of the Legislature who have eaten at his richly-laden boards will testify to his hospitality and geniality. During the war he was liberal to our soldiers. . . .

"He died poor."

VIII

ARABELLA had fared better.

By the end of 1871 — a year after Worsham had returned to Richmond — she was settled at 109 Lexington Avenue, between East Twenty-seventh and Twenty-eighth streets, with her son, her mother, and possibly her sister Emma. John, the younger of her brothers, was just beginning his successful career with the Chesapeake and Ohio Railroad, then in its second year under the control of Collis P. Huntington. Four successive editions of the city directory list "Bell D. Worsham" at the Lexington Avenue address.

Gramercy Park, only six blocks away, gave to the neighborhood a certain social grace. The affluent families gathered there had less wealth than the great rich of Fifth Avenue, but they had a far livelier and more sophisticated interest in the arts. Some of the families around the park were southern. They included among their number Burton Harrison, who had served as the private secretary of Jefferson Davis, and his wife, Constance (Cary) Harrison, novelist and memoirist (*Reflections Grave and Gay*). The Harrisons had both spent much of the war in Richmond before their marriage. So, even had she needed to, Arabella could not have sought them out, for they would have known about Johnny Worsham.

During the years she lived on Lexington Avenue, Arabella's life underwent a crucial change, one that of its nature had to be carefully concealed, at least in its early stages. In her biographical appreciation of Arabella, Miss Evans makes no mention of No. 109, but instead places Arabella in Texas during that period. In the Evans account, Arabella seems to have gone to Texas almost immediately after Worsham's "death" and to have remained there for about five years. She first visited her sister Emma and her brother Richard in San Marcos (a chronological confusion: neither had yet moved to Texas), and then settled down in Austin, where she boarded for the remainder of her protracted visit with a family of some local prominence. (The *Austin Statesman* in 1877 identified her as a Texan, a resident of Blanco, near San Marcos.)

The "young widow" with her infant son, visiting relatives, and forming lifelong friendships with new acquaintances who were to recall long afterward her beauty and charm — of such is the idyll Miss Evans has sketched in a few sentences. One is only sorry that the generous sympathy of Arabella's new friends for her early widowhood was based upon a lie, albeit a brave one.

Contemporary documents and newspaper reports in San Marcos and Austin dispute the telescoping of dates in Miss Evans's appreciation, and also serve to flesh out its superficiality. Arabella did, indeed, visit Texas (perhaps paving the way for her sister and brother — the record remains clouded), and she did make enduring friendships there, particularly with the family of David L. Campbell, a cotton buyer, in whose house she boarded in Austin. (Years later, Campbell's daughter Caroline would join Arabella's household as a paid companion who was considered a member of the family.)

However, not only did Arabella arrive in their midst as an impostor of sorts — "a young widow" — but she boldly imposed on her Texas friends a new lie, in which they could only innocently conspire. In order to understand the strategy behind the lie, one must look as closely as possible at Arabella at that time, and examine the conditions of title to 109 Lexington Avenue — that is, its ownership. Two documents, the first a remarkable portrait with the eloquence of poetry, and the second a terse conveyance registration, dry but evocative, enable us to see Arabella in her twenties and to discover the owner of her house, a way station on her progress to Fifth Avenue.

Several years ago a small oval painting of Arabella by an unidentified artist came to light, revealing precisely the one fact that the chilling Birley portrait so successfully conceals: Belle Worsham was a young woman of seductive beauty. One looks at her and almost immediately wishes to know more about her. Soft, dark eyes — luminous, one supposes. Dark hair, parted at the center, brushed to either side, and gathered at her neck in a large, loose bun. A small mouth, set upon determination.

In the portrait, Arabella wears a Marie Antoinette fichu: a black lace scarf covering her bodice and upper arms, and probably tucked through her belt. At her neck, standing up from the rolled collar of her fichu, one sees a narrow band of white, the collar of her dress. It is held closed by a silk ribbon tied in a flat bow, with the ends falling below her waist. What little one can see of her costume in the small oval portrait suggests that Arabella was alert to postwar high fashion and that she could afford a wardrobe of the sort illustrated in *Harper's Bazaar,* a new magazine begun in 1867 that addressed itself "to ladies whose households were staffed with servants," according to Stella Blum, a historian of American dress.

Her nose is straight — English and comely — and she has a long upper lip. We know that she was tall, and the head-and-shoulder portrait shows her to have had a full bust. She must, indeed, have taken away the breath of many men. The slightly prim touch of the band of white collar showing above the black lace contrasts with the vague sensuality in her eyes — an adroit touch, feminine and alluring, that might beguile a man out of his wits.

No man would turn away from this portrait.

What one cannot read in the picture is Arabella's courage. According to a Richmond oral tradition, verified in part, but only in part,

by circumstantial details and Worsham family memories, Johnny
Worsham abandoned Arabella after she had followed him to New
York and become pregnant. Like Miss Howard, who, as Mme.
Maurois has written, "could not bear the thought that society would
hold her son in contempt," Arabella "was prepared to dare all." She
had already taken certain risks to protect her son, and she was ready
to take more.

Her beauty stood her well. When she moved uptown from Bond
Street and the deteriorating Broadway neighborhood to the fashionable blocks above Gramercy Park she acquired the advantage not
only of a socially preferred environment, but she acquired as well a
very rich landlord. On April 19, 1872 — according to the conveyance
registration, the second of the documents that illuminate the changes
that were coming into Arabella's life — Collis P. Huntington bought
109 Lexington Avenue, a half-lot, for $14,000, assuming additionally
a $6,000 mortgage.

Huntington was not a man to speculate in small Lexington Avenue lots: his large capital was fully committed to his railroad and
shipbuilding ventures. He is believed to have owned only two other
pieces of residential property in New York City at that time, his Park
Avenue house and a nearby stable, both of which he had purchased
in his wife's name. He held No. 109 in his own name.[21] Arabella had
entered his life to stay.

As time passed Arabella seemed to want to defy the world: paradise regained brought her fresh boldness in the proportion. On December 8, 1877, the *Austin Statesman* published the following report
in its "Personal and Local" notes:

"Mrs. B. D. Worsham, mother, and son . . . are in the city, stop-
ping at the Raymond House. Mrs. Worsham is *a niece of Collis P.
Huntington,* the railroad man."

One can only admire Arabella's arrogant daring (here emphasized
by italics) . She had buried a husband who had not died and to whom
she could not legally have been married. Now she was circulating in
Texas the fact that she was the niece of one of the best-known men in
the country, to whom she was not related.

It is a fact that will come as a surprise to Huntington biographers
and genealogists.

TWO

IX

In 1863, in the midst of the war, Collis P. Huntington, a native of New England who had been in business as a storekeeper in Sacramento, California, since the height of the gold rush, had returned east and settled in New York. He had had three goals: to interest eastern financiers in the proposed Central Pacific Railroad, to get every privilege, cash subsidy, and land grant he could possibly wrest from Congress, and to purchase the matériel to build the railroad through the Sierra Nevada, the last a complex logistical undertaking that could have kept a man of ordinary zeal and energy fully occupied.

Huntington had a vision, wholeheartedly pragmatic, in which his interests and those of California merged: a transcontinental railroad which would enrich both. He became "the great persuader," one of the most successful lobbyists in history. He had proved in Washington, and had made good use of there the simple fact that most people are most easily persuaded by money.

A husky, energetic man who stood just over six feet, Huntington once said that work was his pleasure, and that he never spent more than $200 a year on himself. He was proud of the fact that unlike most financiers he could actually *run* a railroad, and that in contrast to many railroad operators he *built* his own roads.

Huntington had been born in Harwinton Township, Connecticut, October 22, 1821, the sixth of nine children of "a surly, improvident" tinkerer who had built his house on a rise above a swamp called Poverty Hollow.[22] When he was thirteen, Huntington was bound out to a local farmer by the township selectmen. He got seven dollars a month for a year, and the farmer's wife taught him the rags-to-riches aphorisms of Benjamin Franklin's *Poor Richard*.

By the time he was fifteen, he was finished with school for good and had begun his successful career as a merchant, a career that led him to New York City, the Deep South (where he was revolted by slavery) , and, finally, to Oneonta, New York, where he worked in a store his brother Solon had built after moving there. Once settled, he returned to his courtship of Elizabeth Stoddard of Cornwall, Connecticut, which had been interrupted by his trips through the South. He and Solon became partners on September 4, 1844, and fourteen days later he married Elizabeth.

Huntington went to California in 1849 during the gold rush to open a hardware store. Five years later he and another Sacramento storekeeper from the East, Mark Hopkins, entered into partnership. On the second floor of their store, the Republican Party in California was born. The political and business interests of the men who met there centered on a coast-to-coast railroad. On June 27, 1861, about ten weeks after the bombardment of Fort Sumter, Huntington and his associates incorporated the Central Pacific Railroad.

Four men, "the big four" — Huntington, Hopkins, Leland Stanford, and Charles Crocker — became the principal figures in the histories of the Central Pacific and the Southern Pacific railroads. After Huntington's death, E. H. Harriman gained control of the Southern Pacific. Camille Weidenfeld, the Wall Street broker who had introduced Harriman to Huntington, once observed to the financial publisher Clarence W. Barron: "Huntington was the cart horse. . . . [He] carried all his associates on his shoulders."

Huntington made his first trip back East on railroad business, taking Elizabeth with him, in December, 1861. They returned to Sacramento the following April. About the time they sailed from New York, Elizabeth learned that her sister Clarissa's husband, Edwin D. Prentice, had died of injuries sustained during a severe flood in Sacramento. Clarissa was left with four children. The Huntingtons, who were childless, persuaded her to allow them to take the youngest of the children, Clara, only one year old, into their home. Thus they became "parents," and, although Huntington never bothered formally to adopt her, Clara Prentice became their "daughter," and was known as Clara Huntington.

After a second business trip to Washington, Huntington moved his family to wartime New York. He installed Elizabeth and Clara in a family suite at the Metropolitan Hotel. Many Union officers were quartered there and they brought to the hotel a sense of urgency and excitement. Downstairs in Niblo's Garden Theatre the most famous musical of the era, *The Black Crook*, opened on September 12, 1866, and did not close its initial run until sixteen months later. However, Elizabeth may have held a poor opinion of the dancing ladies who gave the show its unique interest, for she was "a gentle, quiet, self-effacing woman" who was "an essential source of strength to Collis."[23] She was forty-three, a year older than Huntington.

On October 15, 1867, Elizabeth became the owner of record of a house on the southeast corner of Park Avenue and East Thirty-eighth Street. After four years at the Metropolitan, she and Collis had wearied of hotel life. According to David Lavender, his most recent biographer, Huntington paid for their new house with Central Pacific stock having a total par value of $50,000, but which could then be bought for as little as thirty cents a share. The following year, Elizabeth became the owner of additional property, probably a stable, down the block on Thirty-eighth Street near Lexington Avenue.

Huntington was again an easterner. He disliked California, but he continued to go there on business trips. In addition to his interest in the two western railroads, he assumed control of the Chesapeake and Ohio Railroad, a venture in which his California partners took no interest. The negotiations for the C & O took Collis to Richmond, Virginia, and one series of meetings was held at White Sulphur Springs the first two weeks in July, 1869. Huntington then left for California about mid-August, traveling with his family, business associates, "dignitaries" (including, Lavender notes, "a tame Congressman") , and other guests — a trip that was "something of a royal progress."

Within two years of this trip, Huntington had become Arabella's landlord. Then, within three more years, Arabella and her mother had become wealthy enough to buy a house worth the equivalent of about $430,000 in present-day money. On October 24, 1874, Catherine J. Yarrington bought 68 East Fifty-fourth Street, paying out $30,000 in cash and assuming a $13,000 mortgage — a total cost to her of $43,000. The same day, in an extension of the transaction, Catherine conveyed the same property to Arabella "for and in consideration of natural love and affection and of the sum of One Dollar lawful money."

The double conveyance makes clear that someone who wished to conceal his presence had become Arabella's benefactor. James Henry Duveen, who disliked her, wrote in *The Secrets of an Art Dealer*: "One of the most extraordinary women I have ever known was Arabella Huntington: extraordinary because of her indomitable mind and an outrageous spirit which compelled her to outvie all competitors. Long before I met her, Arabella was the unofficial wife of Collis P. Huntington."

Belle Worsham was about to enter the world of palaces.

Three years after moving to 68 *East* Fifty-fourth Street, Arabella made the first in a series of three purchases on the other side of Fifth Avenue, all of them centering on 4 *West* Fifty-fourth. On April 20, 1877, she sold No. 68 East to Isaac Henderson and on the same day bought the house, stables, and garden at No. 4 West from him. The house had been built by William P. Williams, a steamship company operator, who had bought the land in 1862. Although the New York City building records — construction dockets, architects' plans, and related materials — for the years preceding 1866 have been destroyed, Allan Nevins, the most authoritative of the biographers of John D. Rockefeller, the ultimate owner of the house, has deduced from a letter in the Rockefeller Family Archives that Williams erected a residence and stable on the site in 1864–1865. If, as other New York businessmen of the era often did, Williams used the same architect for both commercial and residential work, the house may have been designed by Andrew Clark, who, in 1866, drew the plans for a freight shed for Williams's steamship line at Pier 44 on the North River at the foot of Jay Street.

In 1868 Williams had sold the property to Roxana Drew, the wife of Daniel Drew, the great bear of Wall Street. The following year, Drew, who along with Jay Gould and Jim Fisk had just defeated Commodore Vanderbilt in the historic "battle of the Erie" Railroad, sold the house to the Henderson family. Drew hadn't lived there. His own mansion was on West Seventeenth Street facing on Union Square.

Arabella paid Henderson $150,000 cash for No. 4, and she also assumed payment of a $100,000 mortgage outstanding on the property — a total commitment of $250,000. She was twenty-seven at the time of the combined transactions.[24] It is amusing to note that she signed the conveyance to Henderson of No. 68 East "Belle D. Worsham," and the conveyance for her purchase from him of No. 4 West "Belle D. Yarrington Worsham." She seems to be saying to us, "I have arrived" — and, indeed, she had arrived, on Fifth Avenue, or at least only one door from the corner.

The lot that Arabella bought from Henderson was sizable: a hundred and thirteen feet on the street front by one hundred feet deep. A year and a half later, on November 1, 1878, she bought the property immediately to the west, with a fifty-foot front, for $33,000. Then, on July 1, 1880, she added the property immediately to the east of her original plot at a cost of $27,500 cash, additionally assuming a mortgage of $15,000, her total commitment being $42,000.

Across the way on the uptown side of the street lay St. Luke's Hospital, which occupied the blockfront from West Fifty-fourth Street to West Fifty-fifth Street on Fifth Avenue, and extended three hundred feet west into the block — more than a third of the way to Sixth Avenue. The grounds of the hospital, an Italianate brick structure with high square towers framing the central chapel bay, were enclosed by a bordering range of trees. The hospital, run by the Protestant Sisters of Charity, had been completed in 1858.

And so, by the summer of 1880, Arabella owned a protected house and stable, free of immediate neighbors and commercial encroachment, on a parcel of land running a hundred and eighty-five feet west along the downtown side of West Fifty-fourth Street from a point about thirty yards west of Fifth Avenue. Her property was a hundred feet deep. She had paid $331,000 for the land "and all the appurtenances thereon," the equivalent in present-day money of more than $3,000,000. One of the deeds conveyed to her bore a restriction: only a "first class residence" could be erected on the property. The clause was unnecessary, for Arabella was a young woman with first-class taste, and access to a first-class purse.

No. 4 West Fifty-fourth Street was not one of the greater mansions of New York history. It once served as part of the setting in a generally forgotten novel (*A Heroine in Bronze* by James Lane Allen), but except for what Arabella did to it, and except, further, for the fact that it became the New York residence of John D. Rockefeller and his family, the house would have remained without consequence, one of the thousands of undistinguished brownstones that have slipped anonymously into the city's past. When Arabella bought it, the house was a dour, foursquare building, whose renaissance decorative devices, long divorced from the stony Florentine and Roman architectural masses they had once relieved, looked stolid rather than bold. The walls of the house were laid up in brick. Only that along the street front was faced with a veneer of brownstone. The brickwork of the side walls looked to the east upon a charming garden with a gazebo and the stables beyond, and to the west upon a large yard filled with trees.

Arabella's house rose four stories above a customary basement podium, half of which lay below the ground level. At the time she moved in, the house had only a few ordinary decorative details to distract the eye from the dark rectitude of its street facade: a stamped metal and wood cornice, plain string courses at the top and bottom floors, a ladder of symmetrical stone quoins at the corners, simple molded window surrounds, and commonplace pediments — flat dripstones above the windows on the upper three stories and segmental-arch pediments above the windows and doorway on the first floor. Arabella converted it into a more ambitious *petit palais,* which, although it was of little architectural interest, now claims a special place in the unwritten history of palace decoration in America during the second half of the nineteenth century.

Her legacy to that history is a set of rooms — documentary souvenirs — permanently on exhibit at the Museum of the City of New York (her bedroom and dressing room) and the Brooklyn Museum (her Moorish parlor). The rooms, which have been seen by several million people since they were installed, were preserved by a rare combination of chance, intelligence, and generosity. (They were given to the museums by John D. Rockefeller, Jr.[25])

Thousands of New York palace *salons,* parlors, libraries, ballrooms, boudoirs, and bedrooms on whose decoration millions of dollars were spent have been destroyed. Arabella's surviving rooms thus command attention beyond the casual pleasure they may bring to the museum visitor.

X

In 1881, Arabella razed the west wall of the house and had the structure widened to almost half again its original breadth at the furthest point of the extension, an estimate based, of necessity, upon photographs taken before and after the changes. (New York City policy calls for the automatic destruction of all building plans, and alteration plans, if any, for any structure in the city that is demolished. No. 4 West Fifty-fourth Street was torn down in 1938 to make way for the garden of the Museum of Modern Art.)

The anonymous architect of Arabella's restructuring enlivened the blank stone wall of the street facade of the new section through the use on the first floor of a blind window, with a surround and pediment matching those on the regular windows, and an aedicular shell-headed panel about one story above. However, his principal decorative contributions were the addition of a projecting entrance portico supported at the outer corners by decorated Ionic columns (Victorian picturesque) and a projecting bay on the second story — a structural extension of the portico — with fluted Ionic corner pilasters, and a parapet-balustrade above. Arabella also added a bay, two windows wide and one window deep, from the basement to the roof at the southeast corner of the house, a vertical range of little garden sunrooms with carved festoon panels beneath the second-story windows. The new west wing (basically a great reception hall with a stairwell bay), the new two-story portico, and the new four-story garden bay together revealed Arabella's palatial intentions, a vision of palaces to come. Her reach may have exceeded her grasp, but only for the moment.

During the structural changes, Arabella also had the entire house stripped of its interior finish down to the lathing. She then had the house completely refinished, redecorated, and refurnished. The cost of the project was great, but probably not as great as the astonishing $800,000 estimate for "the interior furnishings alone" later published by the *New York World* (December 3, 1893). What the estimate, the equivalent of $8,000,000 in present-day money, tells us is the magnitude of Arabella's new wealth. She had entered the ranks of the very rich. Her costly program of alterations and redecoration was undertaken at a time during which the country was still suffering from the most severe depression of the nineteenth century.

In the new wing of the house she installed an Otis Brothers elevator that ran "from cellar to roof," and a broad ceremonial staircase of "black mahogany," a staircase whose well rose through three stories to a stained glass interior skylight "of costly workmanship." The stair was further lit by an ascending group of three stained-glass windows, tall and narrow, which came to be known in the Rockefeller family as "The Three Sisters." The windows, the *World* observed, were "wrought in exquisite lines and coloring in Renaissance designs."

The rails, balusters, posts, newels, underframing panels, fluted and decorated Doric columns, and arches of the staircase remained for almost six decades a handsome summing-up of the superb architectural woodwork executed by the cabinetmakers of that period. (Staircase work had already become a subcontractor specialty.)

In his biography of Rockefeller, Nevins has described the main living room, Arabella's *salon*: it was "perhaps twenty-five feet in width by forty in length, lighted by two tall windows on Fifty-fourth Street, and a third on the garden. The woodwork was rosewood, polished to resemble mahogany; the walls were covered with garnet-colored velvet brocade, and the furniture was massive. . . . This room opened at the rear into a somewhat smaller apartment, decorated in the Moorish style. . . . Still farther back lay the dining-room." Arabella also had "a complete Turkish bath" installed.

One may still see part of what she achieved, and because she was a woman who got what she wanted, her three existing museum-piece rooms — along with Samuel H. Gottscho's superb photographic documentation of her other rooms — may be assumed to bear accurate witness to her taste at the beginning of the 1880's.

Who designed and executed Arabella's new interiors?

"I have furnished the house," George A. Schastey, a New York cabinetmaker, furniture maker, and decorator, wrote to John D. Rockefeller on January 24, 1881. Later that year, on October 29, Schastey elaborated on the matter in another letter to Rockefeller: "We desire to state that the interior woodwork and decoration . . . was designed and executed by us."

Almost nothing is known about Schastey. No furniture he made has yet been identified, nor, apparently, has a stamp, stencil, or label used by him been found by the curators and art historians now studying New York furniture makers. He is listed in successive editions of the city directory (once moving to quarters just vacated by Pottier & Stymus, one of the leading decorators of the era for whom he had previously worked) , and he did exhibit a sideboard, now lost, at the Centennial Exhibition in Philadelphia in 1876, winning an award for it. However, his name has yet to be connected with any major decorating project other than Arabella's.

Margaret Stearns, the Curator of Decorative Arts of the Museum of the City of New York, and Robert E. P. Hendrick, formerly of the Brooklyn Museum, whose collaborative research into the question has uncovered some of the documents used in the present account, continue to search for other data that would support Schastey's sweeping claim, preferring for the present to reserve judgment on it.

Their scholarly wariness is based in part on a letter Mitchell Samuels wrote to John D. Rockefeller, Jr., on March 31, 1938. Samuels, whose firm, French & Company, had sold her some of her palace furnishings of a later date, had come to know Arabella well, and he recalled talking to her about the interiors of 4 West Fifty-fourth Street. "I remember she told me the old firm of Pottier &

Stymus did a good deal of work for her," Samuels wrote. "The wood-work of the house was undoubtedly done by Pottier & Stymus as they were the premier cabinetmakers of the time."

A comparative study of the design and decorative treatment of furniture then being made by Herter Brothers, the leading New York decorators of the day, with the design and inlay work of the sliding doors, doorway surrounds, cabinetry, and the remaining pieces of furniture from the house strongly suggests that they may also have had a hand in Arabella's interiors. (Herters had just com-pleted William H. Vanderbilt's massive tripartite palace on Fifth Avenue, for which they designed both the exteriors and interiors.)

One could examine the merits of the several claims at length, citing work done by Pottier & Stymus for Huntington's partners in San Francisco and for Rockefeller's partners in New York (princi-pally his brother William, and Henry Morrison Flagler), and citing the fact that Herter Brothers maintained an architectural drafting room under Charles B. Atwood, later to gain prominence as the chief designer for Burnham & Root in Chicago, that could have handled the restructuring and extension of Arabella's house as well as its decoration — but, in the end one would have to leave the matter open.

However, it is more than likely that if the definitive documents that would settle the question are found someday, they will reveal that the project was subcontracted to several decorators, cabinet-makers, furniture makers, plasterers, and so on, the common practice of the day, and one that Arabella herself would follow when the time came to decorate her great Fifth Avenue palace.

What can be said of Arabella's costly taste is a more subjective matter.

One may immediately justify her fantasy Moorish sitting room — it was merely a reflection of a romantic vogue that grew out of public fascination with the Alhambra, first stimulated by Washington Irv-ing. Even as sophisticated a palace architect as Richard Morris Hunt had recently designed a Moorish billiard room for the Fifth Avenue palace — a François Premier limestone château — of Alva Vanderbilt and had commissioned the decorator Leon Marcotte to execute it.

The *diwan* and its decoration had passed from the tents — the miragelike desert palaces — of the great Muslim princes to Moorish Spain to Fifth Avenue. (One might here observe that the vision of archetypal splendor realized at Versailles got to France from the vast deserts of the Bedouin wanderings by way of southern Spain, for Louis XIV instinctively turned to the Spanish court for instruction in imperial opulence, as well as for tutoring in imperial *hauteur*, the former a Muslim invention, the latter the vision of a painter, Veláz-quez, who taught his royal patrons how to look like monarchs.)

The walls and ceilings of the rooms on Arabella's first and second floors provide an unusual study in simulation. Embossed and block-printed *trompe-l'oeil* wallpapers were used to simulate leather, painted ceiling panels, the painted beam soffits that framed the fields of the ceiling panels, large wall panels of low-relief carved woodwork, and cornice details such as dentils and egg-and-tongue classical mold-ings. The eye yields willingly to such playful conceits. In the same rooms, the skill of the woodcarvers and cabinetmakers of New York is generously exhibited, and, as has often been remarked, it was high skill indeed. The inlay work of varicolored woods and mother-of-pearl is exquisitely executed, both on furniture and on architectonic details such as door surrounds.

In several of the first-floor reception chambers, the decorative grammar of modified classical design — fluted pilasters, carved col-umn shafts and capitals, and entablature details — created an ambi-ence of ordered serenity in the midst of decorative richness. Nowhere in the house was the refracted classical presence as dominating as it was in the great staircase. There the arches along the first-floor gallery, the fluted columns, and the balustrades introduced a princely certi-tude to the decoration.

The ceiling painting in the main *salon* was simple in spirit and execution: it was no more than a cluster of playful *putti*, charming figures that were echoed in the ceiling framing panels and along the frieze band. Despite the fact that the time favored heavy Victorian *portières* and window curtains, deeply gathered and draped in the-atrical swags that turned doorways into small prosceniums, Arabella's windows were almost chastely framed with curtains cut in relatively narrow panels, embroidered with edge bands, that hung straight to the floor.

It is a risky matter, but one might make this generalization: in a time during which confused Victoriana reigned in all aspects of deco-ration — from fantasy architectonics and ornate wall, ceiling, door, and window treatments based upon a bewildering density of surface enrichment, to a restive profusion of furnishings and decorative ob-jects — Arabella exercised surprising restraint. For example, her bedroom and dressing room, with their Empire resonances, had a modern, uncluttered, post-Victorian look.

Arabella was well ahead of her time in imposing constraints upon the designer of her bedroom and its furnishings, or in accepting them from him. The latter might well have been the case if Christian Herter, the most admired decorator of the period, was the designer, for despite his Beaux-Arts training as a painter in the studio of Pierre-Victor Galland, whom he commissioned to paint a series of murals in the Fifth Avenue palace of William Henry Vanderbilt, Herter had fallen under the spell of Charles L. Eastlake, the English prophet of simplicity in the decorative arts. (One can only guess at the aesthetic tension in a decorator who admired alike Galland and Eastlake.)

However, one condition is perfectly clear in Arabella's interiors: she lacked the lifelong exposure to, and sophistication in, the decorative arts — the authority based upon a combination of knowledge and firsthand experience — that might have led her toward true innovation. Nearby, on Fifth Avenue, Alva Vanderbilt had just installed in her new limestone mansion a François Premier library with carved walnut *boiseries* taken from an early renaissance château, and a Régence-Louis XV *salon,* designed and executed in Paris by Jules Allard, a room of such striking beauty, excellence of craftsmanship, and sound scholarship that it would almost immediately launch a new era in American palace *décor.* But as the world would learn during her vigorous career in women's suffrage, Alva (by then Mrs. O. H. P. Belmont) was born to lead. Arabella would herself become one of Alva's disciples, not in suffrage, but in palace decoration.

Perhaps the most eloquent message one gets from Arabella's costly interiors at No. 4 has best been suggested in an observation Proust would make half a century later: "One of the mistakes of people in society is not to realize that, if they want us to believe in them, it is first necessary that they should believe in themselves, or at least should respect the essential elements of our belief." The time had come for Arabella to assume a high place, if not precisely in "society," then in its magisterial equivalent, the world of the palace builders. And she had accepted her responsibility — to herself and to us. Her rooms at No. 4 tell us quite effectively that she believed in herself. She was ready for the future.

Elizabeth (Stoddard) Huntington died of cancer October 5, 1883, at 65 Park Avenue. She was seriously ill for a long period before her death. The fact that Arabella's relations with Huntington were well enough known for her to be called "the unofficial Mrs. Huntington" suggests that Elizabeth may have been aware of the situation. As early as May 1, 1875, she had had to sign away her dower rights in the property at 109 Lexington Avenue when Huntington sold the house and land. Surely Elizabeth knew that Arabella had been resident in the house as the tenant of record during the previous four years.

Ten weeks after Elizabeth Huntington died, Arabella sold that portion of her property nearest Fifth Avenue to William Henry Vanderbilt for $60,000. No. 4 was receding swiftly into the past. Huntington and Arabella were married there on July 12, 1884. The next day the *New York Tribune* advised its readers that Arabella's "family and that of Mr. Huntington [are] on terms of the closest intimacy. She is wealthy in her own right. Her first husband died several years ago." (Worsham had, in fact, been dead for six years.) Arabella's mother, son, and one of her sisters were present. David Lavender dryly observes that neither of Collis's old partners who were still living came to the wedding, even though both were in New York at the time.

XI

SUDDENLY, Huntington, a man who enjoyed boasting that he had never spent more than $18 a month indulging himself, was launched on a dazzling career as a spender, all in the cause of Arabella's vision of palaces, now amplified and reinforced by her apprenticeship at 4 West Fifty-fourth Street. One must first step back a few months, and then proceed several years into the future, in order to give the coherence it deserves to the story of Huntington's diligent efforts to house Arabella in a regal manner. No. 4 had also served as his apprenticeship.

On April 17, 1884, Charles MacRae, a prominent New York real estate broker whose clients included seven Vanderbilts and Vanderbilt in-laws, two Havemeyers, Pierre Lorillard II, D. O. Mills, Henry M. Flagler, William Rockefeller, Henry Villard, Cyrus W. Field, Robert Bonner, Chauncey Depew, and Joseph Pulitzer, wrote to John D. Rockefeller regarding Rockefeller's negotiations for No. 4. His letter reveals that three years after she had begun her alterations there, Arabella was still adding to her new furnishings. There were, MacRae wrote, "things yet to be unpacked," sitting, one presumes, in crates on the premises.

On June 17 — two months later — Huntington deeded his house at 65 Park Avenue, which had been owned by Elizabeth Huntington until her death seven months earlier, to "Belle D. Worsham," a title transfer that might have suggested much to an alert reporter, including the possibility that Arabella was about to become the official Mrs. Huntington. Several months later, MacRae, in another letter to Rockefeller, mentioned that Arabella "has laid out to live in Mr. Huntington's house . . . at Park Av & 38th Street . . . which she is having entirely altered to suit her." The New York City Alterations Index for 1884 lists Huntington's application for a permit to carry out the work.

Sometime during the spring or early summer of that year, Arabella bought The Homestead, Frederick C. Havemeyer's estate overlooking Long Island Sound at Throg's Neck in the Bronx, for $100,000, according to MacRae, who, as he seems often to have done in his real estate negotiations, represented both parties. Miss Evans writes that Huntington paid $250,000 for the country house and one-hundred-thirteen-acre estate, and that the cost of structural alterations and redecoration, ordered by Arabella, doubled his investment. The Homestead was to become Arabella's and Huntington's legal address. They had already begun to live there at the time of their wedding on July 12, 1884. Alterations at 65 Park Avenue were under way so that the town house would be ready for them to occupy in the fall.

MacRae talked long and often to Arabella during his efforts to sell No. 4 to Rockefeller. Either as a matter of intuition, or simply as a fact that she had confided to him, MacRae came to know that her ultimate goal was to build a palace on Fifth Avenue. On August 12, 1884, a month after the wedding, MacRae mentioned in another letter to Rockefeller that Arabella "now has Mr. Huntington's 8 lots at 5th Av and 81st Street to build on."

Then, in a surprising move, Huntington bought 5 West Fifty-first Street on September 30, 1884, from George Mosle. The house had been designed in 1878 by Detlef Lienau, a prominent New York architect. MacRae, acting as Mosle's agent, had been trying to sell the house to Rockefeller as an alternative to No. 4. Huntington's purchase of the Mosle house put Arabella immediately next door to William H. Vanderbilt, whose great palace between Fifty-first and

Fifty-second streets on Fifth Avenue was one of the wonders of the era.

The following month, on October 24, Arabella, identified in the deed registration as the "wife of Collis P. Huntington of the town of Westchester, County of Westchester," near Throg's Neck, bought nine lots on the northeast corner of Fifth Avenue and Seventy-second Street from John D. and Laura C. Rockefeller for "One Dollar and other good and valuable consideration." The sale had been arranged by MacRae as the first step in a trade-off he had been negotiating for some time. Arabella now had additional Fifth Avenue property "to build on."

Four days later, MacRae arranged for all the parties to sign the contract that would complete the trade-off, and on November 25, Rockefeller bought 4 West Fifty-fourth Street for "One Dollar and other good and valuable consideration." Thus, the trade of properties was concluded. No. 4 had entered a new era, one that would ensure its place among the memorable addresses of New York City.

A question remains: what value should be assigned to the trade? Nevins writes that No. 4 cost Rockefeller $600,000. MacRae advertised that he had resold the Seventy-second Street property — which he had earlier sold to Rockefeller — for $600,000. And in a ledger entitled "Summary: Trial Balance for John D. Rockefeller, December 31, 1888" the value of No. 4 is stated as $515,375.58, and the value of the furniture as $68,000.00 — a total of $583,375.58. The round figure of $600,000 thus appears to be very close to the mark.

One might make a superficial trial balance of Huntington's transactions in the Fifty-fourth Street properties at this point, even though all the figures are not available. Arabella paid $216,000 for her three purchases, and she assumed mortgages of $115,000 — a total commitment of $331,000. To this investment must be added the cost of improvements to No. 4. Here one has available only the *New York World* estimate of $800,000 for "the furnishings alone," an estimate that appears excessive. However, if the figure as originally given to the *World* had been meant to include the cost of structural alterations, it would have fallen within a reasonable magnitude. For want of other data, one is forced to use it as the cost figure for the improvements. Huntington's total investment would thus have been $1,131,-500. The sales of the properties returned $60,000 in cash, and title to properties estimated to have been worth $600,000 (as of 1884) in the real estate market — a total of $660,000. Huntington, on the basis of these available figures, may be said to have "lost" $471,000 overall. His losses may actually have been somewhat less, but it appears almost certain that he came out a loser.

In 1886, Arabella turned her attention to 5 West Fifty-first Street, the former Mosle house whose entrance was but a step west of the doorway to William H. Vanderbilt's art gallery. The alterations index for that year lists Huntington's application for a permit to make structural and other changes there as No. 1542 (a number that suggests the work began during the summer). Among the alterations she made, Arabella had an elevator installed in the house. However, she appears to have changed her mind about living there. Lavender suggests that she and Huntington occupied the house only briefly after the work was completed, returning once again to 65 Park Avenue. Then, on June 14, 1887, they sold the house on Fifty-first Street to Andrew Carnegie for $170,000, plus the cost of the improvements, the title going to Carnegie's wife, Louise. (Carnegie would not start work on his own massive Fifth Avenue palace between Ninety-first and Ninety-second streets until 1899.)

Two years after the Carnegie sale, Huntington bought six lots on Fifth Avenue at Fifty-seventh Street from the children of Robert Bonner, the late editor of the *New York Ledger* and a prominent turfman. William H. Vanderbilt had once tried, without success, to buy the property from Bonner. MacRae handled the sale for the owners: Huntington paid them $450,000 for the lots, which were among the most desirable in the city. The deed transfer was registered May 31, 1889. The purchase indicates that Arabella had decided that neither Eighty-first Street nor Seventy-second Street provided her the setting she desired for her Fifth Avenue palace.[26]

The Fifty-seventh Street intersection of Fifth Avenue — the site of the Bonner lots, which lay on the southeast corner (now occupied by Tiffany's) — had achieved a special distinction on an avenue of costly mansions. There, two blocks below Central Park, Arabella would build her new palace, which would have for its architectural neighbors the great houses built by Cornelius Vanderbilt II (northwest corner), William Collins Whitney (southwest corner), and Mrs. Mary (Mason) Jones (northeast corner), the last a white marble adaptation of a French château designed in 1867 by Robert Mook upon a traditional plan of a central *bloc* and framing end *pavillons*. Mrs. Jones's house was to be memorialized by her grandniece Edith Wharton (née Jones) in *The Age of Innocence*.

George Browne Post had designed Cornelius Vanderbilt II's Louis XIII brick and stone palace, and was then enlarging it to cover the entire blockfront from Fifty-seventh Street to Fifty-eighth Street, where its new main entrance would face the Grand Army Plaza, now known simply as "the Plaza." On December 27, 1889, seven months after Huntington had bought the Bonner lots, Post went to the Department of Buildings and filed his plans for Arabella's addition to the Fifty-seventh Street intersection — her long-rehearsed Fifth Avenue palace.

Two more major purchases rounded out Huntington's great palace spending career. During the spring of 1892, he bought the Colton mansion on Nob Hill in San Francisco for Arabella, and, apparently, during the same year he bought himself a summer retreat, Pine Knot Lodge, in upstate New York. Then, during the winter of 1892–1893, he and Arabella moved into their completed Fifth Avenue residence: 2 East Fifty-seventh Street.

A tradition persists that Arabella, presumably on her own and with her own capital, was a successful real estate speculator. The high period of her real estate operations appears to coincide with the eighteen years between her purchase in 1874 of 68 East Fifty-fourth Street, a singular transaction in which, it will be recalled, she paid her mother $1 for the property, and Huntington's purchase of the Colton house in 1892. The tradition fails in logic, as well as common sense, for it subtracts Huntington from the matter — that is, it ignores his crucial six-figure presence (seven figures in present-day dollars) in, say, Arabella's dealings with Charles MacRae.

There is no clear record of the beginnings of Arabella's Fifth Avenue palace. However, it appears certain that George B. Post was working on the preliminary designs for the house at least three years before Huntington bought the Bonner property. Lavender says that Arabella was involved with the plans by the time she decided in 1887 that she didn't want to live on Fifty-first Street and returned with Huntington to Park Avenue.

Actually, her first choice as architect had been Richard Morris Hunt, the most eminent designer of American palaces in the history of that costly art. In the winter of 1882–1883, William K. Vanderbilt and his wife Alva had occupied the Loire Valley limestone château on the northwest corner of Fifth Avenue and Fifty-second Street, one of the architectural landmarks of the country, that Hunt had designed for them. Arabella must have seen it often, and must have pondered its regal message to the world, its graceful and proud rhetoric.

Hunt's wife, Catherine Clinton (Howland) Hunt, in a memoir written after his death, an unpublished manuscript that forms the centerpiece of *The Richard Morris Hunt Papers, 1828–1895* (edited by Alan Burnham), remarks briefly on Arabella's single encounter with Hunt:

"1886. . . . [Maurice] Fornachon [an architect on Hunt's staff] had bungled his interviews with C. P. Huntington, who had been to the office in regard to a house at the corner of 5th Avenue and 57th, to whom Fornachon had not explained that R[ichard] was coming home [from Paris]. In fact, as soon as he was back, Mrs. Huntington sent for him, but the interview convinced him that they had compromised themselves with George B. Post. Although greatly disappointed, R, with the loyalty which characterized his relations with his brother architects, refused to have anything to do with the work and strongly advised them to let Mr. Post try again, as their complaint was that Mr. Post's original plans were too large."

Despite the fact that Fornachon didn't tell Huntington precisely that Hunt would soon return from Paris, it must have been implicit in the discussion that Hunt wasn't going to stay in Europe forever. The really important fact is that Arabella was in a hurry, so she commissioned Post, who had studied under Hunt, to design the palace (but not, as Mrs. Hunt states, for the Fifty-seventh Street site, which Huntington would not buy for another three years). Mrs. Hunt's memoir also reveals that Arabella didn't like Post's first design, which may have been drawn for the larger area provided by either of Huntington's other Fifth Avenue properties. (It is difficult to discern what role, if any, Huntington played in the design, other than paying for it. Oscar Lewis has written in *The Big Four* that the railroad stations Huntington built in "hundreds of towns and cities in the West," and whose design he personally determined, were "notable examples of unmitigated ugliness." Lewis goes on to quote Willis Polk, one of the most distinguished San Francisco architects of the period, who observed in the middle 1890's: "Mr. Huntington's views on architecture would shame a Digger Indian.")

Post tried again; several times. His plans for the palace filed at the end of 1889 were at first disapproved by the city, for reasons not indicated in the new buildings docket for that year. (The *New York*

Sun of October 19 had already reported the groundbreaking.) Finally, the palace was completed by the winter of 1892–1893.

An English architectural historian has observed that architecture is "an art where censure is more commonly awarded than praise."[27] Perhaps Post has been overcensured for the Huntington palace. But it was, in truth, a very homely building, one that failed in its dubious effort to wed the idiosyncrasy of Henry Hobson Richardson's personal romanesque revival, roughhewn and hearty, with the cool orderliness, the pagan serenity, implicit in the classical aedicular window surrounds, deep and ceremonial, Post designed for two of its three principal stories.

The decorative treatment of windows and doorways as small "rudimentary temples," to use John Summerson's phrase, is a very old practice whose precise beginning has yet to be dated. In a thoughtful and illuminating passage in *Heavenly Mansions and Other Essays in Architecture,* Summerson points out that the practice had its roots in an ancient architectural custom, the creation of *aedicules* (Latin: *little buildings*) — small temples, or shrines — inside large ceremonial buildings. These sometimes took the form of wall niches framed by temple facades, usually holding a statue. India has yielded some of the earliest examples of the practice, which Summerson suspects "is practically as old as architecture itself, and as widespread." Later examples, the stylistic forerunners of Post's surrounds on Arabella's palace, appeared in Roman temples, notably the Temple of Bacchus at Baalbek. With the rebirth of classical architecture in Italy, the aedicular surround became a fixed part of the decorative grammar of Western architecture, but rarely with the brilliance achieved in its use by Michelangelo in the Medici Chapel or the Laurentian Library. By the nineteenth century it had become a pattern-book cliché. A monumental device adapted to dwellings, its ceremonial logic had long been lost, except, perhaps, as it endured in the human unconscious, the original wellspring of the ludic house-within-a-house in Summerson's perceptive view.

In effect, Post tried to impose one style on another — to exaggerate, he tried to force Roman aedicules on a Cistercian monastery. Whatever one may feel about the distinctions of Richardson's bold romanesque style, with its courses of massive stonework, one must admit that he handled his designs with a robust literary swagger. Post lacked flair: he was "interested primarily in the engineering side of architecture," the *Dictionary of American Biography* assures us — his milieu was the large commercial or civic building. He designed a pseudo-romanesque palace with pseudo-classical details for Arabella. Then, he lost the pagan details of the design, its only charm, in a sheath of roughhewn blocks (a complete waste of excellent Indiana limestone). Arabella got, not a temple, not a monastery, but a wayward railroad station for her troubles. But, thanks to Post's cubical massing of its parts, it did look huge.

The inside of the palace merits a moment's reflection. Of its Second Empire interiors, designed by Post, Herter Brothers, and William Baumgarten and Company (Schastey was awarded only the routine carpentry), it should first be noted that Arabella was moving with the contemporary spirit in her oblique search for French eighteenth-century elegance. She had become an openhanded, but not yet very acute, follower of Alva Vanderbilt's French revival movement, a return to the Louis periods in interior design, not as they originally existed but as they had been interpreted in the Paris of Napoleon III and his architect, Hector Lefuel — the Paris also of Pierre Mauguin, the designer of the Hôtel de la Païva, and Charles Garnier, whose masterpiece was the Opera House.

Arabella's American draftsmen (some of them German émigrés) could not match the nonchalant perfection in the work of Jules Allard and his staff in Paris, Alva's decorator at 660 Fifth Avenue (the Régence–Louis XV *salon*), and at Marble House in Newport. Where Post had stumbled in following Richardson on the exterior of Arabella's new palace, he and the Herter and Baumgarten designers had faltered in following Richard Morris Hunt on the interiors. Since the completion of Alva's château at 660 Fifth Avenue in December, 1882, Hunt had made Allard his virtual partner in the execution of the interiors of his great palace projects.

Hunt knew that French *décor* — the imperial opulence of Versailles, the ordered classical charm of the Petit Trianon, the subtle grace of the Hermitage of Madame de Pompadour at Fontainebleau — was extremely difficult to replicate correctly and was almost impossible to adapt without great knowledge and greater skill. As the protégé of Lefuel in Paris, he had learned from a master of interpretation, and as the leading palace architect in America, he had gone back to Paris, to Allard, for the high quality of collaboration he required.

During the first wave of the "period" vogue that Hunt and Allard had launched under Alva's commission, library-shelf *décor* — designs based upon books of French interiors to be found in the offices of almost every New York architect and decorator — became commonplace. Arabella's interiors had the look of the library about them — earnest, pedantic, and graceless; but wearing the air of costliness. It may be said that the Second Empire was the greatest trap of all in the zealous pursuit by clients, architects, and decorators of French *décor* during that era. It was the trap into which Arabella fell. The stodgy splendor of her varicolored marble columns, gilded bronze capitals, and repeated pattern frieze bands (all lacking the handsome vigor of ancient classical models, a vigor which had been sacrificed to the pictorial fantasies of nineteenth-century decorators everywhere) said simply that she was rich. Nothing more.

Hunt seems to have been the only American who truly understood the perplexing opulence of the best decoration of the Second Empire, the time of Napoleon III. He demonstrated this uniqueness in the imperial splendor of the state chambers of The Breakers and Marble House in Newport, the former designed for him in Paris, probably from his own preliminary sketches, by Richard-Hermann-Antoine Bouwens van der Boijen. The principal rooms in these monuments of the age of the American palaces may one day be recognized as of the same rank as: (1) Lefuel's fine *salons* in the Ministry of Finance in "the new Louvre," his theater in the palace at Compiègne, both still standing, and his royal apartments in the Palais des Tuileries, destroyed by the Commune; (2) Manguin's *hôtel particulier* on the Champs-Elysées for the courtesan Thérèse Lachmann, "*later* Mme. Villoing, *later* Mme. la Marquise de Païva, *later* Countess Henckel von Donnesmarck (la Païva)," a succession thus dryly cited by Joanna Richardson in a passage on Mlle. Lachmann (whose *hôtel* today houses the Travellers Club); and (3) Garnier's famous Opera House, the last great court project of the era.

Hunt had been Lefuel's student, and the complete authority of his Second Empire interiors continues to honor his *maître*. It was a style with a rhetoric that suited the vision of the last French emperor, a decorative rhetoric whose exuberance constantly skirted the edge of vulgarity, but one that has never again been matched for imperial *élan*.

It was not a style for the designers in Post's, Herter's, and Baumgarten's drafting rooms — or, for most American drafting rooms. Arabella had aimed at something luminous and splendid: photographs reveal that her decorators gave her, not imperial panache, but heavy-handed imperiousness.

Post had one excellent notion — he had Hunt's protégé, the outstanding Austrian sculptor Karl Bitter, carve the marble frieze in the central court of Arabella's palace, a band that circled the court just below the second-floor gallery. And Arabella commissioned murals for the palace from Elihu Vedder, Edwin H. Blashfield, H. Siddons Mowbray, and Francis M. Lathrop, all of them of the highest rank in American decorative painting at that time. But even their work, except perhaps for that of Mowbray, had a certain attenuation and diffidence in its design and execution. (Arabella's murals are now owned by Yale University.)

Beginning in 1884, Arabella had gradually involved Huntington in art. He accumulated an outstanding collection of eighteenth- and nineteenth-century paintings which Archer Huntington later gave to the Metropolitan Museum of Art. He made his first large purchase at the Mary Jane Morgan sale conducted under the auspices of the American Art Association in 1886. There he paid $25,500 for Item 231, Jean Georges Vibert's anecdotal painting *The Missionary's Story,* a picture that remained his favorite.[28] "I sometimes sit half an hour looking at that picture," he said.[29] He enormously enjoyed imagining the tales the missionary was telling the group of cardinals in the painting. In time, Huntington became so active in the New York auctions that a staff member of one gallery bid for him, and even scouted the market for him, using the code name "Carlos." Arabella appears to have stayed carefully in the background, guiding Huntington's spending.

In 1892, the year the Fifth Avenue palace was completed, Huntington bought the San Francisco mansion of an old railroad associate, David D. Colton, by then deceased, for $500,000. The house stood at the northeast corner of California and Taylor streets on Nob Hill, or "Knob Hill," as the headline on the report of the sale in the *New York Daily Tribune* (May 5, 1892) spelled it. The Colton palace, which had first been occupied in 1872, was faced with wood, cut and painted to simulate stone. Colton had been proud of the fact that the design of the house was based on that of "an Italian palace" — which "Italian palace" no one seemed to know. Arabella's subsequent alterations and redecorating led Huntington to insure the house for $1,000,000.

Also in 1892, Huntington sent his nephew, Henry Edwards Huntington, to San Francisco to manage his western railroad and allied
interests. His absolute trust in his nephew's judgment and his deep
affection for him were to be reflected in his will, in which, as was
earlier noted, he left Henry one-third of his estate.

A body of childish lore has grown up with respect to Huntington
and his Fifth Avenue palace. In it he is treated as a burly giant of a
man who preferred sleeping under the stars to spending the night in
a bed bought in Paris, a cross between Paul Bunyan and George
Hearst. He refused to live in the palace. He lived in the palace, but
every time he sat down, one of the French period chairs broke. And
so on. One might presume from these tractlike fantasies that, as the
years passed, Huntington retreated to the curbstone along East Fifty-
seventh Street in his search for an indestructible seat.

It is true, however, that he did have a favorite among his many
dwellings: Pine Knot Lodge on the shore of Racquette Lake, far
north in New York State in the Adirondack Mountains. He paid
more than $350,000 for the lodge and the forest land around it.
There he could gather his friends about him and relax. J. Pierpont
Morgan visited him there in the summer of 1894, a visit that led
Morgan to establish his own lodge in the neighborhood.

And there, on August 13, 1900, Huntington died.

XII

T HE richest woman in the world."
The facile newspaper phrase may have been rather close to the
mark, for Arabella's share of Huntington's fortune may have been
worth $150,000,000. She herself did her best to prove the description
true during the dozen or so years following Huntington's death,
when she "embarked on an incredible spending spree that . . .
turned her, within a few years, into one of the most important [art]
collectors of her generation. It is a breathless episode when dozens of
masterpieces suddenly appear in the house of Fifty-seventh Street.
. . . The story reaches a rather frenzied climax in 1907, when Arabella spent what must have amounted to several million dollars at
one fell swoop in acquisitions from the great Rudolph Kann Collection that was sold in Paris that year" by Duveen Brothers. The

author of these observations, Robert R. Wark, curator of the Huntington Art Gallery, wonders what caused "this incredible burst of
collecting" which brought pictures by Rembrandt, Hals, Vermeer,
Reynolds, Lawrence, Romney, and Corot into the palace.

It may seem too simple an answer, but Arabella had met another
"great persuader," Joseph Duveen, who taught her the rare pleasure
of owning paintings by Hals, Rembrandt, and Velázquez, the satisfaction of beating princes in the auction room. She was intense and
ardent in her pursuit of such pleasures and satisfactions. No woman
in America, however high her station in society, could match Arabella in these pursuits.

Then, once more proving herself equal to Proust's injunction,
Arabella bought a palace in Paris. During July, 1908, she moved into
the Hôtel de Hirsch at No. 2 Rue de l'Elysée, a vast and sumptuous
residence begun three years after the fall of the Second Empire and
completed over the next decade at a total cost that may have exceeded $25,000,000 in equivalent modern value.

Arabella had moved into history and onto the dreamscape of
Proust's epic memory world, for her new *hôtel particulier* had direct
associations with the Marquis Pierre de Beurnonville, a Girondist
leader who had built a *maison privée* on its site on the eve of the
Revolution, the Empress Eugénie, who had renovated and redecorated de Beurnonville's house, and the Baron Maurice de Hirsch de
Gereuth, a capitalist and philanthropist whose elegant and memorable receptions in his private palace (into which he had absorbed
Eugénie's *petit hôtel*) had served the generation of the Commune as
a long rehearsal for the *belle époque* — there, in a *salle des fêtes*
designed to accommodate two thousand privileged guests, the Princes
d'Orléans, the Prince de Galles, the great aristocracy of France, the
Prince of Wales (preparing for his role as Edward VII), the visiting
nobility of Europe, and the senior members of the international
banking families that kept them solvent, gathered to celebrate, and
insure, their historic dispensation.

Eugénie had bought No. 2 in 1861, a year after the Rue de
l'Elysée, formerly a *passage* through the gardens of the Palais de
l'Elysée, had been opened as a public street reserved for residential
use. And although she never lived there, she considered it to be her
demeure particulière (her personal house, as differing from the
Palais des Tuileries, the imperial residence). She had the painter
Jourdan decorate one of the rooms in the house — the Petit Salon

Bleu — with four large pictorial panels, one of them showing the ill-fated Prince Imperial dancing with other young children, a scene of wistful charm.

The neighboring houses at No.'s 4, 6, and 8 were occupied by the nobility, the Vicomte Aguado, a member of a Spanish family very close to the empress, and the Italian ambassador among them, and by Eugène Rouher, Napoleon III's minister of state. Further along the garden street lay an odd range of houses with "flying" front steps crossing above basement entrance wells *à la mode londonienne,* a reflection of the *vogue anglaise* the emperor had helped to stimulate.

During one period, Eugénie installed her mother, the Comtesse de Montijo, in No. 2, and at another time she leased the house to her beloved friend Anna Murat, the Duchesse de Mouchy. Then, following the death of the emperor in England in 1873, she had Rouher sell the house to the Baron de Hirsch.

Hirsch was an enormously rich man whose grandfather had been the first Jew to own land in Bavaria and to have been ennobled. He inherited great wealth, he married great wealth (his wife, Clara Bischoffsheim, was a daughter of the leading Belgian banking family), and his large investments, principally in railroads, yielded him a steady leaf-fall of gold, no matter what the season.

He moved to Paris after the collapse of Napoleon III, and on June 27, 1872, he bought the Château de Beauregard from the Duchesse de Bauffremont for 850,000 gold francs. Hirsch immediately restored the grounds and the château, which had served as a fortified German army headquarters during the siege of Paris.

The year following, he bought No. 2, and in consequence of secret negotiations he was able to add to his property the land between No. 2 and the Avenue Gabriel along the Rue de l'Elysée. The two purchases cost him 6,200,000 francs. (The published account of costs relating to the Hôtel de Hirsch are ambiguous: one cannot be certain whether the amounts shown refer to gold or silver francs.) In a final negotiation, Hirsch purchased No.'s 4, 6, and 8.

He then commissioned architect Léon Chatenay to design the great *hôtel* that was to absorb No. 2, and extend parallel to the Rue de l'Elysée behind his other three houses (which were to serve as a family enclave whose rear courts would provide access to the Hirsch stables — facilities that provided for the stabling and care of twenty-one horses).

The house that Arabella bought had many architectural and decorative distinctions. Its monumental limestone and marble stairway, an *escalier d'honneur* that cost more than 1,400,000 francs to construct and decorate, was designed by another architect, Emile Peyre. The completion of the last of its carved stone details — statues, basins, lyre-profile balusters — was dated 1883. It is unlikely that another staircase of such astonishing scale was created anywhere else in a private house at the close of the nineteenth century.

The inner court, which measured about sixty-four feet by forty-three feet, gave access to the main entrance of the palace. At its far end, opposite the double carriageways leading to and from the Rue de l'Elysée, there was (as the plans reveal) a special entrance for "M. Lucien," the Hirsches' only child.

In the large winter garden on the second floor hung what Germain Seligman has with deliberate care described as a "unique" set of four tapestries woven at Beauvais about 1703, "a royal command — a gift to the Comte de Toulouse, natural son of Louis XIV, from his mother, the Marquise de Montespan." Only this single set of the tapestries, designed by Berain and woven with added threads of gold and silver, was ever executed. (Jacques Seligmann bought them at auction from the estate of the Baroness de Hirsch before Arabella occupied the house. Today they hang in the Banque du France, which occupies the Hôtel de la Vrillière, the house for which they were originally woven.)

The dining room walls were fitted with *boiseries* taken from the Château de Bercy, which had been built by the architect Francois Le Vau in 1670 and razed in 1860. They included overdoor panels painted by Coypel and Monnoyer. These treasures of eighteenth-century decorative art in the style Régence (a stylistic dating made in a monograph on the house published in Paris two years before Arabella moved in) cost Hirsch 90,000 francs.[30]

In other rooms of her *hôtel*, Arabella could look upon *boiseries* removed from the Hôtel d'Evreux on the Place Vendôme, and the Hôtel de Chanaleilles on the Rue de Chanaleilles.[31] It is possible that she herself may have installed one or both of the latter sets of *boiseries* during her refurbishing of the house. She had made a striking advance into the past, the authentic past of French decoration, a costly paradox.

Her *hôtel* had a Petit Salon Louis XIV, a Salon Louis XIV, and a Grand Salon Louis XVI, all executed with consummate authority. The old Petit Salon Bleu had been preserved as the baroness's dressing room. Eugénie visited the Hôtel de Hirsch after her son had been killed in 1879 while fighting with the British army in the Zulu War, and she was deeply moved when she saw again in the blue dressing room the Jourdan painting of the Prince Imperial as a child.

The great receptions at the Hôtel de Hirsch came to an abrupt end in 1887 with the unexpected death at thirty years of age of Lucien Hirsch. The baron and baroness entertained only intimate friends, and relatives, thereafter. They adopted two young men and a young woman, and devoted their lives principally to their charities. Together they gave away more than $80,000,000, mainly to the Jewish Colonization Society and, in America, to the Baron de Hirsch Fund. Maurice Hirsch died in 1896 and Clara Hirsch in 1899. Lady Randolph Churchill wrote of Hirsch that he "was one of the few millionaires I have met who knew thoroughly how to enjoy himself."[32] A fortunate quality, and one, perhaps, that helped him persevere against the wave of anti-Semitism that rose in consequence of the Dreyfus Affair. He himself was viciously caricatured by Gyp, and, as Philippe Jullian has noted, "the figure of Julius Herzen, whose struggles to enter high life are portrayed in Paul Bourget's novel *Cosmopolis*" (1893) , was based on Hirsch.[33]

Arabella's purchase of a monument that led her into the world of French palace art, authentic and resonant of history, was dutifully observed by the press. On March 27, 1908, the *Oakland* (California) *Tribune* reported that she had paid $300,000 for the Hôtel de Hirsch, and was spending $100,000 on renovations. The *American Reporter* on April 4 said that when the changes she had ordered were completed, the *hôtel* would be "one of the most perfect models of classical architecture in Paris," a statement that might have surprised M. Chatenay and M. Peyre, but not M. Chauvin.

The *Boston Morning Herald* reported that the palace had been "entirely redecorated" and that "certain structural alterations" had been made. One would like to know the details of these projects, but the record is silent. The only thing certain is that Arabella modernized the house, at least to the extent of installing fourteen bathrooms.

Arabella had only recently celebrated her fifty-eighth birthday when she moved into the great house on the Rue de l'Elysée. "Her tastes are quiet and her mode of living has been rather reserved," the *New York World* had observed a short time earlier. While awaiting the completion of the bathrooms, she lived at the Bristol Hotel, "where she always retains the royal suite," the *American Register* noted. It is from such a mosaic of news reports that one must attempt to reconstruct Arabella at that moment of her life.

Once she had moved into No. 2, she could look eastward across the gardens of the Palais de l'Elysée to the Avenue de Marigny. Napoleon III had once secretly made his way through the gardens to a gate that gave onto the avenue. From there he had only to take a few steps to the gate that let him into the garden of Miss Howard, whose house faced on the Rue de Cirque. But that was before the emperor's generous English patroness had been forced to yield Louis-Napoleon Bonaparte to Eugénie de Montijo.

Suddenly, for reasons beyond conjecture, Arabella abandoned her Paris palace. About nineteen months after she moved in, she sold the house to the Comte de Pourtalès, according to a report in the *New York World* of March 19, 1910. The account said that she had decided to sell "as the result of a recent flood." There had, indeed, been extensive flooding of the area in January. The great boulevards were under water and the gardens of the Palais de l'Elysée were a lake. Torrential rains had driven the Seine beyond its banks, and "the Paris basin" had resumed its prehistoric appearance. Then the waters retreated and Paris, used to catastrophe, mopped up. But Arabella moved on.

Whatever the reason for it, the sale mattered but little, for another French *palais* lay ahead for Arabella. And this time Duveen and his favorite decorator, Sir Charles Allom, would be there to ensure that the solecisms of Post, Baumgarten, and Herter would not be repeated. Nor would Arabella, after living with the Château de Bercy *boiseries,* accept less than perfectly studied and executed details in decoration and architecture.

Myron Hunt's pencil would be graceful where Post's had been ponderous. The new palace was to be a monument to an autumnal romance. It was a romance ardently pursued by Henry Huntington, and ultimately accepted by Arabella. Huntington's courtship was already proceeding when Arabella lost interest in her grand *hôtel particulier* in Paris. It had, in fact, been remarked by the press four years earlier.

XIII

Social New York was greatly excited last night by the rumor that the widow of Collis P. Huntington was about to marry Henry E. Huntington, the favorite nephew of her late husband."

The rumor appeared in newspapers across the country on Sunday, April 8, 1906. It had probably been set off by the fact that Huntington's wife had divorced him just two weeks earlier. Arabella denied the rumor to "a correspondent who called on her in her New York home last night." She was dressed, the reporter noted, in "a magnificent black lace gown" and wore "a pendant of pearls and small diamonds hanging from a chain about her neck."

Collis Huntington had been dead for six years, but Arabella remonstrated with the reporter: "Why, as you see, I am still in mourning for my husband." And besides, she added, "Henry E. Huntington is my late husband's nephew." The reporter let the non sequitur expire of its own foolishness.

When he was shown copies of the New York dispatches at the Jonathan Club in Los Angeles, then his residence, Henry Huntington merely said, " 'Huh.' " However, "he said it so vigorously . . . [and] with such a snort, half a laugh of disgust, that his glasses fell off." He felt constrained to add: " 'Absolutely without foundation. It's on a par with other stories about me.' " One might paraphrase Whistler and say it takes truth a long time to look like its rumor. Arabella and Huntington were to be married seven years later.

Henry Huntington had been born in Oneonta, New York, on February 25, 1850, the year after his Uncle Collis had left for California. Collis Huntington ultimately found in his nephew the son he never had. And Henry Huntington revealed precisely those abilities — diligence, efficiency, loyalty, and intelligence — that Collis needed in a right-hand man. After serving his uncle for two decades in the construction and operation of his network of railroads east of the Mississippi River, Henry, as has already been noted, moved to San Francisco in 1892, taking along his wife and four children. Henry Huntington there became the eyes and ears of his uncle in the management of the Southern Pacific Company, the holding company for the Central Pacific and Southern Pacific railroads. Collis Huntington was the president of the company and Henry Huntington became its vice-president. Shortly, Henry began to invest heavily in the street railway systems of San Francisco and Los Angeles.

The unexpected death of his uncle in 1900 brought a profound change to Henry Huntington's life. He had been well-to-do; now he was one of the richest men in the United States. He left his wife, moved to Los Angeles, and there began his remarkable career as the visionary developer of that city. He had married Mary Alice Prentice in 1873. Mary Alice was an older sister of Clara Prentice, known from infancy as Clara Huntington, whom Collis and his first wife had raised as their daughter but whom, it will be recalled, they had never formally adopted. Clara had married Prince François-Edmond-Joseph-Gabriel Vit de Hatzfeldt Wildenbourg, the son of the German ambassador to England, in 1889. (The *Topeka State Journal* in a one-sentence news report once dryly advised its fellow Kansans: "The son-in-law of the late C. P. Huntington has arrived in the United States, bringing his entire name.")

Collis Huntington had objected to paying the prince the *dot* of several million dollars the marriage contract required. But Arabella, serving as Clara's romantic advocate, had persuaded him to. In his will Collis left Clara only $1,000,000. She protested this slight, and Mary Alice sided with her. However, Mary Alice's sisterly concern served only to provoke her husband, who had inherited one-third of his uncle's residual estate, an amount possibly one hundred and fifty times greater in value than Clara's legacy.

The dispute seriously aggravated some deep difference between them that Huntington and Mary Alice had, up to that time, abided. Finally, on March 3, 1906, Mary Alice sued for divorce, charging desertion. Huntington, who had been living in Los Angeles for at least four years, denied the charge but did not contest the action. Mary Alice won her decree in seven minutes and thirty seconds. Their four children were, by that time, all adults, and three of them were married.

On his way to San Francisco in 1892, Henry Huntington had visited Los Angeles. While there he had stayed overnight at J. de Barth Shorb's ranch near Pasadena. Shorb called his ranch "San Marino," the name his grandfather had given to the family plantation in Frederick County, Maryland. His grandfather, for reasons long forgotten, had taken the name from the ancient Italian republic. Shorb's house, a Victorian mansion with mansard roofs, "high ceilings, and extensive and wide verandas," commanded "a splendid view of the San Gabriel Valley to the south, and of the mountains to the north and east."[34] Sitting on the Shorb veranda, Henry Huntington was a man bemused by a vision of Eden.

Six years after he arrived in San Francisco, he began to buy into the Los Angeles transit system. Then in 1902, two years after Collis Huntington's death, he and Arabella, whom he undoubtedly advised in such matters, sold their large interest in the Southern Pacific Company to E. H. Harriman, whose Union Pacific Railroad thus gained the controlling interest (45.49 percent) in Collis's old empire.

One career ended, Henry Huntington started a second: the development of modern Los Angeles. The years from 1902 to 1910 were the busiest of his life. He bought control of the Los Angeles streetcar system and completely overhauled and expanded it, providing a transportation grid upon which the city could grow. He then established an interurban transit system of high-speed electric cars that linked the ocean to the mountains and provided the node points for a cluster of satellite communities. He bought vast tracts of land for urban and suburban development, and built the electric power generating and distribution systems necessary to support the growth he foresaw.

Huntington was obsessed by his concept of a vast city, and his obsession prevailed. In the first decade of this century, Los Angeles grew three hundred percent. By 1908, Huntington started to retire, and by 1910 he sold his interurban transit company, withdrawing from the day-to-day operations of his ventures. He was, of course, dead long before his lovely, open, sunlit city became overwhelmed by the untidy fantasies of men with meaner schemes who in time turned it into the world's first inhabited freeway.

XIV

P ERHAPS his most characteristic trait is an infinite capacity for waiting," a contemporary account observed of Huntington.[35] And nothing he ever undertook better demonstrated his methodical patience than his development of San Marino. There he set out to create an Eden of books, architecture, art, and gardens. He had no blueprint, but he had that disciplined mode of thought which slowly and continuously brings order to the shifting, tenuous images of desire. During his years in San Francisco he had begun casually to buy books for those reasons that lie at the heart of collecting: rarity and beauty. But he could not possibly have foreseen that he was to become an awesome figure in the New York auction rooms, the most formidable bidder in the historic book sales that preceded World War I.

His career as an art collector began as casually. In 1901 he bought three colored prints from a well-known New York art dealer simply because they pleased him: *The Blue Boy, Mrs. Siddons as the Tragic Muse,* and *The Pink Boy.* In June, 1903, he again bought a group of colored prints, and among them, once more, were the same three pictures. Eventually, he bought the originals of *Mrs. Siddons* and *The Blue Boy* from his favorite art dealer, Joseph Duveen. His purchase in 1921 of *The Blue Boy* — Gainsborough's portrait of Jonathan Buttall — was, because of Duveen's robust affection for publicity, the most extensively reported art purchase of the era. The portraits of the youth and the distinguished actress became part of Huntington's growing collection of Georgian masterpieces, the finest in America. It seems unlikely that Huntington had had so remarkable a catalogue of English portraits in mind on the day in 1901 on which he bought his first three colored prints from William Schaus in the dealer's Fifth Avenue gallery on Madison Square.

The story of his purchase of *The Blue Boy* not only reveals the way his goals as a collector took focus only gradually in Huntington's mind, but it also tells us much, perhaps too much, about Duveen. During his long career, the great Anglo-American dealer fostered an elaborate body of iconographic lore in which he portrayed himself as an urbane, witty scholar-connoisseur while denigrating the intelligence, taste, knowledge, and sincerity of his clients.

Duveen pretended that the first time Henry Huntington ever saw *The Blue Boy* was in the summer of 1921. He and the Huntingtons were crossing to Europe on the *Aquitania.* One evening Arabella invited Duveen to dine with them. During dinner, Huntington noticed a reproduction of the Gainsborough portrait on the wall of the dining *salon.*

" 'Who's the boy in the blue suit?' " he asked Duveen — according to Duveen.

The Duveen recollection of the conversation that ensued is a banal invention. In it, Huntington is made to appear a fool, with the especially dreary naïveté of the American parvenu, while Duveen is made to appear shrewd, with the tolerant cunning of a worldly art merchant, who instantly laid the groundwork for a dazzling $600,000 sale. No icon in the Duveen galleries shone with more byzantine a splendor than that of the *maître* himself. And Duveen was, in the end, its most credulous admirer.

Oddly, it is Huntington, the victim of Duveen's superciliousness, who reveals to us something of the dealer's humorless pursuit of sales. Henry Huntington in his black suits and black hat, a man of grave courtesy, gave the world a false impression. He loved jokes and savored a particularly good one long after he heard it. James Thorp, the director of the Huntington Library and Art Gallery, has related in a short memoir on Huntington that "Duveen [once] received an invitation from Pola Negri to attend a party for movie people at the Ambassador Hotel [in Los Angeles]. He was flattered and eager to accept, but he was uncertain as to whether the movie people were in a position to buy paintings; he hated to waste an evening where his salesmanship could not be exercised.

"Mr. Huntington, sensing the fun, assured him that the movie people had all the money there was, upon which Duveen gladly accepted. For Duveen, the evening was an utter and absolute failure: the talk was about who was prettier than whom and who would get which part. When he tried to sell paintings, he was asked to bring a supply suitable for hanging over fireplaces, for about $150 — which was some three zeros below his trading range. . . . Huntington heard the account the next morning with much amusement, and several times afterward he asked the abashed Duveen what further invitations the daily mail was bringing from his movie friends."

No one knew better than his rich American clients precisely where Duveen stood: as far to the left of the decimal point as possible.

XV

HUNTINGTON bought the five-hundred-and-fifty-acre Shorb ranch in January, 1903. In December, 1904, a San Gabriel Valley neighbor and business associate, George Smith Patton, Sr., the father of the hero-general, hired a young gardener, William Hertrich, to work on Henry's new estate. For almost a quarter of a century, Hertrich and Huntington worked together, creating decorative gardens and botanical collections that ranked among the finest of their kind in the world. Hertrich's memoirs constitute a record unique in America of the development of a great estate.

Almost from the beginning of his southern California ventures it was clear that Huntington intended to build his final home at San

Marino, a decision he arrived at after considering two other sites, one in Los Angeles proper and the other nearby on another choice elevation looking out across the San Gabriel Valley. Two years *before* Huntington's divorce, E. S. Code, a civil engineer with the Southern Pacific Railroad, made the first sketches — rough plans and elevations — for a house at San Marino. Code made another set a year later (1905). A wash rendering signed "A. T. L." made at that time suggests that what Henry had in mind was a large frame house, an American adaptation of a Georgian country house exemplified by Crossways, the summer home built by the railroad millionaire Stuyvesant Fish at Newport. Crossways is best remembered as the stage from which Mamie Fish issued some of the wittiest and most scathing *mots* of the Victorian twilight. One feature seen in A. T. L.'s rendering remained through all the subsequent permutations in design: the large veranda extending along the main axis of the house, its roof supported by classical Doric columns.

(That summer, Arabella was absorbed by a matter far more compelling than Henry's architectural planning. She was subpoenaed by the prosecution in the sensational trial of Colonel William D'Alton Mann, the blackmailing publisher of the weekly scandal magazine *Town Topics,* to whom she had made "loans" of at least $15,000. The prospect of testifying under oath on the loans alarmed her, and, alerted by her lawyer, she fled during the night from The Homestead at Throg's Neck just before the process server arrived.)

During 1906, the year after the rendering for the new house was completed, Huntington carried his plans a step further: he had the old Shorb house dismantled. He had decided to site his new house precisely as Shorb had done, overlooking the valley. That year his wife divorced him, and Arabella lost her San Francisco palace in the earthquake and fire that devastated the city. About a year later in a transparent gesture of courtship, Huntington had two tall palms that had stood near Arabella's former palace uprooted, transported to San Marino from San Francisco, and replanted. Arabella gave the land on Nob Hill on which her mansion had stood to the city to be used as a children's park. It was a friendly symbolic quitclaim: Collis, Henry, and now Arabella were done with the city.

In 1907, something happened to Huntington's thinking about the house at San Marino. He stopped his amateur groping and commissioned an outstanding Los Angeles architect, Myron Hunt, to design a palace-*manoir* of a relatively modest compass in the mountain setting; large, but not vast. It now became clear that Huntington had long since decided that his Eden would be incomplete without Arabella, for Hunt's preliminary sketches grew under her watchful eye, and his final designs for his scheme were to be drawn in her Fifth Avenue palace.

Huntington had undoubtedly known Arabella from the years when she was listed in the *New York City Directory* as Bell D. Worsham of 109 Lexington Avenue. Which is to say, he had first seen her when she was in the full bloom of her uncommon beauty. They were of an age. They shared certain general tastes. But Arabella was bold, whereas Huntington was restrained; she was anxious, whereas Huntington was patient. Arabella was sophisticated, cosmopolitan, at home equally in Paris and New York. Huntington had never been outside the country. He might, indeed, have become a collector, but Arabella had a native inclination toward the accumulation of very expensive art and she had acquired the nuance and subtlety of a connoisseur.

About a dozen years earlier, at the time Arabella was completely redecorating her San Francisco palace, Collis Huntington had provided his nephew with what turned out to be an unintentional forewarning. Collis, of course, had had to deal endlessly with the contractors, decorators, and suppliers concerned — and with the exacting demands that Arabella made upon them. One day in a letter to Henry, he had been, perhaps a bit testily, moved to observe: "Belle, as you know, is exceedingly particular."

Henry Huntington was about to bear the burden of this costly truth.

XVI

AT the moment that Myron Hunt was making his preliminary sketches for the palace at San Marino, Arabella was having the most extravagant of her multimillion-dollar seasons in the Paris auction rooms. Duveen Brothers, in a very daring coup, had bought the Rudolph Kann Collection in its entirety, an extravagance urged by Joseph Duveen, the youngest of the partners, that could have damaged the firm financially. Part of the investment of about $4,600,000 was paid by the Paris dealers Gimpel and Wildenstein. The Duveens early on proposed to buy out their partners in the venture. "They were such cumbersome and monopolistic associates that we decided to accept," René Gimpel, the husband of one of Joseph Duveen's sisters, remarked in his diary. Gimpel and Nathan Wildenstein accepted $500,000 to release their option on the paintings in the collection.

Count Hector Baltazzi, the uncle of Baroness Maria Vetsera who had been found dead at Mayerling with the Imperial Archduke Rudolph, brought Arabella to the Duveens. Her purchases alone assured the Duveens the recovery of their large investment in the Kann collection. The grateful firm paid Baltazzi some $50,000 for his services. It seems likely that Arabella met the count in the ruritanian wonderland of drifting, courtless nobility, and quasi-nobility, abundant in titles but lacking funds, which centered on Paris early in the century. Arabella herself had been introduced into this world of deceptive nobiliary conceits by her nominal stepdaughter, Clara, the Princess Hatzfeldt de Wildenbourg, a model of solvency. Very shortly — a little more than a year after her great purchases from the Rudolph Kann Collection — Arabella was to buy and refurbish her double mansion in Paris.

One can appreciate Henry Huntington's problem: even were he to persuade her to visit there, how could he possibly hope to keep Arabella on a fruit ranch in California? His strategy centered on the house. And, thus, his problem devolved upon Myron Hunt.

THREE

XVII

W HEN he got his commission from Huntington, Myron Hunt was thirty-nine years old. In common with his college classmates, he had once grown a mustache in order to appear older than he was. But whereas his fellow students shaved off the disguise after graduation, Hunt continued to cultivate his. Finally, his self-assurance increasing, he began to go clean-shaven. And he developed, along with his solid professional reputation, a certain élan. A rich Californian had come to him and asked him to design and build a house *in eight months.* The man said that he would be in Europe on an extended vacation during that time and wanted to move into his new mansion when he returned. Hunt thought the proposal frivolous. He turned the man down.

However, when Huntington, always sober and meticulous in his dealings with others, approached him, Hunt looked to his dignity. "Dad always claimed [his son recalled] that he traded-in our third-hand Willys-Knight on a brand new Columbia Knight — a very swanky car with the appearance of a bathtub — in order to impress Mr. Huntington with the fact that here was a successful architect." Huntington, of course, was already convinced.

Hunt had been born in Sunderland, Massachusetts, on February 27, 1868. Once he had determined upon a career in architecture, he followed a rigorous course of study at Northwestern University (1888–1890) and the Massachusetts Institute of Technology (1890–1892). Then he worked in the offices of architects in Boston and Chicago (1892–1894) and, finally, studied in Europe.

When he started his professional career in Chicago, Hunt had shared the urge for fundamental changes in American architecture that was then stirring his young contemporaries. He fell in with a group that gathered informally around Frank Lloyd Wright to discuss and argue the new directions a native architecture should take. He and Wright, along with George W. Maher and Dwight Perkins, two others among the Chicago pioneers who are much admired today, were charter members in 1895 of the Chicago Arts & Crafts Society, an outgrowth of "the aesthetic movement" begun in England by William Morris. Wright later called the youthful Myron Hunt "my most enthusiastic advocate." But Hunt was his own man, a thorough professional who was never limited by the Calvinistic aridity at the heart of the aesthetic theory of "modern" architecture, a theory that degenerated first into metaphysics, then into academicism.

Hunt moved to Pasadena in 1903 to accommodate his first wife's failing health.[36] He and Elmer Grey, another architect from Chicago, formed a partnership which they were amicably to dissolve on October 1, 1910. Hunt was something of a preceptor by nature — he wrote little but lectured often, and his office became a school in which a number of Los Angeles architects trained. He might be severe, but he quickly tempered his severity. "Hunt could give you a real tongue-lashing," Walter Steilberg, a San Francisco architect and consulting engineer, has recalled. Steilberg served as "a very junior draftsman" in Hunt's office in 1904 before he rejoined Julia Morgan in San Francisco, later going on to a long career as a consultant. "Hunt would give me hell, then a little later say, 'Come on, we'll go look at some houses.' And he'd get me an ice cream soda, a real treat in those days. You know, I wonder where young architects today get the kind of apprenticeship they got with Miss Morgan and Myron Hunt."

Hunt was to have a distinguished career in every aspect of architecture. The range of his projects indicates the wide range of his art: the buildings and campus plan of Occidental College, the Greek theater and music hall at Pomona College, the Rose Bowl, the Ambassador Hotel in Los Angeles, the Santa Barbara and La Jolla art galleries, the First Congregational Church in Riverside, as well as country clubs, hospitals, orphanages, housing projects, courthouses, libraries, banks, commercial and industrial buildings, and vast army and navy facilities. The palace at San Marino was only one of many residences, large and small, most of them bearing some mark of architectural distinction, that came from his drafting room. He loved landscaping: Italian planning and English planting were his ideals. Harold Coulson Chambers, Hunt's partner from 1920 until the latter's death, recently emphasized a peculiar gift that Hunt delighted in: "Myron loved earthwork. He was clever — extremely clever — in moving and handling earth. He liked natural swales, and his own grades looked like they simply had grown that way."

One searching through photographs and drawings of his houses, as well as his larger structures, tentatively concludes that Hunt did not have a *style,* a design trademark. But in the great variety of his work one does find uniformly a highly intelligent professional presence, one that invents freshly from the terms of the requirements. In his address to the Royal Institute of British Architects upon receiving the King's Gold Medal, the distinguished American architect Thomas Hastings observed: "The problem solved makes style."

Of such was Hunt's style.

XVIII

Hunt's commission contained an unwritten but overriding specification: it became his mission to lure Arabella to San Marino. The peculiar complexities of this responsibility led him to design one of his most graceful improvisations (a word that fits exactly his variation on a classical theme). "She was a difficult woman," Chambers has recalled of Arabella. "She was intelligent and had good taste, and, I think, she had a sense of humor, even though most people never noticed it. I'll admit it was a special kind of humor — like that incident about her telling the reporter she was still in mourning all that time after Collis Huntington was dead. He never knew she was pulling his leg.

"If I remember correctly, Myron went to New York almost as soon as he started working on his original sketches. He lived at the Metropolitan Club and all the discussions were held at her house at Fifth Avenue. He worked up the sketches in the office of a New York architect who was an old friend of his. Used their draftsmen.

"Mrs. Huntington probably had stacks of books and magazines with pictures of houses she liked — a mixture of things, I'm sure. You can go through the architectural magazines of 1906, 1907, and 1908 and find many houses in the East, some of them tremendous, that were very similar to the Huntington house in their general style. Finally, Myron probably had to say, 'All right, I understand what you want.' I remember he came back with the sketches and they remained substantially the same. There is a pen-and-ink rendering of the house made about that time. Elmer Grey drew it. I think it was one of the last renderings he did before the firm broke up."[37]

The house was French, and classical: Beaux-Arts in spirit and authority, and American in sinew. It was derived from urban prototypes adapted to country use. The tile roofs, with their shallow slope, are Mediterranean. The house was designed with a horizontal emphasis — long and low, its third story concealed, in the French tradition, behind a neoclassical balustrade. It was meant to sit firmly against the mountains; aristocratic but not severe. The plan is a cleverly resolved adaptation based upon an axial hall scheme that charmingly suggests both French and English antecedents. A study of the plans reveals that the axial hall does not separate two ranges of rooms, as one might expect it to, but rather links the principal rooms to a handsome bay that houses a great double-flighted staircase.

If one were determined to find a stylistic predecessor for Hunt's overall design, one might profitably examine the French house that John Russell Pope designed for Dr. and Mrs. Henry Barton Jacobs at Newport, completed in 1904. Whiteholme, the Jacobs house, was "regarded as one of the outstanding examples of Louis XVI architecture in the United States."[38] The Jacobs veranda, with its columns engaged to rounded piers at the corners, may be seen in an extended version at San Marino. The two houses shared a common decorative vocabulary, although the Jacobs house (now destroyed) was of stone, and the Huntington house of stucco. Pope's garden portico had a monumental look with two-story columns, pilasters, and corner quadrants; Hunt's terrace portico held these details to a single story, thus evoking a sense of measure — of personal scale.

No one has described the San Marino palace better than Porter Garnet writing in *Sunset, the Pacific Monthly,* in July, 1914:

"I hesitate to use the word 'magnificent' in describing Mr. Huntington's residence, for the term may so easily convey a wrong impression. Standing long and white and low against its background of soaring mountains, it attracts the eye by reason of its classical reserve, stateliness, and dignity. Through the possession of these qualities, rather than the quality of showy splendor, it may be said to be the most truly magnificent residence in the whole of California."

The design, by Myron Hunt, "exhibits a peculiarly interesting and happy solution of the problems presented in building a modern structure of the classic type. . . . One feels that, modelled as it is upon prescribed lines, an element of creative design rather than mere copying or adaptation has gone into its construction. I do not know whether or not Mr. Hunt is a Beaux-Arts man [he wasn't], but I should be inclined to think that he is, because the Huntington residence is precisely the sort of thing a Beaux-Arts man (with individuality) would produce."

The project was a large one, and it attracted lively interest among architects and construction men. In April, 1908, Hunt enlarged his offices and drafting room, probably to handle the enormous volume of detail work that would presently be required. Huntington renamed the ranch, calling it "Los Robles," a name one finds in the weekly reports in the *Southwest Builder,* a construction magazine, and in Hunt's office records. However, within a year, Huntington reverted to the original name, San Marino.

A construction gang from Huntington's Pacific Electric Company excavated the site. "It was impressive . . . to see eight horses hitched to a heavy road plow . . . loosening . . . the hard clay soil . . . for most basement excavations would not be large enough to accommodate a plow, let alone a plow and horses that could be turned about at will," William Hertrich has recalled in his memoirs. The span of the house was to be two hundred and seventy-five feet, the *Southwest Builder* announced.

All contracts — those for the reinforced concrete skeleton, the fabric of the house, the plumbing, the electric wiring, the heating, the finishing and so on — were split up by Hunt to hurry the work along for his patient, but eager, client. Huntington indicated to Hunt as early as 1908 that he was anxious to complete the house. He was getting old — and so was Arabella. That October, Huntington had taken Elmer Grey to New York with him. Grey spent a week working on the interior designs with Arabella; inconclusively, one may assume from subsequent events. Then, a month later, Hunt himself made his second visit to New York on the project to meet with Arabella and to try to wind up the exterior details. There was a sense of urgency in these transcontinental consultations. During the construction period that followed, Hunt often rode on horseback from his house at 200 North Grand Street in Pasadena to the construction site in San Marino to keep things moving.

Harold Chambers recalled not long ago the probable reason for Henry Huntington's wish to get the palace built, finished, and furnished: his strategy was working. "We all thought that Mr. Huntington was going to marry Mrs. Huntington when Myron got back from New York in 1908. I remember that when Myron told me about it, I was surprised. I asked him *why* he wanted to marry her. 'He loves her,' Myron said, and he was a serious man about things like that, so I dropped the matter."

The *décor* remained unresolved. Then, Arabella turned to Duveen for advice. He, in turn, brought in Sir Charles Allom's firm, White Allom Ltd., his subcontractors on many famous decorating projects. Apparently, Duveen got approval to go ahead with work on the interiors in January, 1909. The formal contract for the finishing of the principal rooms of the main floor was let to Duveen Brothers in May. White Allom sent models of the rooms from London to Arabella in New York.[39]

However, once the models were approved, the work seemed to bog down. Huntington wanted to get into the house in January, 1910. When it became apparent, as the year wore on, that the interiors could not possibly be installed in time, Hunt had to send his general superintendent, J. L. Hillman, to London to expedite completion of the paneling, column sheathing, and other interior woodwork. One day during the confusion of delays (not all of them the responsibility of White Allom), a cablegram arrived in Hunt's office from Duveen in London. "Considerable changes" would have to be made in the interior designs. Duveen had just led Huntington into his "first really major art purchase . . . the great set of Beauvais tapestries, called the 'Noble Pastoral,' from designs by François Boucher." They were "among the finest eighteenth century tapestries in existence," and had come from the Kann Collection.[40]

The *Southwest Builder* had reported that the library of the mansion was to measure sixty-five feet in length, with a width of thirty-three feet at one end and forty-two feet at the other — an "L" configuration. The dimensions suggested that Huntington would have well over a thousand feet of shelf space for his growing collection of books. Now, he had yielded most of the space to the Boucher tapestries. Arabella's hand may have guided this significant change: her palace, her interiors. Chambers, who was not concerned with Duveen's sale, and the subsequent redesigning of the library, has remembered how astonished he was the day the tapestries were hung: "They fitted inside the molding of the hardwood panels within an eighth of an inch!" They had cost Huntington almost as much as the house.[41]

By the end of 1909 the woodwork had started arriving from London in sealed tin crates, built to protect the work against the sea air. Alexander Black came over from England to supervise its installation. Some of the white woodwork required ten coats of paint, each coat hand rubbed with pumice. Henry F. Bultitude, a draftsman-designer, came from White Allom's New York office, which had been opened in 1905, to oversee the final execution of the London designs. Bultitude, who would soon establish his own decorating firm in New York under the uncommon rubric "Interior Architecture," had only recently completed some work for the Duke of Marlborough. As had the duchess, Consuelo Vanderbilt, Bultitude had found the duke a highly disagreeable man.

White Allom's interiors for San Marino, like those the firm designed for William Randolph Hearst at St. Donat's Castle in Wales, for Edward Townsend Stotesbury at Whitemarsh Hall, and for Henry Clay Frick on Fifth Avenue, were based upon historic precedent, both English and French, and they were executed with high skill. Arabella was well satisfied with the interiors, and with the palace that Hunt had designed for her.

Elmer Grey's pen-and-ink rendering of Hunt's design, executed, as Chambers recalls, sometime during 1910 before Hunt and Grey dissolved their partnership, reveals to us a major change in the grand scheme that may have disappointed Hunt. In the drawing, a handsome ensemble of marble stairs framed by balustrades leads, in the style of Italian renaissance ramps, down the slope in front of the paved terrace that runs along the garden facade. When the palace was built, the garden stair ramps were eliminated. It is said that Arabella and Huntington, both of whom were sixty in 1910, decided they were too old to climb the steps.[42]

XIX

MYRON HUNT had done his work well, bringing subtlety and distinction to Arabella's newest palace. And Joseph Duveen had added to its treasures a historic set of Boucher tapestries. One cannot doubt the allure of the tapestries for Arabella, for she herself may well have cabled Huntington to let him know they were available from Duveen, and thus urged him to buy them. Huntington's strategy, protracted though it had become as the result of Duveen's cunning maneuver, was being carried out with superb style. (How nice, one might reflect, that Duveen had been able, with consummate concern for the interests of both parties, to serve his old clients, Huntington and Arabella, equally, and at the same time to turn a decent profit.)

Huntington could only have felt reassured when, in 1910, Arabella decided to sell her great *hôtel* in Paris. Not long after the sale the press reported that she would return to New York, and, further, that she planned to make her first visit to southern California. "While here," an Oakland newspaper advised its readers, "she may pay a visit to the costly new home of Henry E. Huntington . . . which is to be completed in June." But 1910 passed, and not only was the house not completed, but Arabella did not visit San Marino, or any other place in California.

Then, in 1911, "a change in family plans" further delayed the completion, and occupancy, of the house.[43] We know Huntington's intentions, for San Marino is his eloquent witness. Of Arabella's intentions we know nothing, except what one may care to deduce from her stubborn wish not to be hurried. Huntington persisted, and cables and telegrams continued to arrive at San Marino from Arabella telling him what other treasures Duveen had for sale — messages that tend in their terseness to sound like orders. Belle had remained "exceedingly particular."

In 1912, William Hertrich, Huntington's able landscape gardener who was charged with the development of San Marino's extraordinary botanical gardens, as well as the completion of the formal garden closer to the house, found the time available to go to New York and there serve as a judge in a national flower show. San Marino was becoming an overrehearsed theater piece, a Victorian charade.

Apparently, Huntington never discussed his difficulties in courting Arabella. He had no confidant, no one to whom he could express his frustration, if, indeed, he felt frustrated. He may, however, have unconsciously referred to his problem with Arabella in a conversation with Maurice Ettinghausen, from whom he sometimes bought books. Ettinghausen in his memoirs, *Rare Books and Royal Collectors,* writes:

"I had the opportunity for some private chats with Mr. Huntington [at San Marino], and I asked him what was his favorite manuscript in his collection. He at once replied, 'The letter [dated July 20, 1819] which Charles Lamb addressed to Frances Kelly, the actress, in which he proposed to her.' Mr. Huntington also owned Miss Kelly's reply, written the same day, refusing Lamb's offer."

XX

Finally, Arabella was willing.

In May, 1913, she left for Paris. The following month, Huntington, making his first trip abroad, followed her there. Then, on July 16, 1913, they were married in the American Church in the Rue de Berri. "The wedding," the *Los Angeles Times* reported, somewhat absentmindedly, "was entirely unexpected."

Huntington promptly completed negotiations with the Baron de

Forest (one of the Baron de Hirsch's adopted sons) for the lease of the Château de Beauregard, the handsome country palace that "Miss Howard" had built half a century earlier. Arabella probably knew that Miss Howard was the mysterious Englishwoman who had become Napoleon III's patroness and most favored mistress until his marriage to Eugénie de Montijo. However, she could not have known that Miss Howard had carried to her grave the secret burden of a daring lie. At the Château de Beauregard in Saint-Cloud on the outskirts of Paris on the way to Versailles, Arabella's own lie may have seemed, for the moment, a bit less threatening than it had in New York.

During their honeymoon, Huntington and Arabella visited other châteaux and gardens in the environs of Paris. Huntington was unimpressed. He wrote home to his estate superintendent: "I tell you, Hertrich, I have seen no place as nice as the ranch." But, during the ten years of his marriage to Arabella, he would see relatively little of the Eden he had so patiently developed — never, apparently, more than ninety days in any year, and usually fewer than that.

On January 5, 1914, the *Los Angeles Herald* announced that "Huntington and his bride" were due to arrive in the city on January 10. On January 9, the *Los Angeles Express* said they would arrive in February. On January 17, the *Herald* reported that they were in Newport News, Virginia, and that Arabella had given that city a $200,000 memorial statue of Collis, who had established the largest shipbuilding yards in the United States there.

On January 23, they arrived at San Marino. Unfortunately for Huntington, they were met by a large crowd, and Arabella was utterly "dismayed." So annoyed (or frightened) was Arabella that ten weeks later she and Huntington left for "a year in Europe." There is no reason to assume that Henry Huntington was not happy in the large personal sacrifices he made to please Arabella. He had long adored her.

Which is to say, he understood Arabella, and accepted gladly her whims, which she had spun upon an armature of gold, her own large fortune. One wonders, of course: did Huntington know her secret? Had he known, when he was much younger and was then running a division of his uncle's Chesapeake and Ohio Railroad . . . had he known that Johnny Worsham was still alive, and still very well known, in Richmond, the city in which Collis Huntington had carried off his purchase of the C & O? A city which, in fact, Henry

Huntington may have come to know fairly well himself. The answer lies in the mausoleum he and Arabella share at San Marino.[44]

In time, Huntington built another palace at San Marino, the Huntington Library, an enduring tribute to that most fugitive of human enterprises, intelligent thought. And with characteristic care and thoroughness he arranged to devise the renowned library and his house (now the Huntington Art Gallery) to the public in the care of trustees, and he further provided $8,000,000 to ensure the proper maintenance, use, and growth of these remarkable institutions. There was something fundamentally classical in the equilibrium of his grand scheme for the purchase, the cataloguing and preservation, and the endowment for public use in perpetuity of his rare treasures.

The historian Oscar Lewis has observed that Huntington made San Marino "one of the world's most important storehouses of the literature and history of the English-speaking people." If Arabella, in her great years as a collector-patron, became the American equivalent of Madame de Pompadour and Isabella d'Este, then Huntington must be accounted a latter-day Medici prince for his achievements in the Florentine humanist tradition.

Although his large purposes were marked by care and gravity, Huntington could be witty, even droll, a singularity he once chose to display under somewhat grim circumstances. In the autumn of 1925, he entered the Lankenau Hospital in Philadelphia for prostate surgery. Just before the operation he called to his bedside the two men who had profited most from his collecting, Duveen — by then Sir Joseph Duveen — and Dr. A. S. W. Rosenbach, the prominent book dealer–scholar, who had sold Huntington some of the rarest and finest, as well as the costliest, of his books and manuscripts.

Rosenbach's biographers, Edwin Wolf II and John F. Fleming, assure us that there "was no love lost between these two giants." They then go on, with urbane glee, to reconstruct for us the joint visit of the dealers to Huntington's bedside:

> When the nurse announced that Mr. Huntington was ready to see them, the two men soberly entered the room. Huntington lay on the bed in his hospital shirt, his head only slightly raised and his two arms extended. With a slight motion he pointed to chairs on either side of the bed. . . . The two dealers sat stiff in their chairs, looking at Mr. Huntington and each other and uttering words of encouragement in a manner . . . far from

encouraging. Suddenly, Huntington, rather amused . . . turned to Duveen and asked, "Sir Joseph, do I remind you of anyone?" Nonplussed, Duveen answered, "Why, no, Mr. Huntington, I don't believe so." Then he turned his head toward Dr. Rosenbach. "Tell me, Doctor, do I remind you of anyone?" The Doctor, quite as much at a loss as Duveen, muttered that he really did not know. "Well, gentlemen," said Henry Huntington, still lying flat with his arms outstretched, "I remind myself of Jesus Christ on the cross between the two thieves." The Doctor and Sir Joseph smiled weakly.[45]

Early in 1927, Duveen made his last trip to San Marino, arriving there with "two special express cars literally loaded with fine [French] items: fine porcelain; statuettes of marble, bronze, terra cotta; and exquisite pieces of furniture and tapestries."[46] It was a remarkable inventory of French art. Duveen had assembled it in large part from the discriminating purchases he had made at the recent sales of the Alfred de Rothschild, Lady Carnarvon, and George J. Gould collections. Huntington spent a week examining everything that Duveen had brought. He finally purchased a complete carload in a "mammoth transaction [that] worked a noticeable strain on [his] somewhat precarious health." It was "definitely the largest transfer of art goods" Duveen had ever made to Huntington, Hertrich later recalled. On February 27, 1927, Gimpel wrote in his diary: "Last month Joe sold $4 million's worth to Henry Huntington." Duveen accepted some land near San Marino in partial payment.

The new collection was installed in the library building as a permanent exhibit, *in memoriam*, honoring Arabella. Together with the art that Arabella had herself installed in the palace, the French decorative art to be seen today at San Marino, in its quality, range, and balance, ranks high among the finest collections to be found outside France. The work of Oudry, Boucher, Carlin, Riesener, Saunier, Gouthière, Caffieri, Houdon, Falconet, and others among those whose luminous mastery lay at the heart of "one of the most refined and sophisticated episodes in the whole chronicle of European civilization," may be seen there.[47] Robert R. Wark, the curator of the Huntington gallery, and the author of an appropriately graceful summing up of the achievements of French decorative art in the eighteenth century, quoted in part above, believes that the "uniform standard of excellence" of the collection stands not only as a hand-some tribute to Arabella, but that it honors as well Duveen's "genu-ine artistic judgement and devotion to enlightened collecting."

In the spring of that year, with the new collection in place and his plans for San Marino as a public trust well advanced, Huntington returned to Philadelphia — to the Lankenau Hospital. A second operation was performed on him, but cancer had taken its fatal toll. Rosenbach, who had, with a gourmet's special concern, overseen the preparation of Huntington's food until the end, telegraphed San Marino on the night of May 17, 1927, to tell the library staff that the great collector had died. He was seventy-seven.

Huntington's body was carried back across the continent which had once been spanned by his uncle's railroads. In California his train was met by a troop of Boy Scouts. They were far too young (and far too excited by Charles A. Lindbergh's arrival in Paris only a few days earlier) to understand the symbolism implicit in the cere-monial tolling of the locomotive bell throughout the removal of Huntington's casket from his private car — they were listening to a *dies irae* for an era.

When Henry Huntington died, the country was astonished by the magnitude of generosity his obituaries revealed. He had once told Rosenbach that "the ownership of a fine library is the . . . surest way to immortality." At the time of his death, his library was "the largest ever gathered together by a single man in the United States." And it so remains.

XXI

ARABELLA had died three years earlier on September 14, 1924, in her Fifth Avenue palace after a lingering illness brought on "mostly by old age." (She was seventy-seven.)

She had been in Paris a year or so before her death — it may have been her last visit there — and she had dropped in at the old Palais de Sagan, the splendid house which Jacques Seligmann had long owned, and in which he had established the last of his galleries. Arabella had often called there, despite Duveen, who would exercise any threat, or deceit, to prevent his customers from buying from any other dealer. However, Seligmann was no longer there to greet her: he had died in

October, 1923. Arabella, now old and infirm, was calling on his son, Germain. She had known the younger Seligman since his father, on a visit to the United States, had first brought him to her Fifth Avenue palace to meet her, a visit which had left the young man awed and nervous. In his urbane and charming memoirs, a superb account of a life in art that is filled with perceptive observations and reflections, Germain Seligman (who had long since dropped the second *n* of his patronymic) recounts with sympathy and warmth Arabella's last visit to the Palais de Sagan:

> She had just dropped in to say hello, she said, as she was no longer in a buying mood and had everything she wanted to own. She was in her seventies by then, but still carried her unusual height with a splendid bearing. I seated her in one of the rooms opening onto the garden where we chatted for a while and then, with no other thought than to please her, I showed her a number of objects of a type which I knew she enjoyed, among them a delightful little marble Venus by Falconet. Looking at me somewhat reproachfully through thick-lensed glasses, she said, "You really shouldn't go to so much trouble for me. You know my sight has become so bad that I can hardly see anything." Whereupon she leaned forward for a closer view of the little figure, not over a foot high overall, and exclaimed, "What a lovely thing. Isn't it a shame that the little finger of the left hand is broken!" I couldn't help bursting into laughter as I congratulated her upon her bad eyesight, for the whole hand was certainly not over half an inch long. Almost before I did she threw her head back in a hearty laugh.[48]

Arabella then added that, although she was not really interested in buying, she wondered what the price might be — she liked to keep up with such matters. Seligman named a price, and Arabella promptly bought the costly little figure.

By the time Arabella was purchasing her last Falconet in Paris, John Archer Worsham had been dead for forty-five years. The Palais de Sagan had been the silent witness of many ironies, but surely none of them could have yielded so wry an incongruity as that which Arabella's presence there suggested.[49] Is it possible (one might ask) that the sumptuous vision that had led her to Paris in search of Carlin, Boucher, and Houdon, and their peers among the masters of the decorative ambience of France in the eighteenth century, had first been inspired by the offhand luxury of a Civil War gambling parlor in Richmond, Virginia?

Johnny Worsham belongs in a southern ballad, a lament sung in the lowering evening and filled with ancient modal echoes:

Johnny Worsham . . . he died poor.

FIVE

SHADOW LAWN

V-1

V-1 Shadow Lawn: south facade. Pencil rendering, c. 1927–1928. Horace Trumbauer, architect, and Julian Abele, chief designer. Courtesy of Mrs. Helena S. Fennessy.

V-2 The first Shadow Lawn. Built by John A. McCall, president of New York Life Insurance Company. First occupied in August, 1905. From *The Architectural Record*, vol. 16 (1904). Courtesy of the Avery Architectural Library, Columbia University.

V-3 The second Shadow Lawn. From *The Versailles of America — Shadow Lawn*. Courtesy of Clarence W. Withey.

V-4 Aerial view. Maysie's solarium penthouse is clearly visible at the right end of the roof. Courtesy of Monmouth College.

V-5 West formal gardens, designed by Achille Duchêne. From *The Versailles of America — Shadow Lawn*. Courtesy of Clarence W. Withey.

V-6 North portico. From *The Versailles of America — Shadow Lawn*. Courtesy of Clarence W. Withey.

V-7 North elevation. Horace Trumbauer, architect, and Julian Abele, chief designer, 1928. Courtesy of the Historical Society of Pennsylvania.

V-8 South elevation. Horace Trumbauer, architect, and Julian Abele, chief designer, 1928. Courtesy of the Historical Society of Pennsylvania.

V-9 First-floor plan. Courtesy of Monmouth College.

V-10 Second-floor plan. Courtesy of Monmouth College.

V-11 Achille Duchêne, one of the most distinguished French landscape artists of the century. From *La vie à la compagne* VII (March 15, 1910).

V-12 Duchêne's rendering of his *"Première Solution"* for the grounds at Shadow Lawn. Courtesy of the Historical Society of Pennsylvania.

V-13 Cortile, first Shadow Lawn. Henry Edward Cregier, architect. From *The Architectural Record*, vol. 16 (1904). Courtesy of the Avery Architectural Library, Columbia University.

V-14 Cortile, second Shadow Lawn. From *The Versailles of America — Shadow Lawn*. Courtesy of Clarence W. Withey.

V-15 Music room. From *The Versailles of America — Shadow Lawn*. Courtesy of Clarence W. Withey.

V-16 Reception room. From *The Versailles of America — Shadow Lawn*. Courtesy of Clarence W. Withey.

V-17 Shadow Lawn: sphinx and *amorino* limestone statuary group (one of a pair). Courtesy of Monmouth College.

V-18 Versailles: sphinx and *amorino* marble and bronze group (one of a pair) by Lerambert and Sarrazin, at entrance to the south *parterre* at Versailles. From van der Kemp, *Versailles*, Paris, 1970. Courtesy of Editions d'Art Lys.

V-19 Shadow Lawn: Ionic capitals with pendant festoons on north portico. Courtesy of Monmouth College.

V-20 Versailles: Ionic capitals with pendant festoons. From Bourget and Cattaui, *Jules Hardouin-Mansart*. Paris, 1960. Courtesy of Editions Vincent, Fréal et Cie.

V-21 Shadow Lawn: sunburst mask of Apollo. Courtesy of Monmouth College.

V-22 Louis XIV *prie-Dieu* with sunburst mask of Apollo. From Strange, *French Interiors, Furniture, Decoration, Woodwork & Allied Arts*. London. Courtesy of B. T. Batsford Limited.

V-23 Shadow Lawn: *entrelac* balustrade, showing foliar carving. Courtesy of Monmouth College.

V-24 Petit Trianon, Versailles: *entrelac* balustrades. West elevation of the Petit Trianon. Drawing from *The Petit Trianon, Versailles* by James A. Arnott and John Wilson, New York, 1929.

V-25 Shadow Lawn: peristyle-colonnade and exedra designed by Achille Duchêne in collaboration with Horace Trumbauer. From *The Versailles of America — Shadow Lawn*. Courtesy of Clarence W. Withey.

V-26 Versailles: the colonnade in the Bosquet. Assumed to have been designed by Hardouin-Mansart. Photograph by Robert Descharnes from *The Versailles I Love*. New York, 1959. Courtesy of Tudor Publishing Company.

V-27 Number 72 Avenue du Bois de Boulogne. Photograph by Henry Sorenson, Paris. Author's collection.

V-28 Hubert Templeton Parson. Courtesy of F. W. Woolworth Co.

V-29 Horace Trumbauer and Mrs. Eleanor Elkins Widener at Harvard University. Courtesy of Mrs. Helena S. Fennessy.

V-30 Julian Abele and Horace Trumbauer. Courtesy of Mrs. Helena S. Fennessy.

V-2

The first Shadow Lawn:
"all vocabulary and no
rhetoric."

V-3

The second Shadow Lawn.

V-4

Aerial view from the
south.

V-5

West formal gardens.

V-6

North portico.

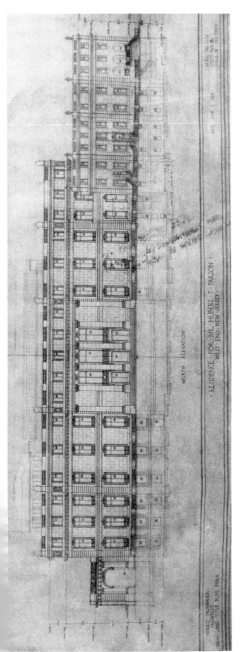

NORTH ELEVATION

· RESIDENCE · FOR · MR · HUBERT · T · PARSON ·
WEST · END · NEW · JERSEY ·

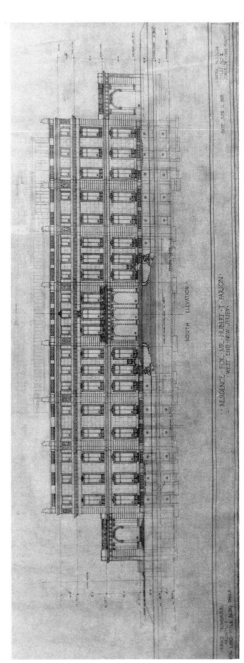

SOUTH ELEVATION

· RESIDENCE · FOR · MR · HUBERT · T · PARSON ·
WEST · END · NEW · JERSEY ·

" 'It's going to look like a municipal building.' "

V-7

V-8

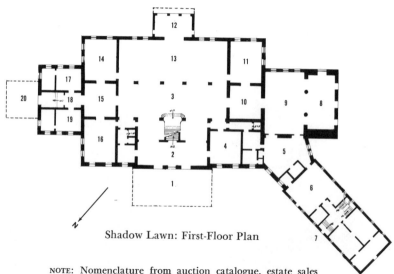

Shadow Lawn: First-Floor Plan

NOTE: Nomenclature from auction catalogue, estate sales brochure (see bibliography for Shadow Lawn), and Clarence W. Withey. Partially conjectural. Only known set of plans by Horace Trumbauer, architect, stolen from Historical Society of Pennsylvania in 1974.

1. North Portico [Main Entrance]. 2. North Foyer [Entrance Hall]. 3. Great Hall [Cortile]. 4. Billiard Room. 5. Pantry. 6. Kitchen. 7. Servants' Rooms. 8. Conservatory. 9. Dining Room. 10. West Rotunda. 11. Morning Room. 12. Sun Room [Loggia]. 13. Reception Room. 14. Library. 15. East Rotunda. 16. Music Room. 17. Ladies' Cloakroom. 18. East Foyer [Carriage Entrance Hall]. 19. Men's Cloakroom. 20. Porte Cochère.

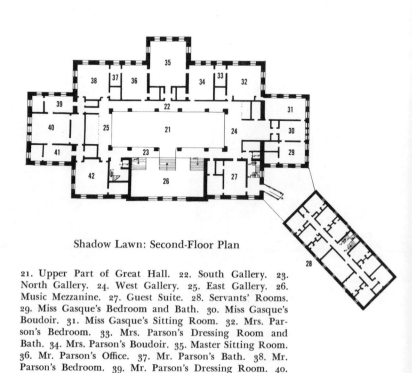

Shadow Lawn: Second-Floor Plan

21. Upper Part of Great Hall. 22. South Gallery. 23. North Gallery. 24. West Gallery. 25. East Gallery. 26. Music Mezzanine. 27. Guest Suite. 28. Servants' Rooms. 29. Miss Gasque's Bedroom and Bath. 30. Miss Gasque's Boudoir. 31. Miss Gasque's Sitting Room. 32. Mrs. Parson's Bedroom. 33. Mrs. Parson's Dressing Room and Bath. 34. Mrs. Parson's Boudoir. 35. Master Sitting Room. 36. Mr. Parson's Office. 37. Mr. Parson's Bath. 38. Mr. Parson's Bedroom. 39. Mr. Parson's Dressing Room. 40. Guest Bedroom. 41. Guest Dressing Room. 42. Guest Suite.

V-11

Achille Duchêne

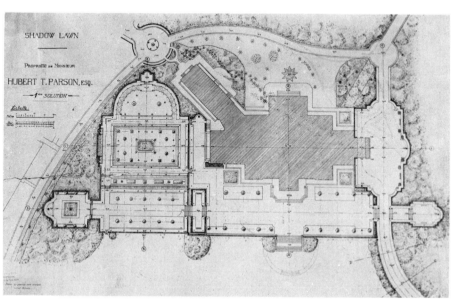

V-12

Duchêne's "Première Solution."

V-13

Cortile, first Shadow Lawn.

V-14

Cortile, second Shadow Lawn.

V-15

Music room.

V-16

Reception room: "Coherence eluded Maysie . . ."

V-17

Shadow Lawn:
sphinx and *amorini.*

V-18

Versailles:
sphinx and *amorini.*

V-19

Shadow Lawn: Ionic capitals
with pendant festoons.

V-20

Versailles: Ionic capitals
with pendant festoons.

V-21

Shadow Lawn: sunburst mask of Apollo.

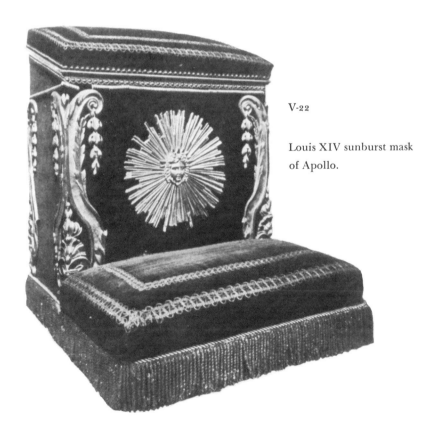

V-22

Louis XIV sunburst mask
of Apollo.

V-23

Shadow Lawn: *entrelac* balustrade.

V-24

Petit Trianon, Versailles:
entrelac balustrades.

V-25

Shadow Lawn: peristyle-colonnade and exedra.

V-26

Versailles:
the colonnade in the Bosquet.

V-27

"... the Parsons and Miss Gasque lived in Paris in a splendid
hôtel particulier."

V-28

Hubert Templeton Parson.

V-29

"If it hadn't been for her, he
would have backed out."

V-30

"Shadow Lawn was their farewell to an age."

> Don't part with your illusions; when they
> are gone you may still exist, but you have
> ceased to live.

Mark twain's wintry epigram was quoted as the thought for the day on Wednesday, September 11, 1929, by the *Wall Street Journal,* the lay breviary of those devoted to that most transcendent of American illusions, the capital share. It was the time of year — the week following Labor Day — during which Hubert Templeton Parson, his wife, Maysie Adelaide (Gasque) Parson, and his wife's sister, F. Bertha Gasque, usually returned to Fifth Avenue from their Paris residence.

While he was away during the summer of 1929, Parson had received a copy of the August issue of the *Magazine of Business* containing an article entitled "What 40,000,000,000 Sales Have Taught Us." Parson was the nominal author of the article. What forty billion sales had taught him personally, a matter he did not discuss with his readers, was that he had become rich enough during his long career with the F. W. Woolworth Company, which he was then serving as president, to own three palaces and to live in Paris each summer with the freehanded indifference to cost of a visiting monarch. (During one of his seasonal visits to Paris, his private secretary passed along to him, via cable, a verified offer of $500,000 in cash for his Fifth Avenue palace. Parsons didn't even bother to answer the cable.)

Between automobile trips into the French countryside in one of the two Rolls-Royces they took abroad with them each year, driven by one of the two chauffeurs they also took abroad, the Parsons and Miss Gasque lived in Paris in a splendid *hôtel particulier.*[1] There they were protected by a handsome wrought-iron fence and partially surrounded by small gardens whose extent was limited, but whose subtlety of design revealed the distinctive mark of Achille Duchêne. The four-story limestone palace, which Parson had constructed several years earlier, but hadn't actually *built* (an ambiguity that will be examined presently) , stood along the northern service zone of the Avenue du Bois de Boulogne, which would be renamed Avenue Foch later that year.

The avenue, a garden-boulevard-promenade which had long been admired as one of the historic monuments of town planning, still displayed in its flower beds, equestrian *allée,* pedestrian *allée,* wide bands of sward, and bordering trees and shrubs — all symmetrically disposed on gentle gradients on either side of a great axial carriage-way — much of the imperial elegance it had first revealed to the lost world of the Second Empire in 1856 under the name Avenue de l'Impératrice.[2]

The celebrated Palais Rose, built by the Marquis Boniface de Castellane with money given to him by his wife, Anna Gould, and consecrated in 1914 by the Curé de Saint-Honoré d'Eylau, stood only a short walk east of Parson's *hôtel* on the same side of the avenue, with its entrance on the Avenue de Malakoff. There on a great stair-case adapted by the architect Paul-Ernest Sanson from drawings of the Escalier des Ambassadeurs, which once had stood at Versailles, Boni and Anna sometimes received two thousand guests at an afternoon reception.

"I took a cab to go to the Prince de Guermantes's house, . . . a magnificent mansion that he had recently built in the Avenue du Bois," Proust's narrator recalls in *Remembrance of Things Past* in a passage describing an afternoon party given by the Princesse de Guermantes a year after World War I, only several years before Parson arrived on the avenue. And although the narrator is disturbed by the fact that his host has left his ancestral *hôtel* in the Faubourg Saint-Germain ("the enchantment cannot be decanted from one vessel to another") , the prince's move to the Avenue du Bois has conferred, as Proust meant it to, a certain distinction on that great promenade.

Parson, had such been his aim, could not have chosen a more sympathetic *mise en scène* in which to present himself to his Paris neighbors, should they, in turn, have cared to notice him. But those Parisians — members of *le gratin:* the upper crust — who, given other circumstances, a different owner, say, might have crowded the *grand salon* of Parson's impressive *hôtel,* or have gathered in the greater intimacy of its *salon de compagnie,* were, in fact, completely unaware of Parson's presence in the city. It was not that they ignored him (which they would have, in any event) , but simply that they were

somewhere else in the summer, as anyone of their status and presumed means would be.

A confidant of his has recalled that Parson "never bothered to
learn a word of French." Given the implications of such indifference,
it is unlikely that he would have bothered, either, to learn that the
gratin quietly left the city each year following the running of the
Grand Prix de Paris at the Hippodrome de Longchamps, the celebrated racecourse in the Bois de Boulogne, on the third Sunday in
June, and that they stayed away — at Deauville, in the mountains, at
family *manoirs* and châteaux — until it was time to return to Paris
and prepare for the *grande saison*. Nor would Parson have understood the significance of the drawn shutters on the *maisons privées* of
those families of the *gratin* whose country places had been sold or
closed because of financial stringency, but who, nonetheless, pretended to the world to be away for the summer.

Parson was a man whose rather dull singularities are worth remembering only because of the consequences of his perverse gifts. He
had an odd competence for being in the right place at the wrong
time, for doing the right thing the wrong way, for pushing small
foolishness to great absurdity, and for arming himself against good
sense with an impenetrable shield of stubbornness. It was his misfortune to have had more than enough money to exercise these strange
gifts without restraint.

Parisians in general, with their tolerance for eccentric behavior,
might have been amused, if only briefly, by hearing about Parson.
He was a humorless parvenu whose wardrobe came from an excellent
tailor, James W. Bell of lower Fifth Avenue, but who managed somehow (perhaps by wearing too large and bright a carnation in his
lapel) to give to those who would later remember him the impression that he had just stepped away from a pari-mutuel window.

He had already spent more than $12,000,000 in an obsessed search
for grandeur. However, his opulent palaces remained hauntingly
silent: his *salons* and gardens were never known to echo to the music
of a ball or the unguarded conversations of delighted guests, good
friends familiar with his vast hall and imperial staircase.[3] It would
have been difficult, perhaps impossible, to have explained Parson, the
master of three palaces, all of them empty alike of great ceremony
and regular receptions, to any Frenchman, for an empty palace is a
stage without actors, a failure of logic.

To Gallic sensibility, with its renewing memories of eighteenth-century *gloire,* Versailles is the archetypal palace, the conceptual model of what a palace should be. And Versailles without its ritual throng, without the liturgical clamor of the king's *cortège* arriving from Marly in the marble entrance court, or without the daily ceremonies of the most privileged of its retinue, attending the king at his morning *levée* in the royal bedchamber or fidgeting at cards as the sputtering candles burned down toward midnight, is an intolerable notion.

For Versailles was, above all things else, the theater in which Europe witnessed the debut of modern France. There, upon an armature of play, Louis XIV slowly created a nation. Its company of players — nobles, state ministers, visiting royalty, ambassadors, and the king's architects, landscape architects, painters, sculptors, cabinetmakers, playwrights, and musicians — was Versailles' *raison d'être.* All had a rôle: the drama was the making of France.

In the French mind, the image of Versailles trembles with life and the tumult of history. Parson on a sudden whim once invited an employee at Shadow Lawn to see a home movie of the house on the Avenue du Bois. "It was interesting because we all wondered what the place looked like," the man has recalled. "But it struck me as very odd — there wasn't a soul to be seen in that huge house, or outside either." Parson, the monarch of silence, might have tempted the comprehension of the French, if only as an American curiosity, but in the end they would have thought him witless.

Nor would an Englishman have understood his want of guests, for the country house implied the presence of visitors. In 1624, Sir Henry Wotton had instructed his countrymen in a much quoted little book, *The Elements of Architecture,* to look upon a country manor as "Everyman's proper *Mansion*-House and Home . . . the *Theatre* of his hospitality." Guests were almost a matter of canon, as well as courtesy. However, like J. Alfred Prufrock, Parson was meant merely "to swell a progress," not to create one.

He would have been unnerved by the graciousness of the Duc and Duchess de Gramont, who entertained more than ninety thousand guests over the years in their *hôtel particulier* in Paris at the corner of the Champs-Elysées and the Rue de Chaillot, a house that stood only several hundred yards east of Parson's house, past the Arc de Triomphe. (Had he walked to the *hôtel* of the Gramonts, Parson would have passed Hittorf's ring of Second Empire apartment residences at the Arc de Triomphe in one of which Alva Erskine Smith had lived as a girl during the Civil War before she became the most distinguished of women palace builders in America, first as Mrs. William Kissam Vanderbilt, then as Mrs. O. H. P. Belmont; and continuing east along the Champs-Elysées he would have come to the *hôtel* long occupied by Mrs. William Astor, the doyenne of the Patriarchs and the Four Hundred, when she came to Paris for the season.)

Remembering her parents' famous hospitality, Elizabeth de Gramont wrote in her memoirs in the late 1920's: "I have kept a vivid memory of the house, perfumed with flowers, gilded and glittering with light, one turmoil of charming people."[4] There Consuelo Vanderbilt, Alva's daughter, and Anna Gould, both of whom were to become mistresses of notable palaces but who were then just being introduced into society in Paris, London, and New York, danced one evening during the *petite saison* shortly before Easter in 1898.

When he completed the fourth and last, as well as the largest and costliest, of his palaces, Parson had a housewarming. He and Maysie met their guests in their one-hundred-and-ten-foot-long *grand salon,* a ceremonial chamber that opened along one side into their one-hundred-and-ten-foot-long cortile, a great hall that rose almost seventy feet through two levels of surrounding galleries to an amber inner skylight lit by one hundred and sixty-five concealed bulbs.

Later that evening, Parson entertained his guests with a film — another home movie, shown by a professional projectionist on one of a pair of theater projectors installed in tandem in his theater-ballroom, a basement chamber large enough to seat an audience of more than three hundred. The invited celebrants numbered "only eighteen in all," a figure remembered four decades later by one of those present, a guest who felt constrained to add: "It was embarrassing. A very strange evening. But that was Parson."

II

On October 11, 1889, Frank Winfield Woolworth wrote a reflective letter to his store managers. A severe illness had warned him that he could no longer run his growing chain of five- and ten-cent stores by himself. "In New York," he wrote, "it [will] be necessary to have a good man responsible for the finances of the company, to take charge of the employees and the office, and see that the books are properly kept."[5]

About two and a half years later he saw a "job-wanted" listing in the *New York World* that interested him. It had been placed there, at a cost of five cents, by H. T. Parson. Woolworth interviewed Parson, and learned that he had been born on September 18, 1872, in Toronto, Ontario, one of three sons of Harry Edwin Parson. Twelve years before Parson was born, his father, once described by the *New York Times* as "a wealthy oil operator," had lost his "fortune."[6] The family moved to Brooklyn when Parson was a boy. He went to Boys' High School, learned bookkeeping, and got a job with the Atlantic Chemical Company for $4 a week. He then became a partner in a chicory importing venture. The partnership failed when chicory was put on the "free list" under the McKinley Tariff Act of 1890.

Parson was nineteen, eager, and ambitious when Woolworth called him in. He was a short, stocky, and somewhat swarthy young man: his large, heavy jaw suggested stubbornness and determination, and he carried his chin high with an air of hauteur. He had a rare gift for handling and ordering numbers, and a photographic memory. Woolworth was impressed by him. The Woolworth chain was then twelve years old; it had fourteen stores and four executives. "What do you think you can do for the company?" Woolworth asked Parson. "Anything you've got for me to do," he replied.[7] Woolworth offered him $8 a week, but Parson wanted $12. He started to work the next day at $12. He was Woolworth's first bookkeeper — "the first career financial man in the organization," a company booklet later observed. His intense, but cool, diligence appealed to Woolworth. Within six years, Parson was running the New York office. He was the "good man" Woolworth needed.

Parson's rise was steady; it coincided with the extraordinary growth of the company. Some of Woolworth's early partners, his brother Charles Sumner Woolworth and Fred Morgan Kirby among them, started their own five 'n' dime chains to meet the tremendous demand that Frank Woolworth's innovation had created. In 1905, Woolworth's years as the paternal sole owner of his company came to an end: the days of employee tea parties in his backyard and conventions of store managers in his parlor were over. A corporation — F. W. Woolworth & Co. — was formed, and Parson was elected its secretary, a member of its executive committee, and a director. Then, on January 1, 1912, the corporation was combined with five other five-and-ten companies, American and British, to form the present F. W. Woolworth Co. Frank Woolworth had opened his first store, a failure, in 1879 with $300 worth of goods bought on credit; the new international corporation was capitalized at $65,000,000 (oddly enough, the estimated probate value of Woolworth's estate). By 1916, Parson was vice-president and general manager of the new company: he was firmly established in the executive hierarchy of American business, the managerial elite.

Parson had learned the tricky five- and ten-cent store business, with its small unit profit and large volume, under Woolworth's proud and watchful eye. He kept the books, ran the headquarters office, prepared the annual inventory, and even clerked behind the counter at Christmas and during other rush seasons. "Parson on his way home met himself coming to work," Woolworth later boasted.[8]

Woolworth had three daughters, but he had no son to succeed him. As time passed, his paternal feeling for Parson grew. He was "always eager to do something for Parson," old associates remembered. John Kennedy Winkler, Woolworth's biographer, learned that Parson first became Woolworth's "trusted lieutenant," and, finally, "the son he never had."[9] While he was still in his thirties, Parson became the heir-apparent to the founder. He was a first-rate modern corporation executive: cost-conscious, impersonal, and financially oriented. Further, he seemed to be a stable sort — a family man. When he had started to work for Woolworth, a fellow employee in the office, F. Bertha Gasque, introduced him to her sister, Maysie. The following year, 1893, Parson and Maysie Adelaide Gasque, both twenty-one, were married. They were to remain childless, but their household was to include Bertha and the sisters' mother, Mrs. Thomas More Gasque. Beyond the fact that she was born in Bayonne, New Jersey, in 1872, almost nothing is known of Maysie's childhood and youth. She is remembered both as "a seamstress" and as a clerk "in a small millinery shop in Brooklyn."

Parson, the corporation's moneyman, able and confident of success, set out to surpass Woolworth, a difficult goal, for Woolworth ranked with Alexander Turney Stewart, George Huntington Hartford, Marshall Field, and John Wanamaker as one of the great merchants of American history. Parson, the surrogate son, slowly developed a second, and probably inevitable, ambition: he wanted to surpass Woolworth's well-known imperial style as a palace builder. This latter aspiration came to light as the result of a naïve gaffe that Parson made as soon as he crossed the line into the world of palaces.

Parson and Maysie were becoming rich. They followed the Woolworths at a respectful distance, but the gap was closing. When the Woolworths summered at Asbury Park in the 1890's, the Parsons established themselves nearby at Allenhurst, one of a cluster of fashionable Jersey shore summer resort villages that included Elberon, Deal, Long Branch, and West Long Branch. By 1914, they had enough money to follow the Woolworths to Fifth Avenue, a move that Frank Woolworth undoubtedly helped to finance.

Mr. Dooley, Finley Peter Dunne's droll observer of American middle-class folkways, once remarked: "If a man is wise, he gets rich an' if he gets rich, he gets foolish, or his wife does." Parson and Maysie both got foolish on October 1, 1914. On that date, "Hubert T. Parson who resides in the Village of Allenhurst State of New Jersey," signed a purchase indenture for 1071 Fifth Avenue, the second house above East Eighty-eighth Street, and the lot on which it stood.[10] The price Parson paid to establish Maysie on Fifth Avenue is not entered in the deed record; however, he assumed payment of a lien of $125,000 outstanding against the property.

Parson immediately got in touch with Helwig Schier of Theo Hoffstatter & Co., a Fifth Avenue decorating firm that had designed and executed the interiors of the City Club, the Downtown Club, nine floors of the Hotel Savoy, and Frank Woolworth's mansions on Fifth Avenue and at Glen Cove, Long Island. Schier was not only Woolworth's decorator, he had become the confidant of the rich merchant's dazzling architectural fantasies. Parson told Schier to strip the house he had just bought at 1071 Fifth Avenue, and completely refinish, redecorate, and refurnish it. His commission included a proviso: "I want everything to be richer and finer than the decorations in Mr. Woolworth's house."[11] Parson had become his own Mephistopheles. Schier, of course, told Woolworth, who "laughed uproariously."

Woolworth had come to Fifth Avenue in 1899. Charles P. H. Gilbert, an architect who was to enjoy a lively traffic in Fifth Avenue mansions for Edmund G. Converse, Isaac D. Fletcher, Felix M. Warburg, Adolph Lewisohn, Jules S. Bache, and Otto H. Kahn, among others, designed a house for Woolworth on the uptown corner of East Eightieth Street. When Woolworth's father, who had long known the frugal life of a small farmer, first saw the house in 1901, he observed: "This must have cost a mint of money." Woolworth replied, "A good deal, father, but it's worth it."[12]

Parson was among the guests who witnessed the startling mixed-media electro-musical light and sound shows Woolworth loved to put on there. With the ingenious help of Frank Taft, a vice-president of the Aeolian-Skinner Organ Company, Woolworth had installed a great dual-system (manual-automatic) organ that sent its music through concealed ducts into stairway newel posts, bedposts, closets, hallways, and chambers throughout the house. Taft created a device that rattled the walls with thunderous storm effects, and a system of indirect colored lighting that Woolworth could control from the organ console as he ran through roll after automatic roll of great musical works. High up in the music room, Woolworth had arrayed a frieze of oil paintings of famous composers: he could call them forth, one by one, from the darkness with his light controls. This elaborate Wagnerian toy had cost him $500,000.

Woolworth, gripped by the urge to build — the mania of kings — next made plans for the skyscraper that bears his name, a work that ranked among the wonders of the world during its first decades. It would, Woolworth reasoned, serve to remind the world to shop at the Woolworth stores in America and elsewhere. But, Henry Goldman, of Goldman, Sachs & Company, the brokerage that had marketed the $65,000,000 in shares of the new Woolworth international corporation in 1912, prevailed against the use of the fresh merger capital for Woolworth's newest architectural fantasy. The stockholders, he reasoned in turn, wanted dividends, not a skyscraper.

So Woolworth built it himself, paying for the massive project in cash: $13,500,000.[13] Louis XIV daily inspecting the progress of Versailles could have had no more pleasure than Woolworth had climbing about his building as it rose story by story. He became involved in every detail and savored every statistic of the structure: twelve miles of marble wainscoting, seventeen million bricks, three thousand windows, seven thousand five hundred tons of terra-cotta (some of it used in a dozen busts placed at the cornice level in the elevator lobbies, caricature portraits of Parson; Louis J. Horowitz, president of the Thompson-Starrett Company, the builders of the skyscraper; Louis E. Pierson, president of the Irving National Exchange Bank and the Broadway-Park Place Company, the nominal owner of the building; Woolworth himself and his brother Charles Sumner Woolworth; and Cass Gilbert, the architect of the building, among others) . The tower rose to a record height of seven hundred ninety-two feet — Woolworth and his friend Frank Taft enjoyed a climb to the top before it was opened.

On the evening of April 24, 1913, President Woodrow Wilson pressed a button in the White House and eighty thousand light bulbs flashed on in the Woolworth Building, marking its completion. Today, the handsome tower designed by Cass Gilbert, whose varied commissions included the Omaha State House, the Detroit Public Library, and the U.S. Customs House in New York, remains one of the few enduringly attractive tall buildings in the world, its gothic detail a delight in a city of barren megaboxes.

Not long after his tower was completed, Woolworth presented each of his daughters with a Fifth Avenue mansion. These were ranged across the street from his own at Nos. 2, 4, and 6 East Eightieth Street. On November 16, 1916, Winfield Hall, Woolworth's country house, a frame villa at Glen Cove, was destroyed by fire. Cass Gilbert and Schier built and decorated a new Winfield Hall, a marble palace that cost an estimated $2,000,000.

However, Woolworth's greatest building project lay ahead. Schier began to plan with him a palace complex that was to cover an entire city block, two hundred feet by eight hundred feet, eastward from upper Fifth Avenue — a hundred and sixty thousand square feet of the costliest residential property in America.[14] The complex was to house Woolworth and his daughters and their families. No one now knows precisely what Woolworth had in mind, but if his visionary family palace had filled the long (east-west) axis of the city block he planned to buy, its length would have exceeded by one hundred and forty feet the span of the grand facade of the Pitti Palace in Florence, and by one hundred feet that of the long axis (including the portico) of the Vatican, the second largest and largest palaces in Italy. Woolworth's death in 1919 ended this remarkable fantasy.

Of such were the architectural works and dreams of the man Parsons had set out to surpass when he commissioned Schier to create a new palace inside the old fabric of 1071 Fifth Avenue. Others in Woolworth's close circle of old friends and associates had been tempted to follow him in his mania, but Parson alone pursued him into the twilight world of irrational grandeur. It took Schier almost four years to complete the new interiors of Parson's Fifth Avenue *palais*.

Parson had decided by then that the time had come for him to provide Maysie a proper country house of her own, so he bought Shadow Lawn, a short automobile ride from their old summer rental in Allenhurst, but light-years away financially. The first thing Parson did was to tell Schier; the first thing Schier did was to tell Woolworth. But this time Woolworth did not laugh. He was now an old man tormented with a fatal illness.

"It will be said that I gave this place to Parson," he complained with paternal disingenuousness to Schier. "I will be blamed for this."[15]

III

IN *Sentimental Education,* Flaubert observes that "royal residences have a melancholy all their own." Shadow Lawn began and ended on a note of melancholy. Here one is in the presence of ruins; not of stone, but of dreams. The palace remains: it was the builders who were destroyed. The magnitude of the troubles that came to Shadow Lawn was heroic, but the troubles themselves were of narrow consequence. One may wish to discover in them something tragic, the inexorable thrust of fate, perhaps, but one finds instead only the uneasy comedy of vanity undone.

During July, 1903, the *Long Branch Record* reported that John Augustine McCall, the president of the New York Life Insurance Company, was building "a handsome country seat" at West Long Branch. McCall is said to have told his architect, Henry Edward Cregier of Chicago, that he wanted a villa "suggestive of the grandeur of the Alhambra, the Petit Trianon, or Sans Souci." McCall dreamed in the ceremonial poetry of Wall Street. His "modified Colonial" frame house, a stylistic label hardly suited to his imposing intentions, was ready for occupancy on August 15, 1905.

The summer palace was two stories high, with an attic, and it had fifty-three rooms ranged around an axial (east-west) cortile that rose through the house to a roof skylight.[16] Huge dormer windows with Greek temple pediments surmounted by acroteria, plinths holding small statues of griffons, broke the slope of the attic roofs. Long spans of pierced parapet-railings (authentically Roman, if the famous reconstruction models of the residential section of ancient Ostia are correct) framed its spacious colonnade-verandas, which bulged into circular belvederes at the corners of the house. Parapet-railings, the classical precursor of renaissance balustrades, were also used to frame the massive turf emplacement on which the house appeared to rest, as well as to enclose a pair of rooftop belvederes — small temples — each of which provided a sweeping view of ocean and countryside.

A two-story hemicycle portico with eight Doric columns projected from the south (greensward) facade, and a two-story rectangular portico with ten Doric columns projected from the north (entrance) facade. The monumentality of its projecting parts — the porticos, the rotunda belvederes, the roof temple-belvederes — tended to overwhelm the central block of the house proper. The one-story Doric columns supporting the roof of the veranda that encircled the house rose to a simple entablature with a range of dentils, above which oversize Greek antifixes — leaf-form sculptured ornaments — were placed at the edge of the roof in line with each column. The large antifixes were also set along the solid parapet above the entablature of each of the two-story porticos, where, once more, they served as decorative terminals for the vertical lines of columns.

All in all, a handsome American improvisation: neoclassical, Greco-Roman seacoast vulgate, a massive carpenter transformation of a Tuscan villa turned outward toward the world instead of inward upon its cortile. It may have been all vocabulary and no rhetoric, but it was white and splendid in the summer sun.

Its interiors were, like its exterior details, monumental. A majestic stairway, probably designed by Cregier, rose through a two-story arch from the axial central hall to a mezzanine, then continued in separate return flights to a second-story gallery that circled the well of the hall and led to the guest suites. No records have been found to tell us who provided the elaborate decoration of McCall's palatial *salons* and chambers. However, it is the opinion of James F. Durnell, a New York City real estate man who was born in Long Branch and who has become an encyclopedic archivist of the Jersey shore, that William Baumgarten & Co. designed and executed the interiors, an attribution with much to recommend it. Baumgarten's was one of the three leading American decorating firms in New York in that era, the others having been Herter Brothers (managed by William Baumgarten for two decades until he established his own large organization in 1891) and Pottier & Stymus. Baumgarten's, as will presently be seen, was to have a long association with Shadow Lawn.

A superintendent of the estate at a later date has recalled being told that its landscaping had been planned by Olmsted, Olmsted & Eliot of Brookline, Massachusetts, the well-known firm founded by Frederick Law Olmsted. However, Durnell has remembered seeing W. G. Eisele, a nurseryman and gardener whose greenhouses were nearby, carrying out all of Shadow Lawn's bedding, planting, and landscaping, which included the damming of a creek to create an artificial lake. The estate took its name from the shadows cast by clusters of great trees planted in the English naturalistic park tradition on the vast lawn that sloped in an easy gradient to the lake south of the villa. McCall had paid $250,000 for "three old family parcels," which he then mortgaged for $100,000. It cost him $850,000 to build and furnish his American Sans Souci. It was, the *New York Times* thought, "the finest country place along the Jersey shore."[17]

The summer of 1905 was McCall's first full season at Shadow Lawn; it was also his last, for by the time autumn came he was one of the central figures in a sensational public investigation of insurance company practices — a scandal that swept across the country. He readily admitted that he had spent $275,000 bribing legislators in various states on behalf of New York Life. The trustees of the company abandoned him: in a ruthless burletta of importuned innocence, they demanded that he return the money. He tried desperately to raise the cash. First, he accepted a surrender value of $100,000 on a $400,000 life insurance policy. Second, he tried, unsuccessfully, to get a $150,000 second mortgage on Shadow Lawn. But it was too late: the tide of public outrage was running against him.

McCall was forced to resign, thus losing his $100,000-a-year salary. In the midst of scandal and financial ruin, he retreated to a resort hotel in Lakewood, New Jersey. There, on February 18, 1906, five months after his troubles began, he died of cancer. His son spoke to the waiting press: "My father earned a good deal of money, but he lived up to almost every cent of it."[18]

IV

THERE *are shadows on the lawn at Shadow Lawn* . . .

The "shadows" referred to in this line from a political poem which was widely quoted in 1916 by those supporting the immediate entry of the United States into World War I were not those cast by the

trees on the vast sward of the old McCall estate. They were instead
the tragic shadows of Americans who lay dead beneath the shipping
lanes of the North Atlantic, victims of German submarine attacks on
the *Lusitania* and other passenger ships. The poem, written by ex-
President Theodore Roosevelt, was an attack on President Woodrow
Wilson, who was then running, almost casually, for reelection, con-
fining himself to a few speeches from the south porch at Shadow
Lawn, the semicircular portico which bore an astonishing likeness to
the familiar garden portico of the White House.

Shadow Lawn was at that moment (the autumn of 1916) becoming the best-known private residence in America, for it was, of necessity, mentioned in every news report of Wilson's campaign. "The
McCall house," as Shadow Lawn was still known along the Jersey
shore, was by that time owned by Joseph B. Greenhut, a New York
City department store owner, who had invited Wilson to use it as a
summer White House.

In March, 1906, a month after McCall had died, Shadow Lawn
had passed from his beleaguered estate to a succession of owners,
none of whom, until Greenhut bought it, could finance such a purchase.[19] The first of the new owners, Myron Oppenheim, who summered in Long Branch, wanted to turn the palace into "a summer
social club," a scheme that failed after he had conveyed partial interest in the deed to several associates in 1906. By August of that year,
Abraham White took title to the estate. Borough records at West
Long Branch reveal that White "gave back a purchase money mortgage of $100,000 on August 20, 1906, and an additional mortgage of
$50,000 on the same day." He immediately changed the name of the
estate to White Park, and revealed his plans to develop a "cottage
colony" on the grounds. However, the Abraham White Realty and
Improvement Corporation was foreclosed on June 19, 1908, for failure to pay the original mortgage of $100,000 given by McCall in
1903.

At the sheriff's sale resulting from the foreclosure, Oppenheim and
his associates again bought the estate to protect their second and
third mortgages. On July 14, they conveyed the house and land to
Robert L. Smith, who, in turn, conveyed it to the Brooklawn Country Club. The country club mortgaged the palace and grounds for
$125,000.

Then, Greenhut bought Shadow Lawn for his own use as a shore
estate in 1909, easily paying the purchase price and assuming all

encumbrances. Joseph Benedict Greenhut had more than enough money to live out McCall's dreams. His father was remembered as the head of the whiskey trust, and he himself was the principal partner in Siegel, Cooper & Company ("The Big Store — A City in Itself"), the earliest of New York City's monumental department stores.

Greenhut hired a professional estate superintendent, Duncan Kelley, and commissioned him to restore the grounds and house to their original condition. He then signified his residential intentions by renaming the estate Shadow Lawn. The few records available disclose that Greenhut paid $200,000 for the deed and that he spent about $400,000 improving the grounds and remodeling the house.

Late in 1915, Greenhut invited President Wilson to use Shadow Lawn the following summer. On September 24, 1916, the President opened his reelection campaign there. He gave Greenhut a check for $2,500 for the rental of the estate (an act of rectitude that today might startle most Americans). Greenhut refused to accept the check from his guest, so Wilson, a former professor of constitutional law, turned it over to local charities.[20]

For a few weeks, Long Branch and West Long Branch enjoyed a flourish of political fame. Railroads ran campaign specials that carried Democratic delegations from states as distant as Ohio and Mississippi to the Jersey shore so they could hear their candidate speak. The Long Branch Chamber of Commerce issued twenty-five thousand Shadow Lawn "Summer White House" stamps.

Joseph P. Tumulty, Wilson's secretary, maintained his headquarters a few miles south at Asbury Park. On Tuesday, November 7, 1916, Wilson motored with his wife to Princeton, New Jersey, to vote, and then returned to Shadow Lawn to await the election returns. Late in the evening, Tumulty called from Asbury Park to tell the President that the *New York World* had conceded the election to Wilson's opponent, Chief Justice Charles Evans Hughes. "Well, Tumulty," Wilson said, "it begins to look as though we have been badly licked." The following morning Wilson's daughter, Margaret, interrupted him while he was shaving to tell him that he had, in fact, been reelected. He finished shaving, then drove to Washington, victor in the nation, but not in West Long Branch. His autumn neighbors had given their majority to Hughes.

A group of wealthy men, probably remembering the prestige that had come to the shore area when another group had purchased a cottage at Elberon for the use of President Grant, then raised $25,000 toward a fund to buy Shadow Lawn as a permanent summer White House. Congressman Thomas J. Scully of Deal, New Jersey, introduced a bill in Congress to facilitate government acceptance. However, the measure died: in 1917 the House of Representatives had far more grievous matters under debate.

V

O N June 11, 1918, Parson became the last of the owners of the original Shadow Lawn. Greenhut's real estate firm, Monmouth Securities, had conveyed the property to the Harsen-Langham Corporation in 1917. Parson bought the estate from the latter firm. He paid $800,000 for the estate, giving additionally a "purchase money mortgage to the Harsen-Langham Corporation in the amount of $150,000," according to the title records. He also "acquired the adjoining tracts."

At that time, the $125,000 lien against his Fifth Avenue house was still outstanding. Parson had plunged heavily into debt, but Woolworth rescued him — for the last time. Woolworth died the following year, and although he did not include Parson in his will, it is clear that he had already taken abundant care of his successor. Woolworth, despite his complaint that he would be "blamed" for encouraging Parson in his extravagant style of living, was very likely the real purchaser of Shadow Lawn, his final gift to his protégé. Under the terms of the will, Parson served, along with Woolworth's two surviving daughters, as an executor of Woolworth's estate. He was also appointed, as Woolworth had wished, the legal guardian of Mrs. Woolworth, who had long been senile. Parson's rôle was clearly that of a surviving son.

He was elected president of the F. W. Woolworth Company in 1919, and by the end of that year he had cleared the lien on 1071 Fifth Avenue. He was now ready to become the laird of Shadow Lawn. On October 15, 1920, he put the estate on a professional footing: he hired George W. Thomson, a Scot who had the care of Robert Collier's estate at Wickatunk, New Jersey, as his superintendent. Thomson's father, grandfather, and great-grandfather had all been professional gardeners in Scotland, and he had served as an apprentice and journeyman on Scotch estates before coming to the

United States.[21] He served Parson thirteen years at Shadow Lawn and came to know him well.

"Parson was a very strict man," he has recalled. "Mind you, he was always a fair man. And the truth is, I admire a strict man. But he could be very nice with it. As a matter of fact, he treated me more like a brother. Of course, if he didn't go for you, you'd go. He used to say to me, 'Thomson, my happiest moments are down here walking around the place.' Oh my, he really loved that place. Every Friday or Saturday he'd come down and go around the estate with me. And if he missed a week or was away visiting the stores around the country, the first thing back he'd go around the grounds with me and his big police dogs. Why, he'd let them jump all over him, and he'd fire any man who abused them.

"He was a short man, and a bit stout. She was just a bit taller than him. Now, I'll tell you, Mrs. Parson was awfully strict and changeable. And domineering, too. To tell the truth, she completely domineered her sister. And Parson would do anything for her. He would have torn the house down if she'd wanted it. *Absolutely!* He'd even move heavy things for her. Now, he shouldn't have done that. Oh my. I used to feel sorry for him. But, as far as the estate was concerned, he was the boss. And a stern little fellow, mind you. I'll bet he was severe up there. They didn't like him, you know, and that's probably why. I went up there once, and there was the little fellow in that big office with that enormous desk."

Up there — the Woolworth Building in New York — Parson successfully restrained the brotherliness he revealed to Thomson in the vast privacy of the Jersey countryside. No man up there knew Parson better than Thomas J. Mullen, who has recalled his thirteen years with him, first as his secretary, then as his assistant and financial confidant.

"Parson was a brilliant financier," Mullen has said. "And he was a good executive, of course, but he wasn't at all well liked in the company. He was a proud and lonely man — I think today you might call him a 'loner.' He was a cold man, and aloof; very distant with people. He wasn't a man who made friends.

"He and his wife were completely self-centered. They didn't have any children, you know. All they had to think about was themselves, and all that ever really concerned him was what she wanted. They were not what you would call sociable people. They liked opera and had a box at the Met, but they never entertained. As far as I know, they never had any parties down there, and I would be the one to know. I even went down there in the summer while they were away, to take the payrolls down."

Once Parson took over *down there,* additions and new construction came rapidly. "In 1920 we relandscaped the whole place," Thomson has recalled. "Then we developed the farm." McCall's sixty-five-acre estate grew to one hundred and eight acres under Parson, and half the land was set aside for farming.

In *The Four Books of Architecture,* Palladio observes that "the city is, as it were, but a great house, and, on the contrary, a country house is a little city." Parson created a little city at Shadow Lawn. Construction included a ten-room house for the superintendent; a new two-story estate garage; eight greenhouses ($250,000) ; a horse barn with six stalls; a cattle barn with twelve stanchions; a poultry house ($45,000) ; a two-story palm house; a bullpen; a ram pen; sheep pens; pheasant pens; rabbit hutches; an icehouse; cottages (refurbished farmhouses Parson had acquired with his land purchases) for the dairyman, the greenhouse man, and the poultryman; and dog kennels for the police dogs that were turned loose on the grounds each midnight. Communal telephone, water, electrical, and sewerage systems were installed.

Five vegetable gardens, flower gardens, raspberry and currant patches, and a grape arbor were set out. The artificial lake was stocked with ducks, geese, and swans. A little summer house was built on the small island in the middle of the lake.

Parson could walk through his truck gardens to the heated palm house and enjoy the beauty of his macaws; he could discuss the condition of his Guernseys with his dairyman; and he could look out his windows like a rich Hesiod and enjoy that most pastoral of visions, sheep grazing on the sward. He fast became a country gentleman in the grand style, even though the "Theatre of his hospitality" remained empty except for himself and Maysie, and her sister Bertha. (The girls' mother, Mrs. Thomas More Gasque, who had been part of the household on Fifth Avenue, died about 1919.)

Parson's executive career flourished as well during his early manorial years. The Woolworth stores enjoyed a boom during his first year as president, and then entered a period of continuous expansion and record profits under his direction. In 1922, Parson made his first appearance in *Who's Who,* and during the same year he discharged his mortgage on Shadow Lawn.

Once the estate grounds, and the farms and farm buildings, were well advanced, Parson commissioned William Baumgarten & Co. to return to Shadow Lawn and completely refinish, redecorate, and re-furnish the house — to strip it down to the fabric and create entirely new interiors, just as Helwig Schier had done at 1071 Fifth Avenue.

Maysie's hour had come at Shadow Lawn, for the interiors were to be her domain. She had served the first phase of her apprenticeship in the complex art of palace decoration in her *petit palais* on Fifth Avenue under Schier. However, because of Schier's formidable posi-tion as Frank Woolworth's decorator and confidant, it is unlikely that Maysie had had much influence on his work. But the Baum-garten staff, which by then had begun to lose its high standing in the world of decoration, would pay close heed to her wishes. She had fifty-four rooms to decorate, a very large commission.

Hans Sieben, a German who had earlier worked in Paris, was put in charge of the project for Baumgarten. The work took two years to complete, 1924 and 1925, and it cost Parson $1,000,000, Thomas Mullen has recalled. Sometime before the work was completed, Sieben left Baumgarten and returned to Paris to go to work there for L. Alavoine et Cie. Parson and Maysie had been well satisfied with his work, a condition that was to bring him both prosperity and sorrow.

About the same time that Baumgarten was completing the costly new interiors at Shadow Lawn, Frank Woolworth's Fifth Avenue palace with its aeolian *Wunderkammer* was being razed to make way for an apartment house. The wrecker's ball: the king is dead. Gold leaf at Shadow Lawn: long live the king.

Parson was about to turn his attention to Maysie's wish to have a place in Paris on the Avenue du Bois de Boulogne.

VI

P ARSON? But of course I remember him."

Parson . . . the name could still evoke laughter in Paris forty years later, could still give rise to a mixture of amused wonder and indifferent scorn in the reception *salon* of Maison Alavoine, an old and distinguished decorating firm at 42 Avenue Kléber near the Arc de Triomphe. Alavoine had seen, and survived, clients of all types. Its long history can be traced back through an unbroken succession of family-owned ventures and partnerships to a pioneer group of eighteenth-century craftsmen, members of the Paris guilds (picture-frame carvers, cabinetmakers, furniture makers, *tapissiers,* and so on) who, departing from tradition, organized an archetypal decorating firm.

This ancient predecessor of Alavoine appears to have been one of the earliest private organizations in the decorative arts to have provided its clients with a range of services rather than only the products of a single craft. It differed from the historic community of workshops at the Gobelins manufactory in that the latter had been established and maintained under royal subsidy (and were, of course, much larger and more comprehensive).

Although its history is largely a matter of oral tradition in the firm, and has yet to be documented, Alavoine feels quite safe in pointing out that it served its first clients — the families of the *ancien régime* and the rich bourgeoisie — during the reign of Louis XVI. However, the claim is put forward simply as a condition of history, existing as little more than a nonchalant *présence* in the firm's reception room.

There one summer morning in the middle 1960's, while he was engaged on "a very interesting commission" for the mother of the Queen of Iran, Henri Samuel, then the *directeur* of Alavoine, recalled for an American visitor the beginnings of Parson's costly efforts to establish Maysie "around the corner" on the Avenue Foch.

Samuel, an urbane and gifted man who now heads his own firm, is considered by his colleagues to be one of the ablest decorators in Europe. He has restored and renovated the famous first-floor *salons* of the Château de Ferrières on the outskirts of Paris for Baron Guy de Rothschild. These interiors were designed by the nineteenth-century painter Eugène Lami. They are the apotheosis of Second Empire splendor, which is all but inseparable from the splendor of *le style Rothschild* — a *décor* of luxuriant and restive opulence with wayward roots in the classical tradition. Samuel's goal at Ferrières was to preserve authenticity while restoring a certain freshness and flair — "a youthful quality" — to the great rooms, a matter of subtly adjusting details while honoring Lami's grand scheme.

Samuel has also designed and installed the interiors of the Paris and Geneva *hôtels* of Baron Edmond de Rothschild, decorated the private family suite at Versailles now occupied by the head curator of the château, Gerald van der Kemp, and overseen the carving of doorframes and overdoors made by Alavoine for the Hôtel de Varengeville Room, which was installed in the Metropolitan Museum of Art, New York City, in 1969. One of his most prestigious commissions came early in the 1960's when he was given the responsibility for the *tapisserie* — the wall hangings, draperies, chair coverings, and carpets — in the renovation of the Grand Trianon at Versailles, a project involving a number of experts whose highly praised restorations were based upon the authoritative research of Denise Ledoux-Lebard.

Samuel knows well the ambience of luxury and elegance, present and past, for he has both created and re-created it. He learned long ago not to be surprised by the fantasies and aesthetic crudities of those rich Americans who wish to buy elegance. He remembered Parson: "Yes, yes. We heard so much about him. Everyone had a story to tell." Samuel first heard about him almost as soon as Parson appeared in Paris, for the decorating community nourishes itself on familial gossip about new commissions, fine pieces coming up at auction, and the vagaries of clients — gossip that is witty, sometimes malicious, and only as accurate as it needs to be.

"Parson, as you know, was a man utterly without taste," Samuel recalled. "But then, how could it have been otherwise?" He made this rhetorical observation with the patient humor of a man lightly ticking off a commonplace professional hazard which requires no further explanation.

"When I first heard about Parson I was only twenty," he went on. "I must explain first that when I finished school, my father — he was a banker — asked me if I wanted to go on to the university or go to America and learn banking. I decided to go to New York, where I worked for the banking house that served as correspondent for my father's firm. I stayed there for two years. It was wonderful, of course. I was young, and a bachelor, and I had the loan of a small apartment — but I wasn't the least bit interested in banking. I was really very keen on decorating.

"I met a decorative painter, a man who did overdoors and that sort of thing. He did a lot of work in New York, and he took me around to the Alavoine office. But they . . . well, they weren't interested in me. There was nothing for me to do there. Curious, isn't it, that I should take charge of Alavoine in Paris twenty-five years later. What happened when I got back from New York was this: I told my father that I wished to become a decorator. He told me to go ahead, but that I would have to sink or swim. I went to work for Jansen and spent five years with them. It was there that I learned to be a decorator.

"When I was just starting at Jansen someone told me that Hans Sieben, who was with Alavoine, was doing an apartment for a man named Parson on the Avenue Foch. So I got in touch with Sieben and sold him some chairs I had bought at auction. Sieben used them in Parson's apartment. That's how I first got to know about this strange American. And that was even before Parson bought the big house on the other side of Avenue Foch. We heard a lot more about Parson after that. About the house, you know. But Martin Becker, who was the head of Alavoine in New York for many years, knows better than anyone else what poor Sieben went through with Parson."

Samuel got up from the Louis XV *fauteuil* in which he had been sitting and crossed the room to the French windows giving onto the Avenue Kléber. He looked out into the morning sunshine and added: "That was a long time ago."

VII

I'll tell you what happened to Parson in Paris."

Martin Becker, the head of Alavoine in New York until he dissolved the American partnership-branch in 1965 and became *président honoraire* of Alavoine in Paris, sat among his paintings, bronzes, and *objets,* collected with a discerning eye over four decades, and discussed his recollections of Parson as a rich innocent abroad. Only the sound of his voice disturbed the deep quiet of his Sutton Place apartment near the East River in Manhattan. From time to time his memories of Parson's arrogance and tastelessness strained his detachment. At such moments he raised his eyebrows and shrugged his shoulders, almost with a French accent.

"Parson first took an apartment at 75bis on the Avenue Foch. I think it was the summer of, say, 1925. They still called it the Avenue du Bois at that time. The house the apartment was in was on the left side as you faced toward the Bois. Parson got in touch with Sieben and asked him to get the place ready for him — to furnish it. Sieben knew the Woolworths and Parson.

"Let me tell you about Hans Sieben, first. He was a German who came to Paris around 1913 to study furniture design and upholstering — to apprentice, and to work. He began with Nelson on the Place Vendôme. Then, because he was a German, he was put in prison as soon as the war broke out. He must have been scared to death because overnight his hair turned white. Incidentally, he did that fine house for Mrs. Harry Lehr [Mrs. Elizabeth Drexel Lehr] in the Rue des Sts. Pères, No. 52, and he did quite a bit of work later on for the Woolworth daughters. Woolworth's granddaughter, Barbara Hutton, used to call him 'Uncle Hans.' He did her London house in Regent's Park.

"After World War I, he didn't want to stay in Paris, so he came to New York and got a job with Baumgarten. They had done those houses on East Eighty-second right off Fifth Avenue for the Woolworth daughters. Woolworth died about the time Sieben got here, I think. And William Baumgarten had been dead for about a dozen years. The firm was going downhill by then, but they were still big. At their peak they had about thirty people in the design department, plus salesmen and the office staff — that's about twenty-five more — and perhaps a hundred people at the plant.

"I was just a kid then, working for Alavoine. My father had come over from Paris to work on the sculpture of the Schwab house. I studied architecture at the Ecole des Beaux-Arts, but I really didn't like it. So my father put me in the design department at Baumgarten's. After the war, in 1920, I went with Alavoine. I heard that Henri Martin, who was the head of Alavoine in Paris, was looking for someone who could speak English, and I thought Sieben was exactly the right man. As I say, I was just a kid, but I recommended Sieben. It took only one interview and he was on his way back to Paris.

"Then Sieben heard from Parson and got the apartment at 75bis ready. He did everything for them. He even bought their plates and silver for them. Poor guy. He really didn't have much taste himself, but he had a problem because Parson had no taste. Actually, it was worse: he had *bad* taste. Sieben put the silver and plates away for them and had the place ready when they got back to Paris from wherever they were vacationing in France.

"Then, they decided the place wasn't big enough, so Parson leased the floor above for the next summer. He told Sieben to have the entire duplex furnished by the time they got back to Paris from New York the following June. And again Sieben took care of everything.

He even hired a chef. And this is the final touch: when they arrived at the apartment from the boat train, Sieben even had dinner on the table waiting for them.

"But, still things weren't right. On the floor above, the help got drunk every night and threw things around. The Parsons always went to bed at ten-thirty and the noise bothered them. So Parson went out and bought the house across the avenue at No. 72."

At this point, memories conflict. In his biography of Woolworth, *Five and Ten,* John K. Winkler states that Parson "built an elaborate mansion in Avenue Foch, Paris." Samuel, when asked to clarify the matter, said, "No, Parson didn't build it. It was already there. I'm quite sure." Thomson has said, "No, no, he didn't buy it. He *built* it — he told me he built it." Mullen has recalled the matter differently: "No. I'm sure he didn't build the house. But he did do it over completely. From top to bottom. Everything in the house was ripped out."

Did Parson build the house or did he not? Becker has provided an extraordinary tale, told to him by Hans Sieben, that proves that Parson may be said to have built the house even though it proves that he didn't:

"Parson took along an architect when he and Sieben went to look at the house. While they were walking around, studying it, the architect observed that it was a pity that it hadn't been better sited on the relatively small plot. It wasn't centered properly. Sieben told me that Parson wanted to know what the architect was saying, so Sieben translated for him. They stopped right there and a long discussion followed. Parson said he had a solution. 'Move the house.' And that's exactly what was done. Parson bought the house and came back to New York. Before the next summer the house was moved — not far, just a few feet."

One may at this point be reminded of an experience the great Thomist scholar Etienne Gilson once had in the manuscript room of the Bibliothèque Nationale while studying the correspondence of Héloïse and Abélard. He saw a scholar wearing the Benedictine robe and approached him. "I wanted him to decide on the spot and without delay the precise sense of the words *conversatio* and *conversio* in the Benedictine Rule," Gilson writes in his essay *Héloïse and Abélard.* " 'And why,' he asked me, 'do you attach such importance to these words?' 'Because,' I replied, 'on the sense of these words depends the authenticity of the correspondence.' Never did a face express greater surprise. Then, after a silence: 'It is impossible for it not to be authentic. It is too beautiful.' "[22]

Was Sieben's tale authentic? One can only beg the question. It is too extravagant not to savor — and too perfectly in keeping with the common memories of Parson to wish to dispute.

"The house was completed and ready for the Parsons the next summer," Becker continued. "Then, they arrived. Poor Sieben. He had, of course, put bidets in all the bathrooms, and when Parson saw them he got furious and yelled: 'What the hell, Sieben, this isn't a whorehouse. Get those things out of here!'

"An appalling man."

VIII

P ARSON in Paris: a cautionary vignette:

"Parson," Mullen has recalled, "didn't read much, and he wasn't an art collector, but he did have some good tapestries. He got them through Georges Haardt, a Belgian, who was his adviser. But there was one time though when Parson went out in Paris on his own and bought some tapestries without any advice, just his own judgment, and he was really had. He got the usual certificates of antiquity, of course, but when we went down to customs after he got back someone told him that the tapestries had been made in the United States. So Parson had them brought to the office and he called Haardt and asked him to please come up and look at them. We prised open the top of the huge box. Haardt could barely see a few inches of the back of one of the tapestries. 'Close it up,' he said. They were not even six months old. It turned out they had been made in Brooklyn."

IX

A question arises: does a $12-a-week bookkeeper from Brooklyn really need two summer palaces, one on the Jersey shore and one in Paris, to keep a Brooklyn shopgirl happy? Parson might have protested the question, for, in his circumscribed view of the matter,

Maysie did, indeed, *need* 72 Avenue Foch. By the time her Paris *hôtel particulier* was ready to occupy, sans bidets, she was bereft of Shadow Lawn. It had burned to the ground at the beginning of the year.

"We always kept the house heated in the winter because Parson loved to come down and use the toboggan slide we built," Thomson has recalled. "And, as you can imagine, it took a lot of coal to heat the place. We usually got in big shipments."

On January 6, 1927, *two hundred tons* of coal were delivered to Shadow Lawn. The following evening, with the temperature at five degrees above zero, a fire started in the basement of the house and spread almost instantly to the vast coal bins. Fire companies came from West Long Branch and nearby Oakhurst, but their task was impossible. A strong, icy wind swept in from the northwest and fanned the flames that rose in great sheets from the massive frame house. The water from the firemen's hoses froze almost instantly. The conflagration, one of the most dramatic of the era along the Jersey shore, drew more than a thousand awed and frozen spectators.

Thomson worked with the firemen through the night. "We had trouble getting the housekeeper out," he has recalled. "Everyone got excited and she kept going back to try to get things out. I was in there trying to save a big orthophonic phonograph when the fireplace blew up and knocked me flat on my back. All the lights went out and I had to crawl out and then I noticed the housekeeper, a big Irish girl, still trying to go back and I had to knock her down to stop her. We couldn't save much. None of the furniture, as I recall. But, with the help of the firemen we got the big reception room rug out. Soaking wet."

During the night Thomson alerted Mullen, and at seven the next morning he got a ride to West End, a short distance away, and called Parson:

"I'll never forget that call. 'Anybody hurt?' he asked me. 'No, thank God,' I said. 'As long as no lives were lost. That's all that matters. The only thing that matters,' he said. Then he said to me, 'Don't worry, the rest can be replaced.' He was only really concerned about one thing: that no one had been badly hurt or killed. After the fire was over a few days and things had calmed down he asked me to make up a list of deserving people — the firemen and others who had tried to help — and he gave them twenty to fifty dollars apiece."

Mullen arrived on the scene during the morning while the rubble of the palace was still smoldering. He began immediately to gather data for the insurance claim. "All that remains this afternoon of the imposing structure are the two chimneys," the *Long Branch Record* reported that day.

Parson collected $759,000 on the ruined house. He had been planning to increase his insurance to $2,000,000 to cover the costly improvements that Baumgarten had completed about a year earlier. The newspapers estimated his losses at $1,250,000. "They were very close," Mullen has observed.

X

P ARSON wasted no time in getting a new palace started — a second Shadow Lawn. Fourteen days after the fire had cooled, a civil engineering firm in Asbury Park completed a map of the foundations of the ruined house.[23] Parson mailed copies of the map to five architects — including C. P. H. Gilbert, who had designed Woolworth's Fifth Avenue house — and asked them to submit designs for a new palace based upon the ground plan of the old.

He and Maysie also began to look at other country mansions in their Rolls-Royce. One day they saw Whitemarsh Hall, the Stotesbury palace in Chestnut Hill. Their search for an architect had ended. Parson called Louis J. Horowitz, the president of the Thompson-Starrett company, the builders of the Woolworth Building, and arranged through Horowitz to meet Horace Trumbauer, the architect of Whitemarsh Hall. Parson also asked Horowitz to build his new palace.

Before the Parsons left for France that summer (to occupy 72 Avenue du Bois de Boulogne), Trumbauer and his chief designer, Julian Abele, were at work on the preliminary sketches. They worked from the ground plan/map Parson had sent to Gilbert. It is one of the few early drawings for the project that remain. (Gilbert had probably returned the map to Parson when he submitted his design proposals for the new palace, and Parson had probably, in turn, sent it on to Trumbauer. The designs submitted by Gilbert, and the four other architects Parson had contacted, were once on file at Monmouth College, the present owner of Shadow Lawn, but were lost in the middle 1960's.)

On November 8 — about nine weeks after Parson had returned from Paris — Trumbauer was able to hand him a "Map Showing Old & New Residence at Shadow Lawn."[24] Included on the map was the ground plan of a new "Lodge," a temporary thirty-three-room dwelling that was already being rushed to completion for the Parsons to use during the construction of their new palace. On December 31, 1927, the *Long Branch Record* had a neighborly New Year's wish for Parson: "A new Shadow Lawn that will eclipse the one built twenty-five years ago."

Peter W. Eller, the general superintendent of Thompson-Starrett at the time, and later its president, could have assured the *Record* that the old villa would, indeed, be eclipsed. "Fred Fall was our resident superintendent on the Parson job," Eller has recalled, "but I went down there several times, and I can remember that when I saw the excavations for the foundation I thought it looked more like a General Motors plant than a residence."

The excavation work also gave Parson a chance to exercise his mature imperial style. "We ran into underground water right where the bowling alley was supposed to go," Eller remembered.[25] "We recommended that the bowling alley be relocated, but Parson wouldn't hear of it. So we had to sink well points and provide a drainage system. As a result, that bowling alley cost him $600,000 — but, he didn't seem to mind." Thomson has a rueful memory of the alleys: "They were beautiful, but they were never used . . . not even once."

Trumbauer went up to New York almost every week and met with Parson in the Woolworth boardroom. But Maysie was the final arbiter of the design. One weekend Parson bundled up the drawings and took them down to Shadow Lawn to show them to Thomson. "I looked at them," Thomson recalls, "and I said, 'My goodness, Mr. Parson, that's going to cost you plenty. And I don't think you'll like it. It's going to look like a municipal building.' Then he rolled up the drawings and said to me, 'Mrs. Parson and I don't care what people think. We're going to have what we want. And this is what we want.' "

Thomson never did learn to like the new palace. However, he admired Trumbauer:

"He had a man here named [Clarence] Freeman, but he came over from Philadelphia pretty frequently himself before I left. (I went to Europe for part of '29 and '30.) I can tell you one thing, Trumbauer was a very outspoken man, and if he didn't like the way something looked, he'd tear it down. You could tell he was a great architect — he knew everything, every detail. And it all had to be perfect; just the way he could see it in his mind."

In April, 1928, Thompson-Starrett signed the construction contract, and in July, William Baumgarten & Co. signed the finishing and decorating contract.[26] Construction moved quickly ahead and it was generally understood that the Parsons would move in before another year was out. On December 31, 1928, the *Long Branch Record,* aware of the steady progress being made on the house, had another New Year's wish for Parson: "Christmas dinner at Shadow Lawn, the finest country estate in the world."

But ahead lay ruin.

XI

$\mathbb{A}$MERICA was nearing the end of a time of fable when Parson returned to New York in the autumn of 1929. All summer long, mesmerized and confident, the country had dreamed of money. There had been warnings, but they had come and gone like heat lightning in August. The stock market had continued rising: all was well. Years afterward, Claud Cockburn, an English observer of the boom market, and subsequently an entertaining chronicler of political and economic vagaries, would write of that time: "If the attitude of the Americans toward the stock market . . . proved anything, it proved that they believed in miracles."[27]

Parson probably saw the quotation from Mark Twain ("Don't part with your illusions") in the *Wall Street Journal* when he got back from Paris. He would have found it reassuring, for he was a man who was not so much devoted to his illusions as imprisoned by them.

Parson's illusions, and the fantasies, each costlier than the other, that sprang from them, present one with a twentieth-century morality play that imposes on one's credulity. Will a man completely destroy himself simply to serve the vanity of an unremarkable middle-aged woman to whom he has been married most of his adult life? The question has the embarrassing ring of soap opera; the answer, even more embarrassing, is *yes.* Parson's illusions, like those of most men, had become articles of faith.

He believed that the economic boom of the twenties would last through the forever of his own mortality, that casual eternity of the ego. He believed that true love, as he had learned to revere it in the gaslit Brooklyn parlors of his Victorian young manhood, must constantly prove itself with costly gifts. And he believed that he could best win attention in a world committed to the headlong pursuit of affluence by creating larger and more opulent palaces than Frank Woolworth.

The first of these illusions was, of course, communal: it was of a piece with the madness that had seized the whole nation. Parson dealt every day in large financial matters; surely he had seen the groundswells of collapse. But if he had, he seems to have been certain they would vanish without causing any real harm to the economy or his own finances. In *Lombard Street,* his classic study of English banking, Walter Bagehot observes: "All people are most credulous when they are most happy."[28] And Parson had reason, indeed, to be a happy man.

Of his second illusion — that love is best proved by gift after gift — one should be wary. Parson may have converted his love into a celebration of devotional gifts, but were they really for Maysie? Or were they ritual gifts to pride? The question is moot, for, as Proust, in *Remembrance of Things Past,* has M. de Norpois observe, "with princes one never does know." And Parson had become an American prince.

How do I love thee? Elizabeth Barrett Browning would have been appalled by Parson's inventory. *Let me count the ways:* thirty-one fur coats, two walk-in vaults filled with silver, four gilded bronze torchères costing $150,000 apiece, three Rolls-Royces, a garden designed by Achille Duchêne, who had re-created the *parterres* at Blenheim Palace for Consuelo Vanderbilt, the Duchess of Marlborough. Parson's ideal grace rose from a ledger. But he was, nonetheless, possessed of a ponderous affection that moved steadily forward, indifferent to cost, careless of disaster.

Of the third of his illusory tenets — that he could compete with Woolworth in the extravagant game of palace building — a contradiction must be noted: Parson was an excellent accountant, and it was precisely this ability that had led Woolworth to single him out as a young man and train him as his successor. What, then, prompted Parson to ask of life a dispensation from reality in his private affairs that he would never have invoked in his highly efficient management of corporate matters?

One must assume that at home Parson yielded utterly to the mesmeric dreams of the bull market. For he had chosen while still in his
thirties to compete as an architectural fantasist with one of the
wealthiest men in the country. As has been seen, Woolworth knew
from the beginning what Parson was trying to do. At first, he was
amused, much as a father might be by a son who flexes a muscle at
him. Later, Woolworth had been deeply troubled by the mounting
cost of Parson's princely commitments, but by then it was too late.
Palace life had become a habit with Parson.

The story of the palace that destroys its obsessed builder has persisted through the ages. "The palace with its furniture, its gardens
and lakes, is quite enchanting . . . [but] its owner is no more. . . .
[His] creditors drove him out; turning his head to look back for
the last time, he died from shock," Jean de La Bruyère wrote in
Caractères (1688).

In his commanding study *The Crisis of the Aristocracy*, Lawrence
Stone has devoted an entire chapter ("Conspicuous Expenditure")
to the ruin of the English nobility who built gigantic "prodigy
houses" whose "sole function was to entertain the sovereign on one
of the summer progresses," or who otherwise built extravagantly "in
order to satisfy a lust for power, a thirst for admiration, an ambition
to outstrip all rivals." Stone points out in his illuminating footnote
to the history of vanity that in England "the building of country
houses between 1570 and 1620 must have been the largest capital
undertaking of the period."[29]

And in America, the young architect Benjamin Henry Latrobe
paid a visit in 1798 to the unfinished, and abandoned, palace in
Philadelphia that had helped to bankrupt Robert Morris, "the financier of the Revolution," who at that time was serving a three-year
sentence in debtors' prison. The house had been designed by Pierre
Charles L'Enfant, creator of the plan for Washington that had also
been abandoned and was not to be adopted until 1901. Latrobe
"gazed upon [the house] with astonishment," and concluded: "It is
impossible to decide which of the two is the madder, the architect or
his employer. Both of them have been ruined by it."[30]

One can understand the medieval abbot building heedlessly, for
he was the victim of the most subtle of vanities, the rage to prove
one's godliness to God. One can also understand the great English
dukes of the sixteenth century going deeply into debt to create their
great prodigy houses in the countryside merely to entertain their

monarch during his, or her, summer progress through the land, an event that might fall their way but once, for they were gambling on winning those crown favors that would restore their purses and give them access to the privileges, and nimbus, of divine power.

But what of Parson?

He had made it clear to Thomson that he and Maysie were going to have what they wanted, no matter what the cost. Reflecting on the implications of this declaration, and the drastic misfortunes they were to bring to Parson, Thomson has observed: "He would do any mortal thing for that woman."

Mullen, his financial confidant, has summed up Parson's irrational plunge into near bankruptcy even more tersely: "She ruined him."

XII

W HICH of you, intending to build a tower, sitteth not down and counteth the cost, whether he have sufficient to finish it?"

Parson was a Baptist, and one may assume that he was familiar with Luke 14:28. When he started to build the new palace at Shadow Lawn for Maysie, Parson had "sufficient" to complete it. His salary as the chief executive officer of Woolworth was $650,000 a year. He owned fifty thousand shares of Woolworth stock, which then had a market value of about $5,000,000. His dividends from these shares added a minimum of $120,000 a year to his income.

He is remembered by Mullen as having been "a brilliant financial man," and his other securities, principally Chilean copper bonds, were substantial. (Although they seem not to have known one another, Parson and Murry Guggenheim, the vice-president of Chilex, the largest American venture of the day in Chilean copper, had neighboring country estates in New Jersey.) There is evidence to suggest that the market value of Parson's other holdings exceeded that of his Woolworth shares, and that the total annual yield in dividends and interest from his other stocks, and from his bonds, was greater than his annual Woolworth dividends. Thus, his overall income was very likely more than $1,000,000 a year. "He had a great deal of money," Mullen has observed, without specifying the precise amount.

By the beginning of September, 1929, the new palace was nearly completed. As was usual in such enormous projects, there was still some cleaning up to be done. However, Parson could easily have paid off the outstanding trade acceptances, closed out with Thompson-Starrett and Baumgarten, and moved in. According to his confidential records, he had already spent more than $7,500,000 on the house.

Then, Maysie had a last-minute whim. She wasn't entirely satisfied with the palace. She wanted a solarium added to it — not on the ground level, but on the roof. An undated rendering in pencil of the south facade of the palace, probably drawn late in 1927 or early in 1928, serves to document what Trumbauer envisioned at Shadow Lawn — a palace in the French neoclassical tradition, precisely balanced in all its parts. There is no roof solarium in the rendering. A study of the elevations of the final design of the new palace dated June 11, 1928, show that a penthouse-solarium had been drawn in, erased, and drawn in again on a smaller scale. There is something tentative about the large structural addition: it is drawn in very lightly — reluctantly, one suspects. Apparently, it was eliminated, for construction had been completed without it. But Maysie, remembering her huge temple-belvederes on the roof of the original palace, now decided that she must have the solarium.

Mullen has recalled the consequences of the decision. Trumbauer, whom he has described as "looking more like a congressman than an architect," went up to New York from his office in Philadelphia determined to veto Maysie's scheme. Thomson's vivid recollections of Trumbauer during the building of Shadow Lawn help one to sense something of the tension of the meeting in Parson's office:

"Now, there was a clever man, Trumbauer. He would listen to suggestions, but he wouldn't stand for any nonsense. He was a big, stout man with a rough voice, and he was rough with Parson. It got so that Parson wouldn't go around the place with him unless I went along. He'd call ahead from New York when he was coming down to meet Trumbauer and tell me to get ready."

Sitting in the Woolworth boardroom, a cigar held firmly between his thumb and fingers as he talked, Trumbauer advised Parson to forget Maysie's foolish notion and to move into the palace. He pointed out that the roof had not been built to carry so great a load. . . .

But Trumbauer argued in vain, for he argued against Maysie. "Mrs. Parson wants it," Parson said.

Then, Louis J. Horowitz, the president of Thompson-Starrett, called on Parson. He was an experienced persuader. He too argued against the penthouse-solarium. "Mrs. Parson wants it," Parson said.

Illusions . . . Parson worked in an office that Frank Woolworth, an ardent enthusiast of Napoleon (who was never so pleased as when writers and reporters called him "a Napoleon of commerce"), had personally conjured, with the help of professional decorators, from documents and from memories of visits he had made to the emperor's studies and throne room. It was probably the most sumptuous private office in America, a state chamber with marble walls, marble pilasters with gilded bronze capitals, gilded bronze door panels, a mahogany desk that was nine feet long and was decorated with gilded bronze mounts, and a pair of rigorously exact copies of the round-backed throne that Charles Percier had designed for Napoleon. The office, as it was so intended to do, brought to mind the emperor busy with his imperial destiny in the "Empire room" at Compiègne and the throne room at Fontainebleau. Napoleon rode in bronze above the inkstand on the desk, and looked out in bronze from a pedestal in the corner of the office.

Mrs. Parson wants it: Napoleon gave the order to Trumbauer to proceed at once with the design of the solarium. Suddenly, it was Black Thursday — October 24, 1929. The stock market crashed: Parson, the paper emperor, was trapped. The value of his securities fell off steeply. But the work on Maysie's solarium went steadily ahead.

XIII

T HE world had changed, but the news hadn't reached Maysie, even though Parson had begun to hedge against the future. On November 27, about a month after Black Thursday had brought to a tragic end the long season of fable in America, Parson transferred the deed to 1071 Fifth Avenue to Maysie.[31] He also transferred a number of his Woolworth shares to her. During the summer the shares had reached a high 108 on the market; soon the stock would drop into the 20's and Parson would see nearly eighty percent of the value of his Woolworth holdings wiped out.

Throughout 1930, work on the vexing solarium proceeded. William O. Frank, Trumbauer's structural expert, made the calculations for the additional support required for the large roof sun house and prepared new structural drawings for the east wing of the palace. Then the construction men under Fred Fall took over. They removed broad strips of the limestone facing courses from ground to roof, removed the sections of the walls thus exposed (destroying in the process some of the fine interior finishing that had been installed by the Baumgarten crews under the supervision of William Groh), put in the new steelwork, including that for the penthouse structure itself, and replaced the walls and facing. Finally, Groh's Scotch plasterers, Swedish carpenters, and Italian decorative painters and gilders again refinished the rooms affected by the reconstruction.

As the year wore on, the Great Depression gathered its terrible momentum. By the end of November, 1930, unemployment had risen to the seven million mark, and wages had begun to fall severely. Once more the palace was completed, and after Thanksgiving Parson went through the formal closing procedures. He had by then lost millions on the stock market collapse. In order to take possession of the palace, he mortgaged Maysie's Fifth Avenue mansion to the Metropolitan Life Insurance Company for $300,000 at five and a half percent on a short-term basis.[32] The mortgage was recorded December 9 — the principal was due only twenty-six months later.

Maysie's rooftop playroom was ready for her at last. Baumgarten had provided it with Aztec decoration. The penthouse and its decoration had cost Parson $500,000. The total cost of the palace now came to $8,000,000, exclusive of the mortgage on the Fifth Avenue house. Mullen has recalled the financing of this extraordinary project: "I was responsible for all the details. I opened a special bank account in which Parson deposited $500,000, and it was my job to maintain the balance at that amount. I paid all the bills; every bit of the money went through my hands. I paid out $4,000,000 for the house, and another $4,000,000 for the interiors. If Parson had taken possession of the house, paid the remaining bills, and closed the account when he got back from Paris in 1929, he would have been all right. But it was her doing — she ruined him."

Parson had again proven himself: to Maysie and to pride. It does not damage Maysie's priority to suggest that in spending $8,000,000 on the palace, Parson had also been more than loyal to his other mistress as well. One would not want to deny either that Parson had taken leave of good sense, or that, as Mullen has recalled, he was a proud man. Above all, the palace was an impressive addition to the astonishing inventory of gifts he had given to Maysie. How do I love thee? One palace more.

XIV

W HEN Napoleon III had Charles Garnier design the Paris Opera, the architect created one of the most engaging of the city's Second Empire monuments. However, when he first brought his designs to the emperor, his bravura adaptation of renaissance forms puzzled the Empress Eugénie. "And what style is this?" she asked. "It isn't Greek, it isn't Louis XIV, and it isn't Louis XV. What is it?" Garnier replied: "It's Napoleon III, your Majesty. Are you complaining of that?"

Had Maysie had the wit to ask Trumbauer the same questions, one suspects that he might have answered, "Pure Trumbauer, madam, and aren't you fortunate?" A professional colleague has recalled that Trumbauer once rejected the picturesque fancies of a rich client's wife by telling her, "Madam, if I built the house you want, you wouldn't live in it, and I wouldn't want it to be seen."

Trumbauer was an ambitious pragmatist who kept a clear and critical eye on his own work. He is remembered as having paid the highest drafting-room salaries in Philadelphia, and as having, in consequence, demanded a high volume of quality production from his staff, an exaction monitored in part by an office time clock and in part by his stringent daily review of work in progress. When one of his own projects failed his standards he could be scathing, as he was the day he told some of his draftsmen that his design for the auditorium of the University of Pennsylvania, a pyramidal mass of stone rising to a spire, looked like "hemorrhoidal gothic: pile on pile."

During the four decades leading up to Shadow Lawn, Trumbauer had provided his palace clients with Northumberland castles, Tudor manor houses, Palladian country mansions in the Georgian tradition, and classic French *hôtels* and *manoirs*.[33] His palaces stood in the city and the countryside, and some of them may still be seen in and around Philadelphia, from the Main Line to Chestnut Hill and Jenkintown; in New York City; and in Newport and Washington.

Trumbauer had served the Widener and Elkins families of Philadelphia much as Richard Morris Hunt had earlier served the Vanderbilts — each was the royal *premier architecte* of a family kingdom — and he had eventually succeeded to Hunt's prestige as the foremost of the American palace architects. However, the distinction was an ironic one in that it assured his aesthetic death sentence, signed by the academic conservators of the new orthodoxy in architecture.

He had turned to classical models — to Greece and Rome reborn in the humanist vision of the master architects of the renaissance — for many of his most famous palace projects. He looked back and turned to gold, and the Puritans of modernism have never forgiven him. Nor have they absolved the pagan grace, serenity, bold certitude, panache, and charm of his best work, most of it designed in close collaboration with Julian Abele, his protégé and associate of thirty-six years.

Little has been published about Trumbauer, partly in consequence of academic disdain, but principally because of his own fear of publicity.[34] Despite his great success, which made him a wealthy man, he felt very deeply his lack of formal education beyond the tenth grade. He seems never to have been interviewed, and his stepdaughter, Mrs. Edward H. Fennessy, has recalled that "he tried never to have his picture taken. I can't tell you how deeply he felt about his lack of schooling. The thought that he might say something wrong terrified him. It bothered him all his life, and caused him to refuse many invitations to receptions given by his clients.

"He didn't even want to go to Cambridge when Harvard gave him an honorary degree after he had designed the library there. It was Mrs. [George D.] Widener who got him to go. She practically took him by the lapels and said, 'Now see here, this is important and you must make up your mind to get there.' She was the one who rigged him out in his gown for the ceremony. If it hadn't been for her, he would have backed out."

Mrs. Widener, née Eleanor Elkins, had built the Harry Elkins Widener Memorial Library at Harvard University in memory of her son who died, along with his father, in the sinking of the S.S. *Titanic*. The Library was dedicated July 24, 1915, the same day the university awarded Trumbauer his honorary master of arts degree.

Long after his large commissions had taken him away from the drawing board, Trumbauer was remembered professionally as an excellent draftsman. After Trumbauer's death, Abele recalled that he had always demanded "far more quality in drawing than was really necessary." In his commitment to fine draftsmanship, Trumbauer was an intuitive disciple of those architects of eighteenth-century Paris who brought drafting to the level of art. "The designs of this period," Michel Gallet has written in his brilliant survey, *Stately Mansions: Eighteenth Century Paris Architecture,* "were submitted on laid paper from Holland. . . . Elevations and sections might be touched up with water color mixed from a palette containing smalt [deep] blue, green earth, yellow lake, gallstone, carmine, and bistre."[35] Accuracy and elegance alike were cultivated, and drawings became both beautiful and highly disciplined.

Trumbauer was also a disciple of the Paris architects in his profound concern with the design and decoration of interiors. Despite the fact that the styles of decoration of the "Louis" periods have been imitated uncounted thousands of times in costly residences in the United States, they constantly betray those who do not understand their nuance, their treacherous subtleties of scale, of refinement and delicacy. Martin Becker has bluntly observed that "Trumbauer was the only one of the American architects who really knew what he was doing inside those big houses. He had the taste and the style. His sense of scale was excellent. He was marvelous to work with, a true classicist."

Trumbauer learned early — probably from examining Hunt's great palaces in Newport and elsewhere — to depend for the detailed design and execution of his superb French interiors upon Jules Allard et Fils and Lucien Alavoine et Cie.[36] Allard had been Hunt's decorator, and there is evidence that Trumbauer may have begun to use the firm even before Hunt's death — as early, that is, as 1892. Alavoine, according to Becker, had carried out the installation of Allard's American palace interiors during the 1890's, and by 1905 had bought out the older firm, a purchase that included its American operations. From that time on, Trumbauer had considered Alavoine to be his decorator, even though he had been obliged on some projects to use other decorating firms, as he was at Shadow Lawn.

"He knew what he wanted, just as Julian Abele did later on after Trumbauer's death," Becker has said. "Our designers spent a lot of time on detail drawings for him. He wanted everything done with great care — the designs, the models, the drawings for the client to look at. He even used to ask us to do full-scale plaster mock-ups of certain details. Things like a section of a cornice, or the capital of a pilaster. We would take them to the site, mount them in the room they were designed for, and study them under different light conditions. With Trumbauer, nothing was left to chance."

Trumbauer had worked well in a variety of architectural styles and traditions. One of his most famous projects had been the two campuses of Duke University, commissioned by the tobacco millionaire James Buchanan Duke and completed in 1932. (A portrait of Trumbauer hangs in the university library.) Trumbauer and Abele designed the women's campus in the Georgian tradition and the men's campus in the style known as "collegiate gothic." After visiting the university, Aldous Huxley observed in the British magazine *Time and Tide:* "It may be that, in buildings like [these], future historians of art will recognize the best examples of large scale gothic architecture ever produced."[37]

However, in his palace commissions Trumbauer had revealed an intuitive affinity for the French classical tradition, which embraces in its long inventory of residential monuments François Mansart's Château de Maisons and Jacques-Ange Gabriel's Petit Trianon at Versailles, together considered by some students of the matter to be the ultimate expression of French classic taste, perfect models of Gallic neoclassicism. Beyond some rudimentary training as a draftsman, Trumbauer was self-taught, but one may assume that his early French bias was further nourished by Abele, who had studied in Paris.

"He learned mostly by osmosis, you might say," Mrs. Fennessy has recalled of Trumbauer. "He was a great reader, and don't forget, his work was his whole life. He couldn't even take a vacation without hurrying off in a few days to some building site. When he came home for dinner he never took time to change or relax. He ate and started to read. He sat in a stiff-backed chair and read French history and French novels mostly. And, of course, he had a superb architectural library at his office."

Ogden Codman, the classicist coauthor with Edith Wharton of *The Decoration of Houses* and an outstanding architect-decorator, paid Trumbauer a rare tribute. Codman knew more about French domestic architecture than any other American who ever lived, compiling a remarkable collection of notes, photos, postcards, and drawings of all the known châteaux of France which he willed to the French Government, and which is now on deposit in the Ministry of Cultural Affairs, Paris. Architect Frederick Rhinelander King, who worked with Codman, recalled that "Trumbauer was the only architect of his time for whom Ogden Codman had any real admiration."[38] More recently, one of Trumbauer's New York houses has been singled out for praise by a widely admired contemporary architect, Philip C. Johnson. "The Duke house," he has said, "is almost more dignified than its French forebears. It is the one revival house that is a total success."[39] Becker has summed up the matter of Trumbauer's designs in the French tradition: "No other American architect had as intelligent a grasp of the French classical house as Trumbauer had."

In the history of American palace architecture, Trumbauer may be said to have been to the French classical tradition what Richard Morris Hunt had been to the Loire Valley châteaux tradition, a generalization that must admit exceptions such as Hunt's classical masterpiece, Marble House, at Newport. The architect and decorator John Barrington Bayley has added a perceptive observation that illuminates Trumbauer's success in adapting the external features of French residential architecture to American town houses set upon narrow plots. "The French never really developed town houses the way the English and the Dutch did," Bayley has pointed out. "There are, historically, no town houses at all in Europe — on the continent, that is — except in Holland. In Rome all you have are palaces and flats. The same is true in Paris. In the eighteenth century, Paris developed the ground plan called *entre cour et jardin,* the central *bloc* lying between the entrance court and the garden. What Trumbauer did that was so great was to put a French facade on an English plan, thus creating the Trumbauer French town house. Very clever."[40]

XV

T RUMBAUER'S ability to adapt the French classical tradition in residential architecture to alien conditions was severely tested at Shadow Lawn. His problem there was unique, as was his solution to it. He was unable to turn for guidance to a historic prototype, but by that time he was well versed in the grammar of the classical style as it had evolved in France beyond the basic elements of column and entablature (themselves the ancient decorative elaboration for liturgical purposes of the post and lintel) .

In effect, he built a very large and very sober French residence, noble in magnitude and subtle in its felicities, around a pseudo-Italian floor plan. He had little elbow room, for during their years in the McCall villa, Maysie and Parson had become deeply attached to its general scheme, which might be said to have wed front-porch America (the encircling veranda) to bastion north Italy (the protected inner court).

The Parsons wanted Trumbauer to retain the old foundation plan with the servants' wing canting off from a corner of the main block; the long, high, central cortile-hall; the great staircase, which had risen through a two-story arch along the north wall of the cortile; the second-story gallery around the central hall that gave access to the guest suites; and the two-story rectangular portico projecting from the north (main entrance) facade, on top of which Maysie had set out great potted plants, chairs, torchères, and tables for rooftop garden parties for herself, her husband, and her sister. Apparently, the two-story semicircular "White House" portico on the south (greensward) facade was sacrificed early, even though it was to be remembered in a small decorative projection.

If the problems were difficult, the magnitudes of the project offered Trumbauer one of the finest opportunities, in terms of size alone, that he had enjoyed since he had built Lynnewood Hall, a Palladian-Georgian echo of Rome, for P. A. B. Widener in 1898. Further, he was not to be alone in bringing under control the contending requirements of creatively intelligent design and Maysie's schoolgirl visions of a courtly realm.

For eighteen years Julian Abele had been serving as his chief designer. By the time they started work on the preliminary sketches for the new Shadow Lawn in 1927, Abele had become Trumbauer's aesthetic alter ego, the man who could perfectly express Trumbauer's ideas as they had evolved in client conferences, who could refine and compose into excellent renderings and elevations his rough sketches drawn hurriedly on whatever was available, who could swiftly grasp the sense of a proposed plan, facade, concave quadrant, trophy, or festoon and make those subtle adjustments in scale and treatment (depth of relief, say) that give to a style its inner coherence — who could, in sum, dramatize for a client precisely what Trumbauer had been talking about (much as Lassurance had done for Hardouin-Mansart, whose client had been Louis XIV).

The student of Trumbauer and his work soon becomes accustomed to the discreet presence of Abele, whose gifts, like those of his design colleagues Frank Seeburger and William O. Frank, were masked by the communal signature of the firm until they were brought to public attention by Wayne Andrews, biographer, historian, photographer, and novelist, in his entry on Trumbauer in the *Dictionary of American Biography.*

One may learn fairly quickly to respect the stylistic authority of the Trumbauer palaces. However, they yield their subtle eloquence only very slowly, for nuance is their secret. And one may sense at the heart of that secret the presence of Abele at his drafting board gently persisting against the academic absolutism of the modernist era — an eloquent man, who was also, in Ralph Ellison's bitter phrase, an invisible man.

XVI

J ULIAN FRANCIS ABELE was born in Philadelphia on April 29, 1881, the third of the six sons of Charles R. Abele, a physician.[41] One of Abele's brothers, Robert, became an orthopedic specialist; another, Joseph, became an engineer; and a third, Ernest, became a craftsman with Samuel Yellin, a leader in the revival of decorative metals work in the United States after World War I.

Abele attended the Institute for Colored Youth and the Brown Preparatory School, and then entered the University of Pennsylvania in the autumn of 1898. As an undergraduate, he was elected president of the Architecture Society and twice served on the board of editors of the university yearbook, *The Record.* In his senior year he was awarded second place in a design competition sponsored and judged by the Society of Beaux-Arts Architects. He graduated in the spring of 1902 with a degree of bachelor of science in architecture.[42]

Abele had impressed William D. Laird, the founder and dean of the university's school of architecture, and Laird took samples of his work to Trumbauer. Helena Fennessy has recalled her stepfather telling her, long after the event, that "the first minute he saw Mr. Abele's student work he wanted him in his office." Trumbauer immediately interviewed Abele and made arrangements for him to take the entrance examinations at the Ecole des Beaux-Arts in Paris that fall. Abele passed. He then spent the next four years as a student in one of the *ateliers* of the school, supported entirely by Trumbauer.

One may assume that Trumbauer enjoyed some measure of paternal gratification when Abele was awarded the Beaux-Arts *diplôme d'architecte* in the winter of 1905–1906.

On March 6, 1906, Abele joined Trumbauer's staff as an assistant to Seeburger, who had been the firm's chief designer since 1900. When Seeburger left in 1909 to open his own office, Trumbauer appointed Abele to succeed him. In his biographical sketch of Trumbauer, Andrews has written that "as time passed, Abele grew more and more fond of the work of the eighteenth-century French master, Jacques-Ange Gabriel."

Abele was an accomplished renderer, working often in watercolors. He was much influenced by the technique of Jules Guerin, a watercolorist who was highly regarded in the architectural world for the artistic quality of his renderings. In a period during which Maxfield Parrish's moonstruck fantasies (murals, posters, magazine covers, and illustrations) with their famous "Parrish blue" skies were enjoying a popular vogue, Guerin brought to his work for Trumbauer, and other architects, a peculiar "night blue" background — still, quiet, timeless: appropriate to noon or midnight — that gave to the dream palaces he rendered a dramatic ambience of expectancy, as though a *fête* were about to commence in the gardens, or the downbeat fall upon a waltz. If, as has been observed, Sargent's portraits taught his patrons how rich they really were, then Guerin's watercolor renderings assured the American palace builders that they had become princes. (Abele also greatly admired Trumbauer's own renderings, describing them to an old friend, Dr. William Warrick, as "magnificent.")

In 1915, four of Abele's watercolors were published in the yearbook of the Philadelphia chapter of the American Institute of Architects. During the last two decades of his life he made gifts of a number of his paintings to two close friends, Dr. Warrick and the architect Louis Magaziner. Abele also enjoyed mural painting, but he appears to have confined such work to his own house. Some of his architectural drawings and renderings may now be found in the Trumbauer holdings of the Historical Society of Pennsylvania in Philadelphia, but they remain to be positively identified (if, indeed, most of them ever can be).

W. Edward Frank, successor to his father in carrying on "The Office of Horace Trumbauer" (now dissolved), has spoken of Abele's remarkable draftsmanship, particularly his gift for handling shadows in so subtle a way that the observer got the impression of far more detail than Abele had actually drawn. When he was showing Andrews his rendering of the principal facade of the Free Library of Philadelphia (based upon the palaces on the Place de la Concorde), Abele smiled and said, "The shadows are all mine." The design, he thus dryly acknowledged, was Gabriel's. But one may sense behind the witty grace note of Abele's observation a resonance of the ambiguity that was the fundamental condition of his life.

As an undergraduate, he had had to confront a racial crudity so remarkable in university discourse that one may cite it without risking the self-righteousness of most rebukes to the past. In the tradition of the Ecole des Beaux-Arts, young architecture students at the University of Pennsylvania were expected to perform a number of routine tasks for the older students — redoing a drawing in a larger scale, laying out mechanical work, inking in pencil drawings, and so on. The *quid pro quo* was that the older students would lead the apprentice-newcomers to the architectural documents they needed to complete assignments, help them with their renderings, and tutor them in other practical ways.

Under this system the younger students were called "niggers" and their services "niggering." After long use, the terms were formalized in the university's textbook on architectural design, chapters of which were published as early as 1921.[43] Abele and Louis Magaziner, a white classmate who was to become Abele's closest friend and confidant, were thus both called "niggers," without discrimination one might add. The danger of our absurdities, one might further add, is that they sometimes seize us by the throat.

Racial bias was to remain a constant of Abele's professional career. "There was a great deal of feeling against Mr. Abele because of his color," Mrs. Fennessy has recalled from conversations with her stepfather, whom she called Père, a reflection of her schooling in France. "Père was widely criticized for hiring Mr. Abele, and the bias extended right in the office — even after the years had passed. I remember him saying there was an office dinner once, and when several of the men found out that Mr. Abele was coming, they deliberately stayed away. But Père never backed down. He thought very highly of Mr. Abele. And they worked so closely for such a long time. I remember that when Père was buried, Mr. Abele broke down. He was a very reserved man, but that day he wept."

On the basis of his research for a biographical essay on Abele,

Alfred S. Branam, Jr., an architectural historian, has concluded that Abele was the first Negro to practice architecture professionally in the United States. He was undoubtedly the first American Negro to study architecture at the Ecole des Beaux-Arts.

Abele was deeply committed to his Beaux-Arts training, and throughout his life he insisted, in accordance with that training, that a good plan is the heart of good architectural design. (About the time that Abele was assuming his responsibilities as Trumbauer's chief designer, Julia Morgan, another Beaux-Arts architect, was impressing on the minds of the young draftsmen in her San Francisco *atelier*-office the same precept, emphasizing that there can be no beauty in architecture until the plan has been carefully analyzed and thoughtfully developed.) Julian Abele Cook, Abele's nephew, has recalled taking some of his own work as an architecture student at Howard University to his uncle for criticism. "Don't forget that the plan is the essential element," Abele summed up. "It is the plan that people experience — that they live in."

Martin Becker of Alavoine worked with Abele for almost a quarter of a century. As a sometime architecture student at the Beaux-Arts himself, he had a warm respect for Abele's mastery of the French classical style. As a decorator, he revered Abele's command of the great eras in French decoration: "First, his knowledge was sound — very solid. Then, every line he drew had an authenticity you didn't expect to find in this country. But what was most important, at least from my point of view, was his taste. He had that rare kind of taste you trust absolutely; he and Trumbauer both."

Trumbauer's respect for Abele and his work was reflected in the salary he paid him — $12,000 a year as early as 1919 (the equivalent of $90,000 or more in 1974). Branam's research has led him to suggest that Trumbauer may also have paid Abele bonuses on some of the firm's larger commissions. After Abele's sudden death from a heart attack on April 23, 1950 — six days before his sixty-ninth birthday — his estate was estimated at $135,000 for purposes of probate. He had achieved both financial success and professional acceptance: nine years before his death he had been elected to membership in the American Institute of Architects.

Abele was fond of Paris and went back whenever he could after his student days there. On one of his visits he met Margaret Buhl, a young Frenchwoman who was studying in Paris at the Ecole Normale de Musique with Nadia Boulanger, the most esteemed teacher of composition of the era, and a conductor, still active, of consummate musical refinement. Mlle. Boulanger's pupils have included such celebrated composers as Jean Français, Lennox Berkeley, Aaron Copland, Ray Harris, Walter Piston, Virgil Thomson, and Robert Russell Bennett, the distinguished theater orchestrator.

The Abeles were married in 1924 and spent part of their honeymoon at Mlle. Boulanger's house in Bourbon-les-Bains, Haute-Marne. They became part of the ardent circle of students and friends — *les Boulangeristes* — who gathered about the eminent teacher. Mlle. Boulanger served as godmother to their son, Julian Jr., born in 1926, and they named their daughter Nadia, born in 1929, for her.

Their marriage appears to have lasted only half a dozen years or so. They were separated several years after the birth of their daughter. Abele then began to go to the Magaziners' frequently for dinner. He and Magaziner would talk through the evening, possibly recalling the college football games they had attended together as undergraduates, and possibly, at some point, discussing the work that each of them had done for Eva Stotesbury in Chestnut Hill and at Bar Harbor.

"The architect Louis Magaziner was Julian's closest friend — his confidant," Dr. Warrick has recalled. In time, Abele confided to Magaziner what the breakup of his home meant to him. Henry J. Magaziner, a witness to his father's friendship with Abele, has remembered that "Julian Abele was shattered when his wife left him. His world caved in and from then on his work was his whole life."

Abele also enjoyed frequent visits with Dr. Warrick, his closest Negro friend, and like his father a physician. He spent long hours on the Warrick porch, often passing the time without saying very much. "Julian was basically a quiet sort — and he was very meticulous in his dress and in his manner," Dr. Warrick has told Branam. "He loved music and liked to play the piano for his own pleasure and sometimes we talked about music and politics. I learned a lot about architecture from listening to him, even though I wasn't really much interested in the subject at first. I remember him talking a good bit about Horace Trumbauer. He really admired him."

Shadow Lawn was their last palace.

There would be Rose Terrace in Grosse Pointe Farms, Michigan, for Trumbauer and Abele to complete, but it was to be not so much a problem in design as an exercise in scaling-up. Mrs. Anna (Thomson) Dodge, the widow of Horace Dodge, commissioned Trumbauer simply to build her a larger version of a *manoir* she greatly admired: Miramar, in Newport, which he and Abele had designed in 1913.

The age of the American palaces had come to an end. Trumbauer found himself with a large staff and no new work, commercial or residential. He had, like many of his patrons, suffered heavy losses in the stock market crash, but he kept his office open in the futile hope that things would get better fairly quickly. He put his staff to work redrawing old projects, and paid them out of his own pocket.

Then — just about the time Parson began his headlong fall into financial ruin at Shadow Lawn — Trumbauer was forced to bid his staff good-bye. However, in the presence of William O. Frank, his structural designer of many years, Trumbauer turned to Abele and said, "I can't let *you* go, Julian. Someone else would snap you up in a minute." He kept Abele on, a sign that he intended to rehire the others as soon as he could. He did, in fact, reopen the offices in 1937, but within a year he was dead, his long and fruitful association with Abele ended.

Thus, Shadow Lawn was their farewell to an age, a fitting salute to dreams as old as man, as splendid, and as foolish.

XVII

THE best way to examine what they designed for Maysie is to stand on the greensward where the Parson sheep once grazed — now the south lawn of Monmouth College — and simply look at the palace head on, as it were. One's first impression is of mass alone. The huge upthrust of pale Bedford (Indiana) limestone is overwhelming. The palace did turn out much as George Thomson feared it would, for it does, indeed, look like a "municipal building," a description appropriate to the size, if not the architectural felicity, of the structure.

From the *porte cochère* on the east (right) to the Watteauesque exedra that closes the formal "Versailles gardens" on the west (left), one's eye traverses a sweep of almost five hundred feet. The main block of the palace has a three-hundred-foot foundation span along its principal (east-west) axis, and a one-hundred-fifty-foot span along its short (north-south) axis. The servants' wing, which extends at a shallow angle from the north-west corner of the house, adds another eighty feet to the main foundation. The wing is almost completely screened from the viewer on the lawn by the colonnade that closes the north side of the garden, and the trees behind it.

The great horizontal range of the palace is emphasized by four lateral bands: the terrace balustrades on the ground level, a plain projecting stone course above the first floor, a deep formal cornice above the second floor, and a parapet-balustrade along the edge of the roof. Often in the case of such a large French house the roof balustrade appears above the second floor, concealing a smaller third floor. At Shadow Lawn, Trumbauer was serving monarchic pretensions: Versailles has three visible stories, and so has Maysie's palace.

But it is not only the size of the palace that astonishes the eye: one is also immediately impressed by the severity of the south facade, a remote echo of the French neoclassical architect's reaction against the freehanded decorative virtuosity of the rococo. The hand of the designer at Shadow Lawn is restrained by Gabriel — the straight line contains any impulse to fugal wanderings.

There are fifty-seven windows on the south facade, all but one of them plain vertical rectangles with deep reveals, simple molded surrounds, and mullionlike sashes (even though they are double hung). The one deviant window has a sober segmental arch at its head; it lies precisely at the center of the composition.

The linearity of the facade is relieved by a discreet use of decorative details:

— A shallow, one-story portico in the central bay in which four Doric columns frame three arched French doors that give onto a terrace with steps leading down to a large circular fountain containing a group of sculptured figures.

— A wrought-iron railing above the portico, and a row of block modillions under the deep cornice band above the second floor.

— Small cartouches at the centers of the window heads on the first floor, and decorative brackets — carved volutes — at the centers of the window heads on the second floor.

— Parapet-balustrades along the terrace and along the roof edge, a handsome renaissance invention that may first have been exploited by Brunelleschi at the Pitti Palace in Florence, on which three ranges of balustrades — above the first and second floors and on the roof — sweep across the huge central *bloc:* a device brought to lyric perfection in the work of Gabriel (notably at the Petit Trianon) and his contemporaries in French classical design.

The "movement" of the projecting bays casting their changing shadows back upon the receding wall planes further relieves the austere countenance of the south facade. And one gradually notices the subtle vertical thrust provided in the decorative scheme at the outside corners of the projecting bays — the rusticated stone trim on the first and second floors, the panels of carved low-relief trophies on the third floor, and finally, the groups of *amorini* standing (almost soaring) on the skyline atop the roof balustrade at each of the projecting corners. (These statues may be the work of Charles Keck, a sculptor who did much work for Trumbauer, notably at Duke University.)

Thus, as one moves about on the great lawn, and as one studies the south facade, the decorative nuances slowly reveal themselves, cool, controlled, and subtly effective.

The formal garden to the west of the palace was designed in Paris by Achille Duchêne. The colonnades he used to close the north and west sides of the formal gardens — that on the north a peristyle-teahouse and that on the west a "water organ" (its jet fountains operated from an indoor control panel) serving as an exedra — were adapted from the circular peristyle known as "la Colonnade" in the *bosquet* at Versailles. A study of Duchêne's plans indicates that economies were made both in the execution of his architectural details and in his planting scheme.[44] In the process a seven-hundred-foot axial garden that would have lent a softening touch of formal grace to the terrace facade was eliminated.

Each of the other facades of the palace has interesting features, the most commanding of them being the massive two-story portico on the north facade which serves as the principal entrance. Six smooth columns across the front, and two more on each side, rise two stories to Ionic capitals which support an entablature and parapet (or attic) behind which, on the flat roof, Maysie continued to give summer evening parties for Parson, herself, and Bertha, and an occasional friend. Pendant festoons, a characteristic decorative device of the French renaissance — used with striking effect by Jules Hardouin-Mansart and François d'Orbay at Versailles, and by Jacques Gabriel (the father of Jacques-Ange Gabriel) on the Hôtels de la Douane et de la Bourse at Bordeaux — fall from the volutes of the Ionic capitals down the face of the massive smooth columns about thirty inches. The device is peculiarly French, a knowledgeable accent that reminds the viewer that the portico is more French than Italian, although he might have concluded differently.

If there is a major fault in the design of the palace, it must be laid to Maysie's solarium. Here the evidence of her want of knowledge, visual perception, and sensitivity is complete, for her penthouse does nothing less than destroy the whole point of Trumbauer's classic scheme — its symmetry.

XVIII

THE interiors were Maysie's domain — Trumbauer did the cortile, Baumgarten & Co. the rest. The great central hall is all architectural: it is plastered to simulate courses of limestone, and its bays of French basket-handle arches on the first floor and rectangular gallery openings above, rising through three stories, are separated by *fleur de pêche* marble pilasters. It defines the grandeur of the state *salons* and master chambers upstairs. It is one hundred ten feet long, twenty-five feet wide, and rises almost seventy feet to an amber skylight. Adjoining it to the south is a one-story extension of the cortile, a vast reception area which is also one hundred ten feet long, and thirty-five feet wide.

As in the original house, a wide marble stairway ascends to a large mezzanine through the central arch in the north wall of the cortile. McCall, it will be recalled, had a single balcony-gallery circling the cortile; Maysie had two. The hand-tufted Seville runners covering the side passages of her galleries measured one hundred twenty-two feet in length.

A four-manual Aeolian-Skinner organ, which automatically played a hymn for Parson each morning during breakfast before he was driven up to New York, used the great hall as a vast resonating chamber that amplified the sound until God's praise shook the palace. Its pipe and echo lofts are concealed at the ends of the galleries; its manual console, rarely touched, is on the first gallery; and its Duo-Art automatic playing mechanism, used daily, is on the mezzanine. The organ cost Parson $100,000.

Maysie had one hundred twenty-eight rooms — twenty-two of them in the servants' wing — to decorate and oversee. There were eight state *salons* on the first floor: two master suites, each with a bedroom, boudoir, dressing room, and two baths; and three guest suites, each with a bedroom, boudoir, and bath, on the second floor; and, nine guest bedrooms, each with a bath, and nine with boudoirs, on the third floor. Each floor had a flower room with marble counters for cutting and preparing the daily deliveries from the gardens. (Maysie had more than one hundred plants strewn about, and she was very severe with the house staff when she found a dead leaf on any of them.) And, up on the third floor Maysie had a small kitchen where she sometimes made the family dessert.

The labels Maysie put on her upstairs rooms reveal nothing more than conventional vagueness, and conventional aspiration. They tell us only that one would have found in her private rooms the sometimes ill-designed variety of imitative decoration and furniture found in the average American palace, a reflection both of the decorator's limitations as an artist and the condition of his warehouse. Among the rooms were an Adam Study (Parson's), a French Sitting Room, a Marie Antoinette Bedroom (Maysie's — she also had a Marie Antoinette Music Room on the ground floor), a Chinese Chippendale Bedroom (Bertha's), a Directoire Guest Bedroom, a Venetian Sun Room, a Queen Anne Boudoir, a Modern Directoire Bedroom, a Spanish Renaissance Bedroom, a Louis Seize Boudoir, an Orchid Walnut Bedroom, a Chinese Living Room, and a Tudor Oak Bedroom.

The quality of the decoration in the palace is wildly variable. There is a curious mixture of opulent intentions opulently realized and certain design crudities — a case, in part, of Baumgarten's German design staff speaking a bookish and uncertain French, as it were.

A decorator who was with Baumgarten at the time, but who had nothing to do with Shadow Lawn, has observed: "They took a beautiful house and ruined it." His ambiguous *they* embraced both Baumgarten's designers and Maysie. "They started down in the basement with some prehistoric caveman decorations, absolutely awful stuff in a house, then went through all the Louis periods upstairs. I saw the drawings for all those pseudo-Louis rooms. It was pathetic; plain awful. Not one thing in the house was original — everything was bad reproduction. Heavy-handed. And none of it had any intrinsic merit. She paid $6,000 to have a bedspread copied in Paris, and the minute it was finished it wasn't worth any more than the material that was used to make it — a few dollars, say."

The criticism is severe, but fair in its own terms; its professional bias favors authentic antique interiors, a difficult ideal to achieve in ninety-six rooms. There is nothing wrong with reproduction. Pierre Verlet, the great scholar of French eighteenth-century decorative art, has dryly disposed of the matter: "Is not Louis XVI's desk at Versailles a faithful copy of Louis XV's?"[45] The true problem is one of logic. If one is to play successfully the exacting game of *témoignage* — the precise reconstitution of a room that existed in the past — or any of its less stringent variants, one must have both knowledge and wisdom.

Edith Wharton played a knowing variation of the game at the Pavillon Colombe in Sainte Brice. Mrs. Wharton was the absolute perfectionist. "Shall I make a confession?" a French noblewoman later asked. "The perfection of her taste . . . chilled me. I have often noticed among Americans attracted by our civilization and our traditions, something for which we ourselves are scarcely prepared, something that exceeds our measure. In nearly every French interior you will notice a clock that betrays the bad taste of the mother-in-law. . . . With Mrs. Wharton I was intimidated by the aesthetic perfection of everything about her."[46] The little stuffed fox on the mantel — expertise takes it away, wisdom puts it back.

But it wasn't wisdom that led Maysie to the luxurious hodgepodge of her decoration. She had already decorated three palaces, but she seems to have learned nothing basic. Coherence eluded her. She had an amiable deficiency most of us will recognize: she could put five pieces of furniture in an empty ballroom, and the place would look cluttered. She was no Edith Wharton: her errors were not those of dehumanized perfection but of awkward splendor.

In the best of the state *salons* at Shadow Lawn — in the Music Room and the Morning Room, say — one can still see a muscular bravura, a bit overdone to be sure, that must have conveyed to Maysie the pomp and glitter of the eighteenth-century French courts. But delicacy and nuance, subtleties of scale, and the wit and charm of true elegance are absent. Coarseness prevails.

Maysie tinkered constantly with the interiors during the finishing and decorating. Time and again, Thomson has recalled, William Groh, the Baumgarten supervisor on the project, had to tear out the plastering or take down the *boiserie* and replace it to suit Maysie's changing specifications.

Maysie was the victim of uncertainty: she couldn't make up her mind. "She would call and ask me to bring some men up to the house," Thomson has said, "and we would spend the afternoon moving heavy furniture from one room to another. Then she would say, 'How does it look, Mr. Thomson?' and I'd have to say, 'Not good, ma'am,' and we'd move everything back again."

"She was slightly eccentric," Clarence W. Withey, who was head poultryman on the estate and who later returned to Shadow Lawn and served as a vice-president of Monmouth College, has observed. "She dyed her hair a coppery color, and she wore a fair amount of makeup, which was considered fast in those days. We used to hear that she had been a seamstress."

Four decades later the Parsons still puzzle him.

XIX

I arrived at Shadow Lawn on Labor Day, 1932," Withey has recalled. "The man in charge of the poultry had died suddenly, and the superintendent asked me to take over for a while. This stretched out to six months. It was during the Depression, so when Parson asked me to stay permanently, I agreed.

"My job was to provide a variety of fowl. Parson had some sort of trouble, and he required a special diet of fowl and lamb. I bred all types of fowl: capons, turkeys, chickens, turkey capons, capon ducks, mallards, Pekin ducks, and the largest flock of artificially raised guinea hens in the East.

"We kept a flock of sheep that ranged from twenty-five up to thirty-five. And we also had fifteen head of cattle, and two bulls named Shadow I and Shadow II.

"I was paid $100 a month. In addition we had an apartment, and we were provided with fresh vegetables and fresh dairy products — and fowl, of course.

"When things were going full tilt there was a staff of close to one hundred working here who went off the grounds at night. There were, I believe, fourteen people working in the house on restricted service, as it was called — maids, cooks, servants, and so on, who lived in the servants' wing of the house. On the grounds, besides a superintendent, there was a dairyman, an assistant dairyman, a head gardener, an assistant gardener, the poultry superintendent (myself) and his three assistants, and the greenhouse superintendent and his assistants.

"Most of us lived in apartments in the big superintendent's house. The two chauffeurs lived off the grounds. Besides the three Rolls-Royces, there was a Ford station wagon and a Reo panel truck to take flowers, vegetables, and poultry to the Fifth Avenue house. (There was also a Cadillac that Parson gave to the superintendent to drive.) At Christmas the Reo carried a full load of dressed turkeys and poinsettias to New York, and at Easter it was loaded with capon or spring ducklings, all wrapped separately, and Easter lilies.

"Parson enjoyed the place tremendously. He walked around thoroughly enjoying the pride of ownership. Once he asked me along and told me about the great losses he had taken in his Chilean copper stocks. He didn't seem to have any friends, men friends, that is. The very few guests who ever came were usually women — her friends, I guess.

"Mrs. Parson had a little canning kitchen over the garage. She liked to come down and put up preserves. At the time I was there, Miss Gasque — Mrs. Parson's sister — acted as the housekeeper. She was gray-haired and charming. She had the Chinese suite in the house. (It's now the office of the president of the college.) Mrs. Parson also liked to sew, and she made some of the drapes in the superintendent's house, and the other cottages, by hand.

"Parson was neat. A meticulous man. I remember that he was deathly afraid of contagious diseases. He had strict rules. No one on the staff was allowed to have an automobile on the grounds. If you went off the grounds in the evening, you had to be back by midnight because the gates were locked then, and six dogs were turned loose. If you had any guests, you had to walk them to the gate before that time. Most of the staff were Scotch, English, and Irish. The shore in those days seemed like the first stop after the boat from Ireland arrived.

"Parson had a brother who lived in Bayonne. His daughters would come down and they were allowed to stay in one of the cottages in the woods and pick their own vegetables. I don't think any of the Woolworth people ever set foot on the place.

"Parson seemed to me like a man who wanted to start a conversation, but didn't know how. He was like the new boy in the neighborhood who stands by a tree and wishes he'd be invited to play. As time passes, I tend to think of him as a rather pathetic sort.

"We didn't have any way of knowing what he was going through of course. Things just went along from day to day for us, then suddenly, furniture began arriving by the vanloads from New York — from the Fifth Avenue house. Then, not long afterwards, mirrors and statues and a lot of heavy furniture, and furnishings, began to show up from France in huge crates. I remember one crate was so big you could drive a car into it.

"Of course, it's easy to look back now and see what was happening. Time was running out on Parson."

It had, in fact, started running out on him long before the crates from Paris arrived.

XX

ON New Year's Eve, 1930, the usual good wishes of the *Long Branch Record* could have counted for but little at Shadow Lawn.

Parson owed more than $500,000 for the additional work on the palace. He owed the Metropolitan Life Insurance Company $300,000, the amount of the mortgage on 1071 Fifth Avenue. He still had his salary of $650,000, but it cost him $300,000 a year to maintain Shadow Lawn, and another $100,000 a year to run his New York and Paris houses. And, the new year brought new debts.

Fred M. Kirby, Charles S. Woolworth, and one or two others among the oldtime Woolworth directors, decided personally to lend Parson about $1,000,000 on Shadow Lawn and his Paris house, assigning the mortgages to the Fremkir Corporation, an anagram on Kirby's name. They were far more concerned with Woolworth's public relations than they were with Parson's personal difficulties.

Breadlines and soup kitchens had appeared in the cities, and people were frightened and angry. A bankruptcy action by Parson's creditors would have taken him into court, and into the headlines. It was no time for the public to learn that the president of Woolworth had recently moved into a $10,000,000* palace in which three people shared ninety-six rooms and were attended by an estate staff of almost one hundred. The Fremkir associates wanted to keep Parson out of court.

Throughout his difficulties, Parson eluded bankruptcy proceedings. Sometimes he waited until the last minute to forestall a threatened action. During 1932, for example, he paid off a $250,000 bank debt almost on the courthouse steps. As a result, no one ever learned

---

* Parson's own final estimate of the cost of Shadow Lawn, a figure that included the Fremkir mortgage and the Metropolitan Life Insurance Company mortgage on 1071 Fifth Avenue.

how much of his dwindling assets he had transferred to Maysie's name, a fact he would have had to disclose to the court in a bankruptcy procedure. (However, Parson provided well for Maysie: she outlived him by sixteen years, until April 28, 1956, in a Park Avenue apartment.[47])

During 1932, Parson reached sixty, the mandatory retirement age at Woolworth at that time. His fellow directors, who could have done so, did not ask him to stay on: his salary stopped. On March 1, 1933, the $300,000 loan on his Fifth Avenue house was due. He could not pay it, and was granted an extension. By the end of the year he was in arrears in his federal income and West Long Branch real estate taxes.

The drum roll of troubles quickened. During 1936, the Metropolitan Life Insurance Company finally foreclosed its mortgage on 1071 Fifth Avenue, and bought the house at public auction on December 18 for $200,000. Parson closed the greenhouses at Shadow Lawn and started selling the estate's butter and milk in the village market. Thomson was injured by one of the police dogs and left the estate.

In 1937, the borough of West Long Branch threatened to cut off Shadow Lawn's sewerage service. Withey sold off the poultry and followed Thomson off the estate. In desperation, Parson tried to sell Shadow Lawn with the help of a large illustrated brochure entitled "The Versailles of America."[48] But no one wanted a $10,000,000 palace in 1937.

In 1938, Kirby became ill and withdrew from the Woolworth board. His son, Allan P. Kirby, who was to become one of America's best known financiers, foreclosed Shadow Lawn and 72 Avenue Foch. "We came out with a final net loss of a couple hundred thousand dollars," Kirby has recalled. At the time of the Fremkir foreclosures, the federal government filed a tax lien of more than $300,000 against Parson. That year he was quietly dropped from the Woolworth board. Peter Eller has recalled that his firm, Thompson-Starrett, absolved most of Parson's unpaid account for the construction of the palace. "Our people were very kind to him," Eller has said.

Before the end of 1938, Maysie and Parson left Shadow Lawn. Parson may still have had his illusions, but he had parted with all three of his palaces.

On September 25, 1939, Undersheriff Dorman McFaddin of Monmouth County sold Shadow Lawn at public auction to the sole bidder, the Borough of West Long Branch.[49]

The price: $100.

XXI

THE shadow of John A. McCall, the man who had created the original Shadow Lawn, hung over Parson a moment longer.

Maysie, after paying a tax lien of $30,592, held a four-week auction of her furniture in 1940. The sale opened on May 25. Among the 2,889 items that went under the hammer was a remarkable commode, a copy of one of the most famous pieces in the French royal inventory, made by Antoine Gaudreaux, from designs by the Slodtz brothers, who furnished it with gilded bronze mounts. It was offered for bidding under two contradictory descriptive titles — "Prince Condé Kingwood Commode," and "Prince Conti Kingwood Commode" — both of them inaccurate, a condition which, at that unhappy moment, reflected silently on the shallowness of Maysie's costly search for elegance.[50]

On June 8, the auctioneer told a reporter that Maysie was realizing only about ten cents on the dollar.[51] Six days later, the German army occupied Paris.

A week after the auction began, Parson was stricken with a heart seizure in a rented house in Allenhurst, the Jersey shore village where he and Maysie had first summered in the 1890's to get away from the Brooklyn heat and be near the Woolworths. He was rushed to New York Hospital. He died there of another heart attack on July 9, leaving an estate of $2,500.[52]

Parson had no son to tell the press that he had made a good salary, and had lived up to every cent of it.

ACKNOWLEDGMENTS
NOTES
BIBLIOGRAPHY

ACKNOWLEDGMENTS

NAÏVETÉ and the bounty of generous intelligence: both went into the making of this book. I brought the former quality to the venture, others gave to it the abundance of their knowledge and insights. Only the reader can determine whether or not this odd partnership was an equitable one. My greenness and imprudence are, I suppose, my own concern. But the kindness and thoughtfulness that sustained me through a long season of research and writing are matters I want to discuss.

I am deeply obliged to the Jerome Foundation, Inc., and to Classical America, Inc., for financial aid. Classical America acted favorably, and with benevolent dispatch, on my petition for a grant to bring the present book to completion. Funds for the grant were authorized by the Directors of the Jerome Foundation, and I am indeed grateful to them.

Mr. Ethan Ayer — poet, short-story writer, opera librettist, and novelist — has shown his generous concern for the work in many ways. He read a succession of intermediate drafts, and his comments on technical matters in architecture and decoration were consistently enlightening and pertinent.

I have depended much on the writing of others and I have in the appropriate places acknowledged this debt to the extent possible. I have made extensive use of newspaper materials. However, many of the news reports and feature stories I have used, and cited in the text, notes, and bibliographies, were written and edited by anonymous reporters and copy desk men and women, who daily turn out the stuff of history under great pressure. I salute and thank them.

I have used the holdings and facilities of a number of libraries, principally the library of the New-York Historical Society, the Avery Memorial Architectural Library of Columbia University, and the New York Public Library, Central Building (particularly the Art and Architecture and Local History and Genealogy divisions). The New York Public Library allowed me the privilege of working in the Wortheim Study during two phases of my research, and I should like to express my appreciation for this courtesy. Other libraries that provided me with congenial surroundings, access to their holdings, and expert help were:

The Henry E. Huntington Library and Art Gallery, San Marino, California; the Asheville (North Carolina) Public Library; the Sarasota (Florida) Public Library; the West Palm Beach (Florida) Public Library; the Long Branch (New Jersey) Public Library; the New York Society Library; the Library of Congress (Manuscript Division), Washington, D.C.; the library of the General Society of Mechanics and Tradesmen of the City of New York; the library of the Metropolitan Museum of Art, New York City; and the library of the American Institute of Architects, Washington, D.C.

I am indebted to the Austin (Texas) Public Library (Austin-Travis County Collection); the San Marcos (Texas) Public Library; the Free Library of Philadelphia; the California State Library, Sacramento, California; and the Richmond (Virginia) Public Library for searches conducted on my behalf, and for copies of documentary and other materials. The National Archives and Records Service, Washington, D.C., supplied microfilm copies of documents I requested, and the Southern California, Northern California, New York City, and Buffalo, New York, chapters of the American Institute of Architects graciously assisted me in various ways.

Much of my work was carried out in museums, principally: the Metropolitan Museum of Art, the Frick Collection, the Museum of the City of New York, the New-York Historical Society, and the Brooklyn Museum, all in New York; the Musée des Arts Décoratifs de l'Union Centrale des Arts Décoratifs, and the Musée National du Louvre, both in Paris; the Boston Museum of Fine Arts; the Philadelphia Museum of Art; and the Henry E. Huntington Library and Art Gallery, San Marino, California.

Perhaps the most significant overall contribution to the content of the book was made by those people who brought to it their personal recollections. I am most grateful to them for their patience and generosity in submitting to extended interviews. Some of them had to interrupt busy schedules, and some had to travel long distances to meet with me. All shared their memories and observations openhandedly, and none placed any restrictions upon my use of what they told me.

Following are the names of those who submitted to interviews, with the places and dates of our meetings indicated. (The list conforms to the chapter headings) :

I. *Whitemarsh Hall:* Mr. James H. R. Cromwell, New York City, January 14, 1967, and subsequent conversations. Mrs. Edward H. Fennessy, Lincoln, Massachusetts, October 24 and 25, 1967. Mr. Martin Becker: for details see Shadow Lawn, below. Mrs. Flora S. Straus (Mrs. Hugh Grant Straus), Mt. Kisco, New York, October 31, 1974 (by telephone).

II. *Ca' D'Zan:* Mr. Frank C. Martin, Sarasota, Florida, March 3, 1965. Mr. Robert Webb, Jr., Sarasota, March 5, 1965. Mr. Frank Fielli, Sarasota, March 5, 1965. Mr. Eugene Pohunek, Sarasota, March 6, 1965. Mrs. Frances Hoersting, Sarasota, March 6, 1965 (by telephone). Mr. Henry Ringling North, New York City, April 10 (by telephone) and April 15, 1965. Mr. John H. Thiesen, New York City, April 15, 1965, and subsequent conversations. Mr. Earl Purdy, New Rochelle, New York, May 20 and (by telephone) June 7, 1965.

III. *Vizcaya:* Miss Lillian Gish, Washington, Connecticut, September 22, 1964. Mrs. Nell Dorr, Washington, Connecticut, September 22, 1964. Mr. Eustace Edgecombe, Miami, March 12, 1965. Mr. F. Burrall Hoffman, Jr., New York City, April 14, 1965. Mr. Diego Suarez, New York City, April 20 and June 4, 1965. Mr. Robert Tyler Davis, New York City, May 20, 1965. Mrs. Marianita C. Ranger, August 10, 1965. Mr. Spencer A. Samuels, New York City, April 16, 1971. Mr. Allyn Cox, New York City, June 5, 1972.

IV. *San Marino:* Mr. William Hertrich, San Marino, California, April 30 and May 3, 1965. Mr. Harold Coulson Chambers, Pasadena, California, May 2, 1965. Mr. Edwin H. Carpenter, San Marino: a succession of interview-discussions between April 27 and May 3, 1965.

V. *Shadow Lawn:* Mr. Thomas J. Mullen, New York City, March 31, 1965, and West Long Branch, New Jersey, July 14, 1965. Mr. Peter W. Eller, New York City, June 1, 1965 (by telephone). Mr. Clarence W. Withey, West Long Branch, July 13 and 14, 1965. Mr. George W. Thomson, Long Branch, New Jersey, July 15 and 16, 1965. Mr. Benno de Térey, New York City, July 10, 1966 (by telephone). Mrs. Edward H. Fennessy: for details see Whitemarsh Hall, above. M. Henri Samuel, Paris, September 22, 1967, and New York City, December 26 and 29, 1967. Mr. Martin Becker, November 15, 1967 (by telephone), December 11, 1967, February 8, 1968.

(NOTE: Mr. Alfred S. Branam, Jr., made available to the author several quotations concerning Julian Abele and his work drawn from interviews he conducted with the following people for use in his forthcoming study of Trumbauer's architecture: Mr. Julian Abele Cook, Mr. W. Edward Frank, Mr. Henry J. Magaziner, and Dr. William Warrick.)

Many people helped me in my research by providing data, background information, copies of documents, letters, old clippings, catalogues, memorabilia, photographs, floor plans, and a wide variety of other materials. I am especially indebted to the following for their generosity:

Albany, New York: Mr. Raymond D. Salman. *Bethel, Connecticut:* Mrs. Anna Hyatt Huntington. *Bloomington, Indiana:* Mr. John B. Patton. *Boston:* Mrs. R. E. Danielson. *Chicago:* Mrs. Marvin Aspen. *Evanston, Illinois:* Mrs. Deva R. Howard.

Miami: Mrs. Louise Howland Drake, Mr. Jefferson T. Warren. *Morristown, New Jersey:* Mr. Allan P. Kirby, *Newport News, Virginia:* Miss Cerinda W. Evans. *New York City:* Mr. Milton Caniff, Mr. David Combs, Mr. James F. Durnell, Mr. Joseph W. Ernst, Mrs. Regina Kellerman, Mr. Stewart Klonis, Mr. Robert T. McLeod, Mr. Lewis Ross, Mr. John Russell, Mr. Charles G. K. Warner, Miss Helen Williams.

Orleans, Massachusetts: Mrs. G. C. Foresman. *Philadelphia:* Mr. Gary Christopher, Mrs. Joan Younger Dickinson, Mr. William Dickinson, Mr. Sidney T. Dvorak, Mr. W. Edward Frank, Mr. John M. Freeman, Mr. Frank P. Graham, Mr. Henry J. Magaziner, Mr. Charles Martyn, Mr. Howard K. Simpson, Mr. George B. Tatum. *Richmond, Virginia:* Col. F. S. Duling, Mr. John G. Worsham, Col. J. M. Wright.

San Diego, California: Rear Admiral Charles B. Hunt, U.S.N. (Ret.). *San Marino, California:* Mr. Robert R. Wark. *Sarasota, Florida:* Miss Florence Gilmore, Mr. Mel Miller, Mr. Karl Nickel, Mr. Robert O. Parks, Mr. Waldo Proffitt. *Tampa, Florida:* Mr. Joseph B. Dobkin, Mr. Paul E. Camp. *Upper Montclair, New Jersey:* Mrs. Lillian Zeffaro. *Washington Court House, Ohio:* Mrs. Kathleen Dolphin, Mr. George Robinson. *West Long Branch, New Jersey:* Miss Betty Baderman, Mr. Ralph G. Binder, Mr. J. Russell Woolley.

London, England: Mr. G. W. Whale.

Paris, France: Mme. Y. Amic.

Once I began work on the book I entered into a network of experts who introduced me one to the other:

Mr. Alan Burnham, Director of Research, New York City Landmarks Preservation Commission, New York City, until recent years a practicing architect, the editor of *New York Landmarks* and the unpublished "Richard Morris Hunt Papers," teacher of Architecture: U.S.A., a history of American architecture, at the New School for Social Research, and a Fellow of the American Institute of Architects.

Mr. Henry Hope Reed, Curator of Central Park, New York City, author of *The Parks of New York City: A History and a Guide* and *The Golden City;* coauthor (with Christopher Tunnard) of *American Skyline* and (with Sophia Duckworth) of *Central Park: A History and a Guide;* coeditor (with William A. Coles) of *Architecture in America: A Battle of Styles,* and an ardent and eloquent champion of the classical tradition in architecture, landscape architecture, and decoration.

Mr. John Barrington Bayley, designer of the new wing of the Frick Collection; an architect, decorator, and photographer whose camera has documented in thousands of photographs much of the history of architecture and decoration in Europe, a history he can discuss, or draw, with equal felicity and scholarship.

Mr. James Parker, Curator of Western Art, the Metropolitan Museum of Art; a widely admired and distinguished authority on architecture, decoration, and the decorative arts, under whose regime the Metropolitan Museum has made outstanding additions to its permanent display of authentic period rooms, which he has documented with meticulous scholarship.

M. Henry Sorensen of Paris, scholar, photographer, author (i.e., "La geniale esquisse de Versailles," *Connaissance des arts,* Juin, 1968), and a brilliant guide to his country's treasured architectural monuments.

It would require an essay to explain what my contacts with these able specialists has meant to me in the course of my work on this book. Briefly, each, in his own way, has been a patient, stimulating, and kindly tutor.

I have elsewhere cited specific materials provided to me by Mr. Alfred S. Branam, Jr., of Philadelphia, an architectural historian. I should like here to thank him for his scholarly generosity in making available to me, right up to press time, data and background information from his ongoing documentation of Horace Trumbauer's work.

In the course of my research I spent many hours discussing historical aspects of the American palaces with Mr. John L. Wadsworth of the History Department of Rutgers University. I will remark elsewhere and at greater length about Mr. Wadsworth's kindness in providing me with both working quarters and access to an abundance of rare materials.

Legal details — language, procedure, specific points of law, and so on — often baffled me during my research into deeds, titles, mortgages, and similar property and estate documents. My recourse was simple: I imposed upon the time and knowledge of Mrs. Joan Cappelli, lawyer and family friend. Time and again she clarified the confusions I brought to her.

Here I must set out a proviso. Although I have had the help of many experts in the preparation of this book, I am the responsible parent of its errors.

During a long period in which I importuned his good humor and patience, my agent, Mr. Donald K. Congdon, never faltered in his encouragement and practical guidance. He was the permissive uncle of a project that went its own way. Mr. Llewellyn Howland III, my editor, reined the matter in, as it were, giving to the final draft a tolerant but meticulous reading from which evolved a number of handsome suggestions. His has been a thoughtful and disciplined advocacy.

As she has done for me in the past, Miss Joellyn Ausanka again brought to the typing of the several "final" drafts of the manuscript a cool and professional editorial eye. Her care and skill were mainstays of a very substantial and uncommon sort.

NOTES

ONE. WHITEMARSH HALL

1. Lippincott, Horace Mather, "Edward T. Stotesbury," *Old York Road Historical Society Bulletin* VI (1942): p. 15. Lippincott also wrote and published a small book entitled *A Narrative Account of Chestnut Hill, Philadelphia, with Some Account of Springfield, Whitemarsh, and Cheltenham Townships in Montgomery County, Pennsylvania* in 1948. These two works, and the obituaries prepared by the Associated Press (originally distributed to member papers April 5, 1929) and the *Evening Bulletin* (May 17, 1938), referred to in the text as the *Philadelphia Bulletin*, are the basic sources used for biographical data on Stotesbury.
2. Ibid., Lippincott, "Stotesbury."
3. Branam, Alfred S., Jr. See Acknowledgments.
4. The author's description of the condition of Whitemarsh Hall is based upon a visit to the house and gardens in 1965. Since that time the premises have been thoroughly vandalized.
5. "Stotesbury Estate." Company memorandum on house data. Pennsalt Chemicals Corporation (now Pennwalt Corporation), n.d.
   Tompkins, Calvin, *Merchants and Masterpieces*, p. 238. Data on the Metropolitan Museum of Art's use of Whitemarsh Hall during World War II.
6. Kimball Fiske, "The Stotesburys." Chapter 16, *Triumph on Fairmont*, by George and Mary Roberts, p. 233.
7. Ibid. David DuBon, Curator, Medieval and Renaissance Decorative Art, Philadelphia Museum of Art, has kindly advised the author (letter, October 18, 1974) that Kimball eventually "lost his enthusiasm" for this attribution, concluding that the problem of attributing the plaster nymphs definitively was more complex than he had at first imagined. The museum exhibits its eight Stotesbury nymphs without attribution. The Metropolitan Museum of Art owns two very similar nymphs, which it also exhibits without attribution.
8. *A New Home for an Old House*, p. 10.
9. Lippincott, "Stotesbury," p. 11.
10. Ibid., p. 5.
11. Ibid., p. 10.
    Stotesbury obituary. Associated Press. Distributed April 5, 1929.
12. Lippincott, "Stotesbury," op. cit., p. 13.
    "Stotesbury House Has Noted History," unidentified, undated newspaper clipping, Philadelphia, *c.* May 20, 1925.
13. Allen, Frederick Lewis, *The Great Pierpont Morgan*, p. 239.
14. Baltzell, E. Digby, *An American Business Aristocracy*, p. 188.
15. Burt, Nathaniel, *The Perennial Philadelphians*, p. 23.

16. Ibid., p. 26.
17. Barron, Clarence W., *They Told Barron*, p. 268.
18. Stone, Lawrence, *The Crisis of the Aristocracy, 1558–1641*, p. 23.
19. Jullian, Philippe, *Prince of Aesthetes*, pp. 16, 17.
20. Burt, Struthers, *Philadelphia: Holy Experiment*, p. 363.
21. Burt, Nathaniel, op. cit., p. 251.
22. Baltzell, op. cit., p. 382.
23. Ibid., pp. 382, 384.
24. Ibid., p. 383.
25. Nicolson, Harold, *Kings, Courts, and Monarchy*, p. 220.
26. Data for Section VI drawn primarily from *A New Home for an Old House* (anonymous) ; Baltzell; N. Burt; and Robert Sobel, *The Big Board*.
27. Lippincott, "Stotesbury," op. cit., p. 4.
28. Baltzell, op. cit., p. 270.
29. Kimball, op. cit., p. 229.
30. Biddle, Cornelia Drexel, *The Happiest Millionaire*, pp. 19–20.
31. Satterlee, Herbert L., *J. Pierpont Morgan*, pp. 148–149.
32. Ibid.
33. Branam, op. cit.
34. Quoted by Josephson, Matthew, *The Robber Barons*, p. 404.
35. *Philadelphia Bulletin*, May 17, 1938.
36. Lippincott, "Stotesbury, op. cit., pp. 9–10.
37. For specific data on his early paintings, see *Collection of Paintings* (printed for E. T. Stotesbury) , 1897.
38. Kimball, op. cit., p. 230.
39. LeBrun, George P., *It's Time to Tell*, p. 212.
40. Cromwell is the primary source of data on the Roberts and Cromwell families.
41. "Two Bachelors Charming Hosts," unidentified, undated newspaper clipping, New York City, *c.* February 18, 1895.
42. Ibid.
43. *New York Times*, December 22, 1909.
44. *Philadelphia Bulletin*, May 3, 1910.
45. Ibid., January 12, 1926.
46. Moore, Charles, *The Life and Times of Charles Follen McKim*, p. 37.
47. "Stotesbury House Has Noted History," op. cit.
48. Cromwell has identified each of the four as having participated in the ongoing changes undertaken at the Walnut Street house.
49. Fleming, John; Honour, Hugh; and Pevsner, Nikolaus, "Mansart" in *The Penguin Dictionary of Architecture*.
50. Gimpel, René, *Diary of an Art Dealer*, p. 142.
    Behrman, S. N., *Duveen*, p. 8.
51. Savage, George, *A Concise History of Interior Decoration*, p. 251.
52. Jullian, Philippe, *Edward and the Edwardians*, p. 200.
53. Berlioz's essay is included in *Source Readings in Music History*, selected and annotated by Oliver Strunk, p. 809.
54. Fennessy, Mrs. Edward H., interviews. See Acknowledgments.
55. Ibid.
56. Moore, op. cit., p. 37.
57. Van Trump, James D., "A Castellated Metamorphosis: Grey Towers into Beaver College," *Charette* 44: No. 2., p. 17.
58. King, Moses, ed., *Philadelphia and Notable Philadelphians*, p. 77.
59. Ibid., p. 76. King is the source of the style labels for this and the succeeding two houses.
60. Lees-Milne, James, "Ralph Allen at Prior Park," *Apollo*, November, 1973, p. 366.
61. Roberts, George and Mary, *Triumph on Fairmount*, p. 182.
62. *Chetwode: Former Home of John J. Astor, Newport, Rhode Island* (New York: Joseph P. Day, n.d.) , 8 pp. Sales brochure.

63. Seligman, Germain, *Merchants of Art*, p. 73.
64. Gallet, Michel, *Stately Mansions: Eighteenth Century Paris Architecture*, p. 19.
65. Vors, Frédéric, article on the Hôtel de la Païva in *The Art Amateur*, August, 1879, p. 52.
    Kashey, Robert, and Reymert, Martin L. H., *Western European Bronzes of the Nineteenth Century*, notes for plate 39.
66. Jervis, Simon, *Victorian Furniture*, plate 2.
    Savage, op. cit., p. 230, fig. 182.
67. Becker, Martin, interviews. See Acknowledgments.
68. Kimball, op. cit., p. 230.
69. Behrman, op. cit., p. 73.
70. *Philadelphia Bulletin*, December 10, 1911.
71. Report on Stotesbury-Cromwell wedding in unidentified, undated newspaper clipping, Philadelphia, *c.* January 18, 1912.
72. *Philadelphia Bulletin*, January 18, 1912.
73. Ibid., January 19 and February 13, 1912.
74. This and the two preceding quotations are constants of Philadelphia oral tradition. They vary with the teller.
75. Burt, N., op. cit., p. 162.
    Wecter, Dixon, *The Saga of American Society*, p. 67.
76. *Newsweek*, June 5, 1967, p. 63.
77. *Philadelphia Bulletin*, October 15, 1911.
78. Delaire, E. et al., *Les architectes élèves de l'école des Beaux-Arts, 1793–1907*.
    Lavedan, Pierre, Gréber obituary-tribute in *La vie urbaine* (Janvier–Mars, 1963).
    Passillé, Raymond de, "Les jardins français aux Etats-Unis: créations De MM. Dûchene et Gréber," *La gazette illustrée des amateurs de Jardins*, 1963.
79. *Philadelphia Bulletin*, April 11, 1916, and October 14, 1919.
80. Letter: Eva R. Stotesbury to Horace Trumbauer, August 6, 1917.
    Philadelphia Bulletin, October 14, 1919.
81. Ibid., February 1, 1923; April 29, 1924; June 17, 1925; January 11, 1964.
82. Gray, David, *Thomas Hastings, Architect*, p. 239.
83. Letter: Robert T. McLeod, George A. Fuller Company, to author, July 30, 1969.
    Philadelphia Bulletin, October 20, 1916.
    Philadelphia Inquirer, October 9, 1921.
84. Letter published courtesy of Mrs. Fennessy: permission of Mr. Cromwell.
85. Letter: McLeod to author, op. cit.
86. De Passillé, op. cit. Henry Hope Reed, Curator of Parks, New York City, has made the following translation (excerpted) of de Passillé's observations on the gardens at Whitemarsh Hall:

> The site of the gardens of Mr. E. T. Stotesbury . . . offered exceptionally favorable conditions for a grand scheme. Although made up of several assembled properties, the estate seemed to be ready, as if decreed by nature, for its transformation into a pleasure ground, and, in a remarkably precise way, prescribed the site, aspect, and even style of the house.
> To the south a great natural opening in the woods already indicated the future axis of the composition. A valley cutting across the land at an angle permitted the development of a perspective on one side, and, on the other, of enframing gardens which rose in a succession of terraces at the foot of the mansion. The site of this last was fixed beforehand by a bare hillock, from the top of which the beholder discovered a truly commanding panorama in all directions, seen through century-old trees.
> The terrain required only simple development and orderly clearing to become, at relatively little cost, a park which recalled Vaux-le-Vicomte and Hampton Court in its style.

87. Gréber, Jacques, *L'architecture aux Etats-Unis*, plate 109.
88. Kimball, op. cit., p. 230.

89. Lavedan, op. cit. Translated by Henry Hope Reed.
90. Gimpel, op. cit., p. 185.
91. The interiors of Whitemarsh Hall have yet to be documented, and perhaps never can be. The records of White Allom Ltd. were destroyed during World War II. Martin Becker, who closed down the firm in 1965, destroyed the Alavoine records. Dozens of interior elevations were stored in the house as of 1965, but have since disappeared. They have probably been destroyed.
92. Amory, Cleveland, *The Last Resorts*, p. 301.
93. Widener, P. A. B., *Without Drums*, p. 267.
94. Burt, N., op. cit., pp. 26–27.
95. *Philadelphia Bulletin*, May 29, 1933; July 27, 1946; November 4, 1947; December 5, 1950; February 8, 1954.
96. Leuchtenberg, William E., *Franklin D. Roosevelt and the New Deal*, p. 23.
97. Ibid., p. 25n.
98. Ibid., p. 18.
99. Ibid.
100. Brooks, John, *Once in Golconda*, p. 210.
101. Leuchtenberg, op. cit., p. 28.
102. Kimball, op. cit., p. 233.

NOTE: The present account does not attempt to make a complete survey of all the houses Stotesbury once owned. However, it should be noted that from June, 1912, until May, 1923, he owned one of the best-known nineteenth-century houses in Philadelphia, the Joseph Harrison House on Rittenhouse Square, designed by Samuel Sloan (built 1855–1857) .

TWO. CA' D'ZAN

1. Rheims, Maurice, *The Strange Life of Objects*, pp. 3–4. Paul Valéry quotation.
2. *Sarasota Herald*, October 4, 1925.
3. North, Henry Ringling, and Hatch, Alden, *The Circus Kings*, p. 165.
4. *Sarasota Herald*, September 9, 1926.
5. Thomas, Richard, *John Ringling*, p. 97.
6. North and Hatch, op. cit., p. 162.
7. *Fortune*, July, 1947, p. 115.
8. *Architecture*, March, 1923, p. 87.
9. Ibid.
10. *Country Life*, October, 1927, p. 53.
11. Fitch, James Marston, *American Building*, captions for plates 141–143.
12. McCarthy, Mary, *Venice Observed*, p. 50.
13. Wiener, Samuel G., foreword in *Venetian Houses and Details*.
14. Pignatti, Terisio, *The Doge's Palace*, p. 5.
15. Spencer, Herbert, quoted in McCarthy, op. cit., p. 6.
16. Gibbon, Edward, quoted in Rosenberg, John D. "Treasure Chest in the Attic," *New York Times, Book Week Paperback Issue*, January 10, 1965, p. 6.
17. Edoardo, Arslan, *Gothic Architecture in Venice*, p. 11.
18. North and Hatch, op. cit., p. 134.
19. Towner, Wesley, *The Elegant Auctioneers*, pp. 124–129.
    Gimpel, René, *Diary of an Art Dealer*, p. 54.
20. Bazin, Germain, *Baroque and Rococo Art*, p. 7.
21. North and Hatch, op. cit., p. 132.
22. Ibid., p. 193.
23. Ibid., pp. 132–133.
24. McCarthy, Mary, *The Stones of Florence*, p. 79.
    Savage, George, *Seventeenth and Eighteenth Century French Porcelain*, p. 11n.

25. North and Hatch, op. cit., p. 204.
26. Green, David, *Sarah Duchess of Marlborough*, pp. 105, 203–206.
27. North and Hatch, op. cit., pp. 201–202.
28. Tapié, Victor-Louis, *The Age of Grandeur*, p. 215.
29. On October 3, 1926, the *Sarasota Herald* reported that Ca' d'Zan, then almost complete, had cost $1,000,000, that Charles Ringling's new mansion just north of Ca' d'Zan had cost $1,000,000, and that the John Ringling Causeway had cost $1,000,000. The figure sounds more like an incantation than a bottom-line total. Today, the following data for the cost of Ca' d'Zan have become standard: fabric — $1,000,000, seawall and swimming pool — $250,000, furnishings — $400,000; a total of $1,650,000 (exclusive of the cost of the art in the palace). These data are attributed, without documentation, to Baum. They must be measured against the following known facts: (A) Ringling told Thomas Martin in 1923 that he had no intention of paying $465,000 for Ca' d'Zan. (B) Thiesen has said that the use of terra-cotta cut finishing costs to one-tenth of what they would have been had dressed and carved stone been used. (C) Ringling ignored Baum's fee. "All I ever got from Ringling for that job was a movie camera, and it didn't work," Baum told Samuel H. Gottscho, the well-known architectural photographer, who photographed the house for him in 1931. After Baum's death (December 14, 1939), his estate sued Ringling's estate for $20,000. What part of the total fee the figure represented is not known, but even if one were to double it the resulting $40,000 does not reflect a $1,650,000 project. (D) Two experts have pointed out that "staff" (a type of stucco used in temporary work such as exposition buildings) was used in some parts of Ca' d'Zan's exterior. (E) The palace fabric was built of reinforced concrete, a material that would not lead to a $1,000, 000 figure for the fabric. One might well conclude that the palace, unfurnished, cost a good deal less than $1,000,000, possibly less than the $465,000 Ringling thought excessive.
30. Thomas, op. cit., p. 159.
31. Ca' d'Zan's charm conceals the desperate cost-cutting that marked its hurried completion. "It was never meant to last," Purdy has pointed out, a statement supported by the presence at certain places on the exterior of staff. Thirty years after it was built, the palace was in a serious state of decay, and the State of Florida had to undertake a costly rehabilitation program (1956–1960). For example, most of the terra-cotta balusters on the terrace had burst open. Ordinary iron rods had been substituted for the galvanized rods specified for use as the core of the cast balusters. The rods rusted badly and grew to twice their thickness over the years, finally splitting the balusters. The bases of the balustrades had been improperly bonded to the marble pavement of the terrace, and they had "walked" (shifted). The numbers cast in the balusters and their capitals, which provided the key for matching the parts of the seven basic designs, and for their sequencing along the balustrade, were ignored by construction workers. And so on. Deterioration had gone far beyond normal wear. The conditions spoke of hasty, careless, and unskilled workmanship, and the improper use of materials.
32. Sears, Roger Franklin, "A Venetian Palace in Florida," *Country Life*, October, 1927, p. 37.
33. Ringling built an eighty-three-hundred-foot-long reinforced concrete causeway from Sarasota across Sarasota Bay to St. Armand's Key as a basic increment in his real estate development program. The first pile for the causeway was driven January 1, 1925. On January 1, 1926, Ringling drove his Rolls-Royce over the raised roadway, which was opened to traffic several weeks later. He thus became, as the *Sarasota Herald* reported, "the first man in history to go from Sarasota to St. Armand's Key by automobile." The causeway is said to have cost Ringling about $750,000. In February, 1926, the lots in "The John Ringling Estates," on St. Armand's Key, now accessible by car, went on sale.

Ringling announced at that time that he and Albert Keller, the head of the Ritz-Carlton Hotel in New York City, were going to build a hotel with the same name on Longboat Key. On April 4, 1926, a news story in the *Herald* reported that the sale of shares in the hotel venture was going very slowly. However, Ringling went ahead with the foundation and structural work. On October 28, the *Herald* published the plans for the hotel and announced that it would open in the fall of 1927. During 1926 the Florida land boom collapsed, and before the end of the year construction of the hotel was suspended. Ringling ordered work started up again in 1927. On August 3 that year, the *Sarasota Times* reported that a hundred and sixty men were at work on the hotel and a hundred and forty others were working on the other Ringling projects on Bird Key and St. Armand's Key, as well as on the John and Mable Ringling Museum of Art.

Work on the hotel, and most of the other Ringling development projects, was terminated before the end of 1927. No accurate data are available to document how much Ringling invested in them, and how much was lost *in toto*. Henry Ringling North has recalled that in the years that followed, the rusting steel work of the hotel looked liked a skeleton rising from the mangrove swamps.

34. *Sarasota Herald*, editorial, September 12, 1926.
35. North and Hatch, op. cit., p. 217.
36. Ibid., pp. 237–238.

THREE. VIZCAYA

1. Garraty, John A., *Right-Hand Man: The Life of George W. Perkins*, pp. 126–146, 189–190. The present account of the formation of the International Harvester Company is drawn primarily from this scholarly biography.
2. Scott, Walter Dill, and Harshe, Robert B., *Charles Deering, 1852–1927*. Biographical data on the several Deerings have been drawn primarily from this privately printed source.
3. Northwestern University and Massachusetts Institute of Technology archives.
4. Barron, Clarence W., *They Told Barron*, p. 283.
5. Hendrick, Burton J., *The Age of Big Business*, p. 152.
6. "Jules Huret" in *Larousse du XXe Siècle*, tome troisième.
7. The spur ran from the Florida East Coast Railroad's Deering Sidetrack, Mile Post 368, to the construction site. The quarry was opened on Windley Key.
8. Hoffman, F. Burrall, interview. See Acknowledgments.
9. *Architectural Review*, July, 1917, p. 123.
10. Fleming, John; Honour, Hugh; and Pevsner, Nikolaus, "Vignola" in *The Penguin Dictionary of Architecture* (revised edition).
11. *Philadelphia Public Ledger*, December 10, 1916. Republished in *Miami Herald*, December 21, 1916.
12. Hoffman, op. cit. Interview.
    Mayer, Grace, *Once Upon a City*, p. 89.
13. Hellman, Geoffrey T., *Mrs. De Peyster's Parties*, p. 165.
14. Leone-Moats, Alice, *Harper's Bazaar*, May, 1949, p. 171.
15. Ibid.
16. Hardy, Thomas, *Jude the Obscure*, pp. ix–x.
    Elsie de Wolfe and Elizabeth Marbury were known, somewhat maliciously, as "the bachelors." The reader is referred to Miss Marbury's eloquent description of their love for one another in her memoirs, *My Crystal Ball*. See dedication and pages 302–303.
17. Leone-Moats, op. cit., p. 168. Elsie de Wolfe may have charged Chalfin a percentage of his income from his contract with Deering. Leone-Moats: "On the various occasions when she has helped unknown decorators by recommending them to prospective clients, she has insisted upon her commission."
18. Data for this biographical sketch of Chalfin have been drawn from letters, newspaper clippings (some unidentified and undated), and memorabilia in the posses-

sion of his family; archives and records of Harvard University, the Art Students'
League, the American Academy in Rome; and, other sources, some confidential.
Most of these materials are listed in the sections headed PAUL CHALFIN in the bib-
liography.

19. Lynes, Russell, *The Art-Makers of Nineteenth Century America*, p. 360.
20. Pennell, Elizabeth R. and Joseph, *The Life of James McNeill Whistler*, Vol. II,
    p. 228. Chalfin's presence as a student in Whistler's *académie* cannot be positively
    established in the Whistler documents. He is the authority for the statement that
    he studied with Whistler, a statement published in a single-sheet "flyer" for his
    lecture at the Arts Club of Chicago, April 21, 1922, and in newspaper accounts of
    the lecture. Letter: Cecilia Chin, Art Institute of Chicago, June 6, 1965, to author.
21. Proske, Beatrice Gilman, *Archer Milton Huntington*, p. 11.
22. Dana, Nathalie, *Young in New York*, p. 149.
23. Cox, Allyn, interview. See Acknowledgments.
24. The Metropolitan Museum of Art has no remaining record of exhibiting the
    "hospital" panels, nor has it ever owned them. "A design for a decorative panel was
    given to the museum in 1919, 'collected from the National Academy of Design.'
    Its size was 18″ by 36″. It was never accessioned, and was sold [to an unknown
    buyer] in 1957. . . . [Chalfin] exhibited in the 1st Industrial Exhibition of Objects
    Showing Museum Influence . . . 1917. The catalogue lists two [Chalfin] exhibits:
    Ceiling canvas, painted in distemper [and a] sketch for ceiling canvas, painted in
    distemper [paired as one exhibit], and 'Motifs from Renaissance Objects in
    Hoentschel Collection.'" Letter: Charlotte W. Appleton, Metropolitan Museum
    of Art, to author, October 3, 1973.
25. Harwood, Kathryn Chapman, *Muse News,* January, 1972, p. 353.
26. Hudson, Virginia Tyler, *Miami Herald,* December 12, 1934. Also, quotation in
    following sentence.
27. Brion, Marcel, *Venice,* pp. 165–166, 169–170. See also the excellent summary his-
    tory of the evolution of *villeggiatura* by Giuseppe Mazzotti, *Palladian and Other
    Venetian Villas,* pp. 7–13. This is an outstanding study of the architecture, decora-
    tion, and social history of "The Brenta Riviera."
28. Fleming, et al., op. cit., "Longhena."
29. Pevsner, Nikolaus, *An Outline of European Architecture,* pp. 282–283.
30. Gibbon, Monk, "Linderhof" in *Great Palaces of Europe,* p. 89.
31. *Architectural Review,* July, 1917 passim. **Source of the quotations describing ware-
    house objects, unless otherwise identified.**
32. Cook, Theodore Andrea, *Twenty-Five Great Houses of France,* pp. 283–284.
    Dunlop, Ian, *Châteaux of the Loire,* pp. 190–191.
    Michelin Guide, English edition, 1964, *Châteaux of Loire,* p. 60.
33. Leffler, Bernice Thompson, *An Italian Villa on Biscayne Bay,* mimeographed, type-
    script, unpublished, p. 22.
34. Ibid., p. 13.
35. Ibid., p. 19.
36. The materials from which this biographical sketch of Mitchell Samuels and the his-
    torical passages on French & Company have been drawn are listed in the MITCHELL
    SAMUELS: FRENCH & COMPANY section of the bibliography. Some of the data were
    drawn from an interview with Spencer Samuels.
37. Louchheim, Aline B., *New York Times,* March 15, 1953. (Mrs. Louchheim later
    enjoyed a distinguished writing and television career as Aline Saarinen.)
38. *Architectural Review,* July, 1917, p. 122.
39. Adams, Adam G., *Tequesta* 15 (1955), p. 29.
    See also Adams's lecture to The Vizcayans, at Vizcaya, November 12, 1963, mimeo-
    graphed, unpublished. These are excellent and essential sources of data on Vizcaya.
40. Suarez, Diego, interview. See Acknowledgments. Source of biographical passages,
    and all subsequent quotes from Suarez, unless otherwise indicated.
41. Dûchene, Achille, *Les jardins de l'avenir: hier, aujourd'hui, demain,* p. 9.
42. Passillé, Raymond de, *La gazette illustrée des amateurs des jardins,* 1923, passim.
    For a more extensive set of citations on the work of the Dûchenes, father and son,

see the section entitled ACHILLE DÛCHENE in the bibliography for Part Five: Shadow Lawn.

43. *Architectural Review*, July, 1917.
44. Patterson, William, *Town & Country*, July 20, 1917, p. 23.
45. Kitchen, Karl K., *New York World Magazine*, March 31, 1918.
46. "The Publishers Department," *Architectural Review*, July, 1917, p. xvii.
47. Ibid.
48. Hudson, op. cit.
49. Harshe, Robert B., and Rich, Daniel Catton, *Vizcaya*, undated handbook, c. 1953, pp. 6, 19n.
50. *Architectural Review*, July, 1917, caption, p. 151.
51. Quoted by Rebecca West in the epigraph to *The Fountain Overflows*.
52. *Trois siècles de papiers peints* (catalogue), Musée des Arts Décoratifs. Paris. 1967, p. 46.
53. Louchheim, op. cit.
54. Ranger, Mrs. Marianita C., interview. See Acknowledgments.
    Mrs. Clara Samuels, the widow of Mitchell Samuels, has recalled that Chalfin sold his house to Ziegfeld Follies star Justine Johnstone and her husband Walter Wanger.
55. Chapman, John Jay, *Vanity Fair*, September, 1919.
56. White, Lawrence Grant, *Sketches and Designs by Stanford White*, p. 26.
57. This brief account of Chalfin's career after Vizcaya is based upon extended study of the pertinent interviews, correspondence, newspaper accounts, magazine articles, documents, and other materials, published and unpublished, listed in Sections 2, 3, and 6 of the bibliography for this chapter.
58. Plan for ground floor of Vizcaya: *Architectural Review*, July, 1917, p. xvii. Plan for ground floor of the Villa Rezzonico: Renato Cevese, *Villa della provincia de Vicenza*, Tomo II, Veneto 2, p. 321.
59. Two other actresses came to Vizcaya as houseguests: Marion Davies and Alla Nazimova. See Fred Lawrence Guiles, *Marion Davies*, pp. 49–51, 53. Miss Davies and her mother, Mrs. Rose Douras, appear to have stayed at Vizcaya in the spring of 1916, about seven months before the villa was completed. The visit bored the young actress. She was a teenager at the time and just beginning her long affair with William Randolph Hearst.
    Deering's close friends in Coconut Grove made a private movie during Nazimova's visit and she appeared in it. Mrs. Barbara D. Danielson has recalled that the film was made by those concerned "strictly for their own amusement." (Letter: Mrs. Danielson to author. Boston, July 14, 1965.) According to tradition, Deering became so annoyed with Nazimova's slovenly ways that one morning she found a oneway railroad ticket to Hollywood under her plate at breakfast. A feature-length Hollywood film shot partly at Vizcaya in April, 1918, has yet to be identified. Remaining still photos indicate it was a World War I movie with an aviator hero.
60. Edgecombe, Eustace, interview. See Acknowledgments.
61. *New York Times*, September 22, 1925.
62. Ibid., January 11, 1953.
63. Letter: A. H. Peavy, Jr., Director, Dade County Park and Recreation Department, to author, April 23, 1971.

FOUR. SAN MARINO

1. On Tuesday, February 5, 1867, the *New York Times*, in a report under the heading "Rents and Real Estate," spoke of "Lexington-avenue and other fashionable localities." (The report observed that high rents were driving people out of the city into the new suburban communities that were growing up.)
2. Lewis, Oscar, *The Big Four*, p. 220.

3. Evans, Cerinda W., *Arabella Duval Huntington*, p. 7.
4. Proske, Beatrice Gilman, *Archer Milton Huntington*, p. 1.
5. Evans, op. cit., pp. 5, 8.
6. Anna Hyatt Huntington, the distinguished sculptor, and the widow of Archer Milton Huntington, very kindly wrote to the author on June 29, 1965, in answer to his letter of inquiry of June 25, 1965, about Mr. Worsham, that she had reread Archer Huntington's "certificate for change of name from Worsham to Huntington and there is no mention of his father Worsham's first name nor anything about him."
7. The quotation in this paragraph assailing Arabella's manners is from James Duveen, *Secrets of an Art Dealer*, p. 171. The contradictory evidence is from Germain Seligman, who has described her warmly in *Merchants of Art*, pp. 138, 139. The "pussy-cat" anecdote may be found in Wesley Towner's remarkable and absorbing *The Elegant Auctioneers*, p. 336.
8. Wark, Robert R., "Arabella Huntington and the Beginnings of the Art Collection" in *The Founding of the Henry E. Huntington Library and Art Gallery: Four Essays*, p. 311.
9. Evans, op. cit., p. 8.
10. Letter: John G. Worsham, Richmond, Virginia, to author, May 20, 1969.
11. Deed of Bargain and Sale. From P. Horton Keach . . . to John A. Worsham, Henrico County Court, deed book 78, reel 38, p. 79. September 4, 1862, recorded September 26, 1862.
12. Chafetz, Henry, *Play the Devil*, p. 225.
13. Dowdey, Clifford, *Experiment in Rebellion*, p. 257.
14. Kimmel, Stanley, *Mr. Davis's Richmond*, p. 93.
15. Ashbury, Herbert, *Sucker's Progress*, p. 397.
16. It may be that in Richmond at that time the two terms were synonymous in that carpenters frequently were trained to run the woodworking machines that had come into common use during the previous several decades.
17. The architects for the Metropolitan Hotel and Niblo's Garden Theatre were George Trench and John Butler Snook. They also designed Commodore Cornelius Vanderbilt's mansion at 10 Washington Place. Snook then designed a Vanderbilt office building and Grand Central Station for W. H. Vanderbilt. His business records, now on deposit at the New-York Historical Society, show that in June, 1879, he charged W. H. Vanderbilt for "making drawings for dwelling house North West Corner Fifth Avenue and 51st Street" and for "making drawings for double dwelling house South West Corner Fifth Avenue and 52nd Street," the reference being to the great triple palace Vanderbilt built for himself (640 Fifth Avenue) and two of his four daughters (642 Fifth Avenue and 2 West Fifty-second Street). In 1882 he designed two more Fifth Avenue palaces (680 and 684 Fifth Avenue) for Vanderbilt's two other daughters. A proviso should be made concerning the triplex Vanderbilt palace between Fifty-first and Fifty-second streets on Fifth Avenue: Snook was, indeed, the architect and construction supervisor of that complex structure, but the design sketches for the palace were drawn in the drafting room of Herter Brothers, probably by Charles B. Atwood, who would later come to prominence for his work at the 1893 World's Columbian Exposition, Chicago.
18. The *New York City Directory* closed its canvass each year on May 1. Each directory thus reflected conditions for the year preceding its closing date. A study by the author of more than one hundred conveyances in the *Block Index of Reindexed Conveyances*, New York City Register, Recorded Deeds and Mortgages, Borough of Manhattan, indicates that directory data for the era with which this chapter is concerned were, in general, about *two years* behind the actual dates of the conveyances. Thus, although Worsham and Schaffer signed a purchase indenture for 17 West Twenty-fourth Street (Block 826, Lot 28, Manhattan) on July 19, 1865, Worsham is not shown resident at that address until the directory that closed May 1, 1867. Dates drawn from the editions of the directory cited in this chapter, unless otherwise indicated, are adjusted to accommodate this time lag, thus allowing a more precise study of events and relationships.
19. Smith, Matthew Hale, *Sunshine and Shadow in New York*, p. 408.

20. Others buried in the same plot include Worsham himself, his brother Washington J. Worsham, and his brother's widow. One can hardly doubt in such a circumstance that Annette was, indeed, Worsham's wife.

21. Collis Potter Huntington signed the purchase indenture for 109 Lexington Avenue on April 15, 1872. A close study of the pertinent documents reveals that what he got for his $20,000 was a curiosity: one of the narrowest houses in New York City, a house (possibly part of a larger structure) on a lot that measured twelve feet four and one-eighth inches along its street front — the east side of Lexington Avenue between East Twenty-seventh and East Twenty-eighth streets — by sixty feet in depth.

22. Lavender, David, *The Great Presuader,* passim. Much of the biographical data used here has been taken from Lavender.

23. Ibid., p. 342.

24. In order to avoid using a numerical superscription at the end of almost every sentence in the account that follows of Arabella's passage from 4 West Fifty-fourth Street to 2 East Fifty-seventh Street — her Fifth Avenue palace — the author has deleted from the text most of the source citations for relevant conveyances, etc.

25. It is probably only just that the rooms should be known to the curatorial world and to the visitors to the museums as "The Rockefeller Rooms." However, the historian of American palace decoration should more accurately describe them as "The Arabella D. Huntington Rooms" (to use the final form of her complex name preferred by Arabella), a reflection of the factual conditions of their origin, which in no way detracts from Rockefeller's generous preservation of these monuments of interior decoration.

26. The Huntingtons were then living at 65 Park Avenue. A special New York City Police Department canvass of 1890 places them at that address. Archer is shown as living with them. He is listed as a "minor" (he was nineteen) rather than as Huntington's "son."

27. Allsopp, Bruce, *The Study of Architectural History,* p. 18.

28. *Priced Catalogue of the Art Collection Formed by the Late Mrs. Mary Jane Morgan to Be Sold at Auction, Without Reserve . . . at Chickering Hall . . . ,* p. 84. Only Jules Breton's *Communicants* (Item 235) commanded a higher price at the auction: $45,500.

29. Lewis, op. cit., p. 233.

30. *Monographie du palais des fue le baron & la baronne de Hirsch,* introduction. The precise dating of such work is difficult, and it might be noted that if the Monnoyer panels were part of the original *boiserie* then it had to have been executed before the Régence, for the painter died in 1690 and the Duc d'Orléans did not begin his regency until 1715.

31. *Chefs-d'oeuvre de la curiosité du monde,* passim.

32. Cornwallis-West, Mrs. George, *The Reminiscences of Lady Randolph Churchill,* p. 284.

33. Jullian, Philippe, *Edward and the Edwardians,* p. 141.

34. Hertrich, William, *The Huntington Botanical Gardens: 1905–1949,* p. 30.

35. *Los Angeles Sunday Times,* February 8, 1914.

36. Hunt's first wife, Harriette Boardman, whom he married May 30, 1894, died October 27, 1913. The Hunts had four sons and one daughter. On July 3, 1915, Hunt married his second wife, Virginia Pease.

37. Hunt's office records have revealed that the earliest work undertaken on San Marino in his drafting room was begun in the fall of 1907. On February 28, 1908, Huntington wrote to Hunt from New York about a rough sketch of the house, noting, "I am in great haste."

38. *Providence Journal,* February 3, 1963.

39. Allom's designs mixed French and English precedent. The oak paneling in the library is based on the French style of the mid-eighteenth century. The drawing room paneling reproduces the Louis XVI style, as does that of the small drawing room. The dining room paneling is based upon English work of the mid-eighteenth century. The small library, originally used by Huntington as an office, was designed

by Myron Hunt, and White Allom executed its late-eighteenth-century English paneling.

40. Wark, op. cit., p. 324.

41. The Boucher tapestries cost Huntington $350,000. At various times he appears to have made summary jottings on construction and finishing costs of San Marino. As of April 25, 1910, the fabric of the house had cost him $406,801.67. The construction costs of the garage, stables, bowling alley, office, and car house (for his railway palace cars) brought the total construction figure to $453,606.68 as of that date. The same day Huntington made a separate list of contractor costs for other than the basic structures, and those figures came to a total of $479,377.25 (including $121,284.96 to Duveen Brothers for White Allom's work on the interiors). The two lists of April 25, 1910, total $932,983.93. It appears, then, that the fabric and finishing of the house and dependencies cost Huntington about $1,000,000 exclusive of the costly furnishings, for which no estimate exists.

42. William Hertrich has recalled that the design for the formal garden staircase-ramps called for one hundred steps from the terrace down into the proposed axial garden below. Huntington didn't like formal gardens. Arabella did, so a small formal garden was created for her nearby, on the same level as the house. The rough designs for the large garden below the terrace, possibly drawn by Hunt, were never executed. Hertrich has also pointed out that the age of the Huntingtons not only caused the elimination of the great stairs below the terrace, but also precluded a ballroom in the plans of the house.

43. Hertrich, op. cit., p. 80.

44. The mausoleum, a circular temple enclosed by a peripteral colonnade, and based like practically all such modern structures on the Tholos of Polycleitos at Epidauros, c. 350 B.C., was designed by John Russell Pope, whose services were recommended to Huntington by Duveen. Hertrich has recalled that Huntington commissioned the design from Pope in 1925, the year after Arabella died, and two years before Huntington's own death. Work was completed in May, 1929, at which time the two bronze caskets containing the remains of the Huntingtons were removed from temporary interment in cement vaults and reinterred in the mausoleum. A circular *tempietto* on the west lawn of the house is sometimes confused with the mausoleum. The *tempietto*, known as The Temple of Love, is an eighteenth-century garden conceit from Porchefontaine, a dependency of Versailles. Its peripteral colonnade encloses a statuary group in French limestone, *L'Amour Captif de la Jeunesse*, identified by Robert R. Wark as "by, or after, Louis-Simon Boizot."

45. Wolf, Edwin II, and Fleming, John F., *Rosenbach*, p. 234.

46. Hertrich, op. cit., p. 123.

47. Wark, Robert R., *French Decorative Art in the Huntington Collection*, p. xi.

48. Seligman, Germain, *Merchants of Art*, pp. 138–139.

49. The *palais* was originally known as the Hôtel de Monaco and was later called the Hôtel de Sagan. It was designed by Alexandre-Théodore Brogniart, one of the finest of the eighteenth-century Paris architects and a member of the Academy, for the Princess of Monaco, *"amie du Prince de Condé,"* and built between 1774 and 1777.

FIVE. SHADOW LAWN

1. Parson once hired a French chauffeur, not in France, but in the United States. When he left for Paris with his Rolls-Royces the following summer, Parson took along his two American chauffeurs as usual and left the French driver behind. The outraged Frenchman went into the garage at Shadow Lawn and filled the gasoline tank of another of Parson's automobiles with shellac. He then left the garage, the grounds, and the baffling world of Hubert Templeton Parson.

2. The Avenue Foch is three-quarters of a mile long and four hundred and fifty feet

wide. It was named Avenue de l'Impératrice from 1854 to 1870, Avenue Général
Ulrich from 1870 to 1875, Avenue du Bois de Boulogne from 1875 to late 1929, and
has been known as Avenue Foch since. It was built under decree of Napoleon III,
traversing private land from the place de l'Etoile, site of the Arc de Triomphe, to
the Porte Dauphine entrance to the Bois de Boulogne. Cost to the nation: $100,000.
The City of Paris spent another $20,000 on flower beds, tree and shrub plantations,
and drainage. The avenue's service zones are framed by iron railings along either
edge. By imperial edict, houses could not be built closer than ten meters to the
railings. The architect Jakob Ignaz Hittorf conceived the boulevard-promenade.
Baron Georges-Eugène Haussmann, the prefect of the Department of the Seine who
carried out the sweeping rebuilding of Paris and the creation of the great network
of boulevards under Napoleon III, dramatically amplified Hittorf's original scheme.

3. As matter of record, it should be noted that Parson once entertained one hundred
twenty-five people. Another time he served a buffet lunch of sandwiches to several
dozen guests. Aside from his housewarming reception, discussed elsewhere, these are
the only receptions recalled by the intimate witnesses of life at Shadow Lawn.

4. de Gramont, E[lizabeth], *Pomp and Circumstance*, p. 221.

5. *Woolworth's First 75 Years*, p. 16.

6. *New York Times*, July 10, 1940.

7. Winkler, John K., *Five and Ten*, p. 109.
New York Times, June 9, 1932.

8. Ibid., July 10, 1940.

9. Winkler, op. cit., p. 231.

10. Parson, Hubert T. and Maysie G., entry in *Block Index of Reindexed Conveyances*,
New York City Register, Block 1500, Lot 2, November 30, 1914. et seq.

11. Winkler, op. cit., p. 230.

12. Ibid., p. 132.

13. Ibid., p. 190.

14. Ibid., p. 230.

15. Ibid., p. 231.

16. *Architectural Record* 16 (1904), 394–406 (residence of John A. McCall, Long Branch,
New Jersey).

17. *New York Times*, February 19, 1906. In point of fact, the country home of Murry
Guggenheim, which stood only several hundred yards from Shadow Lawn, was a
superior piece of architecture. It had won the Gold Medal of the New York Chapter
of the American Institute of Architects in 1903. Art historian Alan Gowans [*Architecture in New Jersey*, p. 107] has remarked "its large, studied and precise renditions
of Louis XVI forms executed with scholarly truth." It was designed by Thomas
Hastings of Carrère & Hastings. The house is now the Murry and Leonie Guggenheim Memorial Library of Monmouth College.

18. *New York Times*, February 19, 1906.

19. Woolley, J. Russell, unpublished ms. about Shadow Lawn's title and conveyance
history. This is the primary source for title data on Shadow Lawn.

20. *Entertaining a Nation*, pp. 126–127.

21. George W. Thomson was born in the Gate House, Cally House Estate, at Kirkcudbright, Kirkcudbrightshire, Scotland. His father was the head gardener of Cally
House, about eight miles southwest of Castle Douglas and not far from Solway Firth
in southernmost Scotland. Thomson served five years as an apprentice at Cally
House. "Then," he has recalled, "I was a journeyman at Keir House in Dunblane,
Perthshire."

22. Gilson, Etienne, *Heloise and Abelard*, pp. xiv–xv.

23. Sincerbeaux, Moore & Shinn, "Map Showing Former Residence . . ." February 26,
1927.

24. Trumbauer, Horace, "Map Showing Old & New . . ." November 8, 1927.

25. Eller, Peter W., interview. See Acknowledgments.

26. Introduction in *Shadow Lawn: Versailles of America* . . . (catalogue).

27. Cockburn, Clyde, *In Time of Trouble*. Quoted by John Brooks, *Once in Golconda*,
p. 84.

28. Bagehot, Walter, *Lombard Street,* p. 151.
29. Stone, Lawrence, *The Crisis of the Aristocracy,* p. 267.
30. Hamlin, Talbot, *Benjamin Henry Latrobe,* p. 132.
31. Parson, Hubert T. and Maysie G., op. cit.
32. Ibid.
33. A chronological list of some important Trumbauer houses follows. If known, the name of the house is given. Lesser-known place-names listed without a state are in Pennsylvania. The date given is for the start of the project in Trumbauer's office. Alfred S. Branam, Jr., has kindly verified the dates.

   Grey Towers: William Welsh Harrison, Glenside, 1892. Chelten House: George Widener Elkins, Elkins Park, 1896. Balangary: Martin Maloney, Spring Lake, New Jersey, 1897. Elstowe Park: William Lukens Elkins, Elkins Park, 1898. Lynnewood Hall: Peter Arrell Brown Widener, Ashbourne, 1898. The Elms: Edward Julius Berwind, Newport, 1899. St. Austel Hall: John B. Gribbel, Wyncote, 1900. Chetwode: William Storrs Wells, Newport, 1900. Wyndhurst: John Milton Colton, Jenkintown, 1900. George Albert Huhn, Philadelphia, 1900. James William Paul, Jr., Radnor, 1900. Mrs. E. G. H. Slater, Washington, 1901.

   Joseph Benton McCall, West Philadelphia, 1901. Edward Collings Knight, Jr., Philadelphia, 1902. Mrs. Alice T. Drexel, New York, 1902. Isaac Townsend Burden, New York, 1903. Clarendon Court: E. C. Knight, Jr., Newport, 1903. C. Hartman Kuhn, Devon, 1904. Perry Belmont, Washington, 1907 (Paul-Ernest Sanson, Paris, Associate Architect). H. M. Nathanson, Rydal, 1907. George F. Huff, Washington, 1907. George J. Gould, New York, 1907. Thomas P. Hunter, Haverford, 1909. Henry Welsh Rogers, New York, 1909. Robert L. Montgomery, Villa Nova, 1909. James Buchanan Duke, New York, 1909. Mrs. Adelaide L. Douglas, New York, 1909. Otto Eisenlohr, Philadelphia, 1911.

   F. P. Mitchell, Washington, 1912. James Speyer, New York, 1912. Miramar: Mrs. George E. Widener, Newport, 1913. Mrs. Amory Carhart, New York, 1913. Brooklands: Mrs. Louise (Cromwell) Brooks, Eccleston, Maryland, 1915. Howard C. Brokaw, Brookville, Long Island, 1916. John S. Phipps, Palm Beach, 1917. Clairemont: Morris Clothier, Villa Nova, 1917. Joseph P. Grace, Long Island, 1920. Mrs. Alexander Hamilton Rice, New York, 1922. John C. Martin, Wyncote, 1923. George McFadden, Rosemont, 1923. Herbert N. Straus, New York, 1927. Mrs. Anna Thomson Dodge, Washington, 1930, and Rose Terrace: Grosse Point, Michigan, 1932.
34. Wayne Andrews's entry on Trumbauer in the *Dictionary of American Biography* (Supplement Two) reopened the whole question of Trumbauer's work, but no one seemed interested in surveying it until recently. Alfred S. Branam, Jr., an architectural historian, is now preparing a critical survey of all of Trumbauer's work (not just the domestic projects which have been the deliberately limited concern of the present account).
35. Gallet, Michel, *Stately Mansions,* p. 19 et seq.
36. It should be noted that Trumbauer also maintained close professional and personal relationships with André Carlhian, a leading Paris decorator and *antiquaire,* who specialized in *boiseries* and *papiers peints* (wallpapers); Robert J. Bagues, of Bagues Frères, Fifth Avenue and Paris; and Henri Bouché, an outstanding decorative painter who lived in New York.
37. Huxley, Aldous, "Notes on the Way," *Time and Tide,* July 3, 1947, pp. 889–891.
38. Reed, Henry Hope. King made the statement to Reed during a discussion of Trumbauer's work. See Acknowledgments.
39. Whitman, Alden. *New York Times,* September 29, 1974.
40. Bailey, John B., See Acknowledgments.
41. Alfred S. Branam, Jr., has generously made available to the author notes from interviews and biographical data relating to Abele which he has gathered for a biographical essay.
42. University of Pennsylvania Archives.
43. Harbeson, John F., *The Study of Architectural Design,* pp. 3, 72, 146, 147, 182, 183.
44. Duchêne, Achille. See Bibliography: SHADOW LAWN *(General)* .
45. Verlet, Pierre, *French Royal Furniture,* p. 82.

46. Connolly, Cyril, and Zerbe, Jerome, *Les pavillons*, p. 62.

47. *New York Herald Tribune*, April 29, 1956.

48. The following passage from the expensive brochure, whose title was printed in silver ink on a royal blue flocked cover, demonstrates that after more than three decades of costly "French" decorating, Parson and his wife were still strangers in the world of sophisticated decoration and its history, recent or distant:

"Across the east rotunda from the Music Room is a charming and dignified library. Panelled in straight grain wood, it is a faithful reproduction of the Henschall [*sic*] Library in Paris."

The reference is to the library of Georges Hoentschel, a leading architect and decorator of late-nineteenth-century Paris. The library was an integral part of Hoentschel's noted art collection. The room is now owned by the Metropolitan Museum of Art, New York City, a gift of J. Pierpont Morgan, along with the rest of Hoentschel's collection of superlative examples of decorative art. Obviously, neither Parson nor Maysie knew about Hoentschel, aside from the fact that they had paid several hundred thousand dollars to "reproduce" his library. The Hoentschel library was also "reproduced" in the house that Trumbauer designed for Mrs. Horace E. Dodge in Washington, and that Alavoine decorated. (It is now the residence of the Belgian ambassador.) However, the two "reproductions" are quite unlike one another.

Germain Seligman has written an appreciative passage on Hoentschel in *Merchants of Art*.

49. *New York Times*, September 26, 1939.

On February 7, 1942, the borough sold the house and property to Eugene F. Lehman, of Tarrytown, New York, for use as the Highland Manor School for Girls. On March 9, 1955, Monmouth College agreed to take over the unfulfilled part of Lehman's obligation.

During the Depression, public school evening classes for adults were begun in Long Branch, as they were throughout the country. The classes in Long Branch evolved into Monmouth Junior College, a community project that prospered so well that on April 1, 1955, the trustees signed a purchase contract with the Borough of West Long Branch for Shadow Lawn. The college made its first payment July 2, 1956, and moved into the palace at the beginning of the 1956–1957 academic year.

In the autumn of the 1957–1958 school year the junior year was added to the college curriculum, and the senior year was added the following autumn. The first bachelors degrees were conferred by Monmouth College as a four-year undergraduate institution in June, 1958.

50. In the 310-page auction catalogue, Item 2671 is listed as "Prince Condé Kingwood Commode." It is illustrated on page 248. In the caption for the photograph it is described as "Prince Conti Kingwood Commode."

The original commode does not appear ever to have been identified with the Prince de Condé or any of the Princes de Conti (of the cadet branch of the house of Bourbon).

The Parson commode was a copy of "Louis XV's medal cabinet, an astounding piece of exuberance in spite of its medals and medallions on a blue horn background inspired by the past . . . supplied by [Antoine] Gaudreaux in 1759 for the 'angle cabinet' of the King at Versailles. The bronzes were made by the Slodtz brothers," who also designed the commode. The description may be found in *French Cabinetmakers of the Eighteenth Century*, edited by Claude Frégnac. Louis XVI gave the commode to the Bibliothèque Nationale, but it has been returned to Versailles and may now be seen there in the royal *cabinet du travail*.

Who made Maysie's copy, and how much did it cost her? And was it, in fact, a good copy? It would take careful study by experts, and further research in the United States and France to answer these questions. However, a superficial examination of the commode, which needs some restoration work, suggests that the workmanship is diligent but not inspired. Nothing, say, to compare to the workmanship of copies executed by Henri Dasson, who turned out remarkably exact replications of royal pieces in the nineteenth century that have commanded six figures in auctions. (See Bibliography: Denise Ledoux-Lebard in Henri Dasson section.) One of Dasson's copies may be seen in the Wallace Collection in London, the finest repository of French eighteenth-century furniture outside France. Such a piece reveals that a copy made by a fine artist remains a work of art.

The catalogue description of the commode, or rather its *two* titles for the piece, might well make the researcher into such matters wary.

The commode was purchased by Mrs. George Washington Kavanaugh and was installed in Mrs. Kavanaugh's fine French house on East Sixty-second Street near Fifth Avenue in New York City.

If, in fact, Maysie bought the commode thinking it was the Prince Condé (or Conti) Kingwood Commode, then one must assume that she was the victim of some rather theatrical salesmanship, a condition that might not augur well for a professional examination of the piece to determine its artistic quality and relative value.

Some honest fellow among the Paris dealers could have warned Maysie that Louis II de Bourbon, Prince de Condé, died seventy years before Gaudreaux made the commode.

51. *New York Times,* June 9, 1940.
52. Ibid., July 10, 1940.
   Ibid., November 23, 1940.

BIBLIOGRAPHY

ONE. WHITEMARSH HALL

General

MISCELLANEOUS

The Architectural Library of the Late Horace Trumbauer (executors' public sale catalogue). Samuel T. Freeman & Co., Philadelphia, February 2, 1939.

Chetwode: Former Home of John J. Astor, Newport, Rhode Island (real estate sales brochure). Joseph P. Day, New York, n.d.

Collection of Paintings (privately published catalogue). E. T. Stotesbury. New York: Knickerbocker Press, 1897.

The Eva R. Stotesbury Collection. XVIII Century French and English Furniture and Objects of Art. Removed from Her Former Residences Whitemarsh Hall, Chestnut Hill, and Marly, Washington, D.C. (public auction leaflet). Samuel T. Freeman & Co., Philadelphia. October 25–28, 1944.

The Eva R. Stotesbury Collection (executors' public auction leaflet). Samuel T. Freeman & Co., Philadelphia. Wingwood House, Bar Harbor. August 20–24, 1946.

Members of the Architectural League of New York. *American Art Annual* 3 (1900–1901) : Section II, 132.

Letter: Robert T. McLeod, Director of Public Relations, George A. Fuller Company, to author. New York City, July 30, 1969.

Letter: Eva R. Stotesbury to Horace Trumbauer. Whitemarsh Lodge, Chestnut Hill, Philadelphia, August 6, 1917.

Stotesbury Estate (hectographed memorandum containing history and data). Pennsalt Chemicals Corporation (now Pennwalt Corporation), c. 1964.

Trumbauer, Horace. "Residence for E. T. Stotesbury, Esq., Chestnut Hill, Pa." Four drawings, each dated "November, 1915": "Front Elevation," "Garden Elevation," "North-East Elevation," "South-West Elevation." Nine drawings, each dated "June 6, 1916": "Front Elevation," "Garden Elevation," "North-East Elevation," "South-West Elevation," "Transverse Section," "Ground Floor Plan," "First Floor Plan," "Second Floor Plan," "Third Floor Plan." Pennwalt Corporation, Philadelphia.

NEWSPAPERS AND PERIODICALS (chronological sequence)

Vors, Frédéric. Article on the Hôtel de la Païva. *The Art Amateur* 1 (August, 1879).

"A New Influence in Philadelphia Architecture." *The Architectural Record* 15 (February, 1904) : 93.

Obituary: Oliver Eaton Cromwell. *New York Times*, December 22, 1909.

Stotesbury buys Glencoe at Rosemont and No. 1923 Walnut from McKean. Unidentified clipping. Philadelphia, May 3, 1910.

"Miss Cromwell Weds." *Baltimore Sun,* May 16, 1911.

Mrs. Cromwell to wed Stotesbury. Unidentified clipping. Philadelphia, *c.* December, 1911.

Cromwell-Stotesbury wedding: he one of world's great financiers. *Philadelphia Bulletin,* December 10, 1911.

Cromwell-Stotesbury wedding: background. Unidentified clipping. Philadelphia, *c.* December 27, 1911.

Cromwell-Stotesbury wedding plans announced. Unidentified clipping. Philadelphia, December 27, 1911.

"Mrs. Cromwell Is 'Entirely Charming.' " *Philadelphia Bulletin,* December 30, 1911.

Stotesbury to remodel Harrison mansion in fall. Unidentified clipping. Philadelphia, 1912.

Stotesbury weds Mrs. Cromwell in her Washington home. Unidentified clipping. Philadelphia, *c.* January 18, 1912.

Train to Stotesbury wedding stops 30 seconds in Philadelphia. *Philadelphia Bulletin,* January 18, 1912.

Stotesbury wedding to Mrs. Cromwell socially important. *Philadelphia Bulletin,* January 18, 1912.

Stotesbury and Mrs. Cromwell wed in Washington. *Philadelphia Bulletin,* January 19, 1912.

Stotesburys to live at Walnut Street house. *Philadelphia Press,* January 19, 1912.

Stotesburys honeymoon quietly at Palm Beach. Unidentified clipping. Philadelphia, January 27, 1912.

Stotesburys leave Palm Beach: bunny hug and turkey trot take social colony by storm. *New York Times,* February 11, 1912.

Minister criticizes Philadelphia. *New York Times,* February 13, 1912.

Mrs. Stotesbury makes Philadelphia "debut" at opera. *Philadelphia Bulletin,* February 13, 1912.

"Mrs. Stotesbury Is Seen at Opera." *Philadelphia Inquirer,* February 13, 1912.

"Nouguès' Quo Vadis Again Presented." *Philadelphia Inquirer,* February 13, 1912.

Quo Vadis: Philadelphia, February 12, 1912. *Musical Courier* 64 (February 14, 1912).

Stotesbury takes title to Harrison mansion on east side of Rittenhouse Square. Unidentified clipping. Philadelphia, June 1, 1912.

Stotesburys to open new ballroom suite on Walnut Street. *Philadelphia Public Ledger,* January 19, 1916.

"Palace for the Stotesburys." *Philadelphia Bulletin,* April 11, 1916.

Stotesbury buys lakefront land at Palm Beach. Unidentified clipping. Philadelphia, *c.* 1917.

Stotesbury pays record $85,000 for lakefront land at Palm Beach. Unidentified clipping. Philadelphia, March 2, 1917.

Stotesbury buys brownstone N.E. corner 18th and Locust: adjoins Rittenhouse Square property purchased in 1912. Unidentified clipping. Philadelphia, September 7, 1917.

"Stotesbury Coal for Poor." *Philadelphia Bulletin,* January 26, 1918.

"Stotesbury Home Loaned as Hospital." *Philadelphia Bulletin,* February 1, 1918.

"U.S. to Quiz Heating of Empty Mansion." *Philadelphia Bulletin,* February 1, 1918.

"Stotesburys' Million-Dollar Country Home Which Will Be Used as Naval Hospital." *Philadelphia Bulletin,* February 5, 1918.

Stotesburys move from Friendship Hall to Dale House: Whitemarsh Hall nearing completion. Unidentified clipping. Philadelphia, October 14, 1919.

Stotesburys' El Mirasol nears completion. Unidentified clipping. Philadelphia, November 5, 1919.

Obituary: James H. Roberts. *New York Times,* June 26, 1920.

"Stotesbury Villa Opens to Society." *Philadelphia Bulletin,* October 8, 1921.

"Stotesburys Open Their Suburban Palace." *Philadelphia Inquirer,* October 9, 1921.

"Stotesbury Villa Enthralls Society." *Philadelphia Bulletin,* October 10, 1921.

Stotesbury offers estate in Green Spring Valley to President as Summer White House. *Philadelphia Bulletin,* February 1, 1923.

Stotesbury sells entire Harrison parcel to Pennsylvania Athletic Club. *Philadelphia Bulletin,* May 16, 1923.

Stotesbury sells Green Spring Valley Estate to chiropractors for $150,000. *Philadelphia Bulletin,* April 29, 1924.

"Stotesbury House Has Noted History." Unidentified clipping. Philadelphia, *c.* May 25, 1925.

Stotesbury buys back Brooklands in Green Spring Valley from National Chiropractic Sanitorium Corporation. *Philadelphia Bulletin,* June 17, 1925.

Photo: Combined town houses of Stotesbury Walnut Street mansion: ground for ballroom was broken in October, 1915. *Philadelphia Bulletin,* October 1, 1925.

Philotropian Club buys No. 1923 Walnut Street for $400,000: for sale by Stotesbury since August, 1922. *Philadelphia Public Ledger,* October 13, 1925.

Stotesbury Walnut Street mansion to be razed, 16-story apartment to be built on site. *Philadelphia Bulletin,* January 12, 1926.

Stotesbury Walnut Street mansion being demolished. *Philadelphia Bulletin,* April 29, 1926.

Patterson, Augusta Owen. "Mr. E. T. Stotesbury's Residence Near Philadelphia." *Town & Country,* December 15, 1926.

Stotesburys establish "New York Home" in Cromwell Arms with James H. R. Cromwells: split top 4 floors of skyscraper apartment. *Philadelphia Bulletin,* February 24, 1927.

"Six Rooms at Whitemarsh Hall." *Town & Country,* February 15, 1928.

"Stately Whitemarsh Hall." *The Spur,* April 1, 1928.

Obituary: Edward T. Stotesbury. *Associated Press,* April 5, 1929. Routine service to members: to be held for use until death of subject.

Stotesburys to sail for Europe in June. *Philadelphia Bulletin,* April 28, 1932.

"Stotesbury Back/ Won't Give Up Home." *Philadelphia Bulletin,* October 7, 1932.

Marceau, Henri et al. "The Stotesbury Collection." *Pennsylvania Museum Bulletin* XXVIII (December, 1932) : 19.

"Stotesburys Reopen Home." *Philadelphia Bulletin,* May 29, 1933.

"Our Airman Flies Low Over the Palacios of Tropical Palm Beach." *Town & Country* 89 (January 15, 1934).

Obituary: Edith L. (Stotesbury) Hutchinson: Mrs. Sydney Emlen Hutchinson. *Philadelphia Inquirer,* May 20, 1935.

Obituary: Edith L. (Stotesbury) Hutchinson: Mrs. Sydney Emlen Hutchinson. *New York Times,* May 21, 1935.

Obituary: Edward T. Stotesbury. *Philadelphia Bulletin,* May 17, 1938.

Stotesbury dies. *Philadelphia Bulletin,* May 17, 1938.

Stotesbury's death: tributes. *Philadelphia Bulletin,* May 17, 1938.

"Drum Hung on Bier of Stotesbury." *Philadelphia Bulletin,* May 19, 1938.

"62 of Stotesbury employees to go." *Philadelphia Bulletin,* June 14, 1938.

Obituary: "Horace Trumbauer/ Noted as Architect." *New York Times,* September 20, 1938.

El Mirasol to rent this season for $8,000 per month. Unidentified clipping. Philadelphia, December 7, 1938.

Government to spend $1,000,000 on research lab at Winoga Farm. Unidentified clipping. Philadelphia, January 12, 1939.

U.S. Dept. of Agriculture building research lab on Stotesbury's Winoga Stock Farm. *Philadelphia Bulletin,* February 10, 1939.

Whitemarsh Hall for sale by executors. *Philadelphia Bulletin,* April 20, 1939.

Plaque at Bar Harbor honors Stotesbury. *Philadelphia Record,* August 6, 1939.

Father Divine offered Whitemarsh Hall: "Ridiculous," says Mrs. Stotesbury's secretary. *Philadelphia Bulletin,* August 11, 1939.

Herbert Pulitzer buys ocean front section of El Mirasol land: mansion unimpaired by sale. *Philadelphia Bulletin,* January 11, 1940.

"Whitemarsh Hall a Forgotten Ghost Town Today." *Philadelphia Bulletin,* February 1, 1940.

"Stotesbury Heirs Win Upkeep Fight." *Philadelphia Bulletin,* May 14, 1940.

Second El Mirasol plot sold: 22-acre site with Malmaison, a guesthouse. *Philadelphia Record,* May 28, 1940.

Mrs. Stotesbury leases Boxwood Farm in New Jersey. Unidentified clipping. Philadelphia, June 19, 1940.

"Mansions a Bargain as Society Goes Streamlined." *Philadelphia Bulletin,* August 2, 1941.

Lippincott, Horace Mather. "Edward T. Stotesbury." *Old York Road Historical Society Bulletin* VI (1942) : 3–23.

"Stotesbury Land Sold." *Philadelphia Bulletin,* January 28, 1942.

"Stotesbury Fence Offered for War/ Could Make 18,000 Machine Guns." *Philadelphia Bulletin,* December 4, 1942.

Proctor, Harry G. "Whitemarsh Hall Sold for Chemical Research Center." *Philadelphia Bulletin,* October 9, 1943.

Cushman, Howard. "Test-Tube-Cluttered Labs Replace Gold-Fitted Rooms at Whitemarsh." *Philadelphia Bulletin,* September 10, 1944.

Mrs. Stotesbury's Washington house to become Belgian Embassy. *Philadelphia Inquirer,* May 5, 1945.

Obituary: Mrs. Eva R. Stotesbury. *New York Herald Tribune,* May 24, 1946.

Obituary: Mrs. Eva R. Stotesbury. *New York Times,* May 24, 1946.

3-way division of Stotesbury residual estate provided by Orphan's Court, Montgomery County. *Philadelphia Bulletin,* 1946. Undated carbon copy of reporter's copy.

Wingwood House for sale: furnishings to be auctioned by Freeman. Unidentified clipping. Philadelphia, July 27, 1946.

"Stotesbury Acres Sold for Homes." *Philadelphia Bulletin,* July 31, 1946.

"El Mirasol Advertised for Sale." Unidentified clipping. Philadelphia, January 10, 1947.

Boyle, Hal. "The Gilt Is Wearing Thin on America's Gold Coast." Unidentified clipping. Philadelphia, February 28, 1947.

Wingwood House, Stotesbury Bar Harbor mansion, sold to Caroline Trippe of New York. *Philadelphia Bulletin,* November 4, 1947.

Obituary: John Kearsley Mitchell. *New York Times,* December 1, 1949.

Obituary: Mrs. John Kearsley Mitchell, née Frances Bergman Stotesbury. *New York Times,* October 15, 1950.

Bar Harbor buys Wingwood House. Unidentified clipping. Philadelphia, December 5, 1950.

Burnham, Alan. "The New York Architecture of Richard Morris Hunt." *Journal of the Society of Architectural Historians,* May, 1952.

Wingwood House, Stotesbury Bar Harbor mansion, razed. *Philadelphia Bulletin,* February 8, 1954.

Old Stotesbury mansion, now Catholic Philotropian Literary Institute, scene of tea dance. Unidentified clipping. Philadelphia, December 28, 1962.

Passillé, Raymond de. "Les jardins français aux Etats-Unis: Créations de MM. Duchêne et Gréber." *La gazette illustrée des amateurs de jardins,* 1963.

Lavedan, Pierre. Obituary-tribute: Jacques Gréber. *La vie urbaine* (Janvier-Mars, 1963) .

Whitemarsh Hall and history described. *Philadelphia Bulletin,* February 23, 1963.

Baptist Church of Maryland buys Brooklands/Rainbow Hill as home for the aged. Unidentified clipping. Philadelphia, January 11, 1964.

Van Trump, James D. "A Castellated Metamorphosis: Grey Towers into Beaver College." *Charette* 44 (February, 1964) .

Springfield Township stalls off high-rise at Whitemarsh Hall. *Philadelphia Bulletin,* March 15, 1964.

Bennett, Ralph K. The story of Stotesbury and Whitemarsh Hall retold. *Philadelphia Inquirer,* August 2, 1964.

"Weeding Out the Saints." *Newsweek,* June 5, 1967.

Branam, Alfred S., Jr. "For Sale: One Palace." *Philadelphia Bulletin* Sunday magazine, February 11, 1968.

Schiller, Johann Christoph Friederich von. "To My Friends" (poem) . *Time,* July 4, 1969.

Thompson, Ray. "Vandals Scar Palace." *Philadelphia Bulletin,* July 10, 1969.

De Wolf, Rose. "Stotesbury 'Palace' Sold for $700,000 to Syndicate Headed by Kaiser-man." *Philadelphia Bulletin,* October 8, 1969.
Maass, Patricia B. "A Pennsylvania Palace Goes on the Block." *Preservation News,* May, 1970.
Lees-Milne, James. "Ralph Allen at Prior Park." *Apollo,* November, 1973.

BOOKS
Amory, Cleveland. *The Last Resorts.* New York: Grosset & Dunlap, 1948.
Baltzell, E. Digby. *An American Business Aristocracy.* New York: Collier Books, 1962. Originally published as *Philadelphia Gentlemen: The Making of a National Upper Class.* New York: Macmillan, 1958.
Bapst, Germain. *Les statues des quatre saisons par Pajou.* Privately printed. Paris, 1922.
Barron, Clarence W. *They Told Barron: Conversations and Revelations of an American Pepys in Wall Street.* Arranged and edited by Arthur Pound and Samuel Taylor Moore. New York: Harper & Brothers, 1930.
Beard, Geoffrey. *Georgian Craftsmen and Their Work.* London: Country Life, 1953.
Behrman, S. N. *Duveen.* London: Hamish Hamilton, 1953.
Berlioz, Hector. "Rossini's 'William Tell.'" Reading 87 in *Source Readings in Music History: From Classical Antiquity through the Romantic Era.* Selected and annotated by Oliver Strunk. New York: Norton, 1950.
Biddle, Cornelia Drexel. *The Happiest Millionaire.* As told to Kyle Crichton. New York: Pocket Books, 1963. Originally published as *My Philadelphia Father,* 1955.
Biddle, Francis. *The Llanfear Pattern.* Philadelphia: Richards Press, 1928.
Braham, Allan, and Smith, Peter. *François Mansart.* 2 vols. London: Zwemmer, 1973.
British XVIII Century Portraits by Romney, Hoppner, Lawrence, Raeburn/Two Salon Suites in Aubusson and Royal Beauvais Tapestry/A Series of Beauvais Chinoiserie Tapestries after Boucher/Chinese Porcelains/An Isphahan Palace Carpet/From the Collection of the Late Edward T. Stotesbury (sales catalogue). New York: Parke-Bernet Galleries, November 18, 1944.
Brooks, John. *Once in Golconda: A True Drama of Wall Street, 1920–1928.* New York: Harper & Row, 1969.
Burt, Nathaniel. *The Perennial Philadelphians: The Anatomy of an American Aristocracy.* Boston: Little, Brown, 1963.
Burt, Struthers. *Philadelphia, Holy Experiment.* New York: Doubleday, Doran, 1945.
Cohen, Charles Joseph. *Rittenhouse Square, Past and Present.* Privately printed, 1922.
Collins, Henry LeRoy, and Jordan, Wilfred. *Philadelphia: A Story of Progress.* 5 vols. New York: Lewis Historical Publishing Co., 1941.
Delaire, E. et al. *Les architectes élèves de l'Ecole des Beaux-Arts, 1793–1907.* 2nd ed. Paris: Librarie de la Construction Moderne, 1907.
Eriksen, Svend. *Early Neo-Classicism in France: The Creation of the Louis Seize Style in Architectural Decoration, Furniture and Ormolu, Gold and Silver, and Sèvres Porcelain in the Mid-Eighteenth Century.* Translated and edited by Peter Thornton. London: Faber, 1974.
Feree, Barr. *American Estates and Gardens.* New York: Munn, 1906.
Flaubert, Gustave. *The Dictionary of Accepted Ideas.* Translated, with introduction and notes, by Jacques Barzun. New York: New Directions Paperback, 1954.
Gallet, Michel. *Stately Mansions: Eighteenth Century Paris Architecture.* Translated by James C. Palmes. New York: Praeger, 1972.
Gimpel, René. *Diary of an Art Dealer.* Translated by John Rosenberg. Introduction by Sir Herbert Read. New York: Farrar, Straus & Giroux, 1966.
Gray, David. *Thomas Hastings, Architect: Collected Writings, Together with a Memoir by David Gray.* Boston: Houghton Mifflin, 1933.
Gréber, Jacques. *L'architecture aux Etats-Unis: Preuve de la force d'expansion du génie français.* 2 vols. Introduction by Victor Cambon. Paris: Payot, 1920.
Gribble and Elkins Families. Privately printed by John Gribble II, Huntington Valley, 1962.

Harris, John. *Georgian Country Houses*. London: Country Life Books, 1968.

Ide, John Jay. *Some Examples of Irish Country Houses of the Georgian Period*. Published by the author. New York, 1959.

Jervis, Simon. *Victorian Furniture*. London: Ward Lock, 1968.

Johnston, Alva. *The Legendary Mizners*. New York: Farrar, Straus & Young, 1953.

Josephson, Matthew. *The Robber Barons: The Great American Capitalists, 1861–1901*. New York: Harcourt, Brace & World, 1934.

Jullian, Philippe. *Edward and the Edwardians*. Translated by Peter Dawnay. New York: Viking, 1967.

———. *Prince of Aesthetes: Count Robert de Montesquiou, 1855–1921*. Translated by John Haylock and Francis King. New York: Viking, 1968.

Kashay, Robert, and Reymert, Martin L. H., et al. *Western European Bronzes of the Nineteenth Century: A Survey* (catalogue). New York: Shepherd Gallery, 1973.

Kimball, Fiske. "The Stotesburys." Chapter 16 of *Triumph on Fairmount: Fiske Kimball and the Philadelphia Museum of Art*. George and Mary Roberts. Philadelphia: Lippincott, 1959.

King, Moses, ed. *Philadelphia and Notable Philadelphians*. New York: Moses King, 1902.

LeBrun, George F. *It's Time to Tell*. As told to Edward D. Radin. New York: Morrow, 1962.

Leslie's History of the Greater New York. Vol. III: *Encyclopedia of New York Biography and Genealogy*. New York: Arkell, 1898.

Leuchtenberg, William E. *Franklin D. Roosevelt and the New Deal, 1932–1940*. New York: Harper & Row, 1963.

Lippincott, Horace Mather. *A Narrative of Chestnut Hill, Philadelphia, with Some Account of Springfield, Whitemarsh and Cheltenham Townships in Montgomery County*. Jenkintown, Pennsylvania: Old York Road Publishing Co., 1948.

Matz, Mary Jane. *The Many Lives of Otto Kahn*. New York: Macmillan, 1963.

Miller, Hope Ridings. *Great Houses of Washington, D.C.* Chapter VIII: "The Belgian Ambassador's Residence," p. 91. New York: Clarkson N. Potter, 1969.

Moore, Charles. *The Life and Times of Charles Follen McKim*. Boston: Houghton Mifflin, 1929.

Nicolson, Harold. *Kings, Courts, and Monarchy*. New York: Simon & Schuster, 1962.

Palladio, Andrea. *The Four Books of Architecture*. Introduction by Adolf K. Placzek. Translated and plates redrawn by Isaac Ware. New York: Dover Publications, 1965. Originally published in 1738. First Italian edition, 1570.

Philadelphia and Popular Philadelphians. Philadelphia: The North American, 1891.

The Philadelphian and His City: Who's Who in Wartime Philadelphia. Philadelphia: Stafford's National News Service, 1920.

Prominent Families of New York: New York: Historical Publishing Co., 1897.

Roberts, George and Mary. *Triumph on Fairmount: Fiske Kimball and the Philadelphia Museum of Art*. Philadelphia: Lippincott, 1959.

Savage, George. *A Concise History of Interior Decoration*. New York: Grosset & Dunlap, 1966.

Seligman, Germain. *Merchants of Art, 1880–1960: Eighty Years of Professional Collecting*. New York: Appleton-Century-Crofts, 1961.

Stone, Lawrence. *The Crisis of the Aristocracy, 1558–1641*. Abridged ed. New York: Oxford University Press, 1967.

Strong, George T. *The Diary of George Templeton Strong: Post-War Years, 1865–1875*. Vol. IV. Allan Nevins and Milton Halsey Thomas, eds. New York: Macmillan, 1952.

———. *Diary of the Civil War, 1860–1865*. Allan Nevins, ed. New York: Macmillan, 1962.

Sturgis, Russell, et al. "Decorative Art." *A Dictionary of Architecture and Building: Biographical, Historical, and Descriptive*. 3 vols. New York: Macmillan, 1902. Republished by Gale Research Co., Detroit, 1966.

Summerson, John. *Architecture in Britain, 1530–1830*. Nikolaus Pevsner, ed. Baltimore: Penguin Books, 1953. 5th revised ed., 1969.

———. *Georgian London*. Baltimore: Penguin Books, 1945. Revised ed., 1962.

Tarbell, Ida M. *Florida Architecture of Addison Mizner.* New York: William Helburn, c. 1928.

Tatum, George B. *Penn's Great Town: 250 Years of Philadelphia Architecture Illustrated in Prints and Drawings.* Philadelphia: University of Pennsylvania Press, 1961.

Tompkins, Calvin. *Merchants and Masterpieces: The Story of the Metropolitan Museum of Art.* New York: Dutton, 1970.

Towner, Wesley. *The Elegant Auctioneers.* Completed by Stephen Varble. New York: Hill & Wang, 1970.

Wecter, Dixon. *The Saga of American Society: A Record of Social Aspiration, 1607–1937.* New York: Charles Scribner's Sons, 1937.

White, Theo B., ed. *Philadelphia Architecture in the Nineteenth Century.* Philadelphia: University of Pennsylvania Press, 1953.

Widener, P. A. B. *Without Drums.* New York: G. P. Putnam's Sons, 1940.

Widener-Dunton, Elkins-Broomhall and Allied Families. Privately printed. New York: American Historical Society, 1935.

Wolf, Edwin II, with Fleming, John F. *Rosenbach: A Biography.* Cleveland: World Publishing Co., 1960.

Third Street: Drexel/Morgan

MISCELLANEOUS, NEWSPAPERS AND PERIODICALS, BOOKS

Adams, Frederick B., Jr. *An Introduction to the Pierpont Morgan Library* (booklet). New York: Pierpont Morgan Library, 1964.

Allen, Frederick Lewis. *The Great Pierpont Morgan.* New York: Harper & Brothers, 1949.

Andrews, Wayne. *Mr. Morgan and His Architect* (booklet). New York: Pierpont Morgan Library, 1957.

"Drexel, Morgan & Co." Unidentified clipping. New York, c. January 2, 1895.

Drexel employees to give Stotesbury dinner on his 50th anniversary with bank. Unidentified clipping. Philadelphia, October 20, 1916.

Garraty, John A. *Right-Hand Man: The Life of George W. Perkins.* New York: Harper & Brothers, 1960.

"Girard's Talk of the Day." *Philadelphia Inquirer,* May 26, 1933.

Letter: Announcement from Drexel & Co., Philadelphia, and Drexel, Morgan & Co., New York, December 31, 1894: 1) Copartnership of these firms expires on this date. 2) New copartnership formed by J. P. Morgan & Co., New York, and Drexel & Co., Philadelphia. 3) The Paris copartnership Drexel, Harjes & Co. will be continued from this date under firm name of Morgan, Harjes & Co.

Letter: Announcement from J. S. Morgan & Co., London, April 17, 1890. John Pierpont Morgan will take the place of Junius Spencer Morgan, his recently deceased father, in the copartnership, which will continue. Signature specimen: "J. P. Morgan."

Letterbook of George Bliss. Vol. 2. Morton, Bliss & Co., Letter: May 8, 1878, New York City. To —— Grenfell, London. Re alterations/expansion Drexel, Morgan & Co., New York. New-York Historical Society.

Morgan names Stotesbury senior partner: he says "I will remain in Philadelphia." *Philadelphia Public Ledger,* April, 1913.

A New Home for an Old House. Privately printed. Philadelphia: Drexel & Co., 1927.

Satterlee, Herbert L. *J. Pierpont Morgan: An Intimate Portrait.* New York: Macmillan, 1939.

Sobel, Robert. *The Big Board: A History of the New York Stock Market.* New York: Free Press, 1965.

——. *Panic on Wall Street: A History of America's Financial Disasters.* New York: Macmillan, 1968.

Stotesbury celebrates 70 years at Drexel & Company. *Philadelphia Inquirer,* October 22, 1936.

Stotesbury denies rumors he will move to New York. Unidentified clipping. Philadelphia, June 2, 1922.

Winkler, John K. *Morgan the Magnificent: The Life of J. Pierpont Morgan (1837–1913)*. Garden City, New York: Garden City Publishing, 1930.

Stotesbury and Hammerstein

NEWSPAPERS, BOOKS

Cone, John Frederick. *Oscar Hammerstein's Manhattan Opera Company*. Norman: University of Oklahoma Press, 1966.

Davis, Ronald L. *Opera in Chicago: A Social and Cultural History, 1850–1965*. New York: Appleton-Century, 1966.

Kolodin, Irving. *The Metropolitan Opera, 1883–1966: A Candid History*. New York: Knopf, 1966.

Name of Philadelphia Opera House changed to the Metropolitan Opera House. *Philadelphia Ledger*, April 28, 1910.

Sheean, Vincent. *Oscar Hammerstein I: The Life and Exploits of an Impressario*. New York: Simon & Schuster, 1956.

TWO. CA' D'ZAN

General

MISCELLANEOUS

Baum, Dwight James. "First Floor Plan. Preliminary Sketches of Residence for Mrs. John Ringling at Sarasota, Florida. Dwight James Baum, Architect" (blueprint). Signed "EBS," January 8, 1924.

"Revised First Floor Plan . . ." (blueprint). Signed "EP" [Earl Purdy], January 21, 1924.

Untitled watercolor rendering of residence for Mrs. John Ringling. Elevation of west facade. Unsigned. Artist: Earl Purdy, c. 1925.

Untitled watercolor rendering of residence for Mrs. John Ringling. Elevation of east facade. Unsigned. Artist: Earl Purdy, c. 1925. NOTE: The above-listed architectural materials are in the holdings of the John and Mable Ringling Museum of Art, Sarasota, Florida.

[Böhler, Julius W.] *John Ringling: Art Collector, Museum Builder* (18 pp. typescript). N.d. John and Mable Ringling Museum of Art, Sarasota, Florida.

Ca' d'Zan: Ringling Residence (pamphlet). Sarasota, Florida: John and Mable Ringling Museum of Art, n.d.

Fifty Masterpieces in the John and Mable Ringling Museum of Art: A Short Guide (pamphlet). Revised ed. Sarasota, Florida: John and Mable Ringling Museum of Art, March, 1963.

"A Tour of the Ringling Residence" (14 pp. typescript). Unsigned. Written by Creighton Gilbert. Sarasota, Florida: John and Mable Ringling Museum of Art, n.d.

NEWSPAPERS AND PERIODICALS (chronological sequence)

Passillé, Raymond de. "Les jardins français aux Etats-Unis: Créations de MM. Duchêne et Gréber." *La gazette illustrée des amateurs des jardins*. Paris, 1923.

"Expect Causeway Will Launch Big Building Boom." *Sarasota Herald*, October 4, 1925.

"A. B. Edwards was City's First Real Estate Man." *Sarasota Herald*, October 4, 1925.

Merle Evans to bring band back this year. *Sarasota Herald*, October 4, 1925.

"Ringling Bank to Be Expanded." *Sarasota Herald*, October 4, 1925.

Mrs. Potter Palmer discovered Sarasota's charm. *Sarasota Herald*, October 4, 1925.

Advertisement: Rich Sarasota estate owners. *Sarasota Herald*, October 10, 1925.

Advertisement: Mizner Development Corporation. *Sarasota Herald*, November 19, 1925.

Drawing: Home of Owen Burns III. Architect: Dwight James Baum. *Sarasota Herald*, November 29, 1925.

"Realty Concern Adds Orchestra." *Sarasota Herald*, December 4, 1925.

"Ringling Causeway Open for Traffic in Two Weeks." *Sarasota Herald*, December 6, 1925.

"Great [Czech] Band Will Arrive on Monday." *Sarasota Herald*, December 8, 1925.

"Gondola Is Now Moored in Bay." *Sarasota Herald*, December 9, 1925.

"Slovakian Band Today to Begin its Engagement." *Sarasota Herald*, December 14, 1925.

"John Ringling to Reach City Saturday/ Will Bring Valuable Statuary/ Band on Same Train/ Build Shell." *Sarasota Herald*, December 18, 1925.

"Czechoslovakian Band Here for Concerts/ John Ringling Back in Sarasota." *Sarasota Herald*, December 20, 1925.

Ringling is Santa Claus to Sarasota: band to give Christmas concert. *Sarasota Herald*, December 25, 1925.

"Czechoslovakian Band in Concert." *Sarasota Herald*, December 26, 1925.

Ringling sets new causeway completion date. *Sarasota Herald*, December 31, 1925.

Walker takes office as New York mayor: will visit Sarasota. *Sarasota Herald*, January 1, 1926.

Story of the Czech band: Bartik's rôle. *Sarasota Herald*, January 3, 1926.

Public letter of thanks to "Good Neighbor" John Ringling. *Sarasota Herald*, January 9, 1926.

Ringling donates Czech band to Catholic Women's Club for concert and dance. *Sarasota Herald*, January 9, 1926.

"Causeway Is Proof of John Ringling's Courage/ All Sarasota Benefits by Prominent Resident's Great Building Project." *Sarasota Herald*, January 10, 1926.

Society notes: Ringling to New York for two weeks: Mrs. Ringling to Tampa. *Sarasota Herald*, January 10, 1926.

"Czech Musicians to Leave Here April 20th." *Sarasota Herald*, April 3, 1926.

Ringling wires sale of Ritz-Carlton shares failing. *Sarasota Herald*, April 4, 1926.

"Builders of Sarasota — Col. Ralph G. Caples." *Sarasota Herald*, April 9, 1926.

Society note: Mrs. John Ringling returning from New York Monday. *Sarasota Herald*, April 11, 1926.

"City Architect Attracts State-Wide Attention/ Thomas Reed Martin . . ." *Sarasota Herald*, September 9, 1926.

"Expect Czecho Band Here Again." *Sarasota Herald*, September 11, 1926.

"News of the Czechs' Welcome" (editorial) . *Sarasota Herald*, September 12, 1926.

Winter life in Sarasota for "Mrs. Visitor": Mrs. John Ringling's yachting parties. *Sarasota Herald*, October 3, 1926.

Major Sarasota construction projects in 1926: Ringling brothers' houses. *Sarasota Herald*, October 3, 1926.

Ringling causeway cost $1,000,000. *Sarasota Herald*, October 3, 1926.

John Ringling returns, inspects real estate projects. *Sarasota Herald*, October 19, 1926.

"Completes Miniature of Ringling Estates Here." *Sarasota Herald*, October 24, 1926.

"John Ringling Approves Project" (Ritz-Carlton to open in fall, 1927.) *Sarasota Herald*, October 28, 1926.

Society notes: Ringlings leave for North. *Sarasota Herald*, October 28, 1926.

"John Ringling Coming Today." *Sarasota Herald*, November 25, 1926.

"Charles Ringling Dies at Home." *Sarasota Herald*, December 4, 1926.

Ringling orders work resumed on Ritz-Carlton. *Sarasota Herald*, December 10, 1926.

Late Charles Ringling's mansion described. *Sarasota Herald*, December 15, 1926.

Leading Sarasota houses. *Sarasota Herald*, December 15, 1926.

"Czechoslovakian Band to Return to City Tuesday." *Sarasota Herald*, December 19, 1926.

Czech band warmly greeted on arrival. *Sarasota Herald*, December 22, 1926.

"John Ringling to Head Sarasota Chamber of Commerce." *Sarasota Herald*, January 18, 1927.

"John Ringling Announces Vast Project Here." *Sarasota Herald*, February 6, 1927.

"More Than 300 Employed on Ringling Work." *Sarasota Times*, August 3, 1927.

Sears, Roger Franklin. "A Venetian Palace in Florida." *Country Life*, October, 1927.

"Ringling Wrangling." *Fortune*, July, 1947.

Taylor, Robert Lewis. "The Triumph of Hoopla" (profile of John Ringling North, Parts 1 and 2). *The New Yorker*, April 10 and 17, 1954.

"Renaissance Splendor on Gramercy Park." *Gramercy Graphic*, February, 1956.

Feature story on Ca' d'Zan and its history. *Sarasota Herald Tribune* (carbon copy of original typescript), *c.* 1957.

Soby, James Thrall. "The Ringling Art Museum." *Saturday Review*, January 5, 1957.

Sutton, Horace. "John's House." *Saturday Review*, March 2, 1957.

Murray, Marian. "The Ringling Museum." *Palm Beach Life*, March 26, 1957.

Harper, Mr. "Palms and Circuses." *Harper's Magazine*, July, 1958.

Rosenberg, John D. "Treasure Chest in the Attic." *New York Times Book Review*, Paperback Section, January 10, 1965. Quotations from Edward Gibbon.

Logan, Andy. "That Was New York. Palace of Delight" (profile of Madison Square Garden). *The New Yorker*, February 27, 1965.

"Resurgence" (Interview with Henry Ringling North). "Talk of the Town," *The New Yorker*, April 10, 1965.

"North, Now East, Touts His Circus." *New York Times*, May 9, 1965.

Sutton, Horace. "Culture and Sun in Sarasota." *New York Herald Tribune*, December 5, 1965.

Durant, John. "Sarasota, Florida's Circus City, Comes of Age." *New York Times*, May 8, 1966.

Maher, James T. "A View of the Water: American Palaces by the Sea." *Holiday*, July, 1966.

Saarinen, Aline. "He Saw Architecture as the Permanent Stage Set of an Age." Essay accompanying article entitled "The Splendid World of Stanford White." *Life*, September 16, 1966.

BOOKS

Baldwin, Charles G. *Stanford White*. New York: Dodd, Mead, 1931. Facsimile reprint. Da Capo Press. New York, 1971.

Bazin, Germain. *Baroque and Rococo*. New York: Praeger, 1964.

Beebe, Lucius. *Mansions on Rails: The Folklore of the Private Railway Car*. Berkeley: Howell-North Books, 1959.

Durant, John and Alice. *Pictorial History of the American Circus*. New York: Barnes, 1957.

Dutton, Ralph. *The Châteaux of France*. London: Batsford, 1957.

Folsom, Merrill. *Great American Mansions and Their Stories*. New York: Hastings House, 1963.

Gimpel, René. *Diary of an Art Dealer*. Translated by John Rosenberg. New York: Farrar, Straus & Giroux, 1966.

Grismer, Karl H. *The Story of Sarasota*. Tampa: M. E. Russell, 1946.

Hamlin, Talbot. *Architecture: An Art for All Men*. New York: Columbia University Press, 1947.

Knowles, Ruth Sheldon. *The Greatest Gamblers: The Epic of American Oil Exploration*. New York: McGraw-Hill, 1959.

Kolodin, Irving. *The Metropolitan Opera, 1883–1966: A Candid History*. New York: Knopf, 1966.

Lister, Martin. *A Journey to Paris*. 1698. Quoted by George Savage. *Seventeenth and Eighteenth Century French Porcelain*. London: Spring Books, 1960.

McCarthy, Mary. *The Stones of Florence*. New York: Harcourt, Brace, n.d.

McCullough, Edo. *Good Old Coney Island: A Sentimental Journey into the Past*. New York: Charles Scribner's Sons, 1957.

Marks, Edward B. *They All Sang: From Tony Pastor to Rudy Vallee*. As told to Abbott J. Liebling. New York: Viking, 1934.

Mayer, Grace. *Once Upon a City: New York from 1890 to 1910 as Photographed by Byron and Described by Grace M. Mayer*. New York: Macmillan, 1958.

North, Henry Ringling, and Hatch, Alden. *The Circus Kings: Our Ringling Family Story.* New York: Doubleday, 1960.

Rheims, Maurice. *The Strange Life of Objects: 35 Centuries of Art Collecting and Collectors.* Translated by David Pryce-Jones. New York: Atheneum, 1961. Quotation from Paul Valéry.

Rochefoucauld, François, Duc de la. *Maxims.* Quoted by Louis Kronenberger. *The Wit of Worldlings. New York Times Book Review,* August 7, 1966.

Savage, George. *Seventeenth and Eighteenth Century French Porcelain.* Reprint. London: Spring Books, 1969.

Seltsam, William H., compiler. *Metropolitan Opera Annals: A Chronicle of Artists and Performances.* New York: H. Wilson Co., 1947.

Tapié, Victor-Lucien. *The Age of Grandeur: Baroque Art and Architecture.* 2nd ed. Translated by A. Ross Williamson. New York: Praeger, 1966.

Thomas, Richard. *John Ringling, Circus Magnate and Art Patron.* New York: Pageant Press, 1960.

Towner, Wesley. *The Elegant Auctioneers.* Completed by Stephen Varble. New York: Hill & Wang, 1970.

White, Lawrence Grant. *Sketches and Designs by Stanford White: With an Outline of His Career by His Son Lawrence Grant White.* New York: Architectural Book Publishing Co., 1920.

Venetian Gothic Architecture

BOOKS AND PERIODICALS

Arslan, Edoardo. *Gothic Architecture in Venice.* Translated by Anne Engel. New York: Phaidon, 1972.

Briggs, Martin S. *Architecture in Italy: A Handbook for Travellers and Students.* London: J. M. Dent & Sons, 1961.

Brion, Marcel. *Venice: The Masque of Italy.* Translated by Neil Mann. New York: Crown, 1962.

Chambers, D. S. *Patrons and Artists in the Italian Renaissance.* Columbia, South Carolina: University of South Carolina Press, 1971.

Chubb, Thomas Caldecott. *The Venetians: Merchant Princes.* New York: Viking, 1968.

Fletcher, Bannister. *A History of Architecture on the Comparative Method.* 17th ed. Revised by R. A. Cordingly. New York: Charles Scribner's Sons, 1963.

Frankl, Paul. *Gothic Architecture.* Translated by Dieter Pevsner. Baltimore: Penguin Books, 1962.

McCarthy, Mary. *Venice Observed.* New York: Reynal, 1956.

McGrew, Charles B. *Italian Doorways.* Cleveland: J. H. Jansen, 1929.

Muraro, Michelangelo. *Invitation to Venice.* Translated by Isabel Quigly. New York: Trident, 1963.

Murray, Peter J. *The Architecture of the Italian Renaissance.* New York: Schocken Books, 1963.

Pignatti, Terisio. *The Doge's Palace.* New York: Reynal in association with William Morrow, n.d.

Ruskin, John. *The Stones of Venice.* Edited and abridged by J. G. Links. New York: Hill & Wang, 1964.

Summerson, John. *Heavenly Mansions: And Other Essays on Architecture.* New York: Norton, 1963.

Wiener, Samuel G. *Venetian Houses and Details: Wherein Is Contained Drawings and Photographs of Houses and Smaller Palaces in and Near Venice Together with Many Details of Architectural Interest.* New York: Architectural Book Publishing Co., 1929.

Dwight James Baum

NEWPAPERS AND PERIODICALS (chronological sequence)
Baum Wins Gold Medal. *Architecture,* March 23, 1923.
A survey of Dwight James Baum's Florida work. *The American Architect,* August 20,
1926.
Baum, Dwight James. "The Architecture of Homes." *Country Life,* October, 1927.
Obituary: Dwight James Baum. *New York Times,* December 14, 1939.

BOOKS
Fitch, James Marston. *American Building: The Forces That Shape It.* Boston: Houghton
Mifflin, 1948.
Green, David. *Sarah Duchess of Marlborough.* New York: Charles Scribner's Sons, 1967.
Price, Matlack. *The Work of Dwight James Baum, Architect.* New York: Architectural
Book Publishing Co., 1927.

THREE. VIZCAYA

General

MISCELLANEOUS
Adams, Adam G. Lecture, November 12, 1963, at Vizcaya for "The Vizcayans." Mime-
ographed typescript. Dade County Art Museum library, Miami, Florida.
Cambridge, Massachusetts. Harvard University archives. Re F. Burrall Hoffman, Jr.
———. Massachusetts Institute of Technology archives. Re James Deering.
Evanston, Illinois. Northwestern University archives. Re James Deering.
———. Northwestern University Preparatory School archives. Re James Deering.
*Handbook of the House, Formal Gardens and Fountains of Vizcaya: Dade County Art
Museum* (pamphlet). Material partially adapted from an earlier handbook by
Robert B. Harshe and Daniel Catton Rich. *c.* 1953.
*Handbook of the House, Formal Gardens and Fountains of Vizcaya: Dade County Art
Museum* (pamphlet). Revised ed. Material partially adapted from an earlier hand-
book by Robert B. Harshe and Daniel Catton Rich. Undated.
Harshe, Robert B., and Rich, Daniel Catton. A guide to Vizcaya (title unknown).
Miami, Florida, 1933.
Leffler, Bernice Thompson. "An Italian Villa on Biscayne Bay" (background study
material for tour guides). Undated mimeograph. Dade County Art Museum library,
Miami, Florida.
Map of Vizcaya: "Home of the Late James Deering of Chicago and Miami. Deering
Plaza" (guide to grounds: "Two Drives through Vizcaya"). Miami, Florida, *c.* 1934.
Motion picture (still photographs). Vizcaya as the *mis-en-scène* for an unidentified
film, April, 1918. Dade County Art Museum library, Miami, Florida.
"No. 9 Rue St. James, Neuilly, Paris" (photo album). James Deering. Scenes of re-
construction, redecoration of the house, *pavillon,* concierge's house. Dade County
Art Museum library, Miami, Florida.
*Official Retrospective Exhibition of the Development of Harvesting Machinery for the
Paris Exposition of 1900* . . . French and English text. Chicago: Deering Harvester
Co., 1900.
Photo albums, untitled. 3 vols. Vizcaya (principally interiors). Photographer: Frank
Bell, Chicago. Dade County Art Museum library, Miami, Florida.
Trois siècles de papiers peints (catalogue for exhibit). Musee des Arts Décoratifs, Paris,
June 22–October 15, 1967.
Vizcaya (booklet). Miami, *c.* 1935.
"Vizcaya" (unpublished catalogue). American Art Association–Anderson Galleries. New

York City, *c.* 1932. (AAA–AG files now owned by Parke-Bernet Galleries, New York City.)

"Vizcaya" (photo albums). 12 vols. James Deering. Several thousand photographs: construction, completed grounds and gardens. Dade County Art Museum library, Miami, Florida.

Vizcaya: An Italian Palace in Miami (tourist folder). Miami, Florida, n.d.

Vizcaya: Handbook of the House, Formal Gardens and Fountains (leaflet). Miami, Florida, n.d.

"Vizcaya Scrapbook." James Deering. Newspaper clippings, etc. Dade County Art Museum library, Miami, Florida.

Warren, Jefferson T. *Vizcaya: Dade County Art Museum: Guide to the Palace and Grounds* (leaflet). Miami, Florida, n.d.

NEWSPAPERS AND PERIODICALS (chronological sequence)

Deering to build $1,000,000 winter palace. *The Florida Homeseeker, c.* 1913.

"Mr. James Deering's Venetian Residence at Miami." *New York American, c.* 1917.

Kitchen, Karl K. "The Grandest House in America Is Located — in Florida." *New York World Magazine,* March 31, 1918.

Passillé, Raymond de. "Les jardins français aux Etats-Unis: Créations de MM. Duchêne et Gréber." *La gazette illustrée des amateurs des jardins,* 1923.

James Deering pays highest income tax in Florida. *New York Times,* September 2, 1925.

Obituary: James Deering. *New York Times,* September 22, 1925.

Burial plans for James Deering. *New York Times,* September 24, 1925.

Art bequests of late James Deering. *New York Times,* February 18, 1926.

Obituary: Charles Deering. *New York Times,* February 7, 1927.

"A Tour Through the World's Most Magnificent Estate." *The Magazine of Sigma Chi,* February, 1936.

Nicholas, William H. "Vizcaya: An Italian Palazzo in Miami." *National Geographic Magazine,* November, 1950.

"James Deering's Lonely Kingdom." *American Weekly,* March 25, 1951.

"Souvenir of Vizcaya" (cover title of special issue). *Tropical Homes and Gardening,* August, 1953.

Adams, Adam G. "Vizcaya." *Tequesta* XV (the Journal of the Historical Association of Southern Florida), 1955.

"The Splendors of Vizcaya." *Interior Design,* September, 1955.

Davis, Robert Tyler. "Vizcaya." *The Florida Architect,* July, 1956.

Blackwell, Harriet. "The Quiet Man Liked Parties." *Miami Herald,* November 12, 1961.

Ash, Agnes. "Mansion in Miami." *New York Times,* February 23, 1964.

Mastai, M-L. d'Ortrange. "Vizcaya: James Deering's Italian Villa in Miami." *The Connoisseur,* March, 1964.

Ennis, Thomas W. "Gracie Mansion Getting 18th-Century Style." *New York Times,* January 12, 1965.

"Mrs. Chauncey McCormick Dies/ Chicago Patron of Arts Was 78." *New York Times,* January 14, 1965.

Wilson, Beverley. "Vizcaya's Wild Party Ghosts Re-Visited." *Miami Herald,* March 10, 1966.

Clarke, Jay. "Miami's Vizcaya Palace Under Bright Lights." *New York Times,* May 5, 1968.

Werne, Jo. "Structure Must Be Made Stronger: Crumbling Concrete Threatens Vizcaya." *Miami Herald,* August 23, 1971.

BOOKS

Ackerman, James S. *Palladio.* Baltimore: Penguin Books, 1966.

Acton, Harold. *Memoirs of an Aesthete.* London: Methuen, 1948.

Andrews, Wayne. *Battle for Chicago.* New York: Harcourt, Brace, 1946.

Baedeker, Karl. *Northern Italy.* Leipzig: Baedeker, 1913.

Barron, Clarence W. *They Told Barron: Conversations and Revelations of an American Pepys in Wall Street.* Edited and arranged by Arthur Pound and Samuel Taylor Moore. New York: Harper and Brothers, 1930.

Bowles, Oliver. *The Stone Industries.* New York: McGraw-Hill, 1934.

Château of the Loire. 4th ed. Michelin guide, English ed. London: Dickens Press, 1967.

Cook, Theodore Andrea. *Twenty-Five Great Houses of France: The Story of the Noblest French Châteaux.* London: Country Life, n.d.

Duchêne, Achille. *Les jardins de l'avenir: hier, aujourd'hui, demain.* Paris: Vincent, Fréal, 1935.

Dunlop, Ian. *Châteaux of the Loire.* New York: Taplinger, 1969.

Garraty, John A. *Right-Hand Man: The Life of George W. Perkins.* New York: Harper & Brothers, 1960.

Gibbon, Monk. "Linderhof" in *Great Palaces of Europe.* New York: G. P. Putnam's Sons, 1964.

Guiles, Fred Lawrence. *Marion Davies.* New York: McGraw-Hill, 1972.

Hendrick, Burton J. *The Age of Big Business: A Chronicle of the Captains of Industry.* New Haven: Yale University Press, 1919.

Huret, Jules. *En Amérique de New-York à la Nouvelle-Orleans.* Paris, 1904.

"Jules Huret" in *Larousse du XXᵉ Siècle.* Vol. 3. Paris: Librarie Larousse, 1930.

Masson, Georgina. *Italian Gardens.* New York: Harry N. Abrams, *c.* 1961.

Monneret de Villard, Ugo. *I monumenti del lago di Como.* (Series title: *L'Italia Monumentale.*) Milan: E. Bonomi, 1912.

Painter, George D. *Proust: The Early Years.* Boston: Little, Brown, 1959.

————. *Proust: The Later Years.* Boston: Little, Brown, 1965.

Reed, Henry Hope. *The Golden City.* New York: Norton, 1970.

Scott, Walter Dill, and Harshe, Robert B. *Charles Deering, 1852–1927: An Appreciation . . . Together with His Memories of William Deering and James Deering.* Privately printed. Boston, 1929.

Towner, Wesley. *The Elegant Auctioneers.* Completed by Stephen Varble. New York: Hill & Wang, 1970.

Tunnard, Christopher, and Reed, Henry Hope. *American Skyline: The Growth and Form of Our Cities and Towns.* New York: New American Library, 1956.

Valeri, Diego, ed. *In Milan and on the Lakes of Lombardy with Stendhal.* London: Macdonald, 1961.

West, Rebecca. *The Fountain Overflows.* New York: Viking Press, 1956.

Paul Chalfin (Chalfin Family Papers)

NOTE: The materials listed in this section are privately held.

CONSOLIDATED

The Alley Festa (souvenir program). Fred T. Ley, June, 1917. World War I fund-raising street fair in Macdougal Alley, New York City. "Paul Chalfin, Designer and Architect of the Alley Festa."

"Association for Befriending Children/House No. 316 West Fourteenth Street." Unidentified clipping. New York City, before 1880. Re fund-raising concert at "Mrs. [Samuel Fletcher] Chalfin's elegant residence in Forty-seventh Street, near the Fifth Avenue . . ."

Certificate of Award to Paul Chalfin. The South Florida Chapter of the American Institute of Architects. For Villa Vizcaya, May 8, 1956.

Certificate of Honorary Membership to Paul Chalfin. American Institute of Decorators, April 22, 1956.

Certificate Number 371, University of the State of New York, State Board for the Registration of Architects. Granted to Paul Chalfin. Date on silver seal: December 1, 1916. (This is not the date of certification, but the date on which the Board of

Registration first granted such certificates under state law.) Signed by the president of the university and members of the board.

Chalfin, Paul. "Roof of Cedars: A Play in Three Acts with Ballets and Epilogue" (revised typescript, copy no. 2). Copyright March 2, 1935. Unproduced. The cast included 29 characters, and a corps de ballet of 37.

————. *The Io of Correggio: Four Versions and Their Interrelations, as Influenced by the Inquisition* (pamphlet). [Greenwich, Connecticut], 1947. Analysis, provenance, and succession of owners of four Correggio paintings: the *Io*. Two-page letter from Chalfin to Mr. McCormick (Mr. Chauncey McCormick, president, Chicago Art Institute) dated February 9, 1948, folded into the pamphlet; handwritten, apparently a draft. Tells how the painting (one of the set of four) came into his possession. Chalfin wants to get the painting authenticated and sell it.

Letter: Charles E. Prendergast to Mrs. J. V. Chalfin (Mrs. Samuel Fletcher Chalfin, mother of Paul Chalfin). New York, March 25, 1906. Contains biographical passages on Colonel Samuel Fletcher Chalfin extracted from a history of the Georgia hussars compiled by Captain Duncan. Prendergast was the author of the section on Colonel Chalfin.

Letter: Mrs. C. A. McVicker to Paul Chalfin. Miami, Florida, November 13, 1957. Questions re "a man named Suarez." Notes for reply on back of sheet, dictated by Chalfin to Mrs. Donald B. Foresman.

Letter: Mrs. John Seebach to "Family of Paul Chalfin." Brooklyn, February 16, 1959. Mrs. Seebach's recollections of incidents in Paul Chalfin's childhood.

Mayor's Committee of Welcome to Home-Coming Troops: Review and Parade of the 27th Division, March 25, 1919 (souvenir booklet). Executive Committee portraits: Paul Chalfin (from portrait painted by Albert Sterner).

Philanthropy of Ralph Voorhees, Clinton, New Jersey. Three unidentified, undated newspaper clippings. Re church and family gifts of Paul Chalfin's great-uncle. Clippings relate Chalfin to "Governor Voorhees" of New Jersey, a blind man "with large banking interests."

Photograph: "Church at Warrenville, Connecticut." 8" x 11" glossy print. Dineen Studio, Willimantic, Connecticut. Handwritten legend on back of photo: "Designed by Paul Chalfin about 1947."

R. C. [Royal Cortissoz] "Art Exhibitions: The Annual Show of the Architectural League." *New York Daily Tribune*, February 2, 1910. Review includes favorable comment on "Anacreonic-Decorative Panel" by Paul Chalfin, painter.

Paul Chalfin (Other Sources)

MISCELLANEOUS

Decorative Broadcasting by Paul Chalfin (advertisement for a lecture). The Arts Club of Chicago, April 21, 1922. Ryerson Library, pamphlet file. Art Institute of Chicago.

Advertisement in *Town & Country*, June 10, 1916 (also appeared in *Country Life* and *House & Garden*, June, 1916) by George Sykes Co. It correctly credits F. Burrall Hoffman, Jr., as "Architect" of Vizcaya.

Advertisement flyer, Miami, Florida, c. February, 1935. Announcing a lecture series by Paul Chalfin, February 8, 15, 22, 1935, in the gardens at Vizcaya.

Architectural League of New York, 25th Annual Exhibition: 1910 (catalogue). American Society of Fine Arts. January 30–February 19, 1910. Special exhibition by the American Academy in Rome. "134. Anacreonic. Decorative Panel." Paul Chalfin, painter, Lazarus Scholarship, 1905–1908.

Art Students League of New York. Catalogues for 1896, 1897, 1901, 1902, 1903.

Cambridge, Massachusetts. Harvard University archives. Re Paul Chalfin.

Chalfin, Paul. *Japanese Wood Carvings: Architectural and Decorative Fragments from Temples and Palaces* (descriptive catalogue). Boston: Museum of Fine Arts, 1903.

1st Industrial Exhibition of Objects Showing Museum Influence (catalogue). New York: Metropolitan Museum of Art, 1917.

Letter: Mrs. Marvin Aspen, Chicago, to author, May 17, 1971, re lectures on interior decoration by Chalfin on March 28, April 4 and 11, 1922, in Chicago under auspices of Vassar Alumni Association.

Letter: Raymond D. Salman, Acting Supervisor, Division of Professional Licensing Services, University of the State of New York, to author. Albany, New York, September 2, 1965. Re granting of New York State license to practice architecture to Paul Chalfin, c. 1916–1917 (waiver of educational requirement).

New York City. Art Students League archives. Re Paul Chalfin.

———. Columbiana Collection (archives), Columbia University. Re Paul Chalfin.

Rome. American Academy in Rome. Jacob H. Lazarus Traveling Scholarship archives for 1905–1906. Re Paul Chalfin.

NEWSPAPERS AND PERIODICALS (chronological sequence)

Mackay, Gordon. "The Story of the House That James Deering Built." *Philadelphia Public Ledger,* December 10, 1916. Republished in the *Miami Herald,* December 21, 1916.

"Miami Homes Described in the Magazines." *Miami Herald,* June 27, 1917.

Vizcaya. *The Architectural Review,* July, 1917. Entire issue devoted to Vizcaya. Three essays: " 'Vizcaya,' the Villa and Grounds," "The gardens at 'Vizcaya,' " and "The Interiors at 'Vizcaya.' " Unsigned author: Paul Chalfin.

Vizcaya. *Harper's Bazaar,* July, 1917.

"Paul Chalfin's 'The Blue Dog,' Is an Unique American House Boat." *Vanity Fair,* July, 1917.

"The Gardens of Vizcaya." *Vogue,* July 15, 1917.

Patterson, William. "A Florida Echo of the Glory of Old Venice." *Town & Country,* July 20, 1917.

"A Venetian Palace at Miami/ Decorations by Paul Chalfin." *Vogue,* August 1, 1917.

Chalfin, Paul. "The Decorations of the Avenue of Victory." *Architecture,* April, 1919.

Hastings, Thomas. "New York's Arch of Victory." *Architecture,* April, 1919.

Chapman, John Jay. "McKim, Mead and White." *Vanity Fair,* September, 1919.

"Says Hylan Wasted Celebration Funds." *New York Times,* October 13, 1919.

Unidentified, undated newspaper clipping. (Chicago. c. March, 1922.) Art Institute of Chicago, Ryerson Library. Re Paul Chalfin: Vassar Alumni (Chicago) fund-raising lectures on interior decorating.

Hudson, Virginia Tyler. "Architect Tells How James Deering Planned Vizcaya Estate." *Miami Herald,* December 12, 1934.

Chalfin, Paul. Series of ten articles in *Miami Herald.* I. "Romance of History in the Language of Art." December 23, 1934. II. Same title. December 30, 1934. III. "Gardens Are Jewels of Beauty from Air or Ground." January 6, 1935. IV. "Three Rich Burial Chests of Ancient Art, Feature of Vizcaya Fountain of Frogs, Recalls Days Before Caesar." January 13, 1935. V. "Marble Tables at Deering Estate Weathered Tempestuous Days of Pompeii." January 20, 1935. VI. "Stone Tables at Vizcaya." January 27, 1935. VII. "The Open Air Casino at Vizcaya." February 3, 1935. VIII. "Symbolic Tables of the Renaissance Period Represented Genius of Florentine Artists in 16th Century Days." February 10, 1935. IX. "Splendid Ceilings and Furnishings of Renaissance Halls: Grand Style of XVI Century Is Seen at Its Best." February 17, 1935. X "Spanish Masterpieces in Rugs Adorn Renaissance Hall." February 24, 1935.

Reno, Doris. "Dade's Showplace Puts Us in Front Ranks of Culture." *Miami Herald,* March 22, 1953. First in a series of four Sunday articles.

Obituary: "Paul Chalfin, 84, Artist, Architect." *New York Times,* February 16, 1959.

Harwood, Kathryn Chapman. "The Life and Times of Vizcaya." *Muse News,* January, 1972. First of two parts.

BOOKS

Dana, Nathalie. *Young in New York: A Memoir of a Victorian Childhood.* Garden City, New York: Doubleday, 1963.

Gish, Lillian, with Ann Pinchot. *The Movies, Mr. Griffith and Me.* New York: Avon, 1970.

Lynes, Russell. *The Art-Makers of Nineteenth Century America*. New York: Atheneum, 1970.
McCarthy, Mary. *The Stones of Florence*. New York: Harcourt, Brace, 1959.
McClelland, Nancy. *The Practical Book of Decorative Wall Treatments*. Philadelphia: Lippincott, 1926.
Parry, Albert. *Garrets and Pretenders: A History of Bohemianism in America*. New York: Dover Publications, 1960.
Patterson, Augusta Owen. *American Homes of Today: Their Architectural Style, Their Environment, Their Characteristics*. New York: Macmillan, 1924. Establishes Paul Chalfin as the anonymous author of the three essays on Vizcaya in *The Architectural Review*, July, 1917.
Pennell, Elizabeth R. and Joseph. *The Life of James McNeill Whistler*. 2 vols. London: Heinemann, 1908.
Proske, Beatrice Gilman. *Archer Milton Huntington*. New York: The Hispanic Society of America, 1963.
White, Lawrence Grant. *Sketches and Designs by Stanford White: With an Outline of His Career by His Son Lawrence Grant White*. New York: Architectural Book Publishing Co., 1920.

Elsie De Wolfe and Elisabeth Marbury

NEWSPAPERS AND PERIODICALS (chronological sequence)
"The Gayest Week of the Season." *New York Herald*, August 28, 1887.
Moats, Alice-Leone. "The Elsie Legend." *Harper's Bazaar*, May, 1949.

BOOKS
Connolly, Cyril, and Zerbe, Jerome. *Les Pavillons*. New York: Macmillan, 1952.
De Wolfe, Elsie (Lady Mendl). *After All*. New York. 1935.
———. *The House in Good Taste*. New York: Century, 1916.
French, Leigh, Jr., and Eberlein, Harold Donaldson. *The Smaller Homes and Gardens of Versailles from 1680 to 1815*. New York: Pencil Points Press, 1926.
Hardy, Thomas. *Jude the Obscure*. London: Macmillan, 1895. "Pocket Edition" (Wessex Edition), 1912.
Hellman, Geoffrey T. *Mrs. de Peyster's Parties and Other Lively Stories from The New Yorker*. New York: Macmillan, 1963.
Jullian, Philippe. *Prince of Aesthetes: Count Robert de Montesquiou, 1855–1921*. Translated by John Haylock and Francis King. New York: Viking, 1967.
Marbury, Elisabeth. *My Crystal Ball: Reminiscences*. New York: Boni & Liveright, 1923.
Mayer, Grace. *Once Upon a City*. New York: Macmillan, 1958.
Morris, Lloyd. *Incredible New York: High Life and Low Life of the Last Hundred Years*. New York: Random House, 1951.
Seligman, Germain. *Merchants of Art, 1880–1960: Eighty Years of Professional Collecting*. New York: Appleton-Century-Crofts, 1961.
Wodehouse, P. G., and Bolton, Guy. *Bring on the Girls!: The Improbable Story of Our Life in Musical Comedy, with Pictures to Prove It*. New York: Simon & Schuster, 1953.

Mitchell Samuels (French & Company)

MISCELLANEOUS
French & Company, Inc. (inaugural exhibition booklet). New York, October 1958.

NEWSPAPERS AND PERIODICALS (chronological sequence)
Thruelsen, Richard. "Ghosts for Sale." *Saturday Evening Post*, September 21, 1946.
"Percy W. French, Decorator, Dead." *New York Times*, July 21, 1956.

"Mr. Huntington's Powerful Lobby at Washington." *San Francisco Call,* May 6, 1891.

"Has Happiness Followed the Huntington Millions?" *Los Angeles Sunday Times,* March 10, 1901.

Prince arrives in U.S. with all his names. *Topeka* (Kansas) *State Journal,* April 10, 1901.

Prince Hatzefeldt Wildenbourg arrives in U.S. *Portland Oregonian,* April 10, 1901.

"Mrs. H. E. Huntington Seeks Divorce." *San Francisco Chronicle,* March 22, 1906.

"Huntingtons Divorced in 7 Minutes." *San Francisco Examiner,* March 23, 1906.

"Seven Minutes in Court for Wife of Traction Magnate." *San Francisco Chronicle,* March 23, 1906.

H. E. Huntington divorced by wife. *New York Sun,* March 24, 1906.

"Henry E. Huntington's Engagement Is Rumored." *Los Angeles Examiner,* April 6, 1906.

"To Be a Nephew's Bride?" *Kansas City Star,* April 6, 1906.

"Marriage Rumor Denied." *Seattle Times,* April 8, 1906.

Rumor: H. E. Huntington to wed. *New York Town Tattler,* December 13, 1907.

Obituary: Mansfield Lovell Hillhouse. *New York Times,* February 8, 1908.

Burglars scared away from Huntington house. *New York Evening World,* April 10, 1909.

"Railway Employees Throng Beach/ Annual Picnic Guests at Redondo." *Los Angeles Express,* August 25, 1913.

Huntington one of founders of L.A. Little Theatre. *Los Angeles Examiner,* September 15, 1913.

"Huntingtons Back In U.S./$20,000 Duties Tendered." *Los Angeles Tribune,* October 28, 1913.

"Henry E. Huntington Named Head of L.A. Symphony Orchestra." *Los Angeles Herald,* October 31, 1913.

"Million, 1920 Is Too Small/ W. M. Garland Alters Slogan." *Los Angeles Examiner,* November 7, 1913.

H. E. Huntington's vast expansion plans. *Los Angeles Examiner,* December 3, 1913.

"72,000,000 Passengers Carried by P.E. in 1912." *Los Angeles Examiner,* December 3, 1913.

"H. E. Huntington Gives $1,000 to Shrine Xmas." *Los Angeles Herald,* December 23, 1913.

"Notes to Santa Intercepted by Herald." *Los Angeles Herald,* December 23, 1913.

"Henry E. Huntington and Bride Due January 10." *Los Angeles Herald,* January 5, 1914.

"Huntington to Return Home in February." *Los Angeles Express,* January 9, 1914.

Huntington and bride left New York for L.A. today. *Los Angeles Herald,* January 17, 1914.

H. E. Huntington and bride stop in Newport News. *Los Angeles Examiner,* January 21, 1914.

"Huntington and His Bride in Pasadena." *Los Angeles Express,* January 23, 1914.

Huntington and Bride Arrive at San Marino. *Los Angeles Daily Times,* January 24, 1914.

Huntington arrives with bride: he's done with business. *Los Angeles Tribune,* January 24, 1914.

" 'More Profit in Real Estate Than Ever' Opinion Is Advanced by H. E. Huntington." *Los Angeles Examiner,* January 24, 1914.

Huntington signs $14,000,000 in bonds. *Los Angeles Examiner,* February 7, 1914.

"A Modest Master of Millions" (profile) . *Los Angeles Sunday Times,* February 8, 1914.

Jonathan Club to honor Huntington at "High Jinks." *Los Angeles Examiner,* February 20, 1914.

Huntington buys Chatsworth Library for $1,500,000. *Los Angeles Examiner,* March 19, 1914.

Huntington buys Lamon's Lincoln letters. *Los Angeles Times,* March 24, 1914.

Huntington bids "Southland" farewell: leaves for Paris. *Los Angeles Evening Herald,* April 10, 1914.

Huntingtons to leave L.A. for one year. *Los Angeles Examiner,* April 10, 1914.

"Widow of the Huntington Millions Comes to San Antonio." *San Antonio Express,* November 4, 1917.

Mrs. H. E. Huntington injures hand. *Los Angeles Herald,* September 19, 1918.

Mrs. Huntington's luncheons for L.A. women. *Los Angeles Sunday Times,* March 11, 1923.

Mrs. Huntington's will. *Los Angeles Daily Times,* October 29, 1924.

"Public Gains Treasure in Huntington Library." *New York Times,* May 29, 1927.

Obituary: Archer M. Huntington. *New York Times,* December 11, 1955.

BOOKS

Asbury, Herbert. *Sucker's Progress: An Informal History of Gambling in America from the Colonies to Canfield.* New York: Dodd, Mead, 1938.

Barea, Ilsa. *Vienna.* New York: Knopf, 1967.

Barron, Clarence W. *More They Told Barron: Conversations and Revelations of an American Pepys in Wall Street. The Notes of the Late Clarence W. Barron.* Arranged and edited by Arthur Pound and Samuel Taylor Moore. New York: Harper & Brothers, 1931.

Behrman, S. N. *Duveen.* London: Hamish Hamilton, 1953.

Birmingham, Stephen. *"Our Crowd": The Great Jewish Families of New York.* New York: Harper & Row, 1967.

Blum, Stella, ed. *Victorian Fashions and Costumes from Harper's Bazar: 1867–1898.* New York: Dover Publications, 1974.

Chafetz, Henry. *Play the Devil: A History of Gambling in the United States from 1492 to 1955.* New York: Clarkson N. Potter, 1960.

Crump, Spencer. *Henry Huntington and the Pacific Electric: A Pictorial Album.* Los Angeles: Trans-Anglo Books, 1970.

Dowdey, Clifford. *Experiment in Rebellion.* New York: Doubleday, 1952.

Duveen, James Henry. *Art Treasures and Intrigue.* New York: Doubleday, Doran, 1935.

———. *The Rise of the House of Duveen.* New York: Knopf, 1957.

———. *Secrets of an Art Dealer.* New York: E. P. Dutton, 1938. Chapter XI: "How a 'Twenty Million' Widow Lost Me 27,000."

Ettinghausen, Maurice. *Rare Books and Royal Collectors: Memoirs of an Antiquarian Bookseller.* New York: Simon & Schuster, 1966.

Evans, Cerinda W. *Collis Potter Huntington.* 2 vols. Newport News, Virginia: The Mariners Museum, 1954.

Fads and Fancies of Representative Americans at the Beginning of the Twentieth Century; Being a Portrayal of Their Tastes, Diversions and Achievements. New York: Town Topics, 1905.

Gimpel, René. *Diary of an Art Dealer.* Translated by John Rosenberg. New York: Farrar, Straus & Giroux, 1966.

Harrison, Mrs. Burton. *Recollections Grave and Gay.* New York: Charles Scribner's Sons, 1912.

Josephson, Matthew. *The Robber Barons: The Great American Capitalists, 1861–1901.* New York: Harcourt, Brace & World, 1962.

Kimmel, Stanley. *Mr. Davis's Richmond.* New York: Coward-McCann, 1958.

Lavender, David. *The Great Persuader.* New York: Doubleday, 1970.

Lewis, Oscar. *The Big Four: The Story of Huntington, Stanford, Hopkins, and Crocker.* New York: Knopf, 1938. Chapter on Huntington.

Logan, Andy. *The Man Who Robbed the Robber Barons.* New York: W. W. Norton, 1965.

Myers, Gustavus. *History of the Great American Fortunes.* New York: Modern Library. Original copyright by author, 1907.

Smith, Matthew Hale. *Sunshine and Shadow in New York.* Hartford: J. Burr, 1868.

Towner, Wesley. *The Elegant Auctioneers.* Completed by Stephen Varble. New York: Hill & Wang, 1970.

Vail, R. W. *Knickerbocker Birthday: A Sesqui-Centennial History of the New-York Historical Society, 1804–1954.* New York: New-York Historical Society, 1954.

Wark, Robert R. *French Decorative Art in the Huntington Collection.* San Marino, California: Huntington Library, 1962.

———. *Sculpture in the Huntington Collection.* San Marino, California: Henry E. Huntington Library and Art Gallery, 1962.

Wecter, Dixon. *The Saga of American Society: A Record of Social Aspiration, 1607–1937.* New York: Charles Scribner's Sons, 1937.
Wolf, Edwin, II, with John F. Fleming. *Rosenbach: A Biography.* Cleveland: World, 1960.

Metropolitan Hotel

BOOKS

Dayton, Abram C. *Last Days of Knickerbocker Life in New York.* New York: G. P. Putnam's Sons, 1897.
Dorsey, Leslie, and Devine, Janice. *Fare Thee Well: A Backward Look at Two Centuries of Historic American Hostelries, Fashionable Spas & Seaside Resorts.* New York: Crown, 1964.
Jenkins, Stephen. *The Greatest Street in the World: The Story of Broadway, Old and New, from the Bowling Green to Albany.* New York: G. P. Putnam's Sons, 1911.
Morris, Lloyd. *Incredible New York: High Life and Low Life of the Last Hundred Years.* New York: Random House, 1951.
Mowatt, Anna Cora. *Autobiography of an Actress; Or Eighty Years on the Stage.* Boston: Ticknor, Reed & Fields, 1854.
Strong, George Templeton. *The Diary of George Templeton Strong.* 4 vols. Allan Nevins and Milton Halsey Thomas, eds. New York: Macmillan, 1952.

Bleecker and Bond Streets

NEWSPAPERS AND PERIODICALS

Lockwood, Charles. "The Bond Street Area." *New-York Historical Society Quarterly* 56 (October, 1972).

BOOKS

Kavaler, Lucy. *The Astors: A Family Chronicle of Pomp and Power.* New York: Dodd, Mead, 1966.
Lockwood, Charles. *Bricks & Brownstones: The New York Row House, 1783–1929: An Architectural & Social History.* New York: McGraw-Hill, 1972.
McCabe, James D., Jr. *Lights and Shadows of New York Life; Or the Sights and Sensations of the Great City.* Philadelphia: National Publishing Co., 1872. Chapter XXIV: "Bleecker Street."
O'Connor, Harvey. *The Astors.* New York: Knopf, 1941.

4 West Fifty-fourth Street, 65 Park Avenue, 5 West Fifty-first Street, 2 East Fifty-seventh Street

MISCELLANEOUS (chronological sequence)

NOTE: Items identified by the abbreviation RFA are drawn from materials in the Rockefeller Family Archives.

New Buildings Docket. Vol. 1866–1867. Department of Buildings, City of New York. Plan No. 148. Submitted September 1, 1866. Pier 33 North River, foot of Jay Street. Owner: William P. Williams.
Plaque. Signatures of employee-donors of engraved silver punch bowl to Auguste Pottier, May 1, 1869, in honor of the tenth anniversary of the partnership of Pottier and William P. Stymus.
Centennial Exposition (official catalogue). Philadelphia, 1876.
Lienau, Detlef. Architectural drawings for residence for George Mosle, 5 West Fifty-first Street, New York City. Columbia University, Avery Library, c. 1878.

Palais de San Donato. Catalogue des objets d'art et d'ameublement. Tableaux dont la vente aux enchères publiques aura lieu à Florence, au palais de San Donato. Le 15 Mars 1880 . . . (auction catalogue).

Letter: Charles MacRae to John D. Rockefeller. New York City, April 9, 1880. RFA.

Alterations Index. Vol. 1880–1881. Bureau of Buildings, Manhattan-Bronx, New York. F. 1881. 4 West Fifty-fourth Street. Alteration number 598. Mrs. B. D. Worsham.

Letter: Charles MacRae to John D. Rockefeller. New York City, January 28, 1881. RFA.

Alterations Index. Vol. 1882–1884. Bureau of Buildings, Manhattan-Bronx, New York. P. 1884. 65 Park Avenue (corner of Thirty-eighth Street). Alteration number 1395. Collis P. Huntington.

Letters: Edward B. Cowles to John D. Rockefeller. New York City, various dates in 1884. Cowles was Rockefeller's lawyer for the purchase of 4 West Fifty-fourth Street. RFA.

Letter: George A. Schastey to John D. Rockefeller. New York City, January 21, 1884. RFA.

Letter: John D. Rockefeller to George A. Schastey. New York City, January 22, 1884. RFA.

Letter: Charles MacRae to John D. Rockefeller. New York City, April 17, 1884. RFA.

Letter: Charles MacRae to John D. Rockefeller. New York City, July 16, 1884. RFA.

Letter: John D. Rockefeller to Charles MacRae. New York City, July 19, 1884. RFA.

Letter: Charles MacRae to John D. Rockefeller. New York City, August 12, 1884. RFA.

Letter: John D. Rockefeller to Charles MacRae. New York City, August 13, 1884. RFA.

Letter: Charles MacRae to John D. Rockefeller. New York City, October 27, 1884. RFA.

Letter: George A. Schastey to John D. Rockefeller. New York City, October 29, 1884. RFA.

John D. Rockefeller journal entries. Journal 308, E-F-G (November 27, 1884 to August 2, 1886). New York City. RFA.

Alterations Index. Vol. 1886. Bureau of Buildings, Manhattan-Bronx, New York. F. 5 West Fifty-first Street. Alteration number 1542. Collis P. Huntington.

Catalogue of Magnificent Furniture, Rich Upholstery and Stuffs, Articles of Vertu, Etc., Etc. . . . Pottier & Stymus Manufacturing Co. . . . No. 489 Fifth Avenue. Auction beginning Friday, April 20th. . . . Thomas E. Kirby, auctioneer. American Art Association, managers. New York, 1888.

"Trial Balance for John D. Rockefeller" (accountant's summary). December 31, 1888. RFA.

Post, George Browne. *Architectural Drawings: Three Interiors.* C. P. Huntington Residence, 2 East Fifty-seventh Street. New York City, Pen and ink perspective: alcove of a reception room, music room, fireplace, c. 1889. New-York Historical Society, Print and Map Division, New York City.

New Buildings Docket. Vol. 1888–1889. Department of Buildings, City of New York. Plan No. 2033. Submitted December 27, 1889. Location: S.E. corner Fifth Avenue and Fifty-seventh Street. Owner: Collis P. Huntington. Architect: George B. Post.

Advertisement. Charles MacRae, real estate broker, 533 Fifth Avenue, New York City. List of outstanding real estate negotiations and clients on large leaflet-style letterhead, c. 1890. RFA.

"Richest Girls in America: Alta and Edith, Daughters of John D. Rockefeller . . ." *New York World*, December 3, 1893. RFA.

Twenty-First Annual Report of the Indiana Department of Geology and Natural Resources. State of Indiana, 1896. List of residential structures in New York City faced with Indiana limestone: "C. P. Huntington Residence."

Letter: Mitchell Samuels to John D. Rockefeller. New York City, March 31, 1938. RFA.

Letter: John D. Rockefeller, Jr., to Mitchell Samuels. Williamsburg, Virginia, April 26, 1938. RFA.

Letter: John D. Rockefeller, Jr., to Charles Nagel. New York City, January 7, 1954.

French and Company, Inc. Inaugural exhibition. New York, October, 1958.

Johnson, Marilynn; Schwartz, Marvin D.; and Boorsch, Suzanne. *19-Century America: Furniture and Other Decorations: An Exhibition in Celebration of the Hundredth*

Anniversary of the Metropolitan Museum of Art. April 16 through September 7, 1970. New York: New York Graphic Society, 1970.

Letter: Mrs. Alice M. Vestal to Margaret Stearns. George Arents Research Library, Syracuse University, Syracuse, New York, March 4, 1971.

Separate file of photographs. Mounted and identified. Re 4 West Fifty-fourth Street, New York City. New York Public Library, Local History and Genealogy Division, New York, n.d.

Scrapbook. "New York City. Numbered Streets. 31–60 Streets" (mounted clippings: articles and photographs). New York Public Library, Local History and Genealogy Division, New York, n.d.

Samuel H. Gottscho Collection: 40,000 photographic negatives. Depositories: Museum of the City of New York; Avery Library, Columbia University; Brooklyn Museum.

NEWSPAPERS AND PERIODICALS (chronological sequence)

C. P. Huntington breaks ground for palace on Fifth Avenue. *New York Sun,* October 19, 1889.

[Taylor, Edwin C.]. "American Mural Decoration." *Bulletin of the Associates of Fine Arts at Yale University.* December, 1926.

"Old 54th St. Home Reflects Rising Land Values." Unidentified, undated clipping. New York City, before 1938.

"Rockefeller Bed Shown by Museum of the City of New York." *New York Times,* March 22, 1938.

"Wreckers Take Over a Famous House" (photo and caption). *New York Sun,* June 15, 1938.

"Rockefeller Home Being Torn Down." *New York Times,* June 16, 1938.

Thruelsen, Richard. "Ghosts for Sale." *Saturday Evening Post,* September 21, 1946.

BOOKS

Ackerman, James S. *The Architecture of Michelangelo.* New York: Viking, 1961.

Artistic Houses: Being A Series of Interior Views of a Number of the Most Beautiful and Celebrated Homes in the United States. 4 vols. in 1. 2nd ed. New York: Benjamin Blom, 1971. First published for subscribers, New York, 1883.

Bing, Samuel. *Artistic America, Tiffany Glass, and Art Nouveau.* Translated (in part) by Benita Eisler. Cambridge, Mass.: MIT Press, 1970.

Clark, Robert Judson. *The Arts and Crafts Movement in America, 1876–1916* (catalogue). Princeton, New Jersey: Princeton University Press, 1972.

Dennis, James M. *Karl Bitter: Architectural Sculptor, 1867–1915.* Madison, Wisconsin: University of Wisconsin Press, 1967.

Fifth Avenue. New York: The Fifth Avenue Bank of New York, 1915.

Harding, G. Lankester. *Baalbeck: A New Guide.* Beirut: Khayats, 1967.

King, Moses, ed. *King's Handbook of New York City: An Outline History and Description of the American Metropolis.* Boston: Moses King, c. 1895.

———: *King's Photographic Views of New York.* Boston: Moses King, 1895.

Nevins, Allan. *John D. Rockefeller: The Heroic Age of American Enterprise.* 2 vols. New York: Charles Scribner's Sons, 1940.

Otto, Celia Jackson. *American Furniture of the Nineteenth Century.* New York: Viking, 1965.

Richardson, Joanna. *Princess Mathilde.* New York: Charles Scribner's Sons, 1969.

Schuyler, Montgomery. *American Architecture and Other Writings.* William H. Jordy and Ralph Coe, eds. 2 vols. Cambridge, Massachusetts: Harvard University Press, 1961.

Summerson, John. *Heavenly Mansions, and Other Essays in Architecture.* New York: Norton, 1963.

Van Brunt, Henry. *Architecture and Society: Selected Essays of Henry Van Brunt.* Edited and with introductory monograph by William A. Coles. Cambridge, Massachusetts: Harvard University Press, 1969.

Walker, Francis A., *United States Centennial Commission: International Exhibition, 1876. Reports and Awards.* Vol. IV (group VII): Furniture, Upholstery, etc. Vol. VII (group SSVII): Plastic and Graphic Art. Class 442. Decoration of Interiors. "Industrial and Architectural Designs; Interior Decorations . . ." Donald G. Mitchell. Washington, D.C.: Government Printing Office, 1880.

Wheeler, Mortimer. *Roman Art and Architecture.* New York: Praeger, 1964.

Richard Morris Hunt: Second Empire Décor

MISCELLANEOUS

Christ, Yvan. Chap. II: "La décoration intérieure" in *L'Art au XIXe siècle. Vol. II: du Second Empire à la fin du siècle.* Paris: Flammarion, 1962.

L'Hôtel du ministre des finances au palais du Louvre (guidebook) . 2nd ed. 1956.

Kashey, Robert, and Reymert, Martin L. H. Appendix III: "Notes on Methods of Bronze Casting Followed by a List of Founders, Foundries and Their Marks" in *Western European Bronzes of the Nineteenth Century: A Survey.* New York: Shepherd Gallery, 1973.

NEWSPAPERS AND PERIODICALS (chronological sequence)

"Presentation of the Royal Gold Medal." *Royal Institute of British Architects Journal of Proceedings, 1892–1893* 9 (June 22, 1893) .

Burnham, Alan. "The New York Architecture of Richard Morris Hunt." *Journal of the Society of Architectural Historians* XI (May, 1952) , pp. 9–14.

BOOKS

Burnham, Alan, ed. "The Richard Morris Hunt Papers." Unpublished.

Croffut, W. A. *The Vanderbilts and the Story of Their Fortune.* Chicago: Belford, Clarke, 1886.

Hess, Thomas B., and Ashbery, John, eds. Chapter XII: "Grand Opera," by John Jacobus, in *The Academy: Five Centuries of Grandeur from the Carracci to Mao Tse-Tung.* New York: Macmillan, 1967.

Richardson, Joanna. *The Courtesans.* Cleveland: World Publishing Co., 1967.

Strong, George Templeton. *Diary of the Civil War, 1860–1865.* Allan Nevins, ed. New York: Macmillan, 1962.

Von Pelt, John Vredenburgh. *A Monograph of the William K. Vanderbilt House, Richard Morris Hunt, Architect.* Eugene Clute, ed. Published by the author, New York, 1925.

Throgs Neck

BOOKS

Jenkins, Stephen. *The Story of the Bronx.* New York: G. P. Putnam's Sons, 1912.

San Francisco: The Colton Mansion

MISCELLANEOUS

Letter: Collis P. Huntington to Henry E. Huntington. San Francisco, June 4, 1896. The Huntington Library, San Marino, California.

NEWSPAPERS AND PERIODICALS

"Mr. Huntington Buys Knob Hill Property." *New York Daily Tribune,* May 6, 1892.

BOOKS

Desmond, Harry W., and Croly, Herbert. *Stately Homes in America: From Colonial Times to the Present Day.* New York: Appleton, 1903.

Kirker, Harold. *California's Architectural Frontier: Style and Tradition in the Nineteenth Century.* San Marino, California: Huntington Library, 1960.

Olmsted, Roger, and Watkins, T. H. *Here Today: San Francisco's Architectural Heritage.* San Francisco: Chronicle Books, 1968.

Pine Knot Lodge: Racquette Lake

BOOKS
Satterlee, Herbert L. *J. Pierpont Morgan: An Intimate Portrait.* New York: Macmillan, 1939.

Paris: No. 2 Rue de L'Elysée

MISCELLANEOUS
Catalogue de quatre tapisseries de Beauvais . . . en l'hôtel de feu Mme. La Baronne De Hirsch. 2, rue de l'Elysée, à Paris le jeudi 22 fevrier 1906 . . . (auction catalogue).

NEWSPAPERS AND PERIODICALS (chronological sequence)
Mrs. H. E. Huntington at Bristol: Paris house being readied. *American Register* (Paris), April 25, 1908.
Mrs. Huntington and son, Archer, at Bristol till Paris house ready. *New York World,* April 26, 1908.
Mrs. Huntington's Paris house. *New York City Press,* July 5, 1908.
"Royal Palace Ready for Mrs. Huntington." *Boston Morning Herald,* July 5, 1908.
"Mrs. Collis P. Huntington Sells Her Paris Home." *New York City Journal,* March 10, 1910.
(Mrs. Huntington sells Paris mansion. *Oakland* (California) *Tribune,* March 27, 1910.

BOOKS
Braibant, Charles; Mirot, Albert; and Le Moël, Michel. *Guide historique des rues de Paris.* Paris: Librarie Hachette, 1965.
Chefs-d'oeuvre de la curiosité du monde (catalogue no. 127). Musée des Arts Décoratifs, Paris, 1954.
Cornwallis-West, Mrs. George. *The Reminiscences of Lady Randolph Churchill.* New York: Century, 1909.
Goodwin, Albert. *The French Revolution.* New York: Harper & Row, 1953.
Hillairet, Jacques. *Dictionnaire historique des rues de Paris.* 4th ed. 2 vols. Paris: Editions de Minuit, 1963.
Huisman, Georges, and Poisson, Georges. *Les monuments de Paris.* Paris: Librarie Hachette, 1966.
Jullian, Philippe. *Edward and the Edwardians.* Translated by Peter Dawnay. New York: Viking, 1967.
Maurois, Simone André. *Miss Howard and the Emperor.* Translated by Humphrey Hare. New York: Knopf, 1957.
Monographie du palais des feu le baron & la baronne de Hirsch: décoration, intérieures & extérieures. Paris: Armand Guérinet, 1906.
Pillement, Georges. *Paris inconnu: itinéraires archéologiques.* Paris: Bernard Grasset, 1965.
Seligman, Germain. *Merchants of Art, 1880–1960: Eighty Years of Professional Collecting.* New York: Appleton-Century-Crofts, 1961.
Thompson, J. M. *The French Revolution.* New York: Oxford University Press, 1943.
———. *Leaders of the French Revolution.* New York: Harper & Row, 1929.

San Marino, Myron Hunt, Charles Allom, William Hertrich

MISCELLANEOUS
Grey, Elmer. Architectural rendering of terrace facade at San Marino, *c.* 1910. Privately owned.

Hanafin, Therese T. "The Eclectic Architecture of Myron Hunt." Master's thesis, San Diego State University, 1969.

Hunt, Myron, and Grey, Elmer. Architectural drawings of San Marino (H. E. Huntington residence). Yearbook of the Philadelphia Chapter American Institute of Architects and the T Square Club. Seventeenth Architectural Exhibition, 1911. "Index of Exhibits."

Hunt, Mrs. Myron (née Virginia Pease). "Memoirs" (unpublished). San Marino, California: Huntington Library.

Year Book, Los Angeles Architectural Club, 1911.

Year Book, Los Angeles Architectural Club, 1912.

Year Book, Los Angeles Architectural Club, 1913.

NEWSPAPERS AND PERIODICALS (chronological sequence)

Work of Myron Hunt and Elmer Grey. *The Architectural Record,* February, 1905.

Jacobs residence: Newport, R.I. *Town & Country,* August 5, 1905.

"The Residence of Mrs. Henry Barton Jacobs." *The Architectural Review,* March, 1908.

Hunt & Grey to enlarge offices. *Southwest Builder and Contractor,* April 3, 1908.

Hunt & Grey perfecting plans for $75,000 Huntington house. *Southwest Builder and Contractor,* June 11, 1908.

Hunt & Grey nearing completion of final plans for Huntington. *Southwest Builder and Contractor,* June 25, 1908.

P. E. construction gang starts Huntington house. *Southwest Builder and Contractor,* August 20, 1908.

Huntington excavation completed: bids for concrete fabric to be opened. *Southwest Builder and Contractor,* 1908.

Contracts let: Grey in New York with Huntington: skeleton target date is February. *Southwest Builder and Contracor,* October 15, 1908.

Plumbing contracts let for Huntington house. *Southwest Builder and Contractor,* January 7, 1909.

Electrical contracts to be let for Huntington residence. *Southwest Builder and Contractor,* March 25, 1909.

Duveen Bros., London, gets interior work at Huntington house. *Southwest Builder and Contractor,* May 13, 1909.

Concrete and marble work at Huntington house to be completed in November. *Southwest Builder and Contractor,* June 22, 1909.

$100,000 in Huntington contracts have been let. *Southwest Builder and Contractor,* June 24, 1909.

Richards-Neustadt announces subcontracts on Huntington house. *Southwest Builder and Contractor,* July 1, 1909.

"Announcement" (Hunt and Grey dissolve partnership). *Southwest Builder and Contractor,* September 29, 1910.

Huntington residence plans completed. *Southwest Builder and Contractor,* October 6, 1910.

Huntington buys complete Japanese garden. *Los Angeles Herald,* March 7, 1914.

Garnett, Porter. "The Huntington Home at Oak Knoll." *Sunset, the Pacific Monthly,* June, 1914.

"Has Designed Structures of Merit" (Myron Hunt). *Pasadena* (California) *Star-News,* undated clipping.

"Myron Hunt, Southland's Famous Architect Dies." unidentified clipping, *c.* May 27, 1952.

BOOKS

Adams-Acton, Murray. *Domestic Architecture and Old Furniture.* London, 1929.

Condit, Carl. *The Chicago School of Architecture.* Chicago: University of Chicago Press, 1964.

Embury, Aymar, II. *One Hundred Country Houses: Modern American Examples.* New York: Century, 1909.

Garnett, Porter. *Stately Homes of California.* Boston: Little, Brown, 1915.

Hamlin, Talbot Faulkner. *The American Spirit in Architecture*. New Haven: Yale University Press, 1926.

Hertrich, William. *The Huntington Botanical Gardens, 1905–1949: Personal Recollections*. San Marino, California: Huntington Library, 1949.

Hunt, Myron, and Hooker, Katharine. *Farmhouses and Small Provincial Buildings in Southern Italy*. New York: Architectural Book Publishing Co., 1925.

Lewis, Oscar. *Here Lived the Californians*. New York: Reinhart, 1957.

McCoy, Esther. *Five California Architects*. New York: Reinhold, 1960.

Padilla, Victoria. *Southern California Gardens: An Illustrated History*. Berkeley: University of California Press, 1961.

Peisch, Mark L. *The Chicago School of Architecture: Early Followers of Sullivan and Wright*. New York: Random House, 1946.

Some Interesting Homes Executed by White Allom, 15 George Street, Hanover Square, London, and 19 East 52nd Street, New York. London, *c.* 1919.

Wright, Frank Lloyd. *A Testament*. New York: Bramhall House, 1957.

FIVE. SHADOW LAWN

General

MISCELLANEOUS

Duchêne, Achille. "Shadow Lawn. Propriété de Monsieur Hubert T. Parson, Esq." "Premier Solution" (plan for formal garden adjacent to house), *c.* 1928–1929. The Historical Society of Pennsylvania, Philadelphia.

————. "Salle en treillage servant de motif décoratif dans l'axe transversal de la roserie" (garden plan), *c.* 1928–1929. The Historical Society of Pennsylvania, Philadelphia.

Eighty Acres of Opportunity (pamphlet). Monmouth College, West Long Branch, New Jersey, 1956.

Long Branch, New Jersey: Summer Capital of the United States: Queen of American Seaside Cities. Department of Publicity, Long Branch, New Jersey, *c.* 1916.

Monmouth College Catalogue, 1965–1966. Monmouth College, West Long Branch, New Jersey, 1965.

McNelis, Catherine, and Weir, Hugh. *Fifty Years of Woolworth: 1879–1929* (pamphlet). New York: F. W. Woolworth, n.d.

Parson, Hubert T. and Maysie G. *Block Index of Reindexed Conveyances*. New York City Register, Recorded Deeds and Mortgages, Borough of Manhattan. Section 15, Block 1500, Lot 2. August 13, 1914, et seq.

Philadelphia: University of Pennsylvania archives. Re Julian F. Abele.

Shadow Lawn — The Versailles of America (pamphlet). Privately published sales brochure. New York, *c.* 1937–1938.

Shadow Lawn. Versailles of America. The Original Contents of an Estate — Real and Personal, Costing $10,000,000. Palatial Mansion Consisting of 128 Rooms, 8 Auxiliary Cottages, 108 Acres of Choice Exclusive Real Estate All Known as Shadow Lawn. West Long Branch, New Jersey (sales catalogue). Sold by order of Mrs. Hubert T. Parson. Sale conducted by J. A. Fleischer, Arthur Ross, S. LeNoble. Concord Galleries, New York, 1940.

Sincerbeaux, Moore & Shinn, Civil Engineers, Asbury Park, New Jersey. "Map Showing Former Residence of Hubert T. Parson, Esq., West Long Branch, N.J." February 26, 1927. The Historical Society of Pennsylvania, Philadelphia.

Trumbauer, Horace. "Residence of Hubert T. Parson, West End [West Long Branch], New Jersey." Summary of six drawings by title and date only: north elevation, July 11, 1928; east elevation, July 11, 1928; south elevation, July 11, 1928; west elevation, July 11, 1928. Map showing old and new residences at Shadow Lawn, November 8, 1927; revised December 1, 1927. Sketch showing relation of new and old house plans, December 13, 1927. The Historical Society of Pennsylvania, Philadelphia.

Views of Long Branch (pamphlet) , c. 1903.

Woolley, J. Russell, Borough Clerk, West Long Branch, New Jersey. Shadow Lawn title and conveyance history (Thermofax of typescript; no title) , c. 1958.

Woolworth's First 75 Years: The Story of Everybody's Store. New York: F. W. Woolworth, 1954.

NEWSPAPERS AND PERIODICALS (chronological sequence)

McCall to build shore mansion: house described. *Long Branch Record,* July (?) , 1903.

"American Residences of Today" (photographic portfolio; residence of John A. McCall, Long Branch, New Jersey) . *The Architectural Record,* 1904.

Obituary: John A. McCall. *New York Times,* February 19, 1906.

Wilson accepts nomination in Shadow Lawn speech. *New York Times,* September 3, 1916.

Senator James heads notification ceremonies at Shadow Lawn. *New York Times,* September 3, 1916.

Wilson check for Shadow Lawn rental to charities. *New York Times,* September 15, 1916.

Wilson opens campaign at Shadow Lawn. *New York Times,* September 24, 1916.

Wilson closes campaign at Shadow Lawn. *New York Times,* November 5, 1916.

New Year's wishes from editor. *Long Branch Record,* December 31, 1926.

Parson, Hubert T. Letter to the editor. *Long Branch Record,* January 4, 1927.

"Shadow Lawn, Home of Hubert T. Parson, Is Totally Destroyed . . ." *Long Branch Record,* January 8, 1927.

"Foremen Working on Smouldering Ruins." *Long Branch Record,* January 10, 1927.

"Entries Received from Shadow Lawn." *Long Branch Record,* September 10, 1927.

Shadow Lawn wins two flower show cups. *Long Branch Record,* September 15, 1927.

George Thomson scores 86 points in show. *Long Branch Record,* September 17, 1927.

New Year's wishes from the editor. *Long Branch Record,* December 31, 1927.

New Year's wishes from the editor. *Long Branch Record,* December 31, 1928.

Parson, Hubert T. "What 40,000,000,000 Sales Have Taught Us." *Magazine of Business,* August, 1929.

New York Stock Exchange: Woolworth Co. *New York Times,* September 4, 1929.

New York Stock Exchange: Woolworth Co. *New York Times,* October 29, 1929.

New York Stock Exchange: Woolworth Co. *New York Times,* November 1, 1929.

New York Stock Exchange: Woolworth Co. *New York Times,* December 31, 1929.

Parson announces 20-cent items for Woolworth stores. *New York Times,* February 28, 1932.

"Woolworth's Head, Parson, Quits at 60." *New York Times,* June 9, 1932.

"Shadow Lawn Goes for $100 at Auction." *New York Times,* September 26, 1939.

"Pays $30,592 Tax Lien." *New York Times,* March 23, 1940.

"Tax Lien Paid on Furnishings at Parson Estate." *New York Herald Tribune,* March 23, 1940.

"Tax Sale to Clear old Jersey Mansion." *New York Times,* May 26, 1940.

"Parson Sale Raises $12,000." *New York Times,* June 6, 1940.

"$65,000 Realized at Sale." *New York Times,* June 9, 1940.

"More Parson Art Sold." *New York Times,* June 16, 1940.

"H. T. Parson Dead/A Woolworth Aide." *New York Times,* July 10, 1940.

"Shadow Lawn Deal Off." *New York Times,* November 10, 1940.

"H. T. Parsons [sic] Left Only $2,500 Estate." *New York Times,* November 23, 1940.

Shadow Lawn sold again. *New York Times,* February 21, 1942.

Huxley, Aldous. "Notes on the Way." *Time and Tide,* July 3, 1947.

Obituary: Maysie Gasque Parson: Mrs. Hubert T. Parson. *New York Herald Tribune,* April 29, 1956.

Monmouth College ready for fall semester. *New York Journal American,* August 2, 1959.

"Shore Haven for Many Presidents." *Newark Sunday News,* March 11, 1962.

Parker, James. "The Hotel de Varengeville Room and the Room from the Palais Paar: A Magnificent Donation." *The Metropolitan Museum of Art Bulletin,* November, 1969.

Whitman, Alden. "Philip Johnson Gazes Sadly on the City." *New York Times,* September 29, 1974.

BOOKS

Bagehot, Walter. *Lombard Street: A Description of the Money Market.* 14th ed. London: John Murray, 1927.

Barron, Clarence W. *They Told Barron: Conversations and Revelations of an American Pepys in Wall Street.* Edited and arranged by Arthur Pound and Samuel Taylor Moore. New York: Harper & Brothers, 1930.

Brooks, John. *Once in Golconda: A True Drama of Wall Street 1920–1938.* New York: Harper & Row, 1969. Quotation from Clyde Cockburn's *In Time of Trouble.* New York, 1956.

Castellane, Boniface de. *Confessions of the Marquis de Castellane.* (American title: *How I Discovered America.*) London: Thornton Butterworth, 1924.

Entertaining a Nation: The Career of Long Branch. American Guide Series, Writers' Project, Works Project Administration, 1940.

Galbraith, John Kenneth. *The Great Crash, 1929.* Boston: Houghton Mifflin, 1961.

Gallet, Michel. *Stately Mansions: Eighteenth Century Paris Architecture.* Translated by James C. Palmes. New York: Praeger, 1972.

Garraty, John A. *Right-Hand Man: The Life of George W. Perkins.* New York: Harper & Brothers, 1960.

Gilson, Etienne. *Heloise and Abelard.* Translated by L. K. Shook. London: Hollis & Carter, 1953.

Gowans, Alan. *Architecture in New Jersey.* Vol. 6. Princeton, New Jersey: Van Nostrand, 1964.

Gramont, E[lizabeth] de. *Pomp and Circumstance.* Translated by Brian W. Downs. New York: Jonathan Cape & Harrison Smith, 1929.

Harbeson, John F. *The Study of Architectural Design, with Special Reference to the Program of the Beaux-Arts Institute of Design.* New York: Pencil Points Press, 1927.

Hill, Oliver, and Cornforth, John. *Caroline: 1625–1685.* London: Country Life, 1966. Quotation from Henry Wotton's *The Elements of Architecture,* 1694.

Miller, Hope Ridings. *Great Houses of Washington, D.C.* New York: Clarkson N. Potter, 1969.

Verlet, Pierre. *French Royal Furniture: An Historical Survey Followed by a Study of Forty Pieces Preserved in Great Britain and the United States.* New York: Clarkson N. Potter, 1963.

Wheeler, Mortimer. *Roman Art and Architecture.* New York: Praeger, 1964.

Wilson, Harold F. *The Story of the Jersey Shore.* Vol. 4. Princeton, New Jersey: Van Nostrand, 1964.

Winkler, John K. *Five and Ten: The Fabulous Life of F. W. Woolworth.* New York: Robert McBride, 1940.

Avenue du Bois de Boulogne (Avenue Foch)

BOOKS

Braibant, Charles; Mirot, Albert; Le Moel, Michel. *Guide historique des rues de Paris.* Paris: Librairie Hachette, 1965.

Clunn, Harold P. *The Face of Paris.* London: Spring Books, n.d.

Crafty. *Paris au bois.* Paris: E. Plon, Nourrit, 1890.

Muirhead, L. Russell. *Paris.* 2nd ed. New York: Rand McNally, 1960.

Pinkney, David H. *Napoleon III and the Rebuilding of Paris.* Princeton, New Jersey: Princeton University Press, 1958.

Saalman, Howard. *Haussmann: Paris Transformed.* New York: George Braziller, 1971.

Skinner, Cornelia Otis. *Elegant Wits and Grand Horizontals*. Boston: Houghton Mifflin, 1962.

Achille Duchêne

CONSOLIDATED

Balsan, Consuelo Vanderbilt. *The Glitter and the Gold*. New York: Harper & Brothers, 1952.

Bourget, Pierre, and Cattaui, Georges. *Jules-Hardouin Mansart*. Paris: Vincent, Fréal, 1956.

Connolly, Cyril, and Zerbe, Jerome. *Les Pavillons*. New York: Macmillan, 1952.

Duchêne, Achille. *Les jardins de l'avenir: hier aujourd'hui, demain*. Paris: Vincent, Fréal, 1935.

Duchêne, Achille, and Fouquier, M. *De divers styles des jardins*. Paris: Emile Paul, 1914.

French, Leigh, Jr., and Eberlein, Harold Donaldson. *The Smaller Homes and Gardens of Versailles from 1680 to 1815*. New York: Pencil Points Press, 1926.

Ganay, Ernest de. "Les jardins d'Achille Duchêne." *Art et industrie*, September, 1935.

Gille, Philippe. *Versailles et les deux Trianons*. Vol. II. Tours: Maison Alfred Mame et Fils, 1900.

Maumené, Albert; Duchêne, Achille; and Gibault, Georges. "Quatre siècles de jardins à la français." *La vie à la compagne*. March 15, 1910.

Passillé, Raymond de. "Les jardins français aux Etats-Unis: créations de MM. Duchêne et Gréber. *La gazette illustrée des amateurs des jardins*. Paris, 1923.

Financial Ruin of Palace Builders

BOOKS

Frégnac, Claude, et al. *Les châteaux de l'Isle de France*. Paris: Hachette, 1963. Quotation from La Bruyère's *Caractères*, 1688.

Hamlin, Talbot. *Benjamin Henry Latrobe*. New York: Oxford University Press, 1955.

Lavedan, Pierre. *French Architecture*. Baltimore: Penguin Books, 1956.

Stone, Lawrence. Chapter X: "Conspicuous Expenditure" in *The Crisis of the Aristocracy, 1558–1641*. Abridged ed. London: Oxford University Press, 1967.

C. P. H. Gilbert: Fifth Avenue Commissions

NEWSPAPERS AND PERIODICALS (chronological sequence)

C. P. H. Gilbert: Residence for E. C. Converse, 3 East Seventy-eighth Street. *The American Architect*, February 24, 1900.

C. P. H. Gilbert: Residence for Isaac D. Fletcher, 2 East Seventy-ninth Street. *The American Architect*, March 31, 1900.

C. P. H. Gilbert: residence for Jules S. Bache, 8 East Seventy-sixth Street. *The American Architect*, July 28, 1900.

C. P. H. Gilbert: residence for Adolph Lewisohn. *The Architectural Record*, July, 1918.

C. P. H. Gilbert: residence for Otto H. Kahn, 1 East Seventy-ninth Street. *Architecture and Building* 51 (1919) .

The "Prince Condé/Conti" Commode

CONSOLIDATED

Aprà, Nietta. *Il mobile Luigi XIV, Luigi XV, Luigi XVI*. I Documentari. October, 1970.

Bayley, John Barrington. "The House on Sixty-Second Street." *The Classical Forum* 1.

Frégnac, Claude et al. *French Cabinetmakers of the Eighteenth Century*. Paris: Hachette, 1965.

Gonzalez-Palacios, Alvar. *Il mobili nei secoli*. Vol. 1. Milan: Fratelli Fabbri Editori, 1969.
Verlet, Pierre. *The Eighteenth Century in France: Society, Decoration, Furniture*. Translated by George Savage. Rutland, Vermont: Charles E. Tuttle, 1967.

Henri Dasson

BOOKS
  NOTE: Dasson signed his work "Henry Dasson," but is known as "Henri." For an illustration of his mark, see Mme. Ledoux-Lebard, below, p. 122.

Ledoux-Lebard, Denise. *Les ébénistes parisiens du XIXᵉ siècle (1795–1870): leurs oeuvres et leurs marques*. Paris: F. De Nobele, 1965.
Lostalot, Alfred de. *Les arts du bois: dessins et modèles*. 2nd ed. Paris: Bibliothèque de la Gazette des Beaux-Arts, c. 1890.
Savage, George. "Pierre Dasson" in *Dictionary of Antiques*. New York: Praeger, 1970.

INDEX

Hoffman, F. Burrall, Jr.: and Chalfin, 177–178, 180–181, 200–204; and Deering, 204, 209–210; and the Deering collection, 180–182, 185; early life and education, 174–175; in Italy, 187–188; and Vizcaya, 180–181, 187, 195, 205–207

Hoffman, Murray, 174

Hoffman, Wickham, 174

Hoffstatter, Theo, and Company, 336

Holabird & Roche, 106

Homestead, The, 273

Hopkins, Mark, 262

Horowitz, Louis J., 337, 355, 361–362

Hôtel de Botterel-Quintin, 20

Hôtel de Chanaleilles, 285

Hôtel d'Evreux, 285

Hôtel de la Bourse, 377

Hôtel de la Douane, 377

Hôtel de la Vrillière (Banque du France), 285

Hôtel de Maisons, 199

Hôtel de Rothelin, 87

Hôtel de Tessé, 59

Howard, Miss, 241–242, 287, 304

Hughes, Charles Evans, 343

Hughes, Charles Evans, Jr., 113

Hunt, Myron, 287, 293–302

Hunt, Richard Morris, 49, 51–52, 54–57, 269, 276–277, 279–280, 364–366

Huntington, Arabella Duval (Yarrington) Worsham Huntington: and art, 240, 281–283, 286, 294–295; character, 244–245; death, 307–308; early life and family, 242, 249–250; Fifth Avenue palace, 276–281; 4 West Fifty-fourth St., 264–273; Hôtel de Hirsch, 283–287; and Collis P. Huntington, 239–240, 260, 263, 271–273, 281–282; and Henry E. Huntington, 241, 244, 288, 302–304; mysteries in life, 237–238, 241–243; portraits: by Birley, 239, 243–246, anonymous, 259–260; real estate dealing, 263–265, 272–276; and San Marino, 293–294, 298–299, 304–305; wealth, 240, 263, 282–283; as "widow," 257–259; and Worsham, 242, 246–247, 250, 254–257

Huntington, Archer Milton, 173, 240, 255, 281

Huntington, Clara. See de Hatzfeldt Wildenbourg, Clara (Prentice)

Huntington, Collis Potter: and Arabella, 239–240, 242–243, 260, 263, 272–273, 281–282; and art, 281; death, 282; early life and career, 261–263; and Henry E. Huntington, 241, 282, 288–289; real estate dealing, 272–276, 281; marriage to Elizabeth Stoddard, 262–263

Huntington, Elizabeth (Stoddard), 262–263, 271–272

Huntington, Henry Edwards: and Arabella, 241, 244, 288, 302–304; and art, 291–292, 301; death, 307; early life, 288; and Collis P. Huntington, 241, 282, 288–289; and Los Angeles, 290; portrait, 238–239; marriage to Mary Alice Prentice, 289; and San Marino, 289–293, 299–301, 305–307

Huntington, Mary Alice (Prentice) (Mrs. Henry Edwards Huntington), 289

Huntington, Solon, 262

Huntington, Henry E., Library and Art Gallery, 238–239, 305, 307

Huret, Jules, 162–164

Hutchinson, Edith L. (Stotesbury) (Mrs. Sydney Emlyn Hutchinson), 36

Hutchinson, Sydney Emlyn, 36

Hutton, Barbara, 351

Hyde Park, 183

Idle Hour, 66

Ingalls, Harry Creighton, 180, 189, 202–203

International Harvester Company, 159–161

Irving, Washington, 269

Jackson and Graham, 54

Jacobs, Henry Barton, 299

James, Arthur Curtiss, 187

Jansen, 349–350

Jenkins, Lynn, 71

Jerome, Leonard, 252

Joffre, Joseph, 19

Jomar (railroad car), 105

Jones, Mary (Mason), 275

Jourdan, Adolphe, 283

Joy, Thaddeus, 204

Kahn, Otto H., 336

Kann, Randolph, Collection, 282, 294–295, 301

Keck, Charles, 377

Keenan, Anna Marie (Dot King), 36

Keller, Albert, 137

Kelley, Duncan, 343

Kelly, Frances, 303

Kemp, Gerald van der, 348

Kent, William, 76

Kent-Costikyan Trading Company, 196

Kern, Jerome, 169

Ketcham, Oram W., Inc., 123, 130

Ketterer, Gustav, 81, 83

Kirby, Allan P., 384

Kirby, Fred M., 334, 383–384

Koons, Louis, 207

Koons, Thomas, 207

A

B